DOVER·THRIFT·EDITIONS

The Cherry Orchard
ANTON CHEKHOV

DOVER PUBLICATIONS, INC.
New York

DOVER THRIFT EDITIONS
Editor: Stanley Appelbaum

Published in Canada by General Publishing Company, Ltd.,
30 Lesmill Road, Don Mills, Toronto, Ontario.
Published in the United Kingdom by Constable and Company, Ltd.,
3 The Lanchesters, 162–164 Fulham Palace Road, London W6 9ER.

This Dover edition, first published in 1991,
is an unabridged republication of the text of the play as published in
The Works of Anton Chekhov: One Volume Edition,
Black's Readers Service Company, N.Y., n.d. (ca. 1929; translator not credited).
A few typographical errors have been corrected tacitly.
The Note and the list of characters were prepared
specially for the present edition.

Manufactured in the United States of America
Dover Publications, Inc.
31 East 2nd Street
Mineola, N.Y. 11501

Library of Congress Cataloging-in-Publication Data

Chekhov, Anton Pavlovich, 1860–1904.
[Vishnevyĭ sad. English]
The cherry orchard / Anton Chekhov.
p.   cm.—(Dover thrift editions)
Translation of: Vishnevyĭ sad.
"An unabridged republication of the text of the play as published
in The works of Anton Chekhov: one volume edition.
Black's Readers Service Company, N.Y., n.d., ca. 1929 . . ."—T.p. verso.
ISBN 0-486-26682-6
I. Title. II. Series.
PG3456.V5E5 1991   90-19508
891.72'3—dc20   CIP

Note

EVER SINCE ITS CREATION in January of 1904 by the fledgling Moscow Art Theatre (with the playwright's wife, Olga Knipper, as Madame Ranevsky and with Stanislavsky as Gayef), Anton Pavlovich Chekhov's last play (born in 1860, he died six months after the premiere) has been acclaimed as one of the great theatrical experiences. A triumph of natural action and dialogue, it is at the same time a brilliantly constructed mechanism.

On the interpersonal plane, *The Cherry Orchard* offers razor-sharp characterizations of real human beings who, for all their personal attractiveness, are capable of smothering genuine cries of anguish with their own selfish tics and trivialities. On the social plane, the play is the danse macabre of a culture in violent transition: among the masters and the servants alike, and among the various age groups, lovable but fuzzy-minded and weak-willed traditionalists are preyed upon by efficient but vulgar and heartless upstarts. Characteristically for Chekhov, the words of sanity and healing are uttered by a powerless, spurned observer, the "perpetual student" Trophimof.

Contents

	page
Characters	ix
Act I	1
Act II	17
Act III	28
Act IV	40

Characters

(*in order of speaking*)

Yermolai Alexeyitch LOPAKHIN, a wealthy neighbor

DUNYASHA (Avdotya Fyodorovna Kozoyedov), a maidservant

Simeon Panteleyitch EPHIKHODOF, a clerk

FIRS Nikolayevitch, an old servant

ANYA, younger daughter of Madame Ranevsky

MADAME Lyubof (Lyuba) Andreyevna RANEVSKY, joint owner of the estate, sister of Gayef

BARBARA (Varvara Mikhailovna), elderly daughter of Madame Ranevsky

Leonid (Lenya) Andreyitch GAYEF, joint owner of the estate, brother of Madame Ranevsky

CHARLOTTE Ivanovna, Anya's governess

Simeonof-PISHTCHIK, a neighboring landowner

YASHA, a manservant

Peter TROPHIMOF, a tutor

STATIONMASTER

POSTMASTER (silent role)

The Cherry Orchard

Act I

A room which is still called the nursery. One door leads to ANYA'S *room. Dawn, the sun will soon rise. It is already May, the cherry trees are in blossom, but it is cold in the garden and there is a morning frost. The windows are closed.*

Enter DUNYASHA *with a candle, and* LOPAKHIN *with a book in his hand.*

LOPAKHIN. Here's the train, thank heaven. What is the time?
DUNYASHA. Near two. [*Putting the candle out.*] It is light already.
LOPAKHIN. How late is the train? Two hours at least. [*Yawning and stretching.*] A fine mess I have made of it. I came to meet them at the station and then I went and fell asleep, as I sat in my chair. What trouble! Why did you not rouse me?
DUNYASHA. I thought that you had gone. [*She listens.*] I think they are coming.
LOPAKHIN [*listening*]. No; they have got to get the baggage and the rest. [*A pause.*] Madame Ranévsky has been five years abroad. I wonder what she is like now. What a fine character she is! So easy and simple. I remember when I was only fifteen my old father (he used to keep a shop here in the village then) struck me in the face with his fist and my nose bled. We were out in the courtyard, and he had been drinking. Madame Ranévsky, I remember it like yesterday, still a slender young girl, brought me to the wash-hand stand, here, in this very room, in the nursery. 'Don't cry, little peasant,' she said, 'it'll be all right for your wedding.' [*A pause.*] 'Little peasant!' . . . My father, it is true, was a peasant, and here am I in a white waistcoat and brown boots; a silk purse out of a sow's ear; just turned rich, with plenty of money, but still a peasant of the peasants. [*Turning over the pages of the book.*] Here's this book that I was reading without any attention and fell asleep.

DUNYASHA. The dogs never slept all night, they knew that their master and mistress were coming.

LOPAKHIN. What's the matter with you, Dunyásha? You're all . . .

DUNYASHA. My hands are trembling, I feel quite faint.

LOPAKHIN. You are too refined, Dunyásha, that's what it is. You dress yourself like a young lady, and look at your hair! You ought not to do it; you ought to remember your place.

[*Enter* EPHIKHODOF *with a nosegay. He is dressed in a short jacket and brightly polished boots which squeak noisily. As he comes in he drops the nosegay.*]

EPHIKHODOF [*picking it up*]. The gardener has sent this; he says it is to go in the dining-room. [*Handing it to* DUNYASHA.]

LOPAKHIN. And bring me some quass.

DUNYASHA. Yes, sir.

[*Exit* DUNYASHA.]

EPHIKHODOF. There's a frost this morning, three degrees, and the cherry trees all in blossom. I can't say I think much of our climate; [*sighing*] that is impossible. Our climate is not adapted to contribute; and I should like to add, with your permission, that only two days ago I bought myself a new pair of boots, and I venture to assure you they do squeak beyond all bearing. What am I to grease them with?

LOPAKHIN. Get out; I'm tired of you.

EPHIKHODOF. Every day some misfortune happens to me; but do I grumble? No; I am used to it; I can afford to smile. [*Enter* DUNYASHA, *and hands a glass of quass to* LOPAKHIN.] I must be going. [*He knocks against a chair, which falls to the ground.*] There you are! [*In a voice of triumph.*] You see, if I may venture on the expression, the sort of incidents *inter alia*. It really is astonishing!

[*Exit* EPHIKHODOF.]

DUNYASHA. To tell you the truth, Yermolái Alexéyitch, Ephikhódof has made me a proposal.

LOPAKHIN. Hmph!

DUNYASHA. I hardly know what to do. He is such a well-behaved young man, only so often when he talks one doesn't know what he means. It is all so nice and full of good feeling, but you can't make out what it means. I fancy I am rather fond of him. He adores me passionately. He is a most unfortunate man; every day something seems to happen to him. They call him 'Twenty-two misfortunes,' that's his nickname.

LOPAKHIN [*listening*]. There, surely that is them coming!

DUNYASHA. They're coming! Oh, what is the matter with me? I am all turning cold.
LOPAKHIN. Yes, there they are, and no mistake. Let's go and meet them. Will she know me again, I wonder? It is five years since we met.
DUNYASHA. I am going to faint! . . . I am going to faint!

[*Two carriages are heard driving up to the house.* LOPAKHIN *and* DUNYASHA *exeunt quickly. The stage remains empty. A hubbub begins in the neighbouring rooms.* FIRS *walks hastily across the stage, leaning on a walking-stick. He has been to meet them at the station. He is wearing an old-fashioned livery and a tall hat; he mumbles something to himself but not a word is audible. The noise behind the scenes grows louder and louder. A voice says: 'Let's go this way.'*

[*Enter* MADAME RANEVSKY, ANYA, CHARLOTTE, *leading a little dog on a chain, all dressed in travelling dresses;* BARBARA *in greatcoat with a kerchief over her head,* GAYEF, SIMEONOF-PISHTCHIK, LOPAKHIN, DUNYASHA, *carrying parcel and umbrella, servants with luggage, all cross the stage.*]

ANYA. Come through this way. Do you remember what room this is, mamma?
MADAME RANEVSKY [*joyfully through her tears*]. The nursery.
BARBARA. How cold it is. My hands are simply frozen. [*To* MADAME RANEVSKY.] Your two rooms, the white room and the violet room, are just the same as they were, mamma.
MADAME RANEVSKY. My nursery, my dear, beautiful nursery! This is where I used to sleep when I was a little girl. [*Crying.*] I am like a little girl still. [*Kissing* GAYEF *and* BARBARA *and then* GAYEF *again.*] Barbara has not altered a bit, she is just like a nun, and I knew Dunyásha at once. [*Kissing* DUNYASHA.]
GAYEF. Your train was two hours late. What do you think of that? There's punctuality for you!
CHARLOTTE [*to* SIMEONOF-PISHTCHIK]. My little dog eats nuts.
PISHTCHIK [*astonished*]. You don't say so! Well, I never!

[*Exeunt all but* ANYA *and* DUNYASHA.]

DUNYASHA. At last you've come!

[*She takes off* ANYA's *overcoat and hat.*]

ANYA. I have not slept for four nights on the journey. I am frozen to death.
DUNYASHA. It was Lent when you went away. There was snow on the ground, it was freezing; but now! Oh, my dear! [*Laughing and kissing*

her.] How I have waited for you, my joy, my light! Oh, I must tell you something at once, I cannot wait another minute.

ANYA [*without interest*]. What, again?

DUNYASHA. Ephikhódof, the clerk, proposed to me in Easter week.

ANYA. Same old story.... [*Putting her hair straight.*] All my hairpins have dropped out. [*She is very tired, staggering with fatigue.*]

DUNYASHA. I hardly know what to think of it. He loves me! oh, how he loves me!

ANYA [*looking into her bedroom, affectionately*]. My room, my windows, just as if I had never gone away! I am at home again! When I wake up in the morning I shall run out into the garden.... Oh, if only I could get to sleep! I have not slept the whole journey from Paris, I was so nervous and anxious.

DUNYASHA. Monsieur Trophímof arrived the day before yesterday.

ANYA [*joyfully*]. Peter?

DUNYASHA. He is sleeping outside in the bath-house; he is living there. He was afraid he might be in the way. [*Looking at her watch.*] I'd like to go and wake him, only Mamzelle Barbara told me not to. 'Mind you don't wake him,' she said.

[*Enter* BARBARA *with bunch of keys hanging from her girdle.*]

BARBARA. Dunyásha, go and get some coffee, quick. Mamma wants some coffee.

DUNYASHA. In a minute.

[*Exit* DUNYASHA.]

BARBARA. Well, thank heaven, you have come. Here you are at home again. [*Caressing her.*] My little darling is back! My pretty one is back!

ANYA. What I've had to go through!

BARBARA. I can believe you.

ANYA. I left here in Holy Week. How cold it was! Charlotte would talk the whole way and keep doing conjuring tricks. What on earth made you tie Charlotte round my neck?

BARBARA. Well, you couldn't travel alone, my pet. At seventeen!

ANYA. When we got to Paris, it was so cold! there was snow on the ground. I can't talk French a bit. Mamma was on the fifth floor of a big house. When I arrived there were a lot of Frenchmen with her, and ladies, and an old Catholic priest with a book, and it was very uncomfortable and full of tobacco smoke. I suddenly felt so sorry for mamma, oh, so sorry! I took her head in my arms and squeezed it and could not let it go, and then mamma kept kissing me and crying.

BARBARA [*crying*]. Don't go on, don't go on!

ANYA. She's sold her villa near Mentone already. She's nothing left, absolutely nothing; and I hadn't a farthing either. We only just managed to get home. And mamma won't understand! We get out at a station to have some dinner, and she asks for all the most expensive things and gives the waiters a florin each for a tip; and Charlotte does the same. And Yásha wanted his portion too. It was too awful! Yásha is mamma's new man-servant. We have brought him back with us.

BARBARA. I've seen the rascal.

ANYA. Come, tell me all about everything! Has the interest on the mortgage been paid?

BARBARA. How could it be?

ANYA. Oh dear! Oh dear!

BARBARA. The property will be sold in August.

ANYA. Oh dear! Oh dear!

LOPAKHIN [*looking in at the door and mooing like a cow*]. Moo-o.

[*He goes away again.*]

BARBARA [*laughing through her tears and shaking her fist at the door*]. Oh, I should like to give him one!

ANYA [*embracing* BARBARA *softly*]. Barbara, has he proposed to you? [BARBARA *shakes her head.*] And yet I am sure he loves you. Why don't you come to an understanding? What are you waiting for?

BARBARA. I don't think anything will come of it. He has so much to do; he can't be bothered with me; he hardly takes any notice. Confound the man, I can't bear to see him! Everyone talks about our marriage; everyone congratulates me, but, as a matter of fact, there is nothing in it; it's all a dream. [*Changing her tone.*] You've got on a brooch like a bee.

ANYA [*sadly*]. Mamma bought it for me. [*Going into her room, talking gaily, like a child.*] When I was in Paris, I went up in a balloon!

BARBARA. How glad I am you are back, my little pet! my pretty one! [DUNYASHA *has already returned with a coffee-pot and begins to prepare the coffee.*] [*Standing by the door.*] I trudge about all day looking after things, and I think and think. What are we to do? If only we could marry you to some rich man it would be a load off my mind. I would go into a retreat, and then to Kief, to Moscow; I would tramp about from one holy place to another, always tramping and tramping. What bliss!

ANYA. The birds are singing in the garden. What time is it now?

BARBARA. It must be past two. It is time to go to bed, my darling. [*Following* ANYA *into her room.*] What bliss!

[*Enter* YASHA *with a shawl and a travelling bag.*]

YASHA [*crossing the stage, delicately*]. May I pass this way, mademoiselle?
DUNYASHA. One would hardly know you, Yásha. How you've changed abroad!
YASHA. Ahem! and who may you be?
DUNYASHA. When you left here I was a little thing like that. [*Indicating with her hand.*] My name is Dunyásha, Theodore Kozoyédof's daughter. Don't you remember me?
YASHA. Ahem! You little cucumber!

[*He looks round cautiously, then embraces her. She screams and drops a saucer. Exit* YASHA, *hastily.*]

BARBARA [*in the doorway, crossly*]. What's all this?
DUNYASHA [*crying*]. I've broken a saucer.
BARBARA. Well, it brings luck.

[*Enter* ANYA *from her room.*]

ANYA. We must tell mamma that Peter's here.
BARBARA. I've told them not to wake him.
ANYA [*thoughtfully*]. It's just six years since papa died. And only a month afterwards poor little Grisha was drowned in the river; my pretty little brother, only seven years old! It was too much for mamma; she ran away, ran away without looking back. [*Shuddering.*] How well I can understand her, if only she knew! [*A pause.*] Peter Trophímof was Grisha's tutor; he might remind her.

[*Enter* FIRS *in long coat and white waistcoat.*]

FIRS [*going over to the coffee-pot, anxiously*]. My mistress is going to take coffee here. [*Putting on white gloves.*] Is the coffee ready? [*Sternly, to* DUNYASHA.] Here, girl, where's the cream?
DUNYASHA. Oh, dear! Oh dear!

[*Exit* DUNYASHA, *hastily.*]

FIRS [*bustling about the coffee-pot*]. Ah, you . . . job-lot! [*Mumbling to himself.*] She's come back from Paris. The master went to Paris once in a post-chaise. [*Laughing.*]
BARBARA. What is it, Firs?
FIRS. I beg your pardon? [*Joyfully.*] My mistress has come home; at last I've seen her. Now I'm ready to die.

[*He cries with joy. Enter* MADAME RANEVSKY, LOPAKHIN, GAYEF *and* PISHTCHIK; PISHTCHIK *in Russian breeches and coat of fine cloth.* GAYEF *as he enters makes gestures as if playing billiards.*]

MADAME RANEVSKY. What was the expression? Let me see. 'I'll put the red in the corner pocket; double into the middle——'
GAYEF. I'll chip the red in the right-hand top. Once upon a time. Lyuba, when we were children, we used to sleep here side by side in two little cots, and now I'm fifty-one, and can't bring myself to believe it.
LOPAKHIN. Yes; time flies.
GAYEF. Who's that?
LOPAKHIN. Time flies. I say.
GAYEF. There's a smell of patchouli!
ANYA. I am going to bed. Good-night, mamma. [*Kissing her mother.*]
MADAME RANEVSKY. My beloved little girl! [*Kissing her hands.*] Are you glad you're home again? I can't come to my right senses.
ANYA. Good-night, uncle.
GAYEF [*kissing her face and hands*]. God bless you, little Anya. How like your mother you are! [*To* MADAME RANEVSKY.] You were just such another girl at her age, Lyuba.

[ANYA *shakes hands with* LOPAKHIN *and* SIMEONOF-PISHTCHIK *and exit, shutting her bedroom door behind her.*]

MADAME RANEVSKY. She's very, very tired.
PISHTCHIK. It must have been a long journey.
BARBARA [*to* LOPAKHIN *and* PISHTCHIK]. Well, gentlemen, it's past two; time you were off.
MADAME RANEVSKY [*laughing*]. You haven't changed a bit, Barbara! [*Drawing her to herself and kissing her.*] I'll just finish my coffee, then we'll all go. [FIRS *puts a footstool under her feet.*] Thank you, friend. I'm used to my coffee. I drink it day and night. Thank you, you dear old man. [*Kissing* FIRS.]
BARBARA. I'll go and see if they've got all the luggage. [*Exit* BARBARA.]
MADAME RANEVSKY. Can it be me that's sitting here? [*Laughing.*] I want to jump and wave my arms about. [*Pausing and covering her face.*] Surely I must be dreaming! God knows I love my country. I love it tenderly. I couldn't see out of the window from the train, I was crying so. [*Crying.*] However, I must drink my coffee. Thank you, Firs; thank you, dear old man. I'm so glad to find you still alive.
FIRS. The day before yesterday.
GAYEF. He's hard of hearing.
LOPAKHIN. I've got to be off for Kharkof by the five o'clock train. Such a nuisance! I wanted to stay and look at you and talk to you. You're as splendid as you always were.
PISHTCHIK [*sighing heavily*]. Handsomer than ever and dressed like a Parisian . . . perish my waggon and all its wheels!

LOPAKHIN. Your brother, Leoníd Andréyitch, says I'm a snob, a money-grubber. He can say what he likes. I don't care a hang. Only I want you to believe in me as you used to; I want your wonderful, touching eyes to look at me as they used to. Merciful God in heaven! My father was your father's serf, and your grandfather's serf before him; but you, you did so much for me in the old days that I've forgotten everything, and I love you like a sister—more than a sister.

MADAME RANEVSKY. I can't sit still! I can't do it! [*Jumping up and walking about in great agitation.*] This happiness is more than I can bear. Laugh at me! I am a fool! [*Kissing a cupboard.*] My darling old cupboard! [*Caressing a table.*] My dear little table!

GAYEF. Nurse is dead since you went away.

MADAME RANEVSKY [*sitting down and drinking coffee*]. Yes, Heaven rest her soul. They wrote and told me.

GAYEF. And Anastási is dead. Squint-eyed Peter has left us and works in the town at the Police Inspector's now.

[GAYEF *takes out a box of sugar candy from his pocket, and begins to eat it.*]

PISHTCHIK. My daughter Dáshenka sent her compliments.

LOPAKHIN. I long to say something charming and delightful to you. [*Looking at his watch.*] I'm just off; there's no time to talk. Well, yes, I'll put it in two or three words. You know that your cherry orchard is going to be sold to pay the mortgage: the sale is fixed for the twenty-second of August; but don't you be uneasy, my dear lady; sleep peacefully; there's a way out of it. This is my plan. Listen to me carefully. Your property is only fifteen miles from the town; the railway runs close beside it; and if only you will cut up the cherry orchard and the land along the river into building lots and let it off on lease for villas, you will get at least two thousand five hundred pounds a year out of it.

GAYEF. Come, come! What rubbish you're talking!

MADAME RANEVSKY. I don't quite understand what you mean, Yermolái Alexéyitch.

LOPAKHIN. You will get a pound a year at least for every acre from the tenants, and if you advertise the thing at once, I am ready to bet whatever you like, by the autumn you won't have a clod of that earth left on your hands. It'll all be snapped up. In two words, I congratulate you; you are saved. It's a first-class site, with a good deep river. Only of course you will have to put it in order and clear the ground; you will have to pull down all the old buildings—this house, for instance, which is no longer fit for anything; you'll have to cut down the cherry orchard. . . .

MADAME RANEVSKY. Cut down the cherry orchard! Excuse me, but you don't know what you're talking about. If there is one thing that's interesting, remarkable in fact, in the whole province, it's our cherry orchard.

LOPAKHIN. There's nothing remarkable about the orchard except that it's a very big one. It only bears once every two years, and then you don't know what to do with the fruit. Nobody wants to buy it.

GAYEF. Our cherry orchard is mentioned in Andréyevsky's Encyclopaedia.

LOPAKHIN [*looking at his watch*]. If we don't make up our minds or think of any way, on the twenty-second of August the cherry orchard and the whole property will be sold by auction. Come, make up your mind! There's no other way out of it, I swear—absolutely none.

FIRS. In the old days, forty or fifty years ago, they used to dry the cherries and soak 'em and pickle 'em, and make jam of 'em; and the dried cherries . . .

GAYEF. Shut up, Firs.

FIRS. The dried cherries used to be sent in waggons to Moscow and Kharkof. A heap of money! The dried cherries were soft and juicy and sweet and sweet-smelling then. They knew some way in those days.

MADAME RANEVSKY. And why don't they do it now?

FIRS. They've forgotten. Nobody remembers how to do it.

PISHTCHIK [*to* MADAME RANEVSKY]. What about Paris? How did you get on? Did you eat frogs?

MADAME RANEVSKY. Crocodiles.

PISHTCHIK. You don't say so! Well, I never!

LOPAKHIN. Until a little while ago there was nothing but gentry and peasants in the villages; but now villa residents have made their appearance. All the towns, even the little ones, are surrounded by villas now. In another twenty years the villa resident will have multiplied like anything. At present he only sits and drinks tea on his verandah, but it is quite likely that he will soon take to cultivating his three acres of land, and then your old cherry orchard will become fruitful, rich and happy. . . .

GAYEF [*angry*]. What gibberish!

[*Enter* BARBARA *and* YASHA.]

BARBARA [*taking out a key and noisily unlocking an old-fashioned cupboard*]. There are two telegrams for you, mamma. Here they are.

MADAME RANEVSKY [*tearing them up without reading them*]. They're from Paris. I've done with Paris.

GAYEF. Do you know how old this cupboard is, Lyuba? A week ago I pulled out the bottom drawer and saw a date burnt in it. That cupboard was made exactly a hundred years ago. What do you think of that, eh? We might celebrate its jubilee. It's only an inanimate thing, but for all that it's a historic cupboard.

PISHTCHIK [*astonished*]. A hundred years? Well, I never!

GAYEF [*touching the cupboard*]. Yes, it's a wonderful thing. . . . Beloved and venerable cupboard; honour and glory to your existence, which for more than a hundred years has been directed to the noble ideals of justice and virtue. Your silent summons to profitable labour has never weakened in all these hundred years. [*Crying.*] You have upheld the courage of succeeding generations of our human kind; you have upheld faith in a better future and cherished in us ideals of goodness and social consciousness. [*A pause.*]

LOPAKHIN. Yes. . . .

MADAME RANEVSKY. You haven't changed, Leoníd.

GAYEF [*embarrassed*]. Off the white in the corner, chip the red in the middle pocket!

LOPAKHIN [*looking at his watch*]. Well, I must be off.

YASHA [*handing a box to* MADAME RANEVSKY]. Perhaps you'll take your pills now.

PISHTCHIK. You oughtn't to take medicine, dear lady. It does you neither good nor harm. Give them here, my friend. [*He empties all the pills into the palm of his hand, blows on them, puts them in his mouth and swallows them down with a draught of quass.*] There!

MADAME RANEVSKY [*alarmed*]. Have you gone off your head?

PISHTCHIK. I've taken all the pills.

LOPAKHIN. Greedy fellow! [*Everyone laughs.*]

FIRS [*mumbling*]. They were here in Easter week and finished off a gallon of pickled gherkins.

MADAME RANEVSKY. What's he talking about?

BARBARA. He's been mumbling like that these three years. We've got used to it.

YASHA. Advancing age.

[CHARLOTTE *crosses in a white frock, very thin, tightly laced, with a lorgnette at her waist.*]

LOPAKHIN. Excuse me, Charlotte Ivánovna, I've not paid my respects to you yet. [*He prepares to kiss her hand.*]

CHARLOTTE [*drawing her hand away*]. If one allows you to kiss one's hand, you will want to kiss one's elbow next, and then one's shoulder.

LOPAKHIN. I'm having no luck today. [*All laugh.*] Charlotte Ivánovna, do us a conjuring trick.

MADAME RANEVSKY. Charlotte, do do us a conjuring trick.

CHARLOTTE. No, thank you. I'm going to bed.

[*Exit* CHARLOTTE.]

LOPAKHIN. We shall meet again in three weeks. [*Kissing* MADAME RANEVSKY's *hand.*] Meanwhile, good-bye. I must be off. [*To* GAYEF.] So-long. [*Kissing* PISHTCHIK.] Ta-ta. [*Shaking hands with* BARBARA, *then with* FIRS *and* YASHA.] I hate having to go. [*To* MADAME RANEVSKY.] If you make up your mind about the villas, let me know, and I'll raise you five thousand pounds at once. Think it over seriously.

BARBARA [*angrily*]. For heaven's sake do go!

LOPAKHIN. I'm going, I'm going.

[*Exit* LOPAKHIN.]

GAYEF. Snob! . . . However, *pardon!* Barbara's going to marry him; he's Barbara's young man.

BARBARA. You talk too much, uncle.

MADAME RANEVSKY. Why, Barbara, I shall be very glad. He's a nice man.

PISHTCHIK. Not a doubt about it. . . . A most worthy individual. My Dáshenka, she says . . . oh, she says . . . lots of things. [*Snoring and waking up again at once.*] By the by, dear lady, can you lend me twenty-five pounds? I've got to pay the interest on my mortgage to-morrow.

BARBARA [*alarmed*]. We can't! we can't!

MADAME RANEVSKY. It really is a fact that I haven't any money.

PISHTCHIK. I'll find it somewhere. [*Laughing.*] I never lose hope. Last time I thought: 'Now I really am done for, I'm a ruined man,' when behold, they ran a railway over my land and paid me compensation. And so it'll be again; something will happen, if not today, then to-morrow. Dáshenka may win the twenty-thousand-pound prize; she's got a ticket in the lottery.

MADAME RANEVSKY. The coffee's finished. Let's go to bed.

FIRS [*brushing* GAYEF'S *clothes, admonishingly*]. You've put on the wrong trousers again. Whatever am I to do with you?

BARBARA [*softly*]. Anya is asleep. [*She opens the window quietly.*] The sun's up already; it isn't cold now. Look, mamma, how lovely the trees are. Heavens! what a sweet air! The starlings are singing!

GAYEF [*opening the other window*]. The orchard is all white. You've not forgotten it, Lyuba? This long avenue going straight on, straight on, like a ribbon between the trees? It shines like silver on moonlight nights. Do you remember? You've not forgotten?

MADAME RANEVSKY [*looking out into the garden*]. Oh, my childhood, my pure and happy childhood! I used to sleep in this nursery. I used to look out from here into the garden. Happiness awoke with me every morning! and the orchard was just the same then as it is now; nothing is altered. [*Laughing with joy.*] It is all white, all white! Oh, my cherry orchard! After the dark and stormy autumn and the frosts of winter you are young again and full of happiness; the angels of heaven have not abandoned you. Oh! if only I could free my neck and shoulders from the stone that weighs them down! If only I could forget my past!

GAYEF. Yes; and this orchard will be sold to pay our debts, however impossible it may seem. . . .

MADAME RANEVSKY. Look! There's mamma walking in the orchard . . . in a white frock! [*Laughing with joy.*] There she is!

GAYEF. Where?

BARBARA. Heaven help you!

MADAME RANEVSKY. There's no one there, really. It only looked like it; there on the right where the path turns down to the summer-house; there's a white tree that leans over and looks like a woman. [*Enter* TROPHIMOF *in a shabby student uniform and spectacles.*] What a wonderful orchard, with its white masses of blossom and the blue sky above!

TROPHIMOF. Lyubóf Andréyevna! [*She looks round at him.*] I only want to say, 'How do you do,' and go away at once. [*Kissing her hand eagerly.*] I was told to wait till the morning, but I hadn't the patience.

[MADAME RANEVSKY *looks at him in astonishment.*]

BARBARA [*crying*]. This is Peter Trophímof.

TROPHIMOF. Peter Trophímof; I was Grisha's tutor, you know. Have I really altered so much?

[MADAME RANEVSKY *embraces him and cries softly.*]

GAYEF. Come, come, that's enough, Lyuba!

BARBARA [*crying*]. I told you to wait till to-morrow, you know, Peter.

MADAME RANEVSKY. My little Grisha! My little boy! Grisha . . . my son. . . .

BARBARA. It can't be helped, mamma. It was the will of God.

TROPHIMOF [*gently, crying*]. There, there!

MADAME RANEVSKY [*crying*]. He was drowned. My little boy was drowned. Why? What was the use of that, my dear? [*In a softer voice.*] Anya's asleep in there, and I am speaking so loud, and making a noise. . . . But tell me, Peter, why have you grown so ugly? Why have you grown so old?

TROPHIMOF. An old woman in the train called me a 'mouldy gentleman.'

MADAME RANEVSKY. You were quite a boy then, a dear little student, and now your hair's going and you wear spectacles. Are you really still a student? [*Going towards the door.*]
TROPHIMOF. Yes, I expect I shall be a perpetual student.
MADAME RANEVSKY [*kissing her brother and then* BARBARA]. Well, go to bed. You've grown old too, Leoníd.
PISHTCHIK [*following her*]. Yes, yes; time for bed. Oh, oh, my gout! I'll stay the night here. Don't forget, Lyubóf Andréyevna, my angel, to-morrow morning . . . twenty-five.
GAYEF. He's still on the same string.
PISHTCHIK. Twenty-five . . . to pay the interest on my mortgage.
MADAME RANEVSKY. I haven't any money, my friend.
PISHTCHIK. I'll pay you back, dear lady. It's a trifling sum.
MADAME RANEVSKY. Well, well, Leoníd will give it to you. Let him have it, Leoníd.
GAYEF [*ironical*]. I'll give it him right enough! Hold your pocket wide!
MADAME RANEVSKY. It can't be helped. . . . He needs it. He'll pay it back.

[*Exeunt* MADAME RANEVSKY, TROPHIMOF, PISHTCHIK *and* FIRS. GAYEF, BARBARA *and* YASHA *remain.*]

GAYEF. My sister hasn't lost her old habit of scattering the money. [*To* YASHA.] Go away, my lad! You smell of chicken.
YASHA [*laughing*]. You're just the same as you always were, Leoníd Andréyevitch!
GAYEF. Who's that? [*To* BARBARA.] What does he say?
BARBARA [*to* YASHA]. Your mother's come up from the village. She's been waiting for you since yesterday in the servants' hall. She wants to see you.
YASHA. What a nuisance she is!
BARBARA. You wicked, unnatural son!
YASHA. Well, what do I want with her? She might just as well have waited till to-morrow.

[*Exit* YASHA.]

BARBARA. Mamma is just like she used to be; she hasn't changed a bit. If she had her way, she'd give away everything she has.
GAYEF. Yes. [*A pause.*] If people recommend very many cures for an illness, that means that the illness is incurable. I think and think, I batter my brains; I know of many remedies, very many, and that means really that there is none. How nice it would be to get a fortune left one by somebody! How nice it would be if Anya could marry a very rich

man! How nice it would be to go to Yaroslav and try my luck with my aunt the Countess. My aunt is very, very rich, you know.

BARBARA [*crying softly*]. If only God would help us!

GAYEF. Don't howl! My aunt is very rich, but she does not like us. In the first place, my sister married a solicitor, not a nobleman. [ANYA *appears in the doorway.*] She married a man who was not a nobleman, and it's no good pretending that she has led a virtuous life. She's a dear, kind, charming creature, and I love her very much, but whatever mitigating circumstances one may find for her, there's no getting round it that she's a sinful woman. You can see it in her every gesture.

BARBARA [*whispering*]. Anya is standing in the door!

GAYEF. Who's that? [*A pause.*] It's very odd, something's got into my right eye. I can't see properly out of it. Last Thursday when I was down at the District Court . . .

[ANYA *comes down.*]

BARBARA. Why aren't you asleep, Anya?

ANYA. I can't sleep. It's no good trying.

GAYEF. My little pet! [*Kissing* ANYA'S *hands and face.*] My little girl! [*Crying.*] You're not my niece; you're my angel; you're my everything. Trust me, trust me. . . .

ANYA. I do trust you, uncle. Everyone loves you, everyone respects you; but dear, dear uncle, you ought to hold your tongue, only to hold your tongue. What were you saying just now about mamma? about your own sister? What was the good of saying that?

GAYEF. Yes, yes. [*Covering his face with her hand.*] You're quite right; it was awful of me! Lord, Lord! save me from myself! And a little while ago I made a speech over a cupboard. What a stupid thing to do! As soon as I had done it, I knew it was stupid.

BARBARA. Yes, really, uncle. You ought to hold your tongue. Say nothing; that's all that's wanted.

ANYA. If only you would hold your tongue, you'd be so much happier!

GAYEF. I will! I will! [*Kissing* ANYA'S *and* BARBARA'S *hands.*] I'll hold my tongue. But there's one thing I must say; it's business. Last Thursday, when I was down at the District Court, a lot of us were there together, we began to talk about this and that, one thing and another, and it seems I could arrange a loan on note of hand to pay the interest into the bank.

BARBARA. If only Heaven would help us!

GAYEF. I'll go on Tuesday and talk it over again. [*To* BARBARA.] Don't howl! [*To* ANYA.] Your mamma shall have a talk with Lopákhin. Of course he won't refuse her. And as soon as you are rested you must go to see your grandmother, the Countess, at Yaroslav. We'll operate from three points, and the trick is done. We'll pay the interest, I'm certain of it. [*Taking sugar candy.*] I swear on my honour, or whatever you will, the property shall not be sold. [*Excitedly.*] I swear by my hope of eternal happiness! There's my hand on it. Call me a base, dishonourable man if I let it go to auction. I swear by my whole being.

ANYA [*calm again and happy*]. What a dear you are, uncle, and how clever! [*Embraces him.*] Now I'm easy again. I'm easy again! I'm happy!

[*Enter* FIRS.]

FIRS [*reproachfully*]. Leoníd Andréyevitch, have you no fear of God? When are you going to bed?

GAYEF. I'm just off—just off. You get along, Firs. I'll undress myself all right. Come, children, bye-bye! Details to-morrow, but now let's go to bed. [*Kissing* ANYA *and* BARBARA.] I'm a good Liberal, a man of the eighties. People abuse the eighties, but I think that I may say I've suffered something for my convictions in my time. It's not for nothing that the peasants love me. We ought to know the peasants; we ought to know with what . . .

ANYA. You're at it again, uncle!

BARBARA. Why don't you hold your tongue, uncle?

FIRS [*angrily*]. Leoníd Andréyevitch!

GAYEF. I'm coming; I'm coming. Now go to bed. Off two cushions in the middle pocket! I start another life! . . .

[*Exit, with* FIRS *hobbling after him.*]

ANYA. Now my mind is at rest. I don't want to go to Yaroslav; I don't like grandmamma; but my mind is at rest, thanks to Uncle Leoníd. [*She sits down.*]

BARBARA. Time for bed. I'm off. Whilst you were away there's been a scandal. You know that nobody lives in the old servants' quarters except the old people, Ephim, Pauline, Evstignéy and old Karp. Well, they took to having in all sorts of queer fish to sleep there with them. I didn't say a word. But at last I heard they had spread a report that I had given orders that they were to have nothing but peas to eat; out of stinginess, you understand? It was all Evstignéy's doing. 'Very well,' I said to myself, 'you wait a bit.' So I sent for Evstignéy. [*Yawning.*] He comes. 'Now then, Evstignéy,' I said, 'you old imbecile, how do you dare . . .' [*Looking at* ANYA.] Anya, Anya! [*A pause.*] She's asleep. [*Taking* ANYA's *arm.*] Let's go to bed. Come along. [*Leading her away.*] Sleep on, my little one! Come along; come along! [*They go towards* ANYA's *room. In the distance beyond the orchard a shepherd plays his pipe.*

TROPHIMOF *crosses the stage and, seeing* BARBARA *and* ANYA, *stops.*] 'Sh! She's asleep, she's asleep! Come along, my love.
ANYA [*drowsily*]. I'm so tired! Listen to the bells! Uncle, dear uncle! Mamma! Uncle!
BARBARA. Come along, my love! Come along.

[*Exeunt* BARBARA *and* ANYA *to the bedroom.*]

TROPHIMOF [*with emotion*]. My sunshine! My spring!

CURTAIN

Act II

In the open fields; an old crooked half-ruined shrine. Near it a well; big stones, apparently old tombstones; an old bench. Road to the estate beyond. On one side rise dark poplar trees. Beyond them begins the cherry orchard. In the distance a row of telegraph poles, and, far away on the horizon, the dim outlines of a big town, visible only in fine, clear weather. It is near sunset.

CHARLOTTE, YASHA *and* DUNYASHA *sit on the bench.* EPHIKHODOF *stands by them and plays on a guitar; they meditate.* CHARLOTTE *wears an old peaked cap. She has taken a gun from off her shoulders and is mending the buckle of the strap.*

CHARLOTTE [*thoughtfully*]. I have no proper passport. I don't know how old I am; I always feel I am still young. When I was a little girl my father and mother used to go about from one country fair to another, giving performances, and very good ones too. I used to do the *salto mortale* and all sorts of tricks. When papa and mamma died an old German lady adopted me and educated me. Good! When I grew up I became a governess. But where I come from and who I am, I haven't a notion. Who my parents were—very likely they weren't married—I don't know. [*Taking a cucumber from her pocket and beginning to eat it.*] I don't know anything about it. [*A pause.*] I long to talk so, and I have no one to talk to, I have no friends or relations.

EPHIKHODOF [*playing on the guitar and singing*].

'What is the noisy world to me?
Oh, what are friends and foes?'

How sweet it is to play upon a mandoline!

DUNYASHA. That's a guitar, not a mandoline. [*She looks at herself in a hand-glass and powders her face.*]

EPHIKHODOF. For the madman who loves, it is a mandoline. [*Singing.*]

'Oh, that my heart were cheered
By the warmth of requited love.'

[YASHA *joins in.*]

CHARLOTTE. How badly these people do sing! Foo! Like jackals howling!
DUNYASHA [*to* YASHA]. What happiness it must be to live abroad!
YASHA. Of course it is; I quite agree with you. [*He yawns and lights a cigar.*]
EPHIKHODOF. It stands to reason. Everything abroad has attained a certain culmination.
YASHA. That's right.
EPHIKHODOF. I am a man of cultivation; I have studied various remarkable books, but I cannot fathom the direction of my preferences; do I want to live or do I want to shoot myself, so to speak? But in order to be ready for all contingencies, I always carry a revolver in my pocket. Here it is. [*Showing revolver.*]
CHARLOTTE. That's done. I'm off. [*Slinging the rifle over her shoulder.*] You're a clever fellow, Ephikhódof, and very alarming. Women must fall madly in love with you. Brrr! [*Going.*] These clever people are all so stupid; I have no one to talk to. I am always alone, always alone; I have no friends or relations, and who I am, or why I exist, is a mystery.

[*Exit slowly.*]

EPHIKHODOF. Strictly speaking, without touching upon other matters, I must protest *inter alia* that destiny treats me with the utmost rigour, as a tempest might treat a small ship. If I labour under a misapprehension, how is it that when I woke up this morning, behold, so to speak, I perceived sitting on my chest a spider of praeternatural dimensions, like that [*indicating with both hands*]? And if I go to take a draught of quass, I am sure to find something of the most indelicate character, in the nature of a cockroach. [*A pause.*] Have you read Buckle? [*A pause.*] [*To* DUNYASHA.] I should like to trouble you, Avdótya Fyódorovna, for a momentary interview.
DUNYASHA. Talk away.
EPHIKHODOF. I should prefer to conduct it *tête-à-tête*. [*Sighing.*]
DUNYASHA [*confused*]. Very well, only first please fetch me my cloak. It's by the cupboard. It's rather damp here.
EPHIKHODOF. Very well, mademoiselle. I will go and fetch it, mademoiselle. Now I know what to do with my revolver.

[*Takes his guitar and exit, playing.*]

YASHA. Twenty-two misfortunes! Between you and me, he's a stupid fellow. [*Yawning.*]

DUNYASHA. Heaven help him, he'll shoot himself! [*A pause.*] I have grown so nervous, I am always in a twitter. I was quite a little girl when they took me into the household, and now I have got quite disused to common life, and my hands are as white as white, like a lady's. I have grown so refined, so delicate and genteel, I am afraid of everything. I'm always frightened. And if you deceive me, Yásha, I don't know what will happen to my nerves.

YASHA [*kissing her*]. You little cucumber! Of course every girl ought to behave herself properly; there's nothing I dislike as much as when girls aren't proper in their behaviour.

DUNYASHA. I've fallen dreadfully in love with you. You're so educated; you can talk about anything! [*A pause.*]

YASHA [*yawning*]. Yes. . . . The way I look at it is this; if a girl falls in love with anybody, then I call her immoral. [*A pause.*] How pleasant it is to smoke one's cigar in the open air. [*Listening.*] There's someone coming. It's the missis and the rest of 'em. . . . [DUNYASHA *embraces him hastily.*] Go towards the house as if you'd just been for a bathe. Go by this path or else they'll meet you and think that I've been walking out with you. I can't stand that sort of thing.

DUNYASHA [*coughing softly*]. Your cigar has given me a headache.

[*Exit* DUNYASHA.]

[YASHA *remains sitting by the shrine. Enter* MADAME RANEVSKY, GAYEF *and* LOPAKHIN.]

LOPAKHIN. You must make up your minds once and for all. Time waits for no man. The question is perfectly simple. Are you going to let off the land for villas or not? Answer in one word; yes or no. Only one word!

MADAME RANEVSKY. Who's smoking horrible cigars here? [*She sits down.*]

GAYEF. How handy it is now they've built that railway. [*Sitting.*] We've been into town for lunch and back again. . . . Red in the middle! I must just go up to the house and have a game.

MADAME RANEVSKY. There's no hurry.

LOPAKHIN. Only one word—yes or no! [*Entreatingly.*] Come, answer the question!

GAYEF [*yawning*]. Who's that?

MADAME RANEVSKY [*looking into her purse*]. I had a lot of money yesterday but there's hardly any left now. Poor Barbara tries to save money by feeding us all on milk soup; the old people in the kitchen get nothing but peas, and yet I go squandering aimlessly. . . . [*Dropping her purse and scattering gold coins; vexed.*] There, I've dropped it all!

YASHA. Allow me, I'll pick it up. [*Collecting the coins.*]
MADAME RANEVSKY. Yes, please do, Yásha! Whatever made me go into town for lunch? I hate your horrid restaurant with the organ and the tablecloths all smelling of soap. Why do you drink so much, Leoníd? Why do you eat so much? Why do you talk so much? You talked too much at the restaurant again, and most unsuitably, about the seventies, and the decadents. And to whom? Fancy talking about decadents to the waiters!
LOPAKHIN. Quite true.
GAYEF [*with a gesture*]. I'm incorrigible, that's plain. [*Irritably to* YASHA.] What do you keep dodging about in front of me for?
YASHA [*laughing*]. I can't hear your voice without laughing.
GAYEF [*to* MADAME RANEVSKY]. Either he or I . . .
MADAME RANEVSKY. Go away, Yásha; run along.
YASHA [*handing* MADAME RANEVSKY *her purse*]. I'll go at once. [*Restraining his laughter with difficulty.*] This very minute.

[*Exit* YASHA.]

LOPAKHIN. Derigánof, the millionaire, wants to buy your property. They say he'll come to the auction himself.
MADAME RANEVSKY. How did you hear?
LOPAKHIN. I was told so in town.
GAYEF. Our aunt at Yaroslav has promised to send something; but I don't know when, or how much.
LOPAKHIN. How much will she send? Ten thousand pounds? Twenty thousand pounds?
MADAME RANEVSKY. Oh, come . . . A thousand or fifteen hundred at the most.
LOPAKHIN. Excuse me, but in all my life I never met anybody so frivolous as you two, so crazy and unbusinesslike! I tell you in plain Russian your property is going to be sold, and you don't seem to understand what I say.
MADAME RANEVSKY. Well, what are we to do? Tell us what you want us to do.
LOPAKHIN. Don't I tell you every day? Every day I say the same thing over and over again. You must lease off the cherry orchard and the rest of the estate for villas; you must do it at once, this very moment; the auction will be on you in two twos! Try and understand. Once you make up your mind there are to be villas, you can get all the money you want, and you're saved.
MADAME RANEVSKY. Villas and villa residents, oh, please, . . . it's so vulgar!

GAYEF. I quite agree with you.

LOPAKHIN. I shall either cry, or scream, or faint. I can't stand it! You'll be the death of me. [*To* GAYEF.] You're an old woman!

GAYEF. Who's that?

LOPAKHIN. You're an old woman! [*Going.*]

MADAME RANEVSKY [*frightened*]. No, don't go. Stay here, there's a dear! Perhaps we shall think of some way.

LOPAKHIN. What's the good of thinking!

MADAME RANEVSKY. Please don't go; I want you. At any rate it's gayer when you're here. [*A pause.*] I keep expecting something to happen, as if the house were going to tumble down about our ears.

GAYEF [*in deep abstraction*]. Off the cushion on the corner; double into the middle pocket. . . .

MADAME RANEVSKY. We have been very, very sinful!

LOPAKHIN. You! What sins have you committed?

GAYEF [*eating candy*]. They say I've devoured all my substance in sugar candy. [*Laughing.*]

MADAME RANEVSKY. Oh, the sins that I have committed . . . I've always squandered money at random like a madwoman; I married a man who made nothing but debts. My husband drank himself to death on champagne; he was a fearful drinker. Then for my sins I fell in love and went off with another man; and immediately—that was my first punishment—a blow full on the head . . . here, in this very river . . . my little boy was drowned; and I went abroad, right, right away, never to come back any more, never to see this river again. . . . I shut my eyes and ran, like a mad thing, and *he* came after me, pitiless and cruel. I bought a villa at Mentone, because he fell ill there, and for three years I knew no rest day or night; the sick man tormented and wore down my soul. Then, last year, when my villa was sold to pay my debts, I went off to Paris, and he came and robbed me of everything, left me and took up with another woman, and I tried to poison myself. . . . It was all so stupid, so humiliating. . . . Then suddenly I longed to be back in Russia, in my own country, with my little girl. . . . [*Wiping away her tears.*] Lord, Lord, be merciful to me; forgive my sins! Do not punish me any more! [*Taking a telegram from her pocket.*] I got this to-day from Paris. . . . He asks to be forgiven, begs me to go back. . . . [*Tearing up the telegram.*] Isn't that music that I hear? [*Listening.*]

GAYEF. That's our famous Jewish band. You remember? Four fiddles, a flute and a double bass.

MADAME RANEVSKY. Does it still exist? We must make them come up some time; we'll have a dance.

LOPAKHIN [*listening*]. I don't hear anything. [*Singing softly.*]

> 'The Germans for a fee will turn
> A Russ into a Frenchman.'

[*Laughing.*] I saw a very funny piece at the theatre last night; awfully funny!

MADAME RANEVSKY. It probably wasn't a bit funny. You people ought to go and see plays; you ought to try to see yourselves; to see what a dull life you lead, and how much too much you talk.

LOPAKHIN. Quite right. To tell the honest truth, our life's an imbecile affair. [*A pause.*] My papa was a peasant, an idiot; he understood nothing; he taught me nothing; all he did was to beat me when he was drunk, with a walking-stick. As a matter of fact I'm just as big a blockhead and idiot as he was. I never did any lessons; my handwriting's abominable; I write so badly I'm ashamed before people; like a pig.

MADAME RANEVSKY. You ought to get married.

LOPAKHIN. Yes, that's true.

MADAME RANEVSKY. Why not marry Barbara? She's a nice girl.

LOPAKHIN. Yes.

MADAME RANEVSKY. She's a nice straightforward creature; works all day; and what's most important, she loves you. You've been fond of her for a long time.

LOPAKHIN. Well, why not? I'm quite willing. She's a very nice girl. [*A pause.*]

GAYEF. I've been offered a place in a bank. Six hundred pounds a year. Do you hear?

MADAME RANEVSKY. You in a bank! Stay where you are.

[*Enter* FIRS *carrying an overcoat.*]

FIRS [*to* GAYEF]. Put this on, please, master; it's getting damp.

GAYEF [*putting on the coat*]. What a plague you are, Firs!

FIRS. What's the use. . . . You went off and never told me. [*Examining his clothes.*]

MADAME RANEVSKY. How old you've got, Firs!

FIRS. I beg your pardon?

LOPAKHIN. She says how old you've got!

FIRS. I've been alive a long time. When they found me a wife, your father wasn't even born yet. [*Laughing.*] And when the Liberation came I was already chief valet. But I wouldn't have any Liberation then; I stayed with the master. [*A pause.*] I remember how happy everybody was, but why they were happy they didn't know themselves.

LOPAKHIN. It was fine before then. Anyway they used to flog 'em.
FIRS [*mishearing him*]. I should think so! The peasants minded the masters, and the masters minded the peasants, but now it's all higgledy-piggledy; you can't make head or tail of it.
GAYEF. Shut up, Firs. I must go into town again to-morrow. I've been promised an introduction to a general who'll lend money on a bill.
LOPAKHIN. You'll do no good. You won't even pay the interest; set your mind at ease about that.
MADAME RANEVSKY [*to* LOPAKHIN]. He's only talking nonsense. There's no such general at all.

[*Enter* TROPHIMOF, ANYA *and* BARBARA.]

GAYEF. Here come the others.
ANYA. Here's the mamma.
MADAME RANEVSKY [*tenderly*]. Come along, come along, . . . my little ones. . . . [*Embracing* ANYA *and* BARBARA.] If only you knew how much I love you both! Sit beside me . . . there, like that. [*Everyone sits.*]
LOPAKHIN. The Perpetual Student's always among the girls.
TROPHIMOF. It's no affair of yours.
LOPAKHIN. He's nearly fifty and still a student.
TROPHIMOF. Stop your idiotic jokes!
LOPAKHIN. What are you losing your temper for, silly?
TROPHIMOF. Why can't you leave me alone?
LOPAKHIN [*laughing*]. I should like to know what your opinion is of me?
TROPHIMOF. My opinion of you, Yermolái Alexéyitch, is this. You're a rich man; you'll soon be a millionaire. Just as a beast of prey which devours everything that comes in its way is necessary for the conversion of matter, so you are necessary too.

[*All laugh.*]

BARBARA. Tell us something about the planets, Peter, instead.
MADAME RANEVSKY. No. Let's go on with the conversation we were having yesterday.
TROPHIMOF. What about?
GAYEF. About the proud man.
TROPHIMOF. We had a long talk yesterday, but we didn't come to any conclusion. There is something mystical in the proud man in the sense in which you use the words. You may be right from your point of view, but, if we look at it simple-mindedly, what room is there for pride? Is there any sense in it, when man is so poorly constructed from the physiological point of view, when the vast majority of us are so gross

and stupid and profoundly unhappy? We must give up admiring ourselves. The only thing to do is to work.

GAYEF. We shall die all the same.

TROPHIMOF. Who knows? And what does it mean, to die? Perhaps man has a hundred senses, and when he dies only the five senses that we know perish with him, and the other ninety-five remain alive.

MADAME RANEVSKY. How clever you are, Peter.

LOPAKHIN [*ironically*]. Oh, extraordinary!

TROPHIMOF. Mankind marches forward, perfecting its strength. Everything that is unattainable for us now will one day be near and clear; but we must work; we must help with all our force those who seek for truth. At present only a few men work in Russia. The vast majority of the educated people that I know seek after nothing, do nothing, and are as yet incapable of work. They call themselves the 'Intelligentsia,' they say 'thou' and 'thee' to the servants, they treat the peasants like animals, learn nothing, read nothing serious, do absolutely nothing, only talk about science, and understand little or nothing about art. They are all serious; they all have solemn faces; they only discuss important subjects; they philosophise; but meanwhile the vast majority of us, ninety-nine per cent., live like savages; at the least thing they curse and punch people's heads; they eat like beasts and sleep in dirt and bad air; there are bugs everywhere, evil smells, damp and moral degradation. . . . It's plain that all our clever conversations are only meant to distract our own attention and other people's. Show me where those crèches are, that they're always talking so much about; or those reading-rooms. They are only things people write about in novels; they don't really exist at all. Nothing exists but dirt, vulgarity and Asiatic ways. I am afraid of solemn faces; I dislike them; I am afraid of solemn conversations. Let us rather hold our tongues.

LOPAKHIN. Do you know, I get up at five every morning. I work from morning till night; I am always handling my own money or other people's, and I see the sort of men there are about me. One only has to begin to do anything to see how few honest and decent people there are. Sometimes, as I lie awake in bed, I think: 'O Lord, you have given us mighty forests, boundless fields and immeasurable horizons, and we, living in their midst, ought really to be giants.'

MADAME RANEVSKY. Oh dear, you want giants! They are all very well in fairy stories; but in real life they are rather alarming. [EPHIKHODOF *passes at the back of the scene, playing on his guitar.*] [*Pensively.*] There goes Ephikhódof.

ANYA [*pensively*]. There goes Ephikhódof.

GAYEF. The sun has set.

TROPHIMOF. Yes.
GAYEF [*as if declaiming, but not loud*]. O Nature, wonderful Nature, you glow with eternal light; beautiful and indifferent, you whom we call our mother, uniting in yourself both life and death, you animate and you destroy. . . .
BARBARA [*entreatingly*]. Uncle!
ANYA. You're at it again, uncle!
TROPHIMOF. You'd far better double the red into the middle pocket.
GAYEF. I'll hold my tongue! I'll hold my tongue!

[*They all sit pensively. Silence reigns, broken only by the mumbling of old* FIRS. *Suddenly a distant sound is heard as if from the sky, the sound of a string breaking, dying away, melancholy.*]

MADAME RANEVSKY. What's that?
LOPAKHIN. I don't know. It's a lifting-tub given way somewhere away in the mines. It must be a long way off.
GAYEF. Perhaps it's some sort of bird . . . a heron, or something.
TROPHIMOF. Or an owl. . . .
MADAME RANEVSKY [*shuddering*]. There's something uncanny about it!
FIRS. The same thing happened before the great misfortune: the owl screeched and the samovar kept humming.
GAYEF. What great misfortune?
FIRS. The Liberation. [*A pause.*]
MADAME RANEVSKY. Come, everyone, let's go in; it's getting late. [*To* ANYA.] You've tears in your eyes. What is it, little one? [*Embracing her.*]
ANYA. Nothing, mamma. I'm all right.
TROPHIMOF. There's someone coming.

[*A* Tramp *appears in a torn white-peaked cap and overcoat. He is slightly drunk.*]

TRAMP. Excuse me, but can I go through this way straight to the station?
GAYEF. Certainly. Follow this path.
TRAMP. I am uncommonly obliged to you, sir. [*Coughing.*] We're having lovely weather. [*Declaiming.*] 'Brother, my suffering brother' . . . 'Come forth to the Volga. Who moans?' . . . [*To* BARBARA.] Mademoiselle, please spare a sixpence for a hungry fellow-countryman.

[BARBARA, *frightened, screams.*]

LOPAKHIN [*angrily*]. There's a decency for even indecency to observe.
MADAME RANEVSKY. Take this; here you are. [*Fumbling in her purse.*] I haven't any silver. . . . Never mind, take this sovereign.

TRAMP. I am uncommonly obliged to you, madam.

[*Exit* TRAMP. *Laughter.*]

BARBARA [*frightened*]. I'm going! I'm going! Oh, mamma, there's nothing for the servants to eat at home, and you've gone and given this man a sovereign.
MADAME RANEVSKY. What's to be done with your stupid old mother? I'll give you up everything I have when I get back. Yermolái Alexéyitch, lend me some more money.
LOPAKHIN. Very good.
MADAME RANEVSKY. Come along, everyone; it's time to go in. We've settled all about your marriage between us, Barbara. I wish you joy.
BARBARA [*through her tears*]. You mustn't joke about such things, mamma.
LOPAKHIN. Amelia, get thee to a nunnery, go!
GAYEF. My hands are all trembling; it's ages since I had a game of billiards.
LOPAKHIN. Amelia, nymphlet, in thine orisons remember me.
MADAME RANEVSKY. Come along. It's nearly supper-time.
BARBARA. How he frightened me! My heart is simply throbbing.
LOPAKHIN. Allow me to remind you, the cherry orchard is to be sold on the twenty-second of August. Bear that in mind; bear that in mind!

[*Exeunt omnes except* TROPHIMOF *and* ANYA.]

ANYA [*laughing*]. Many thanks to the Tramp for frightening Barbara; at last we are alone.
TROPHIMOF. Barbara's afraid we shall go and fall in love with each other. Day after day she never leaves us alone. With her narrow mind she cannot understand that we are above love. To avoid everything petty, everything illusory, everything that prevents one from being free and happy, that is the whole meaning and purpose of our life. Forward! We march on irresistibly towards that bright star which burns far, far before us! Forward! Don't tarry, comrades!
ANYA [*clasping her hands*]. What beautiful things you say! [*A pause.*] Isn't it enchanting here to-day!
TROPHIMOF. Yes, it's wonderful weather.
ANYA. What have you done to me, Peter? Why is it that I no longer love the cherry orchard as I did? I used to love it so tenderly; I thought there was no better place on earth than our garden.
TROPHIMOF. All Russia is our garden. The earth is great and beautiful; it is full of wonderful places. [*A pause.*] Think, Anya, your grandfather, your great-grandfather and all your ancestors were serf-owners, owners

of living souls. Do not human spirits look out at you from every tree in the orchard, from every leaf and every stem? Do you not hear human voices? . . . Oh! it is terrible. Your orchard frightens me. When I walk through it in the evening or at night, the rugged bark on the trees glows with a dim light, and the cherry trees seem to see all that happened a hundred and two hundred years ago in painful and oppressive dreams. Well, well, we have fallen at least two hundred years behind the times. We have achieved nothing at all as yet; we have not made up our minds how we stand with the past; we only philosophise, complain of boredom, or drink vodka. It is so plain that, before we can live in the present, we must first redeem the past, and have done with it; and it is only by suffering that we can redeem it, only by strenuous, unremitting toil. Understand that, Anya.

ANYA. The house we live in has long since ceased to be our house; and I shall go away, I give you my word.

TROPHIMOF. If you have the household keys, throw them in the well and go away. Be free, be free as the wind.

ANYA [*enthusiastically*]. How beautifully you put it!

TROPHIMOF. Believe what I say, Anya; believe what I say. I'm not thirty yet; I am still young, still a student; but what I have been through! I am hungry as the winter; I am sick, anxious, poor as a beggar. Fate has tossed me hither and thither; I have been everywhere, everywhere. But wherever I have been, every minute, day and night, my soul has been full of mysterious anticipations. I feel the approach of happiness; Anya; I see it coming. . . .

ANYA [*pensively*]. The moon is rising.

[EPHIKHODOF *is heard still playing the same sad tune on his guitar. The moon rises. Somewhere beyond the poplar trees,* BARBARA *is heard calling for* ANYA: '*Anya, where are you?*']

TROPHIMOF. Yes, the moon is rising. [*A pause.*] There it is, there is happiness; it is coming towards us, nearer and nearer; I can hear the sound of its footsteps. . . . And if we do not see it, if we do not know it, what does it matter? Others will see it.

BARBARA [*without*]. Anya? Where are you?

TROPHIMOF. There's Barbara again! [*Angrily.*] It really is too bad!

ANYA. Never mind. Let us go down to the river. It's lovely there.

TROPHIMOF. Come on!

[*Exeunt* ANYA *and* TROPHIMOF.]

BARBARA [*without*]. Anya! Anya!

CURTAIN

Act III

A sitting-room separated by an arch from a big drawing-room behind. Chandelier lighted. The Jewish band mentioned in Act II is heard playing on the landing. Evening. In the drawing-room they are dancing the grand rond. SIMEONOF-PISHTCHIK *is heard crying:* 'Promenade à une paire!'

The dancers come down into the sitting-room. The first pair consists of PISHTCHIK *and* CHARLOTTE; *the second of* TROPHIMOF *and* MADAME RANEVSKY; *the third of* ANYA *and the* POST OFFICE OFFICIAL; *the fourth of* BARBARA *and the* STATION-MASTER, *etc., etc.* BARBARA *is crying softly and wipes away the tears as she dances. In the last pair comes* DUNYASHA. *They cross the sitting-room.*

PISHTCHIK. Grand rond, balancez. . . . Les cavaliers à genou et remerciez vos dames.

[FIRS *in evening dress carries seltzer water across on a tray.* PISHTCHIK *and* TROPHIMOF *come down into the sitting-room.*]

PISHTCHIK. I am a full-blooded man; I've had two strokes already; it's hard work dancing, but, as the saying goes: 'If you run with the pack, bark or no, but anyway wag your tail.' I'm as strong as a horse. My old father, who was fond of his joke, rest his soul, used to say, talking of our pedigree, that the ancient stock of the Simeónof-Píshtchiks was descended from that very horse that Caligula made a senator. . . . [*Sitting.*] But the worst of it is, I've got no money. A hungry dog believes in nothing but meat. [*Snoring and waking up again at once.*] I'm just the same. . . . It's nothing but money, money, with me.

TROPHIMOF. Yes, it's quite true, there is something horselike about your build.

PISHTCHIK. Well, well . . . a horse is a jolly creature . . . you can sell a horse.

[*A sound of billiards being played in the next room.* BARBARA *appears in the drawing-room beyond the arch.*]

TROPHIMOF [*teasing her*]. Madame Lopákhin! Madame Lopákhin!
BARBARA [*angrily*]. Mouldy gentleman!
TROPHIMOF. Yes, I'm a mouldy gentleman, and I'm proud of it.
BARBARA [*bitterly*]. We've hired the band, but where's the money to pay for it?

[*Exit* BARBARA.]

TROPHIMOF [*to* PISHTCHIK]. If the energy which you have spent in the course of your whole life in looking for money to pay the interest on your loans had been diverted to some other purpose, you would have had enough of it, I dare say, to turn the world upside down.
PISHTCHIK. Nietzsche, the philosopher, a very remarkable man, very famous, a man of gigantic intellect, says in his works that it's quite right to forge banknotes.
TROPHIMOF. What, have you read Nietzsche?
PISHTCHIK. Well . . . Dáshenka told me. . . . But I'm in such a hole, I'd forge 'em for two-pence. I've got to pay thirty-one pounds the day after to-morrow. . . . I've got thirteen pounds already. [*Feeling his pockets; alarmed.*] My money's gone! I've lost my money! [*Crying.*] Where's my money got to? [*Joyfully.*] Here it is, inside the lining. . . . It's thrown me all in a perspiration.

[*Enter* MADAME RANEVSKY *and* CHARLOTTE.]

MADAME RANEVSKY [*humming a lezginka*]. Why is Leoníd so long? What can he be doing in the town? [*To* DUNYASHA.] Dunyásha, ask the musicians if they'll have some tea.
TROPHIMOF. The sale did not come off, in all probability.
MADAME RANEVSKY. It was a stupid day for the musicians to come; it was a stupid day to have this dance. . . . Well, well, it doesn't matter. . . . [*She sits down and sings softly to herself.*]
CHARLOTTE [*giving* PISHTCHIK *a pack of cards*]. Here is a pack of cards. Think of any card you like.
PISHTCHIK. I've thought of one.
CHARLOTTE. Now shuffle the pack. That's all right. Give them here, O most worthy Mr. Píshtchik. Ein, zwei, drei! Now look and you'll find it in your side pocket.
PISHTCHIK [*taking a card from his side pocket*]. The Eight of Spades. You're perfectly right. [*Astonished.*] Well, I never!
CHARLOTTE [*holding the pack on the palm of her hand, to* TROPHIMOF]. Say quickly, what's the top card?

TROPHIMOF. Well, say the Queen of Spades.
CHARLOTTE. Right! [*To* PISHTCHIK.] Now then, what's the top card?
PISHTCHIK. Ace of Hearts.
CHARLOTTE. Right! [*She claps her hands; the pack of cards disappears.*] What a beautiful day we've been having.

[A *mysterious female* VOICE *answers her as if from under the floor:* 'Yes, indeed, a charming day, mademoiselle.']

CHARLOTTE. You are my beautiful ideal.
THE VOICE. *'I think you also ferry peautiful, mademoiselle.'*
STATION-MASTER [*applauding*]. Bravo, Miss Ventriloquist!
PISHTCHIK [*astonished*]. Well, I never! Bewitching Charlotte Ivánovna, I'm head over ears in love with you.
CHARLOTTE. In love! [*Shrugging her shoulders.*] Are you capable of love? Guter Mensch, aber schlechter Musikant!
TROPHIMOF [*slapping* PISHTCHIK *on the shoulder*]. You old horse!
CHARLOTTE. Now attention, please; one more trick. [*Taking a shawl from a chair.*] Now here's a shawl, and a very pretty shawl; I'm going to sell this very pretty shawl. [*Shaking it.*] Who'll buy? who'll buy?
PISHTCHIK [*astonished*]. Well, I never!
CHARLOTTE. Ein, zwei, drei! [*She lifts the shawl quickly; behind it stands* ANYA, *who drops a curtsy, runs to her mother, kisses her, then runs up into the drawing-room amid general applause.*]
MADAME RANEVSKY [*applauding*]. Bravo! bravo!
CHARLOTTE. Once more. Ein, zwei, drei! [*She lifts up the shawl; behind it stands* BARBARA, *bowing.*]
PISHTCHIK [*astonished*]. Well, I never!
CHARLOTTE. That's all. [*She throws the shawl over* PISHTCHIK, *makes a curtsy and runs up into the drawing-room.*]
PISHTCHIK [*hurrying after her*]. You little rascal . . . there's a girl for you, there's a girl. . . .

[*Exit.*]

MADAME RANEVSKY. And still no sign of Leoníd. What he's doing in the town so long, I can't understand. It must be all over by now; the property's sold; or the auction never came off; why does he keep me in suspense so long?
BARBARA [*trying to soothe her*]. Uncle has bought it, I am sure of that.
TROPHIMOF [*mockingly*]. Of course he has!
BARBARA. Grannie sent him a power of attorney to buy it in her name and transfer the mortgage. She's done it for Anya's sake. I'm perfectly sure that Heaven will help us and uncle will buy it.

MADAME RANEVSKY. Your Yaroslav grannie sent fifteen hundred pounds to buy the property in her name—she doesn't trust us—but it wouldn't be enough even to pay the interest. [*Covering her face with her hands.*] My fate is being decided to-day, my fate. . . .
TROPHIMOF [*teasing* BARBARA]. Madame Lopákhin!
BARBARA [*angrily*]. Perpetual Student! He's been sent down twice from the University.
MADAME RANEVSKY. Why do you get angry, Barbara? He calls you Madame Lopákhin for fun. Why not? You can marry Lopákhin if you like; he's a nice, interesting man; you needn't if you don't; nobody wants to force you, my pet.
BARBARA. I take it very seriously, mamma, I must confess. He's a nice man and I like him.
MADAME RANEVSKY. Then marry him. There's no good putting it off that I can see.
BARBARA. But, mamma, I can't propose to him myself. For two whole years everybody's been talking about him to me, everyone; but he either says nothing or makes a joke of it. I quite understand. He's making money; he's always busy; he can't be bothered with me. If I only had some money, even a little, even ten pounds, I would give everything up and go right away. I would go into a nunnery.
TROPHIMOF [*mockingly*]. What bliss!
BARBARA [*to* TROPHIMOF]. A student ought to be intelligent. [*In a gentler voice, crying.*] How ugly you've grown, Peter; how old you've grown! [*She stops crying; to* MADAME RANEVSKY.] But I can't live without work, mamma. I must have something to do every minute of the day.

[*Enter* YASHA.]

YASHA [*trying not to laugh*]. Ephikhódof has broken a billiard cue.

[*Exit* YASHA.]

BARBARA. What's Ephikhódof doing here? Who gave him leave to play billiards? I don't understand these people.

[*Exit* BARBARA.]

MADAME RANEVSKY. Don't tease her, Peter. Don't you see that she's unhappy enough already?
TROPHIMOF. I wish she wouldn't be so fussy, always meddling in other people's affairs. The whole summer she's given me and Anya no peace; she is afraid we'll work up a romance between us. What business is it of hers? I'm sure I never gave her any grounds; I'm not likely to be so commonplace. We are above love!

MADAME RANEVSKY. Then I suppose I must be beneath love. [*Deeply agitated.*] Why doesn't Leoníd come? Oh, if only I knew whether the property's sold or not! It seems such an impossible disaster, that I don't know what to think. . . . I'm bewildered. . . . I shall burst out screaming, I shall do something idiotic. Save me, Peter; say something to me, say something. . . .

TROPHIMOF. Whether the property is sold to-day or whether it's not sold, surely it's all one? It's all over with it long ago; there's no turning back, the path is overgrown. Be calm, dear Lyubóf Andréyevna. You mustn't deceive yourself any longer; for once you must look the truth straight in the face.

MADAME RANEVSKY. What truth? You can see what's truth, and what's untruth, but I seem to have lost the power of vision; I see nothing. You settle every important question so boldly; but tell me, Peter, isn't that because you're young, because you have never solved any question of your own as yet by suffering? You look boldly ahead; isn't it only that you don't see or divine anything terrible in the future; because life is still hidden from your young eyes? You are bolder, honester, deeper than we are, but reflect, show me just a finger's breadth of consideration, take pity on me. Don't you see? I was born here, my father and mother lived here, and my grandfather; I love this house; without the cherry orchard my life has no meaning for me, and if it *must* be sold, then for heaven's sake sell me too! [*Embracing* TROPHIMOF *and kissing him on the forehead.*] My little boy was drowned here. [*Crying.*] Be gentle with me, dear, kind Peter.

TROPHIMOF. You know I sympathise with all my heart.

MADAME RANEVSKY. Yes, yes, but you ought to say it somehow differently. [*Taking out her handkerchief and dropping a telegram.*] I am so wretched to-day, you can't imagine! All this noise jars on me, my heart jumps at every sound. I tremble all over; but I can't shut myself up; I am afraid of the silence when I'm alone. Don't be hard on me, Peter; I love you like a son. I would gladly let Anya marry you, I swear it; but you must work, Peter; you must get your degree. You do nothing; Fate tosses you about from place to place; and that's not right. It's true what I say, isn't it? And you must do something to your beard to make it grow better. [*Laughing.*] I can't help laughing at you.

TROPHIMOF [*picking up the telegram*]. I don't wish to be an Adonis.

MADAME RANEVSKY. It's a telegram from Paris. I get them every day. One came yesterday, another to-day. That savage is ill again; he's in a bad way. . . . He asks me to forgive him, he begs me to come; and I really ought to go to Paris and be with him. You look at me sternly; but what am I to do, Peter? What am I to do? He's ill, he's lonely, he's unhappy. Who is to look after him? Who is to keep him from doing stupid things? Who is to give him his medicine when it's time? After all, why should I be ashamed to say it? I love him, that's plain. I love him, I love him. . . . My love is like a stone tied round my neck; it's dragging me down to the bottom; but I love my stone. I can't live without it. [*Squeezing* TROPHIMOF's *hand.*] Don't think ill of me, Peter; don't say anything! Don't say anything!

TROPHIMOF [*crying*]. Forgive my bluntness, for heaven's sake; but the man has simply robbed you.

MADAME RANEVSKY. No, no, no! [*Stopping her ears.*] You mustn't say that!

TROPHIMOF. He's a rascal; everybody sees it but yourself; he's a petty rascal, a ne'er-do-well. . . .

MADAME RANEVSKY [*angry but restrained*]. You're twenty-six or twenty-seven, and you're still a Lower School boy!

TROPHIMOF. Who cares?

MADAME RANEVSKY. You ought to be a man by now; at your age you ought to understand people who love. You ought to love someone yourself, you ought to be in love! [*Angrily.*] Yes, yes! It's not purity with you; it's simply you're a smug, a figure of fun, a freak. . . .

TROPHIMOF [*horrified*]. What does she say?

MADAME RANEVSKY. 'I am above love!' You're not above love; you're simply what Firs calls a 'job-lot.' At your age you ought to be ashamed not to have a mistress!

TROPHIMOF [*aghast*]. This is awful! What does she say? [*Going quickly up into the drawing-room, clasping his head with his hands.*] This is something awful! I can't stand it; I'm off . . . [*Exit, but returns at once.*] All is over between us!

[*Exit to landing.*]

MADAME RANEVSKY [*calling after him*]. Stop, Peter! Don't be ridiculous; I was only joking! Peter!

[TROPHIMOF *is heard on the landing going quickly down the stairs, and suddenly falling down them with a crash.* ANYA *and* BARBARA *scream. A moment later the sound of laughter.*]

MADAME RANEVSKY. What has happened?

[ANYA *runs in.*]

ANYA [*laughing*]. Peter's tumbled downstairs. [*She runs out again.*]
MADAME RANEVSKY. What a ridiculous fellow he is!

[*The* STATION-MASTER *stands in the middle of the drawing-room behind the arch and recites Alexey Tolstoy's poem, 'The Sinner.' Everybody* stops to listen, but after a few lines the sound of a waltz is heard from the landing and he breaks off. All dance. TROPHIMOF, ANYA, BARBARA and MADAME RANEVSKY enter from the landing.]

MADAME RANEVSKY. Come, Peter, come, you pure spirit. . . . I beg your pardon. Let's have a dance. [*She dances with* TROPHIMOF. ANYA *and* BARBARA *dance.*]

[*Enter* FIRS, *and stands his walking-stick by the side door. Enter* YASHA *by the drawing-room; he stands looking at the dancers.*]

YASHA. Well, grandfather?

FIRS. I'm not feeling well. In the old days it was generals and barons and admirals that danced at our dances, but now we send for the Postmaster and the Station-Master, and even they make a favour of coming. I'm sort of weak all over. The old master, their grandfather, used to give us all sealing wax, when we had anything the matter. I've taken sealing wax every day for twenty years and more. Perhaps that's why I'm still alive.

YASHA. I'm sick of you, grandfather. [*Yawning.*] I wish you'd die and have done with it.

FIRS. Ah! you . . . job-lot! [*He mumbles to himself.*]

[TROPHIMOF *and* MADAME RANEVSKY *dance beyond the arch and down into the sitting-room.*]

MADAME RANEVSKY. Merci. I'll sit down. [*Sitting.*] I'm tired.

[*Enter* ANYA.]

ANYA [*agitated*]. There was somebody in the kitchen just now saying that the cherry orchard was sold to-day.

MADAME RANEVSKY. Sold? Who to?

ANYA. He didn't say who to. He's gone. [*She dances with* TROPHIMOF. *Both dance up into the drawing-room.*]

YASHA. It was some old fellow chattering; a stranger.

FIRS. And still Leoníd Andréyitch doesn't come. He's wearing his light overcoat *demi-saison*; he'll catch cold as like as not. Ah, young wood, green wood!

MADAME RANEVSKY. This is killing me. Yásha, go and find out who it was sold to.

YASHA. Why, he's gone long ago, the old man. [*Laughs.*]

MADAME RANEVSKY [*vexed*]. What are you laughing at? What are you glad about?

YASHA. He's a ridiculous fellow, is Ephikhódof. Nothing in him. Twenty-two misfortunes!

MADAME RANEVSKY. Firs, if the property is sold, where will you go to?
FIRS. Wherever you tell me, there I'll go.
MADAME RANEVSKY. Why do you look like that? Are you ill? You ought to be in bed.
FIRS [*ironically*]. Oh yes, I'll go to bed, and who'll hand the things around, who'll give orders? I've the whole house on my hands.
YASHA. Lyubóf Andréyevna! Let me ask a favour of you; be so kind; if you go to Paris again, take me with you, I beseech you. It's absolutely impossible for me to stay here. [*Looking about; sotto voce.*] What's the use of talking? You can see for yourself this is a barbarous country; the people have no morals; and the boredom! The food in the kitchen is something shocking, and on the top of it old Firs goes about mumbling irrelevant nonsense. Take me back with you; be so kind!

[*Enter* PISHTCHIK.]

PISHTCHIK. May I have the pleasure . . . a bit of a waltz, charming lady? [MADAME RANEVSKY *takes his arm.*] All the same, enchanting lady, you must let me have eighteen pounds. [*Dancing.*] Let me have . . . eighteen pounds.

[*Exeunt dancing through the arch.*]

YASHA [*singing to himself*].

    'Oh, wilt thou understand
    The turmoil of my soul?'

[*Beyond the arch appears a figure in grey tall hat and check trousers, jumping and waving its arms. Cries of* 'Bravo, Charlotte Ivánovna.']

DUNYASHA [*stopping to powder her face*]. Mamselle Anya tells me I'm to dance; there are so many gentlemen and so few ladies. But dancing makes me giddy and makes my heart beat, Firs Nikoláyevitch; and just now the gentleman from the post office said something so nice to me, oh, so nice! It quite took my breath away. [*The music stops.*]
FIRS. What did he say to you?
DUNYASHA. He said, 'You are like a flower.'
YASHA [*yawning*]. Cad!

[*Exit* YASHA.]

DUNYASHA. Like a flower! I am so ladylike and refined, I dote on compliments.
FIRS. You'll come to a bad end.

[*Enter* EPHIKHODOF.]

EPHIKHODOF. You are not pleased to see me, Avdótya Fyódorovna, no more than if I were some sort of insect. [*Sighing.*] Ah! Life! Life!
DUNYASHA. What do you want?
EPHIKHODOF. Undoubtedly perhaps you are right. [*Sighing.*] But of course, if one regards it, so to speak, from the point of view, if I may allow myself the expression, and with apologies for my frankness, you have finally reduced me to a state of mind. I quite appreciate my destiny; every day some misfortune happens to me, and I have long since grown accustomed to it, and face my fortune with a smile. You have passed your word to me, and although I . . .
DUNYASHA. Let us talk of this another time, if you please; but now leave me in peace. I am busy meditating. [*Playing with her fan.*]
EPHIKHODOF. Every day some misfortune befalls me, and yet, if I may venture to say so, I meet them with smiles and even laughter.

[*Enter* BARBARA *from the drawing-room.*]

BARBARA [*to* EPHIKHODOF]. Haven't you gone yet, Simeon? You seem to pay no attention to what you're told. [*To* DUNYASHA.] You get out of here, Dunyásha. [*To* EPHIKHODOF.] First you play billiards and break a cue, and then you march about the drawing-room as if you were a guest!
EPHIKHODOF. Allow me to inform you that it's not your place to call me to account.
BARBARA. I'm not calling you to account; I'm merely talking to you. All you can do is to walk about from one place to another, without ever doing a stroke of work; and why on earth we keep a clerk at all heaven only knows.
EPHIKHODOF [*offended*]. Whether I work, or whether I walk, or whether I eat, or whether I play billiards is a question to be decided only by my elders and people who understand.
BARBARA [*furious*]. How dare you talk to me like that! How dare you! I don't understand things, don't I? You clear out of here this minute! Do you hear me? This minute!
EPHIKHODOF [*flinching*]. I must beg you to express yourself in genteeler language.
BARBARA [*beside herself*]. You clear out this instant second! Out you go! [*Following him as he retreats towards the door.*] Twenty-two misfortunes! Make yourself scarce! Get out of my sight!

[*Exit* EPHIKHODOF.]

EPHIKHODOF [*without*]. I shall lodge a complaint against you.
BARBARA. What! You're coming back, are you? [*Seizing the walking-stick*

left at the door by FIRS.] Come on! Come on! Come on! I'll teach you! Are you coming? Are you coming? Then take that. [*She slashes with the stick.*]

[*Enter* LOPAKHIN.]

LOPAKHIN. Many thanks; much obliged.
BARBARA [*still angry, but ironical*]. Sorry!
LOPAKHIN. Don't mention it. I'm very grateful for your warm reception.
BARBARA. It's not worth thanking me for. [*She walks away, then looks round and asks in a gentle voice.*] I didn't hurt you?
LOPAKHIN. Oh, no, nothing to matter. I shall have a bump like a goose's egg, that's all.

[*Voices from the drawing-room: 'Lopákhin has arrived! Yermolái Alexéyitch!'*]

PISHTCHIK. Let my eyes see him, let my ears hear him! [*He and* LOPAKHIN *kiss.*] You smell of brandy, old man. We're having a high time, too.

[*Enter* MADAME RANEVSKY.]

MADAME RANEVSKY. Is it you, Yermolái Alexéyitch? Why have you been so long? Where is Leoníd?
LOPAKHIN. Leoníd Andréyitch came back with me. He's just coming.
MADAME RANEVSKY [*agitated*]. What happened? Did the sale come off? Tell me, tell me!
LOPAKHIN [*embarrassed, afraid of showing his pleasure.*] The sale was all over by four o'clock. We missed the train and had to wait till half-past eight. [*Sighing heavily.*] Ouf! I'm rather giddy. . . .

[*Enter* GAYEF. *In one hand he carries parcels; with the other he wipes away his tears.*]

MADAME RANEVSKY. What happened, Lénya? Come, Lénya! [*Impatiently, crying.*] Be quick, be quick, for heaven's sake!
GAYEF [*answering her only with an up and down gesture of the hand; to* FIRS, *crying*]. Here, take these. . . . Here are some anchovies and Black Sea herrings. I've had nothing to eat all day. Lord, what I've been through! [*Through the open door of the billiard-room comes the click of the billiard balls and* YASHA'S *voice: 'Seven, eighteen!'* GAYEF'S *expression changes; he stops crying.*] I'm frightfully tired. Come and help me change, Firs. [*He goes up through the drawing-room,* FIRS *following.*]
PISHTCHIK. What about the sale? Come on, tell us all about it.
MADAME RANEVSKY. Was the cherry orchard sold?

LOPAKHIN. Yes.

MADAME RANEVSKY. Who bought it?

LOPAKHIN. I did. [*A pause*. MADAME RANEVSKY *is overwhelmed at the news. She would fall to the ground but for the chair and table by her.* BARBARA *takes the keys from her belt, throws them on the floor in the middle of the sitting-room, and exit.*] I bought it. Wait a bit; don't hurry me; my head's in a whirl; I can't speak. . . . [*Laughing.*] When we got to the sale, Deriganof was there already. Leoníd Andréyitch had only fifteen hundred pounds, and Deriganof bid three thousand more than the mortgage right away. When I saw how things stood, I went for him and bid four thousand. He said four thousand five hundred. I said five thousand five hundred. He went up by five hundreds, you see, and I went up by thousands. . . . Well, it was soon over. I bid nine thousand more than the mortgage, and got it; and now the cherry orchard is mine! Mine! [*Laughing.*] Heaven's alive! Just think of it! The cherry orchard is mine! Tell me that I'm drunk; tell me that I'm off my head; tell me that it's all a dream! . . . [*Stamping his feet.*] Don't laugh at me! If only my father and my grandfather could rise from their graves and see the whole affair, how their Yermolái, their flogged and ignorant Yermolái, who used to run about barefooted in the winter, how this same Yermolái had bought a property that hasn't its equal for beauty anywhere in the whole world! I have bought the property where my father and grandfather were slaves, where they weren't even allowed into the kitchen. I'm asleep, it's only a vision, it isn't real. . . . 'Tis the fruit of imagination, wrapped in the mists of ignorance. [*Picking up the keys and smiling affectionately.*] She's thrown down her keys; she wants to show that she's no longer mistress here. . . . [*Jingling them together.*] Well, well, what's the odds? [*The musicians are heard tuning up.*] Hey, musicians, play! I want to hear you. Come everyone and see Yermolái Lopákhin lay his axe to the cherry orchard, come and see the trees fall down! We'll fill the place with villas; our grandsons and great-grandsons shall see a new life here. . . . Strike up, music! [*The band plays.* MADAME RANEVSKY *sinks into a chair and weeps bitterly.*] [*Reproachfully.*] Oh, why, why didn't you listen to me? You can't put the clock back now, poor dear. [*Crying.*] Oh, that all this were past and over! Oh, that our unhappy topsy-turvy life were changed!

PISHTCHIK [*taking him by the arm, sotto voce*]. She's crying. Let's go into the drawing-room and leave her alone to . . . Come on. [*Taking him by the arm, and going up towards the drawing-room.*]

LOPAKHIN. What's up? Play your best, musicians! Let everything be as I want. [*Ironically.*] Here comes the new squire, the owner of the cherry orchard! [*Knocking up by accident against a table and nearly throwing down the candelabra.*] Never mind, I can pay for everything!

[*Exit with* PISHTCHIK. *Nobody remains in the drawing-room or sitting-room except* MADAME RANEVSKY, *who sits huddled together, weeping bitterly. The band plays softly. Enter* ANYA *and* TROPHIMOF *quickly.* ANYA *goes to her mother and kneels before her.* TROPHIMOF *stands in the entry to the drawing-room.*]

ANYA. Mamma! Are you crying, mamma? My dear, good, sweet mamma! Darling, I love you! I bless you! The cherry orchard is sold; it's gone; it's quite true, it's quite true. But don't cry, mamma, you've still got life before you, you've still got your pure and lovely soul. Come with me, darling; come away from here. We'll plant a new garden, still lovelier than this. You will see it and understand, and happiness, deep, tranquil happiness will sink down on your soul, like the sun at eventide, and you'll smile, mamma. Come, darling, come with me!

CURTAIN

Act IV

Same scene as Act I. There are no window-curtains, no pictures. The little furniture left is stacked in a corner, as if for sale. A feeling of emptiness. By the door to the hall and at the back of the scene are piled portmanteaux, bundles, etc. The door is open and the voices of BARBARA *and* ANYA *are audible.*

[LOPAKHIN *stands waiting.* YASHA *holds a tray with small tumblers full of champagne.* EPHIKHODOF *is tying up a box in the hall. A distant murmur of voices behind the scene; the* PEASANTS *have come to say good-bye.*]

GAYEF [*without*]. Thank you, my lads, thank you.
YASHA. The common people have come to say good-bye. I'll tell you what I think, Yermolái Alexéyitch; they're good fellows but rather stupid.

[*The murmur of voices dies away. Enter* MADAME RANEVSKY *and* GAYEF *from the hall. She is not crying, but she is pale, her face twitches, she cannot speak.*]

GAYEF. You gave them your purse, Lyuba. That was wrong, very wrong!
MADAME RANEVSKY. I couldn't help it, I couldn't help it!

[*Exeunt both.*]

LOPAKHIN [*calling after them through the doorway*]. Please come here! Won't you come here? Just a glass to say good-bye. I forgot to bring any from town, and could only raise one bottle at the station. Come along. [*A pause.*] What, won't you have any? [*Returning from the door.*] If I'd known, I wouldn't have bought it. I shan't have any either. [YASHA *sets the tray down carefully on a chair.*] Drink it yourself, Yásha.
YASHA. Here's to our departure! Good luck to them that stay! [*Drinking.*] This isn't real champagne, you take my word for it.

LOPAKHIN. Sixteen shillings a bottle. [*A pause.*] It's devilish cold in here.
YASHA. The fires weren't lighted to-day; we're all going away. [*He laughs.*]
LOPAKHIN. What are you laughing for?
YASHA. Just pleasure.
LOPAKHIN. Here we are in October, but it's as calm and sunny as summer. Good building weather. [*Looking at his watch and speaking off.*] Don't forget that there's only forty-seven minutes before the train goes. You must start for the station in twenty minutes. Make haste.

[*Enter* TROPHIMOF *in an overcoat, from out of doors.*]

TROPHIMOF. I think it's time we were off. The carriages are round. What the deuce has become of my goloshes? I've lost 'em. [*Calling off.*] Anya, my goloshes have disappeared. I can't find them anywhere!
LOPAKHIN. I've got to go to Kharkof. I'll start in the same train with you. I'm going to spend the winter in Kharkof. I've been loafing about all this time with you people, eating my head off for want of work. I can't live without work, I don't know what to do with my hands; they dangle about as if they didn't belong to me.
TROPHIMOF. Well, we're going now, and you'll be able to get back to your beneficent labours.
LOPAKHIN. Have a glass.
TROPHIMOF. Not for me.
LOPAKHIN. Well, so you're off to Moscow?
TROPHIMOF. Yes, I'll see them into the town, and go on to Moscow to-morrow.
LOPAKHIN. Well, well. . . . I suppose the professors haven't started their lectures yet; they're waiting till you arrive.
TROPHIMOF. It is no affair of yours.
LOPAKHIN. How many years have you been up at the University?
TROPHIMOF. Try and think of some new joke; this one's getting a bit flat. [*Looking for his goloshes.*] Look here, I dare say we shan't meet again, so let me give you a bit of advice as a keepsake: Don't flap your hands about! Get out of the habit of flapping. Building villas, prophesying that villa residents will turn into small freeholders, all that sort of thing is flapping too. Well, when all's said and done, I like you. You have thin, delicate, artist fingers; you have a delicate, artist soul.
LOPAKHIN [*embracing him*]. Good-bye, old chap. Thank you for everything. Take some money off me for the journey if you want it.
TROPHIMOF. What for? I don't want it.
LOPAKHIN. But you haven't got any.
TROPHIMOF. Yes, I have. Many thanks. I got some for a translation. Here it is, in my pocket. [*Anxiously.*] I can't find my goloshes anywhere!

BARBARA [*from the next room*]. Here, take your garbage away! [*She throws a pair of goloshes on the stage.*]

TROPHIMOF. What are you so cross about, Barbara? Humph! . . . But those aren't *my* goloshes!

LOPAKHIN. In the spring I sowed three thousand acres of poppy and I have cleared four thousand pounds net profit. When my poppies were in flower, what a picture they made! So you see, I cleared four thousand pounds; and I wanted to lend you a bit because I've got it to spare. What's the good of being stuck up? I'm a peasant. . . . As man to man. . . .

TROPHIMOF. Your father was a peasant; mine was a chemist; it doesn't prove anything. [LOPAKHIN *takes out his pocket-book with paper money.*] Shut up, shut up. . . . If you offered me twenty thousand pounds I would not take it. I am a free man; nothing that you value so highly, all of you, rich and poor, has the smallest power over me; it's like thistledown floating on the wind. I can do without you; I can go past you; I'm strong and proud. Mankind marches forward to the highest truth, to the highest happiness possible on earth, and I march in the foremost ranks.

LOPAKHIN. Will you get there?

TROPHIMOF. Yes. [*A pause.*] I will get there myself or I will show others the way.

[*The sound of axes hewing is heard in the distance.*]

LOPAKHIN. Well, good-bye, old chap; it is time to start. Here we stand swaggering to each other, and life goes by all the time without heeding us. When I work for hours without getting tired, I get easy in my mind and I seem to know why I exist. But God alone knows what most of the people in Russia were born for. . . . Well, who cares? It doesn't affect the circulation of work. They say Leoníd Andréyitch has got a place; he's going to be in a bank and get six hundred pounds a year. . . . He won't sit it out, he's too lazy.

ANYA [*in the doorway*]. Mamma says, will you stop cutting down the orchard till she has gone.

TROPHIMOF. Really, haven't you got tact enough for that?

[*Exit* TROPHIMOF *by the hall.*]

LOPAKHIN. Of course, I'll stop them at once. What fools they are!

[*Exit after* TROPHIMOF.]

ANYA. Has Firs been sent to the hospital?

YASHA. I told 'em this morning. They're sure to have sent him.

ANYA [*to* EPHIKHODOF, *who crosses*]. Simeon Pateléyitch, please find out if Firs has been sent to the hospital.
YASHA [*offended*]. I told George this morning. What's the good of asking a dozen times?
EPHIKHODOF. Our centenarian friend, in my conclusive opinion, is hardly worth tinkering; it's time he was dispatched to his forefathers. I can only say I envy him. [*Putting down a portmanteau on a bandbox and crushing it flat.*] There you are! I knew how it would be!

[*Exit.*]

YASHA [*jeering*]. Twenty-two misfortunes.
BARBARA [*without*]. Has Firs been sent to the hospital?
ANYA. Yes.
BARBARA. Why didn't they take the note to the doctor?
ANYA. We must send it after them.

[*Exit* ANYA.]

BARBARA [*from the next room*]. Where's Yásha? Tell him his mother is here. She wants to say good-bye to him.
YASHA [*with a gesture of impatience*]. It's enough to try the patience of a saint!

[DUNYASHA *has been busying herself with the luggage. Seeing* YASHA *alone, she approaches him.*]

DUNYASHA. You might just look once at me, Yásha. You are going away, you are leaving me. [*Crying and throwing her arms round his neck.*]
YASHA. What's the good of crying? [*Drinking champagne.*] In six days I shall be back in Paris. To-morrow we take the express, off we go, and that's the last of us! I can hardly believe it's true. Vive la France! This place don't suit me. I can't bear it . . . it can't be helped. I have had enough barbarism; I'm fed up. [*Drinking champagne.*] What's the good of crying? You be a good girl, and you'll have no call to cry.
DUNYASHA [*powdering her face and looking into a glass*]. Write me a letter from Paris. I've been so fond of you, Yásha, ever so fond! I am a delicate creature, Yásha.
YASHA. Here's somebody coming. [*He busies himself with the luggage, singing under his breath.*]

[*Enter* MADAME RANEVSKY, GAYEF, ANYA *and* CHARLOTTE.]

GAYEF. We'll have to be off; it's nearly time. [*Looking at* YASHA.] Who is it smells of red herring?
MADAME RANEVSKY. We must take our seats in ten minutes. [*Looking

round the room.] Good-bye, dear old house, good-bye, grandpapa! When winter is past and spring comes again, you will be here no more; they will have pulled you down. Oh, think of all these walls have seen! [*Kissing* ANYA *passionately.*] My treasure, you look radiant, your eyes flash like two diamonds. Are you happy? very happy?

ANYA. Very, very happy. We're beginning a new life, mamma.

GAYEF [*gaily*]. She's quite right, everything's all right now. Till the cherry orchard was sold we were all agitated and miserable; but once the thing was settled finally and irrevocably, we all calmed down and got jolly again. I'm a bank clerk now; I'm a financier . . . red in the middle! And you, Lyuba, whatever you may say, you're looking ever so much better, not a doubt about it.

MADAME RANEVSKY. Yes, my nerves are better; it's quite true. [*She is helped on with her hat and coat.*] I sleep well now. Take my things out, Yásha. We must be off. [*To* ANYA.] We shall soon meet again, darling. . . . I'm off to Paris; I shall live on the money your grandmother sent from Yaroslav to buy the property. God bless your grandmother! I'm afraid it won't last long.

ANYA. You'll come back very, very soon, won't you, mamma? I'm going to work and pass the examination at the Gymnase and get a place and help you. We'll read all sorts of books together, won't we, mamma? [*Kissing her mother's hands.*] We'll read in the long autumn evenings, we'll read heaps of books, and a new, wonderful world will open up before us. [*Meditating.*] . . . Come back, mamma!

MADAME RANEVSKY. I'll come back, my angel. [*Embracing her.*]

[*Enter* LOPAKHIN. CHARLOTTE *sings softly.*]

GAYEF. Happy Charlotte, she's singing.

CHARLOTTE [*taking a bundle of rugs, like a swaddled baby*]. Hush-a-bye, baby, on the tree top . . . [*The baby answers, 'Wah, wah.'*] Hush, my little one, hush, my pretty one! ['Wah, wah.'] You'll break your mother's heart. [*She throws the bundle down on the floor again.*] Don't forget to find me a new place, please. I can't do without it.

LOPAKHIN. We'll find you a place, Charlotte Ivánovna, don't be afraid.

GAYEF. Everybody's deserting us. Barbara's going. Nobody seems to want us.

CHARLOTTE. There's nowhere for me to live in the town. I'm obliged to go. [*Hums a tune.*] What's the odds?

[*Enter* PISHTCHIK.]

LOPAKHIN. Nature's masterpiece!

PISHTCHIK [*panting*]. Oy, oy, let me get my breath again! . . . I'm done up! . . . My noble friends! . . . Give me some water.

GAYEF. Wants some money, I suppose. No, thank you; I'll keep out of harm's way.

[*Exit.*]

PISHTCHIK. It's ages since I have been here, fairest lady. [*To* LOPAKHIN.] You here? Glad to see you, you man of gigantic intellect. Take this; it's for you. [*Giving* LOPAKHIN *money.*] Forty pounds! I still owe you eighty-four.

LOPAKHIN [*amazed, shrugging his shoulders*]. It's like a thing in a dream! Where did you get it from?

PISHTCHIK. Wait a bit. . . . I'm hot. . . . A most remarkable thing! Some Englishmen came and found some sort of white clay on my land. [*To* MADAME RANEVSKY.] And here's forty pounds for you, lovely, wonderful lady. [*Giving her money.*] The rest another time. [*Drinking water.*] Only just now a young man in the train was saying that some . . . some great philosopher advises us all to jump off roofs. . . . Jump, he says, and there's an end of it. [*With an astonished air.*] Just think of that! More water!

LOPAKHIN. Who were the Englishmen?

PISHTCHIK. I leased them the plot with the clay on it for twenty-four years. But I haven't any time now . . . I must be getting on. I must go to Znoikof's, to Kardamónof's. . . . I owe everybody money. [*Drinking.*] Good-bye to everyone; I'll look in on Thursday.

MADAME RANEVSKY. We're just moving into town, and to-morrow I go abroad.

PISHTCHIK. What! [*Alarmed.*] What are you going into town for? Why, what's happened to the furniture? . . . Trunks? . . . Oh, it's all right. [*Crying.*] It's all right. People of powerful intellect . . . those Englishmen. It's all right. Be happy . . . God be with you . . . it's all right. Everything in this world has come to an end. [*Kissing* MADAME RANEVSKY'S *hand.*] If ever the news reaches you that *I* have come to an end, give a thought to the old . . . horse, and say, 'Once there lived a certain Simeónof-Píshtchik, Heaven rest his soul.'. . . Remarkable weather we're having. . . . Yes. . . . [*Goes out deeply moved. Returns at once and says from the doorway.*] Dáshenka sent her compliments.

[*Exit.*]

MADAME RANEVSKY. Now we can go. I have only two things on my mind. One is poor old Firs. [*Looking at her watch.*] We can still stay five minutes.

ANYA. Firs has been sent to the hospital already, mamma. Yásha sent him off this morning.

MADAME RANEVSKY. My second anxiety is Barbara. She's used to getting up early and working, and now that she has no work to do she's like a fish out of water. She has grown thin and pale and taken to crying, poor dear. . . . [*A pause.*] You know very well, Yermolái Alexéyitch, I always hoped . . . to see her married to you, and as far as I can see, you're looking out for a wife. [*She whispers to* ANYA, *who nods to* CHARLOTTE, *and both exeunt.*] She loves you; you like her; and I can't make out why you seem to fight shy of each other. I don't understand it.

LOPAKHIN. I don't understand it either, to tell you the truth. It all seems so odd. If there's still time, I'll do it this moment. Let's get it over and have done with it; without you there, I feel as if I should never propose to her.

MADAME RANEVSKY. A capital idea! After all, it doesn't take more than a minute. I'll call her at once.

LOPAKHIN. And here's the champagne all ready. [*Looking at the glasses.*] Empty; someone's drunk it. [YASHA *coughs.*] That's what they call lapping it up and no mistake!

MADAME RANEVSKY [*animated*]. Capital! We'll all go away. . . . *Allez,* Yásha. I'll call her. [*At the door.*] Barbara, leave all that and come here. Come along!

[*Exeunt* MADAME RANEVSKY *and* YASHA.]

LOPAKHIN [*looking at his watch*]. Yes.

[*A pause. A stifled laugh behind the door; whispering; at last enter* BARBARA.]

BARBARA [*examining the luggage*]. Very odd; I can't find it anywhere . . .
LOPAKHIN. What are you looking for?
BARBARA. I packed it myself, and can't remember. [*A pause.*]
LOPAKHIN. Where are you going to-day, Varvára Mikháilovna?
BARBARA. Me? I'm going to the Ragulins'. I'm engaged to go and keep house for them, to be housekeeper or whatever it is.
LOPAKHIN. Oh, at Yáshnevo? That's about fifty miles from here. [*A pause.*] Well, so life in this house is over now.
BARBARA [*looking at the luggage*]. Wherever can it be? Perhaps I put it in the trunk. . . . Yes, life here is over now; there won't be any more . . .
LOPAKHIN. And I'm off to Kharkof at once . . . by the same train. A lot of business to do. I'm leaving Ephikhódof to look after this place. I've taken him on.
BARBARA. Have you?
LOPAKHIN. At this time last year snow was falling already, if you remember; but now it's fine and sunny. Still, it's cold for all that. Three degrees of frost.

BARBARA. Were there? I didn't look. [A *pause*.] Besides, the thermometer's broken. [A *pause*.]
A VOICE [*at the outer door*]. Yermolái Alexéyitch!
LOPAKHIN [*as if he had only been waiting to be called*]. I'm just coming! [*Exit* LOPAKHIN *quickly*.]

[BARBARA *sits on the floor, puts her head on a bundle and sobs softly. The door opens and* MADAME RANEVSKY *comes in cautiously*.]

MADAME RANEVSKY. Well? [A *pause*.] We must be off.
BARBARA [*no longer crying, wiping her eyes*]. Yes, it's time, mamma. I shall get to the Ragulins' all right to-day, so long as I don't miss the train.
MADAME RANEVSKY [*calling off*]. Put on your things, Anya.

[*Enter* ANYA, *then* GAYEF *and* CHARLOTTE. GAYEF *wears a warm overcoat with a hood. The servants and drivers come in.* EPHIKHODOF *busies himself about the luggage*.]

MADAME RANEVSKY. Now we can start on our journey.
ANYA [*delighted*]. We can start on our journey!
GAYEF. My friends, my dear, beloved friends! Now that I am leaving this house for ever, can I keep silence? Can I refrain from expressing those emotions which fill my whole being at such a moment?
ANYA [*pleadingly*]. Uncle!
BARBARA. Uncle, what's the good?
GAYEF [*sadly*]. Double the red in the middle pocket. I'll hold my tongue.

[*Enter* TROPHIMOF, *then* LOPAKHIN.]

TROPHIMOF. Come along, it's time to start.
LOPAKHIN. Ephikhódof, my coat.
MADAME RANEVSKY. I must sit here another minute. It's just as if I had never noticed before what the walls and ceilings of the house were like. I look at them hungrily, with such tender love. . . .
GAYEF. I remember, when I was six years old, how I sat in this window on Trinity Sunday, and watched father starting out for church.
MADAME RANEVSKY. Has everything been cleared out?
LOPAKHIN. Apparently everything. [*To* EPHIKHODOF, *putting on his overcoat*.] See that everything's in order, Ephikhódof.
EPHIKHODOF [*in a hoarse voice*]. You trust me, Yermolái Alexéyitch.
LOPAKHIN. What's up with your voice?
EPHIKHODOF. I was just having a drink of water. I swallowed something.
YASHA [*contemptuously*]. Cad!
MADAME RANEVSKY. We're going, and not a soul will be left here.

LOPAKHIN. Until the spring.

[BARBARA *pulls an umbrella out of a bundle of rugs, as if she were brandishing it to strike.* LOPAKHIN *pretends to be frightened.*]

BARBARA. Don't be so silly! I never thought of such a thing.
TROPHIMOF. Come, we'd better go and get in. It's time to start. The train will be in immediately.
BARBARA. There are your goloshes, Peter, by that portmanteau. [*Crying.*] What dirty old things they are!
TROPHIMOF [*putting on his goloshes*]. Come along.
GAYEF [*much moved, afraid of crying*]. The train . . . the station . . . double the red in the middle; doublette to pot the white in the corner. . . .
MADAME RANEVSKY. Come on!
LOPAKHIN. Is everyone here? No one left in there? [*Locking the door.*] There are things stacked in there; I must lock them up. Come on!
ANYA. Good-bye, house! good-bye, old life!
TROPHIMOF. Welcome, new life!

[*Exit with* ANYA. BARBARA *looks round the room, and exit slowly. Exeunt* YASHA, *and* CHARLOTTE *with her dog.*]

LOPAKHIN. Till the spring, then. Go on, everybody. So-long!

[*Exit.* MADAME RANEVSKY *and* GAYEF *remain alone. They seem to have been waiting for this, throw their arms round each other's necks and sob restrainedly and gently, afraid of being overheard.*]

GAYEF [*in despair*]. My sister! my sister!
MADAME RANEVSKY. Oh, my dear, sweet lovely orchard! My life, my youth, my happiness, farewell! Farewell!
ANYA [*calling gaily, without*]. Mamma!
TROPHIMOF [*gay and excited*]. Aoo!
MADAME RANEVSKY. One last look at the walls and the windows. . . . Our dear mother used to walk up and down this room.
GAYEF. My sister! my sister!
ANYA [*without*]. Aoo!
MADAME RANEVSKY. We're coming. [*Exeunt.*]

[*The stage is empty. One hears all the doors being locked, and the carriages driving away. All is quiet. Amid the silence the thud of the axes on the trees echoes sad and lonely. The sound of footsteps.* FIRS *appears in the doorway* R. *He is dressed, as always, in his long coat and white waistcoat; he wears slippers. He is ill.*]

Firs [*going to the door* L. *and trying the handle*]. Locked. They've gone. [*Sitting on the sofa.*] They've forgotten me. Never mind! I'll sit here. Leoníd Andréyitch is sure to have put on his cloth coat instead of his fur. [*He sighs anxiously.*] He hadn't me to see. Young wood, green wood! [*He mumbles something incomprehensible.*] Life has gone by as if I'd never lived. [*Lying down.*] I'll lie down. There's no strength left in you; there's nothing, nothing. Ah, you . . . job-lot!

[*He lies motionless. A distant sound is heard, as if from the sky, the sound of a string breaking, dying away, melancholy. Silence ensues, broken only by the stroke of the axe on the trees far away in the cherry orchard.*]

CURTAIN

Joshua M. Edgemon

apply the ideas we talked about so far

critique the performance

2/3 page single space typed paper   Feb 3rd

(Doubleness
Immediacy
Spaces
Commentary on Human Nature [Condition]
"way of seeing")

* Performance Differs from the text
what messages were clearer?

* Production vs Expectation
<u>Critique</u> "everything"

Apply the ideas/ish talked about so far

Critique the performance

3-5 page single spaced typed paper. Ref 3x.

(Boulezians

Tanglewood

Spects
Commentary on Great Visitors
"How ad seeing")

※ Performance Different from the text.
what messages were chosen?

※ Production vs Expectation
Critique "everything"

DOVER·THRIFT·EDITIONS

The Misanthrope

MOLIÈRE

DOVER PUBLICATIONS, INC.
New York

DOVER THRIFT EDITIONS

GENERAL EDITOR: STANLEY APPELBAUM
EDITOR OF THIS VOLUME: SHANE WELLER

Published in Canada by General Publishing Company, Ltd., 30 Lesmill Road, Don Mills, Toronto, Ontario.
Published in the United Kingdom by Constable and Company, Ltd., 3 The Lanchesters, 162–164 Fulham Palace Road, London W6 9ER.

This Dover edition, first published in 1992, contains the unabridged text of *The Misanthrope*, based on the translation from the French by Henri van Laun published in Volume III of *The Dramatic Works of Molière*, William Paterson, Edinburgh, 1876.

Manufactured in the United States of America
Dover Publications, Inc., 31 East 2nd Street, Mineola, N.Y. 11501

Library of Congress Cataloging-in-Publication Data

Molière. 1622–1673.
   [Misanthrope. English]
   The misanthrope / Molière.
       p.   cm. — (Dover thrift editions)
   Translation of: The misanthrope.
   ISBN 0-486-27065-3 (pbk.)
   I. Title. II. Series.
[PQ1837.A445 1992]
842'.4—dc20
                                                                                     91-27835
                                                                                            CIP

Note

"MOLIÈRE" WAS THE pseudonym of the French actor-manager and dramatist Jean Baptiste Poquelin (1622–1673). Born in Paris and educated at the Jesuit Collège de Clermont, Molière abandoned his studies and the prospect of a court appointment to form the company of the Illustre Théâtre in 1643. The troupe began touring the French provinces in 1645. Although Molière was himself imprisoned twice for debt, his company returned in 1658 to Paris, where, under the patronage of Philippe, duc d'Orléans (the brother of King Louis XIV), it performed regularly at the theater of the Palais-Royal, becoming the Troupe du roi in 1665.

The Misanthrope, which is among the playwright's finest comedies, was first performed in 1666 at the Palais-Royal. In the original production, Molière himself played the role of Alceste, an implacable commentator on contemporary moral and aesthetic standards; Molière's wife, Armande Béjart, played Célimène. Although the originality of the comic vision in *The Misanthrope* was recognized immediately, the play provoked a mixed response, primarily because neither mocker nor mocked escapes unscathed: while ridiculing the fatuous literary pretentions and moral hypocrisy of the French aristocracy, the play also relishes the propensity for self-delusion that characterizes the intolerant critic of that same society.

Contents

Dramatis Personae	ix
Act I	1
Act II	13
Act III	23
Act IV	33
Act V	43

DRAMATIS PERSONAE

ALCESTE, *in love with Célimène*
PHILINTE, *his friend*
ORONTE, *in love with Célimène*
CÉLIMÈNE, *beloved by Alceste*
ÉLIANTE, *her cousin*
ARSINOÉ, *Célimène's friend*
ACASTE ⎫
CLITANDRE ⎭ *marquises*
BASQUE, *servant to Célimène*
DUBOIS, *servant to Alceste*
A Guard of the Maréchaussée

Scene: *At Paris, in* Célimène's *house*

ACT I.
SCENE I.

Philinte, Alceste.

Philinte. What is the matter? What ails you?
Alceste. [*Seated*] Leave me, I pray.
Philinte. But, once more, tell me what strange whim . . .
Alceste. Leave me, I tell you, and get out of my sight.
Philinte. But you might at least listen to people, without getting angry.
Alceste. I choose to get angry, and I do not choose to listen.
Philinte. I do not understand you in these abrupt moods, and although we are friends, I am the first . . .
Alceste. [*Rising quickly*] I, your friend? Lay not that flattering unction to your soul. I have until now professed to be so; but after what I have just seen of you, I tell you candidly that I am such no longer; I have no wish to occupy a place in a corrupt heart.
Philinte. I am then very much to be blamed from your point of view, Alceste?
Alceste. To be blamed? You ought to die from very shame; there is no excuse for such behavior, and every man of honor must be disgusted at it. I see you almost stifle a man with caresses, show him the most ardent affection, and overwhelm him with protestations, offers, and vows of friendship. Your ebullitions of tenderness know no bounds; and when I ask you who that man is, you can scarcely tell me his name; your feelings for him, the moment you have turned your back, suddenly cool; you speak of him most indifferently to me. Zounds! I call it unworthy, base, and infamous, so far to lower one's self as to act contrary to one's own feelings, and if, by some mischance, I had done such a thing, I should hang myself at once out of sheer vexation.
Philinte. I do not see that it is a hanging matter at all; and I beg of you

ALCESTE.   not to think it amiss if I ask you to show me some mercy, for I shall not hang myself, if it be all the same to you.

ALCESTE.   That is a sorry joke.

PHILINTE.   But, seriously, what would you have people do?

ALCESTE.   I would have people be sincere, and that, like men of honor, no word be spoken that comes not from the heart.

PHILINTE.   <u>When a man comes and embraces you warmly, you must pay him back in his own coin, respond as best you can to his show of feeling, and return offer for offer, and vow for vow.</u>

ALCESTE.   Not so. I cannot bear so base a method, which your fashionable people generally affect; there is nothing I detest so much as the contortions of these great time-and-lip servers, these affable dispensers of meaningless embraces, these obliging utterers of empty words who view every one in civilities, and treat the man of worth and the fop alike. What good does it do if a man heaps endearments on you, vows that he is your friend, that he believes in you, is full of zeal for you, esteems and loves you, and lauds you to the skies, when he rushes to do the same to the first rapscallion he meets? No, no, no heart with the least self-respect cares for esteem so prostituted; he will hardly relish it, even when openly expressed, when he finds that he shares it with the whole universe. Preference must be based on esteem, and to esteem every one is to esteem no one. Since you abandon yourself to the vices of the times, zounds! you are not the man for me. I decline this overcomplaisant kindness, which uses no discrimination. I like to be distinguished; and, to cut the matter short, the friend of all mankind is no friend of mine.

PHILINTE.   But when we are of the world, we must conform to the outward civilities which custom demands.

ALCESTE.   I deny it. We ought to punish pitilessly that shameful pretence of friendly intercourse. I like a man to be a man, and to show on all occasions the bottom of his heart in his discourse. Let that be the thing to speak, and never let our feelings be hidden beneath vain compliments.

PHILINTE.   There are many cases in which plain speaking would become ridiculous, and could hardly be tolerated. And, with all due allowance for your unbending honesty, it is as well to conceal your feelings sometimes. Would it be right or decent to tell thousands of people what we think of them? And when we meet with some one whom we hate or who displeases us, must we tell him so openly?

ALCESTE. Yes.
PHILINTE. What! Would you tell old Emilia that it ill becomes her to set up for a beauty at her age, and that the paint she uses disgusts everyone?
ALCESTE. Undoubtedly.
PHILINTE. Or Dorilas, that he is a bore, and that there is no one at court who is not sick of hearing him boast of his courage, and the lustre of his house?
ALCESTE. Decidedly so.
PHILINTE. You are jesting.
ALCESTE. I am not jesting at all; and I would not spare any one in that respect. It offends my eyes too much; and whether at court or in town, I behold nothing but what provokes my spleen. I become quite melancholy and deeply grieved to see men behave to each other as they do. Everywhere I find nothing but base flattery, injustice, self-interest, deceit, roguery. I cannot bear it any longer; I am furious; and my intention is to break with all mankind.
PHILINTE. This philosophical spleen is somewhat too savage. I cannot but laugh to see you in these gloomy fits, and fancy that I perceive in us two, brought up together, the two brothers described in *The School for Husbands*,* who . . .
ALCESTE. Good Heavens! drop your insipid comparisons.
PHILINTE. Nay, seriously, leave off these vagaries. The world will not alter for all your meddling. And as plain speaking has such charms for you, I shall tell you frankly that this complaint of yours is as good as a play, wherever you go, and that all those invectives against the manners of the age, make you a laughing stock to many people.
ALCESTE. So much the better, zounds! so much the better. That is just what I want. It is a very good sign, and I rejoice at it. All men are so odious to me, that I should be sorry to appear rational in their eyes.
PHILINTE. But do you wish harm to all mankind?
ALCESTE. Yes, I have conceived a terrible hatred for them.
PHILINTE. Shall all poor mortals, without exception, be included in this aversion? There are some, even in the age in which we live . . .
ALCESTE. No, they are all alike; and I hate all men: some, because they

---

* Molière's play *L'École des maris*, first performed in 1661.

are wicked and mischievous; others because they lend themselves to the wicked, and have not that healthy contempt with which vice ought to inspire all virtuous minds. You can see how unjustly and excessively complacent people are to that bare-faced scoundrel with whom I am at law. You may plainly perceive the traitor through his mask; he is well known everywhere in his true colors; his rolling eyes and his honeyed tones impose only on those who do not know him. People are aware that this low-bred fellow, who deserves to be pilloried, has, by the dirtiest jobs, made his way in the world; and that the splendid position he has acquired makes merit repine and virtue blush. Yet whatever dishonorable epithets may be launched against him everywhere, nobody defends his wretched honor. Call him a rogue, an infamous wretch, a confounded scoundrel if you like, all the world will say "yea," and no one contradicts you. But for all that, his bowing and scraping are welcome everywhere; he is received, smiled upon, and wriggles himself into all kinds of society; and, if any appointment is to be secured by intriguing, he will carry the day over a man of the greatest worth. Zounds! these are mortal stabs to me, to see vice parleyed with; and sometimes I feel suddenly inclined to fly into a wilderness far from the approach of men.

PHILINTE.   Great Heaven! let us torment ourselves a little less about the vices of our age, and be a little more lenient to human nature. Let us not scrutinize it with the utmost severity, but look with some indulgence at its failings. In society, we need virtue to be more pliable. If we are too wise, we may be equally to blame. Good sense avoids all extremes, and requires us to be soberly rational. This unbending and virtuous stiffness of ancient times shocks too much the ordinary customs of our own; it requires too great perfection from us mortals; we must yield to the times without being too stubborn; it is the height of folly to busy ourselves in correcting the world. I, as well as yourself, notice a hundred things every day which might be better managed, differently enacted; but whatever I may discover at any moment, people do not see me in a rage like you. I take men quietly just as they are; I accustom my mind to bear with what they do; and I believe that at court, as well as in the city, my phlegm is as philosophical as your bile.

ALCESTE.   But this phlegm, good sir, you who reason so well, could it not be disturbed by anything? And if perchance a friend should betray you; if he forms a subtle plot to get hold of what is yours; if people should try to spread evil reports about you, would you tamely submit to all this without flying into a rage?

PHILINTE. Ay, I look upon all these faults of which you complain as vices inseparably connected with human nature; in short, my mind is no more shocked at seeing a man a rogue, unjust, or selfish, than at seeing vultures eager for prey, mischievous apes, or fury-lashed wolves.

ALCESTE. What! I should see myself deceived, torn to pieces, robbed, without being . . . Zounds! I shall say no more about it; all this reasoning is beside the point!

PHILINTE. Upon my word, you would do well to keep silence. Rail a little less at your opponents, and attend a little more to your suit.

ALCESTE. That I shall not do; that is settled long ago.

PHILINTE. But whom then do you expect to solicit for you?

ALCESTE. Whom? Reason, my just right, equity.

PHILINTE. Shall you not pay a visit to any of the judges?

ALCESTE. No. Is my cause unjust or dubious?

PHILINTE. I am agreed on that; but you know what harm intrigues do, and . . .

ALCESTE. No. I am resolved not to stir a step. I am either right or wrong.

PHILINTE. Do not trust to that.

ALCESTE. I shall not budge an inch.

PHILINTE. Your opponent is powerful, and by his underhand work, may induce . . .

ALCESTE. It does not matter.

PHILINTE. You will make a mistake.

ALCESTE. Be it so. I wish to see the end of it.

PHILINTE. But . . .

ALCESTE. I shall have the satisfaction of losing my suit.

PHILINTE. But after all . . .

ALCESTE. I shall see by this trial whether men have sufficient impudence, are wicked, villainous, and perverse enough to do me this injustice in the face of the whole world.

PHILINTE. What a strange fellow!

ALCESTE. I could wish, were it to cost me ever so much, that, for the fun of the thing, I lost my case.

PHILINTE. But people will really laugh at you, Alceste, if they hear you go on in this fashion.

ALCESTE. So much the worse for those who will.

PHILINTE. But this rectitude, which you exact so carefully in every case, this absolute integrity in which you intrench yourself, do you perceive it in the lady you love? As for me, I am astonished that, appearing to be at war with the whole human race, you yet, notwithstanding everything that can render it odious to you, have found aught to charm your eyes. And what surprises me still more, is the strange choice your heart has made. The sincere Éliante has a liking for you, the prude Arsinoé looks with favor upon you, yet your heart does not respond to their passion; whilst you wear the chains of Célimène, who sports with you, and whose coquettish humor and malicious wit seem to accord so well with the manner of the times. How comes it that, hating these things as mortally as you do, you endure so much of them in that lady? Are they no longer faults in so sweet a charmer? Do not you perceive them, or if you do, do you excuse them?

ALCESTE. Not so. The love I feel for this young widow does not make me blind to her faults, and, notwithstanding the great passion with which she has inspired me, I am the first to see, as well as to condemn, them. But for all this, do what I will, I confess my weakness, she has the art of pleasing me. In vain I see her faults; I may even blame them; in spite of all, she makes me love her. Her charms conquer everything, and, no doubt, my sincere love will purify her heart from the vices of our times.

PHILINTE. If you accomplish this, it will be no small task. Do you believe yourself beloved by her?

ALCESTE. Yes, certainly! I should not love her at all, did I not think so.

PHILINTE. But if her love for you is so apparent, how comes it that your rivals cause you so much uneasiness?

ALCESTE. It is because a heart, deeply smitten, claims all to itself; I come here only with the intention of telling her what, on this subject, my feelings dictate.

PHILINTE. Had I but to choose, her cousin Éliante would have all my love. Her heart, which values yours, is stable and sincere; and this more compatible choice would have suited you better.

ALCESTE. It is true; my good sense tells me so every day; but good sense does not always rule love.

PHILINTE. Well, I fear much for your affections; and the hope which you cherish may perhaps . . .

SCENE II.

ORONTE, ALCESTE, PHILINTE.

ORONTE. [*To* ALCESTE] I have been informed yonder, that Éliante and Célimène have gone out to make some purchases. But as I heard that you were here, I came to tell you, most sincerely, that I have conceived the greatest regard for you, and that, for a long time, this regard has inspired me with the most ardent wish to be reckoned among your friends. Yes; I like to do homage to merit; and I am most anxious that a bond of friendship should unite us. I suppose that a zealous friend, and of my standing, is not altogether to be rejected. [*All this time* ALCESTE *has been musing, and seems not to be aware that* ORONTE *is addressing him. He looks up only when* ORONTE *says to him*]—It is to you, if you please, that this speech is addressed.

ALCESTE. To me, sir?

ORONTE. To you. Is it in any way offensive to you?

ALCESTE. Not in the least. But my surprise is very great; and I did not expect that honor.

ORONTE. The regard in which I hold you ought not to astonish you, and you claim it from the whole world.

ALCESTE. Sir . . .

ORONTE. Our whole kingdom contains nothing above the dazzling merit which people discover in you.

ALCESTE. Sir . . .

ORONTE. Yes; for my part, I prefer you to the most important in it.

ALCESTE. Sir . . .

ORONTE. May Heaven strike me dead, if I lie! And, to convince you, on this very spot, of my feelings, allow me, sir, to embrace you with all my heart, and to solicit a place in your friendship. Your hand, if you please. Will you promise me your friendship?

ALCESTE. Sir . . .

ORONTE. What! you refuse me?

ALCESTE. Sir, you do me too much honor; but friendship is a sacred thing, and to lavish it on every occasion is surely to profane it. Judgment and choice should preside at such a compact; we ought to know more of each other before engaging ourselves; and it may happen that our dispositions are such that we may both of us repent of our bargain.

ORONTE. Upon my word! that is wisely said; and I esteem you all the more for it. Let us therefore leave it to time to form such a pleasing bond; but, meanwhile, I am entirely at your disposal. If you have any business at court, every one knows how well I stand with the King; I have his private ear; and, upon my word, he treats me in everything with the utmost intimacy. In short, I am yours in every emergency; and, as you are a man of brilliant parts, and to inaugurate our charming amity, I come to read you a sonnet which I made a little while ago, and to find out whether it be good enough for publicity.

ALCESTE. I am not fit, sir, to decide such a matter. You will therefore excuse me.

ORONTE. Why so?

ALCESTE. I have the failing of being a little more sincere in those things than is necessary.

ORONTE. The very thing I ask; and I should have reason to complain, if, in laying myself open to you that you might give me your frank opinion, you should deceive me, and disguise anything from me.

ALCESTE. If that be the case, sir, I am perfectly willing.

ORONTE. *Sonnet* . . . It is a sonnet . . . *Hope* . . . It is to a lady who flattered my passion with some hope. *Hope* . . . They are not long, pompous verses, but mild, tender and melting little lines. [*At every one of these interruptions he looks at* ALCESTE]

ALCESTE. We shall see.

ORONTE. *Hope* . . . I do not know whether the style will strike you as sufficiently clear and easy, and whether you will approve of my choice of words.

ALCESTE. We shall soon see, sir.

ORONTE. Besides, you must know that I was only a quarter of an hour in composing it.

ALCESTE. Let us hear, sir; the time signifies nothing.

ORONTE. [*Reads*]

> *Hope, it is true, oft gives relief,*
> *Rocks for a while our tedious pain,*
> *But what a poor advantage, Phillis,*
> *When nought remains, and all is gone!*

PHILINTE. I am already charmed with this little bit.

ALCESTE. [*Softly to* PHILINTE] What! do you mean to tell me that you like this stuff?
ORONTE.

> *You once showed some complaisance,*
> *But less would have sufficed,*
> *You should not take that trouble*
> *To give me nought but hope.*

PHILINTE. In what pretty terms these thoughts are put!
ALCESTE. How now! you vile flatterer, you praise this rubbish!
ORONTE.

> *If I must wait eternally,*
> *My passion, driven to extremes,*
> *Will fly to death.*
> *Your tender cares cannot prevent this,*
> *Fair Phillis, aye we're in despair,*
> *When we must hope for ever.*

PHILINTE. The conclusion is pretty, amorous, admirable.
ALCESTE. [*Softly, and aside to* PHILINTE] A plague on the conclusion! I wish you had concluded to break your nose, you poisoner to the devil!
PHILINTE. I never heard verses more skilfully turned.
ALCESTE. [*Softly, and aside*] Zounds! . . .
ORONTE. [*To* PHILINTE] You flatter me, and you are under the impression perhaps . . .
PHILINTE. No, I am not flattering at all.
ALCESTE. [*Softly, and aside*] What else are you doing, you wretch?
ORONTE. [*To* ALCESTE] But for you, you know our agreement. Speak to me, I pray, in all sincerity.
ALCESTE. These matters, sir, are always more or less delicate, and every one is fond of being praised for his wit. But I was saying one day to a certain person, who shall be nameless, when he showed me some of his verses, that a gentleman ought at all times to exercise a great control over that itch for writing which sometimes attacks us, and should keep a tight rein over the strong propensity which one has to display such amusements; and that, in the frequent anxiety to show their productions, people are frequently exposed to act a very foolish part.
ORONTE. Do you wish to convey to me by this that I am wrong in desiring . . .

ALCESTE. I do not say that exactly. But I told him that writing without warmth becomes a bore; that there needs no other weakness to disgrace a man; that, even if people, on the other hand, had a hundred good qualities, we view them from their worst sides.

ORONTE. Do you find anything to object to in my sonnet?

ALCESTE. I do not say that. But, to keep him from writing, I set before his eyes how, in our days, that desire had spoiled a great many very worthy people.

ORONTE. Do I write badly? Am I like them in any way?

ALCESTE. I do not say that. But, in short, I said to him: What pressing need is there for you to rhyme, and what the deuce drives you into print? If we can pardon the sending into the world of a badly-written book, it will only be in those unfortunate men who write for their livelihood. Believe me, resist your temptations, keep these effusions from the public, and do not, how much soever you may be asked, forfeit the reputation which you enjoy at court of being a man of sense and a gentleman, to take, from the hands of a greedy printer, that of a ridiculous and wretched author. That is what I tried to make him understand.

ORONTE. This is all well and good, and I seem to understand you. But I should like to know what there is in my sonnet to . . .

ALCESTE. Candidly, you had better put it in your closet. You have been following bad models, and your expressions are not at all natural. Pray what is—*Rocks for a while our tedious pain?* And what, *When nought remains, and all is gone?* What, *You should not take that trouble to give me nought but hope?* And what, *Phillis, aye we're in despair when we must hope for ever?* This figurative style, that people are so vain of, is beside all good taste and truth; it is only a play upon words, sheer affectation, and it is not thus that nature speaks. The wretched taste of the age is what I dislike in this. Our forefathers, unpolished as they were, had a much better one; and I value all that is admired now-a-days far less than an old song which I am going to repeat to you:

> *Had our great monarch granted me*
> *His Paris large and fair;*
> *And I straightway must quit for aye*
> *The love of my true dear;*
> *Then would I say, King Hal, I pray,*
> *Take back your Paris fair,*
> *I love much mo my dear, I trow,*
> *I love much mo my dear.*

This versification is not rich, and the style is antiquated; but do you not see that it is far better than all those trumpery trifles against which good sense revolts, and that in this, passion speaks from the heart?

> Had our great monarch granted me
> His Paris large and fair;
> And I straightway must quit for aye
> The love of my true dear;
> Then would I say, King Hal, I pray,
> Take back your Paris fair,
> I love much mo my dear, I trow,
> I love much mo my dear.

This is what a really loving heart would say. [*To* PHILINTE, *who is laughing*] Yes, master wag, in spite of all your wit, I care more for this than for all the florid pomp and the tinsel which everybody is admiring now-a-days.

ORONTE. And I, I maintain that my verses are very good.

ALCESTE. Doubtless you have your reasons for thinking them so; but you will allow me to have mine, which, with your permission, will remain independent.

ORONTE. It is enough for me that others prize them.

ALCESTE. That is because they know how to dissemble, which I do not.

ORONTE. Do you really believe that you have such a great share of wit?

ALCESTE. If I praised your verses, I should have more.

ORONTE. I shall do very well without your approbation.

ALCESTE. You will have to do without it, if it be all the same.

ORONTE. I should like much to see you compose some on the same subject, just to have a sample of your style.

ALCESTE. I might, perchance, make some as bad; but I should take good care not to show them to any one.

ORONTE. You are mighty positive; and this great sufficiency . . .

ALCESTE. Pray, seek some one else to flatter you, and not me.

ORONTE. But, my little sir, drop this haughty tone.

ALCESTE. In truth, my big sir, I shall do as I like.

PHILINTE. [*Coming between them*] Stop, gentlemen! that is carrying the matter too far. Cease, I pray.

ORONTE. Ah! I am wrong, I confess; and I leave the field to you. I am your servant, sir, most heartily.

ALCESTE. And I, sir, am your most humble servant.

SCENE III.

PHILINTE, ALCESTE.

PHILINTE. Well! you see. By being too sincere, you have got a nice affair on your hands; I saw that Oronte, in order to be flattered . . .
ALCESTE. Do not talk to me.
PHILINTE. But . . .
ALCESTE. No more society for me.
PHILINTE. Is it too much . . .
ALCESTE. Leave me alone.
PHILINTE. If I . . .
ALCESTE. Not another word.
PHILINTE. But what . . .
ALCESTE. I will hear no more.
PHILINTE. But . . .
ALCESTE. Again?
PHILINTE. People insult . . .
ALCESTE. Ah! Zounds! this is too much. Do not dog my steps.
PHILINTE. You are making fun of me; I shall not leave you.

ACT II.
SCENE I.

ALCESTE, CÉLIMÈNE.

ALCESTE. Will you have me speak candidly to you, Madam? Well, then, I am very much dissatisfied with your behavior. I am very angry when I think of it; and I perceive that we shall have to break with each other. Yes; I should only deceive you were I to speak otherwise. Sooner or later a rupture is unavoidable; and if I were to promise the contrary a thousand times, I should not be able to bear this any longer.

CÉLIMÈNE. Oh, I see! it is to quarrel with me, that you wished to conduct me home?

ALCESTE. I do not quarrel. But your disposition, Madam, is too ready to give any first comer an entrance into your heart. Too many admirers beset you; and my temper cannot put up with that.

CÉLIMÈNE. Am I to blame for having too many admirers? Can I prevent people from thinking me amiable? and am I to take a stick to drive them away, when they endeavor by tender means to visit me?

ALCESTE. No, Madam, there is no need for a stick, but only a heart less yielding and less melting at their love-tales. I am aware that your good looks accompany you, go where you will; but your reception retains those whom your eyes attract; and that gentleness, accorded to those who surrender their arms, finishes on their hearts the sway which your charms began. The too agreeable expectation which you offer them increases their assiduities towards you; and your complacency, a little less extended, would drive away the great crowd of so many admirers. But tell me, at least, Madam, by what good fortune Clitandre has the happiness of pleasing you so mightily? Upon what basis of merit and sublime virtue do you ground the honor of your regard for him? Is it by the long nail on his little finger that he has acquired the esteem which you display for him? Are you, like all the rest of the fashionable world, fascinated by the dazzling merit of his fair wig? Do his great rolls make you love him? Do his many ribbons charm you? Is it by the attraction of his great German breeches that he has conquered your heart, whilst at the same time he pretended to be your slave? Or have his manner of smiling, and his falsetto voice, found out the secret of moving your feelings?

CÉLIMÈNE. How unjustly you take umbrage at him! Do not you know why I countenance him; and that he has promised to interest all his friends in my lawsuit?

ALCESTE. Lose your lawsuit, Madam, with patience, and do not countenance a rival whom I detest.

CÉLIMÈNE. But you are getting jealous of the whole world.

ALCESTE. It is because the whole world is so kindly received by you.

CÉLIMÈNE. That is the very thing to calm your frightened mind, because my good-will is diffused over all: you would have more reason to be offended if you saw me entirely occupied with one.

ALCESTE. But as for me, whom you accuse of too much jealousy, what have I more than any of them, Madam, pray?

CÉLIMÈNE. The happiness of knowing that you are beloved.

ALCESTE. And what grounds has my lovesick heart for believing it?

CÉLIMÈNE. I think that, as I have taken the trouble to tell you so, such an avowal ought to satisfy you.

ALCESTE. But who will assure me that you may not, at the same time, say as much to everybody else perhaps?

CÉLIMÈNE. Certainly, for a lover, this is a pretty amorous speech, and you make me out a very nice lady. Well! to remove such a suspicion, I retract this moment everything I have said; and no one but yourself shall for the future impose upon you. Will that satisfy you?

ALCESTE. Zounds! why do I love you so! Ah! if ever I get heart-whole out of your hands, I shall bless Heaven for this rare good fortune. I make no secret of it; I do all that is possible to tear this unfortunate attachment from my heart; but hitherto my greatest efforts have been of no avail; and it is for my sins that I love you thus.

CÉLIMÈNE. It is very true that your affection for me is unequaled.

ALCESTE. As for that, I can challenge the whole world. My love for you cannot be conceived; and never, Madam, has any man loved as I do.

CÉLIMÈNE. Your method, however, is entirely new, for you love people only to quarrel with them; it is in peevish expression alone that your feelings vent themselves; no one ever saw such a grumbling swain.

ALCESTE. But it lies with you alone to dissipate this ill-humor. For mercy's sake let us make an end of all these bickerings; deal openly with each other, and try to put a stop . . .

SCENE II.

CÉLIMÈNE, ALCESTE, BASQUE.

CÉLIMÈNE.   What is the matter?
BASQUE.   Acaste is below.
CÉLIMÈNE.   Very well! bid him come up.

SCENE III.

CÉLIMÈNE, ALCESTE.

ALCESTE.   What! can one never have a little private conversation with you? You are always ready to receive company; and you cannot, for a single instant, make up your mind to be "not at home."
CÉLIMÈNE.   Do you wish me to quarrel with Acaste?
ALCESTE.   You have such regard for people, which I by no means like.
CÉLIMÈNE.   He is a man never to forgive me, if he knew that his presence could annoy me.
ALCESTE.   And what is that to you, to inconvenience yourself so . . .
CÉLIMÈNE.   But, good Heaven! the amity of such as he is of importance; they are a kind of people who, I do not know how, have acquired the right to be heard at court. They take their part in every conversation; they can do you no good, but they may do you harm; and, whatever support one may find elsewhere, it will never do to be on bad terms with these very noisy gentry.
ALCESTE.   In short, whatever people may say or do, you always find reasons to bear with every one; and your very careful judgment . . .

SCENE IV.

ALCESTE, CÉLIMÈNE, BASQUE.

BASQUE. Clitandre is here, too, Madam.
ALCESTE. Exactly so. [*Wishes to go*]
CÉLIMÈNE. Where are you running to?
ALCESTE. I am going.
CÉLIMÈNE. Stay.
ALCESTE. For what?
CÉLIMÈNE. Stay.
ALCESTE. I cannot.
CÉLIMÈNE. I wish it.
ALCESTE. I will not. These conversations only weary me; and it is too bad of you to wish me to endure them.
CÉLIMÈNE. I wish it, I wish it.
ALCESTE. No, it is impossible.
CÉLIMÈNE. Very well, then; go, begone; you can do as you like.

SCENE V.

ÉLIANTE, PHILINTE, ACASTE, CLITANDRE, ALCESTE, CÉLIMÈNE, BASQUE.

ÉLIANTE. [*To* CÉLIMÈNE] Here are the two marquises coming up with us. Has anyone told you?
CÉLIMÈNE. Yes. [*To* BASQUE] Place chairs for everyone. [BASQUE *places chairs, and goes out*] [*To* ALCESTE] You are not gone?
ALCESTE. No; but I am determined, Madam, to have you make up your mind either for them or for me.
CÉLIMÈNE. Hold your tongue.
ALCESTE. This very day you shall explain yourself.
CÉLIMÈNE. You are losing your senses.
ALCESTE. Not at all. You shall declare yourself.
CÉLIMÈNE. Indeed!
ALCESTE. You must take your stand.
CÉLIMÈNE. You are jesting, I believe.

ALCESTE. Not so. But you must choose. I have been too patient.
CLITANDRE. Egad! I have just come from the Louvre, where Cléonte, at the levee, made himself very ridiculous. Has he not some friend who could charitably enlighten him upon his manners?
CÉLIMÈNE. Truth to say, he compromises himself very much in society; everywhere he carries himself with an air that is noticed at first sight, and when after a short absence you meet him again, he is still more absurd than ever.
ACASTE. Egad! Talk of absurd people, just now, one of the most tedious ones was annoying me. That reasoner, Damon, kept me, if you please, for a full hour in the broiling sun, away from my sedan-chair.
CÉLIMÈNE. He is a strange talker, and one who always finds the means of telling you nothing with a great flow of words. There is no sense at all in his tittle-tattle, and all that we hear is but noise.
ÉLIANTE. [*To* PHILINTE] This beginning is not bad; and the conversation takes a sufficiently agreeable turn against our neighbors.
CLITANDRE. Timante, too, Madam, is another original.
CÉLIMÈNE. He is a complete mystery from top to toe, who throws upon you, in passing, a bewildered glance, and who, without having anything to do, is always busy. Whatever he utters is accompanied with grimaces; he quite oppresses people by his ceremonies. To interrupt a conversation, he has always a secret to whisper to you, and that secret turns out to be nothing. Of the merest molehill he makes a mountain, and whispers everything in your ear, even to a "good-day."
ACASTE. And Geralde, Madam?
CÉLIMÈNE. That tiresome story-teller! He never comes down from his nobleman's pedestal; he continually mixes with the best society, and never quotes any one of minor rank than a Duke, Prince, or Princess. Rank is his hobby, and his conversation is of nothing but horses, carriages, and dogs. He *thee's* and *thou's* persons of the highest standing, and the word *Sir* is quite obsolete with him.
CLITANDRE. It is said that he is on the best of terms with Bélise.
CÉLIMÈNE. Poor silly woman, and the dreariest company! When she comes to visit me, I suffer from martyrdom; one has to rack one's brain perpetually to find out what to say to her; and the impossibility of her expressing her thoughts allows the conversation to drop every minute. In vain you try to overcome her stupid silence by the assistance of the most commonplace topic; even the fine weather, the rain, the heat and

the cold are subjects, which, with her, are soon exhausted. Yet for all that, her calls, unbearable enough, are prolonged to an insufferable length; and you may consult the clock, or yawn twenty times, but she stirs no more than a log of wood.

ACASTE. What think you of Adraste?

CÉLIMÈNE. Oh! What excessive pride! He is a man positively puffed out with conceit. His self-importance is never satisfied with the court, against which he inveighs daily; and whenever an office, a place, or a living is bestowed on another, he is sure to think himself unjustly treated.

CLITANDRE. But young Cléon, whom the most respectable people go to see, what say you of him?

CÉLIMÈNE. That it is to his cook he owes his distinction, and to his table that people pay visits.

ÉLIANTE. He takes pains to provide the most dainty dishes.

CÉLIMÈNE. True; but I should be very glad if he would not dish up himself. His foolish person is a very bad dish, which, to my thinking, spoils every entertainment which he gives.

PHILINTE. His uncle Damis is very much esteemed; what say you to him, Madam?

CÉLIMÈNE. He is one of my friends.

PHILINTE. I think him a perfect gentleman, and sensible enough.

CÉLIMÈNE. True; but he pretends to too much wit, which annoys me. He is always upon stilts, and, in all his conversations, one sees him laboring to say smart things. Since he took it into his head to be clever, he is so difficult to please that nothing suits his taste. He must needs find mistakes in everything that one writes, and thinks that to bestow praise does not become a wit, that to find fault shows learning, that only fools admire and laugh, and that, by not approving of anything in the works of our time, he is superior to all other people. Even in conversations he finds something to cavil at, the subjects are too trivial for his condescension; and, with arms crossed on his breast, he looks down from the height of his intellect with pity on what everyone says.

ACASTE. Drat it! his very picture.

CLITANDRE. [*To* CÉLIMÈNE] You have an admirable knack of portraying people to the life.

ALCESTE. Capital, go on, my fine courtly friends. You spare no one, and everyone will have his turn. Nevertheless, let but any one of those persons appear, and we shall see you rush to meet him, offer him your hand, and, with a flattering kiss, give weight to your protestations of being his servant.

CLITANDRE. Why this to us? If what is said offends you, the reproach must be addressed to this lady.

ALCESTE. No, gadzooks! it concerns you; for your assenting smiles draw from her wit all these slanderous remarks. Her satirical vein is incessantly recruited by the culpable incense of your flattery; and her mind would find fewer charms in raillery, if she discovered that no one applauded her. Thus it is that to flatterers we ought everywhere to impute the vices which are sown among mankind.

PHILINTE. But why do you take so great an interest in those people, for you would condemn the very things that are blamed in them?

CÉLIMÈNE. And is not this gentleman bound to contradict? Would you have him subscribe to the general opinion; and must he not everywhere display the spirit of contradiction with which Heaven has endowed him? Other people's sentiments can never please him. He always supports a contrary idea, and he would think himself too much of the common herd, were he observed to be of any one's opinion but his own. The honor of gainsaying has so many charms for him, that he very often takes up the cudgels against himself; he combats his own sentiments as soon as he hears them from other folks' lips.

ALCESTE. In short, Madam, the laughers are on your side; and you may launch your satire against me.

PHILINTE. But it is very true, too, that you always take up arms against everything that is said; and that your avowed spleen cannot bear people to be praised or blamed.

ALCESTE. 'Sdeath! spleen against mankind is always seasonable, because they are never in the right, and I see that, in all their dealings, they either praise impertinently, or censure rashly.

CÉLIMÈNE. But . . .

ALCESTE. No, Madam, no, though I were to die for it, you have pastimes which I cannot tolerate; and people are very wrong to nourish in your heart this great attachment to the very faults which they blame in you.

CLITANDRE. As for myself, I do not know; but I openly acknowledge that hitherto I have thought this lady faultless.

ACASTE. I see that she is endowed with charms and attractions; but the faults which she has have not struck me.

ALCESTE. So much the more have they struck me; and far from appearing blind, she knows that I take care to reproach her with them. The more we love any one, the less we ought to flatter her. True love shows itself by overlooking nothing; and, were I a lady, I would banish all those mean-spirited lovers who submit to all my sentiments, and whose mild complacencies every moment offer up incense to my vagaries.

CÉLIMÈNE. In short, if hearts were ruled by you we ought, to love well, to relinquish all tenderness, and make it the highest aim of perfect attachment to rail heartily at the persons we love.

ÉLIANTE. Love, generally speaking, is little apt to put up with these decrees, and lovers are always observed to extol their choice. Their passion never sees aught to blame in it, and in the beloved all things become lovable. They think their faults perfections, and invent sweet terms to call them by. The pale one vies with the jessamine in fairness; another, dark enough to frighten people, becomes an adorable brunette; the lean one has a good shape and is lithe; the stout one has a portly and majestic bearing; the slattern, who has few charms, passes under the name of a careless beauty; the giantess seems a very goddess in their sight; the dwarf is an epitome of all the wonders of Heaven; the proud one has a soul worthy of a diadem; the artful brims with wit; the silly one is very good-natured; the chatterbox is good-tempered; and the silent one modest and reticent. Thus a passionate swain loves even the very faults of those of whom he is enamored.

ALCESTE. And I maintain that . . .

CÉLIMÈNE. Let us drop the subject, and take a turn or two in the gallery. What! are you going, gentlemen?

CLITANDRE *and* ACASTE. No, no, Madam.

ALCESTE. The fear of their departure troubles you very much. Go when you like, gentlemen; but I tell you beforehand that I shall not leave until you leave.

ACASTE. Unless it inconveniences this lady, I have nothing to call me elsewhere the whole day.

CLITANDRE. I, provided I am present when the King retires, I have no other matter to call me away.

CÉLIMÈNE. [*To* ALCESTE] You only joke, I fancy.

ALCESTE. Not at all. We shall soon see whether it is me of whom you wish to get rid.

SCENE VI.

ALCESTE, CÉLIMÈNE, ÉLIANTE, ACASTE, PHILINTE, CLITANDRE, BASQUE.

BASQUE. [*To* ALCESTE] There is a man downstairs, sir, who wishes to speak to you on business which cannot be postponed.
ALCESTE. Tell him that I have no such urgent business.
BASQUE. He wears a jacket with large plaited skirts embroidered with gold.
CÉLIMÈNE. [*To* ALCESTE] Go and see who it is, or else let him come in.

SCENE VII.

ALCESTE, CÉLIMÈNE, ÉLIANTE, ACASTE, PHILINTE, CLITANDRE, a Guard of the Maréchaussée.

ALCESTE. [*Going to meet the* Guard] What may be your pleasure? Come in, sir.
GUARD. I would have a few words privately with you, sir.
ALCESTE. You may speak aloud, sir, so as to let me know.
GUARD. The Marshals of France, whose commands I bear, hereby summon you to appear before them immediately, sir.
ALCESTE. Whom? Me, sir?
GUARD. Yourself.
ALCESTE. And for what?
PHILINTE. [*To* ALCESTE] It is this ridiculous affair between you and Oronte.
CÉLIMÈNE. [*To* PHILINTE] What do you mean?
PHILINTE. Oronte and he have been insulting each other just now about some trifling verses which he did not like; and the Marshals wish to nip the affair in the bud.
ALCESTE. Well, I shall never basely submit.
PHILINTE. But you must obey the summons: come, get ready.
ALCESTE. How will they settle this between us? Will the edict of these gentlemen oblige me to approve of the verses which are the cause of

our quarrel? I will not retract what I have said; I think them abominable.

PHILINTE.   But with a little milder tone . . .

ALCESTE.   I will not abate one jot; the verses are execrable.

PHILINTE.   You ought to show a more accommodating spirit. Come along.

ALCESTE.   I shall go, but nothing shall induce me to retract.

PHILINTE.   Go and show yourself.

ALCESTE.   Unless an express order from the King himself commands me to approve of the verses which cause all this trouble, I shall ever maintain, egad, that they are bad, and that a fellow deserves hanging for making them. [*To* CLITANDRE *and* ACASTE, *who are laughing*] Hang it! gentlemen, I did not think I was so amusing.

CÉLIMÈNE.   Go quickly whither you are wanted.

ALCESTE.   I am going, Madam; but shall come back here to finish our discussion.

ACT III.
SCENE I.

CLITANDRE, ACASTE.

CLITANDRE. My dear marquis, you appear mightily pleased with yourself; everything amuses you, and nothing discomposes you. But really and truly, think you, without flattering yourself, that you have good reasons for appearing so joyful?

ACASTE. Egad, I do not find, on looking at myself, any matter to be sorrowful about. I am wealthy, I am young, and am descended from a family which, with some appearance of truth, may be called noble; and I think that, by the rank which my lineage confers upon me, there are very few offices to which I might not aspire. As for courage, which we ought especially to value, it is well known—this without vanity—that I do not lack it; and people have seen me carry on an affair of honor in a manner sufficiently vigorous and brisk. As for wit, I have some, no doubt; and as for good taste, to judge and reason upon everything without study; at "first nights," of which I am very fond, to take my place as a critic upon the stage, to give my opinion as a judge, to applaud, and point out the best passages by repeated bravoes, I am sufficiently adroit; I carry myself well, and am good-looking, have particularly fine teeth, and a good figure. I believe, without flattering myself, that, as for dressing in good taste, very few will dispute the palm with me. I find myself treated with every possible consideration, very much beloved by the fair sex; and I stand very well with the King. With all that, I think, dear marquis, that one might be satisfied with oneself anywhere.

CLITANDRE. True. But, finding so many easy conquests elsewhere, why come you here to utter fruitless sighs?

ACASTE. I? Zounds! I have neither the wish nor the disposition to put up with the indifference of any woman. I leave it to awkward and ordinary people to burn constantly for cruel fair maidens, to languish at their feet, and to bear with their severities, to invoke the aid of sighs and tears, and to endeavor, by long and persistent assiduities, to obtain what is denied to their little merit. But men of my stamp, marquis, are not made to love on trust, and be at all the expenses themselves. Be the merit of the fair ever so great, I think, thank Heaven, that we have our value as well as they; that it is not reasonable to enthrall a heart like mine without its costing them anything; and that, to weigh everything in a just scale, the advances should be, at least, reciprocal.

CLITANDRE. Then you think that you are right enough here, marquis?

ACASTE. I have some reason, marquis, to think so.

CLITANDRE. Believe me, divest yourself of this great mistake: you flatter yourself, dear friend, and are altogether self-deceived.

ACASTE. It is true. I flatter myself, and am, in fact, altogether self-deceived.

CLITANDRE. But what causes you to judge your happiness to be complete?

ACASTE. I flatter myself.

CLITANDRE. Upon what do you ground your belief?

ACASTE. I am altogether self-deceived.

CLITANDRE. Have you any sure proofs?

ACASTE. I am mistaken, I tell you.

CLITANDRE. Has Célimène made you any secret avowal of her inclinations?

ACASTE. No, I am very badly treated by her.

CLITANDRE. Answer me, I pray.

ACASTE. I meet with nothing but rebuffs.

CLITANDRE. A truce to your raillery; and tell me what hope she has held out to you.

ACASTE. I am the rejected, and you are the lucky one. She has a great aversion to me, and one of these days I shall have to hang myself.

CLITANDRE. Nonsense. Shall we two, marquis, to adjust our love affairs, make a compact together? Whenever one of us shall be able to show a certain proof of having the greater share in Célimène's heart, the other shall leave the field free to the supposed conqueror, and by that means rid him of an obstinate rival.

ACASTE. Egad! you please me with these words, and I agree to that from the bottom of my heart. But, hush.

SCENE II.

Célimène, Acaste, Clitandre.

Célimène. What! here still?
Clitandre. Love, Madam, detains us.
Célimène. I hear a carriage below. Do you know whose it is?
Clitandre. No.

SCENE III.

Célimène, Acaste, Clitandre, Basque.

Basque. Arsinoé, Madam, is coming up to see you.
Célimène. What does the woman want with me?
Basque. Éliante is downstairs talking to her.
Célimène. What is she thinking about, and what brings her here?
Acaste. She has everywhere the reputation of being a consummate prude, and her fervent zeal . . .
Célimène. Psha, downright humbug. In her inmost soul she is as worldly as any; and her every nerve is strained to hook some one, without being successful, however. She can only look with envious eyes on the accepted lovers of others; and in her wretched condition, forsaken by all, she is for ever railing against the blindness of the age. She endeavors to hide the dreadful isolation of her home under a false cloak of prudishness; and to save the credit of her feeble charms, she brands as criminal the power which they lack. Yet a swain would not come at all amiss to the lady; and she has even a tender hankering after Alceste. Every attention that he pays me, she looks upon as a theft committed by me, and as an insult to her attractions; and her jealous spite, which she can hardly hide, breaks out against me at every opportunity, and in an underhand manner. In short, I never saw anything, to my fancy, so stupid. She is impertinent to the last degree . . .

SCENE IV.

Arsinoé, Célimène, Clitandre, Acaste.

Célimène. Ah! what happy chance brings you here, Madam? I was really getting uneasy about you.
Arsinoé. I have come to give you some advice as a matter of duty.
Célimène. How very glad I am to see you!
    [*Exeunt* Clitandre *and* Acaste, *laughing*]

SCENE V.

Arsinoé, Célimène.

Arsinoé. They could not have left at a more convenient opportunity.
Célimène. Shall we sit down?
Arsinoé. It is not necessary. Friendship, Madam, must especially show itself in matters which may be of consequence to us; and as there are none of greater importance than honor and decorum, I come to prove to you, by an advice which closely touches your reputation, the friendship which I feel for you. Yesterday I was with some people of rare virtue, where the conversation turned upon you; and there, your conduct, which is causing some stir, was unfortunately, Madam, far from being commended. That crowd of people, whose visits you permit, your gallantry and the noise it makes, were criticized rather more freely and more severely than I could have wished. You can easily imagine whose part I took. I did all I could to defend you. I exonerated you, and vouched for the purity of your heart, and the honesty of your intentions. But you know there are things in life which one cannot well defend, although one may have the greatest wish to do so; and I was at last obliged to confess that the way in which you lived did you some harm; that, in the eyes of the world, it had a doubtful look; that there was no story so ill-natured as not to be everywhere told about it; and that, if you liked, your behavior might give less cause for censure. Not that I believe that decency is in any way outraged. Heaven forbid that I should harbor such a thought! But the

world is so ready to give credit to the faintest shadow of a crime, and it is not enough to live blameless one's self. Madam, I believe you to be too sensible not to take in good part this useful counsel, and not to ascribe it only to the inner promptings of an affection that feels an interest in your welfare.

CÉLIMÈNE. Madam, I have a great many thanks to return you. Such counsel lays me under an obligation; and, far from taking it amiss, I intend this very moment to repay the favor, by giving you an advice which also touches your reputation closely; and as I see you prove yourself my friend by acquainting me with the stories that are current of me, I shall follow so nice an example, by informing you what is said of you. In a house the other day, where I paid a visit, I met some people of exemplary merit, who, while talking of the proper duties of a well spent life, turned the topic of the conversation upon you, Madam. There your prudishness and your too fervent zeal were not at all cited as a good example. This affectation of a grave demeanor, your eternal conversations on wisdom and honor, your mincings and mouthings at the slightest shadows of indecency, which an innocent though ambiguous word may convey, that lofty esteem in which you hold yourself, and those pitying glances which you cast upon all, your frequent lectures and your acrid censures on things which are pure and harmless; all this, if I may speak frankly to you, Madam, was blamed unanimously. What is the good, said they, of this modest mien and this prudent exterior, which is belied by all the rest? She says her prayers with the utmost exactness; but she beats her servants and pays them no wages. She displays great fervor in every place of devotion; but she paints and wishes to appear handsome. She covers the nudities in her pictures; but loves the reality. As for me, I undertook your defence against everyone, and positively assured them that it was nothing but scandal; but the general opinion went against me, as they came to the conclusion that you would do well to concern yourself less about the actions of others, and take a little more pains with your own; that one ought to look a long time at one's self before thinking of condemning other people; that when we wish to correct others, we ought to add the weight of a blameless life; and that even then, it would be better to leave it to those whom Heaven has ordained for the task. Madam, I also believe you to be too sensible not to take in good part this useful counsel, and not to ascribe it only to the inner promptings of an affection that feels an interest in your welfare.

ARSINOÉ. To whatever we may be exposed when we reprove, I did not expect this retort, Madam, and, by its very sting, I see how my sincere advice has hurt your feelings.

CÉLIMÈNE. On the contrary, Madam; and, if we were reasonable, these mutual counsels would become customary. If honestly made use of, they would to a great extent destroy the excellent opinion people have of themselves. It depends entirely on you whether we shall continue this trustworthy practice with equal zeal, and whether we shall take great care to tell each other, between ourselves, what we hear, you of me, I of you.

ARSINOÉ. Ah! Madam, I can hear nothing said of you. It is in me that people find so much to reprove.

CÉLIMÈNE. Madam, it is easy, I believe, to blame or praise everything; and everyone may be right, according to their age and taste. There is a time for gallantry, there is one also for prudishness. One may out of policy take to it, when youthful attractions have faded away. It sometimes serves to hide vexatious ravages of time. I do not say that I shall not follow your example, one of these days. Those things come with old age; but twenty, as everyone well knows, is not an age to play the prude.

ARSINOÉ. You certainly pride yourself upon a very small advantage, and you boast terribly of your age. Whatever difference there may be between your years and mine, there is no occasion to make such a tremendous fuss about it; and I am at a loss to know, Madam, why you should get so angry, and what makes you goad me in this manner.

CÉLIMÈNE. And I, Madam, am at an equal loss to know why one hears you inveigh so bitterly against me everywhere. Must I always suffer for your vexations? Can I help it, if people refuse to pay you any attentions? If men will fall in love with me, and will persist in offering me each day those attentions of which your heart would wish to see me deprived, I cannot alter it, and it is not my fault. I leave you the field free, and do not prevent you from having charms to attract people.

ARSINOÉ. Alas! and do you think that I would trouble myself about this crowd of lovers of which you are so vain, and that it is not very easy to judge at what price they may be attracted now-a-days? Do you wish to make it be believed, that, judging by what is going on, your merit alone attracts this crowd; that their affection for you is strictly honest, and that it is for nothing but your virtue that they all pay you their court? People are not blinded by those empty pretences; the world is not duped in that way; and I see many ladies who are capable of inspiring a tender feeling, yet who do not succeed in attracting a crowd of beaux; and from that fact we may draw our conclusion that those conquests are not altogether made without some great advances; that no one cares to sigh for us, for our handsome looks only; and that the attentions bestowed on us are generally dearly bought. Do not therefore pull yourself up with vain-glory about the trifling advantages of a poor victory; and moderate slightly the pride on your good looks, instead of looking down upon people on account of them. If I were at all envious about your conquests, I dare say that I might manage like other people; be under no restraint, and thus show plainly that one may have lovers, when one wishes for them.

CÉLIMÈNE.   Do have some then, Madam, and let us see you try it; endeavor to please by this extraordinary secret; and without . . .

ARSINOÉ.   Let us break off this conversation, Madam, it might excite too much both your temper and mine; and I would have already taken my leave, had I not been obliged to wait for my carriage.

CÉLIMÈNE.   Please stay as long as you like, and do not hurry yourself on that account, Madam. But instead of wearying you any longer with my presence, I am going to give you some more pleasant company. This gentleman, who comes very opportunely, will better supply my place in entertaining you.

SCENE VI.

ALCESTE, CÉLIMÈNE, ARSINOÉ.

CÉLIMÈNE.   Alceste, I have to write a few lines, which I cannot well delay. Please to stay with this lady; she will all the more easily excuse my rudeness.

SCENE VII.

ALCESTE, ARSINOÉ.

ARSINOÉ.   You see, I am left here to entertain you, until my coach comes round. She could have devised no more charming treat for me, than such a conversation. Indeed, people of exceptional merit attract the esteem and love of every one; and yours has undoubtedly some secret charm, which makes me feel interested in all your doings. I could wish that the court, with a real regard to your merits, would do more justice to your deserts. You have reason to complain; and it vexes me to see that day by day nothing is done for you.

ALCESTE. For me, Madam? And by what right could I pretend to anything? What service have I rendered to the State? Pray, what have I done, so brilliant in itself, to complain of the court doing nothing for me?

ARSINOÉ. Not everyone whom the State delights to honor, has rendered signal services; there must be an opportunity as well as the power; and the abilities which you allow us to perceive, ought . . .

ALCESTE. For Heaven's sake, let us have no more of my abilities, I pray. What would you have the court to do? It would have enough to do, and have its hands full, to discover the merits of people.

ARSINOÉ. Sterling merit discovers itself. A great deal is made of yours in certain places; and let me tell you that, not later than yesterday, you were highly spoken of in two distinguished circles, by people of very great standing.

ALCESTE. As for that, Madam, everyone is praised now-a-days, and very little discrimination is shown in our times. Everything is equally endowed with great merit, so that it is no longer an honor to be lauded. Praises abound, they throw them at one's head, and even my valet is put in the gazette.

ARSINOÉ. As for me, I could wish that, to bring yourself into greater notice, some place at court might tempt you. If you will only give me a hint that you seriously think about it, a great many engines might be set in motion to serve you; and I know some people whom I could employ for you, and who would manage the matter smoothly enough.

ALCESTE. And what should I do when I got there, Madam? My disposition rather prompts me to keep away from it. Heaven, when ushering me into the world, did not give me a mind suited for the atmosphere of a court. I have not the qualifications necessary for success, nor for making my fortune there. To be open and candid is my chief talent; I possess not the art of deceiving people in conversation; and he who has not the gift of concealing his thoughts, ought not to stay long in those places. When not at court, one has not, doubtless, that standing, and the advantage of those honorable titles which it bestows now-a-days;

but, on the other hand, one has not the vexation of playing the silly fool. One has not to bear a thousand galling rebuffs; one is not, as it were, forced to praise the verses of Mister so-and-so, to laud Madam such and such, and to put up with the whims of some ingenious marquis.

ARSINOÉ. Since you wish it, let us drop the subject of the court: but I cannot help grieving for your amours; and, to tell you my opinions candidly on that head, I could heartily wish your affections better bestowed. You certainly deserve a much happier fate, and she who has fascinated you is unworthy of you.

ALCESTE. But in saying so, Madam, remember, I pray, that this lady is your friend.

ARSINOÉ. True. But really my conscience revolts at the thought of suffering any longer the wrong that is done to you. The position in which I see you afflicts my very soul, and I caution you that your affections are betrayed.

ALCESTE. This is certainly showing me a deal of good feeling, Madam, and such information is very welcome to a lover.

ARSINOÉ. Yes, for all Célimène is my friend, I do not hesitate to call her unworthy of possessing the heart of a man of honor; and hers only pretends to respond to yours.

ALCESTE. That is very possible, Madam, one cannot look into the heart; but your charitable feelings might well have refrained from awakening such a suspicion as mine.

ARSINOÉ. Nothing is easier than to say no more about it, if you do not wish to be undeceived.

ALCESTE. Just so. But whatever may be openly said on this subject is not half so annoying as hints thrown out; and I for one would prefer to be plainly told that only which could be clearly proved.

ARSINOÉ. Very well! and that is sufficient; I can fully enlighten you upon this subject. I will have you believe nothing but what your own eyes see. Only have the kindness to escort me as far as my house; and I will give you undeniable proof of the faithlessness of your fair one's heart; and if, after that, you can find charms in anyone else, we will perhaps find you some consolation.

ACT IV.
SCENE I.

ÉLIANTE, PHILINTE.

PHILINTE. No, never have I seen so obstinate a mind, nor a reconciliation more difficult to effect. In vain was Alceste tried on all sides; he would still maintain his opinion; and never, I believe, has a more curious dispute engaged the attention of those gentlemen. "No, gentlemen," exclaimed he, "I will not retract, and I shall agree with you on every point, except on this one. At what is Oronte offended? and with what does he reproach me? Does it reflect upon his honor that he cannot write well? What is my opinion to him, which he has altogether wrongly construed? One may be a perfect gentleman, and write bad verses; those things have nothing to do with honor. I take him to be a gallant man in every way; a man of standing, of merit, and courage, anything you like, but he is a wretched author. I shall praise, if you wish, his mode of living, his lavishness, his skill in riding, in fencing, in dancing; but as to praising his verses, I am his humble servant; and if one has not the gift of composing better, one ought to leave off rhyming altogether, unless condemned to it on forfeit of one's life." In short, all the modification they could with difficulty obtain from him, was to say, in what he thought a much gentler tone—"I am sorry, sir, to be so difficult to please; and out of regard to you, I could wish, with all my heart, to have found your sonnet a little better." And they compelled them to settle this dispute quickly with an embrace.

ÉLIANTE. He is very eccentric in his doings; but I must confess that I think a great deal of him; and the candor upon which he prides himself has something noble and heroic in it. It is a rare virtue now-a-days, and I, for one, should not be sorry to meet with it everywhere.

PHILINTE. As for me, the more I see of him, the more I am amazed at that passion to which his whole heart is given up. I cannot conceive how, with a disposition like his, he has taken it into his head to love at all; and still less can I understand how your cousin happens to be the person to whom his feelings are inclined.

ÉLIANTE. That shows that love is not always produced by compatibility of temper; and in this case, all the pretty theories of gentle sympathies are belied.

PHILINTE. But do you think him beloved in return, to judge from what we see?

ÉLIANTE. That is a point not easily decided. How can we judge whether it be true she loves? Her own heart is not so very sure of what it feels. It sometimes loves, without being quite aware of it, and at other times thinks it does, without the least grounds.

PHILINTE. I think that our friend will have more trouble with this cousin of yours than he imagines; and to tell you the truth, if he were of my mind, he would bestow his affections elsewhere; and by a better choice, we should see him, Madam, profit by the kind feelings which your heart evinces for him.

ÉLIANTE. As for me, I do not mince matters, and I think that in such cases we ought to act with sincerity. I do not run counter to his tender feelings; on the contrary, I feel interested in them; and, if it depended only on me, I would unite him to the object of his love. But if, as it may happen in love affairs, his affections should receive a check, and if Célimène should respond to the love of any one else, I could easily be prevailed upon to listen to his addresses, and I should have no repugnance whatever to them on account of their rebuff elsewhere.

PHILINTE. Nor do I, from my side, oppose myself, Madam, to the tender feelings which you entertain for him; and he himself, if he wished, could inform you what I have taken care to say to him on that score. But if, by the union of those two, you should be prevented from accepting his attentions, all mine would endeavor to gain that great favor which your kind feelings offer to him; only too happy, Madam, to have them transferred to myself, if his heart could not respond to yours.

ÉLIANTE. You are in the humor to jest, Philinte.

PHILINTE. Not so, Madam, I am speaking my inmost feelings. I only wait the opportune moment to offer myself openly, and am wishing most anxiously to hurry its advent.

SCENE II.

ALCESTE, ÉLIANTE, PHILINTE.

ALCESTE.   Ah, Madam! obtain me justice, for an offence which triumphs over all my constancy.
ÉLIANTE.   What ails you? What disturbs you?
ALCESTE.   This much ails me, that it is death to me to think of it; and the upheaving of all creation would less overwhelm me than this accident. It is all over with me . . . My love . . . I cannot speak.
ÉLIANTE.   Just endeavor to be composed.
ALCESTE.   Oh, just Heaven; can the odious vices of the basest minds be joined to such beauty?
ÉLIANTE.   But, once more, what can have . . .
ALCESTE.   Alas! All is ruined! I am! I am betrayed! I am stricken to death. Célimène . . . would you credit it! Célimène deceives me and is faithless.
ÉLIANTE.   Have you just grounds for believing so?
PHILINTE.   Perhaps it is a suspicion, rashly conceived; and your jealous temper often harbors fancies . . .
ALCESTE.   Ah! 'Sdeath, please to mind your own business, sir. [*To* ÉLIANTE] Her treachery is but too certain, for I have in my pocket a letter in her own handwriting. Yes, Madam, a letter, intended for Oronte, has placed before my eyes my disgrace and her shame; Oronte, whose addresses I believed she avoided, and whom, of all my rivals, I feared the least.
PHILINTE.   A letter may deceive by appearances, and is sometimes not so culpable as may be thought.
ALCESTE.   Once more, sir, leave me alone, if you please, and trouble yourself only about your own concerns.
ÉLIANTE.   You should moderate your passion; and the insult . . .
ALCESTE.   You must be left to do that, Madam; it is to you that my heart has recourse to-day to free itself from this goading pain. Avenge me on an ungrateful and perfidious relative who basely deceives such constant tenderness. Avenge me for an act that ought to fill you with horror.
ÉLIANTE.   I avenge you? How?
ALCESTE.   By accepting my heart. Take it, Madam, instead of the false

one; it is in this way that I can avenge myself upon her; and I shall punish her by the sincere attachment, and the profound love, the respectful cares, the eager devotions, the ceaseless attentions which this heart will henceforth offer up at your shrine.

ÉLIANTE. I certainly sympathize with you in your sufferings, and do not despise your proffered heart; but the wrong done may not be so great as you think, and you might wish to forego this desire for revenge. When the injury proceeds from a beloved object, we form many designs which we never execute; we may find as powerful a reason as we like to break off the connection, the guilty charmer is soon again innocent; all the harm we wish her quickly vanishes, and we know what a lover's anger means.

ALCESTE. No, no, Madam, no. The offence is too cruel; there will be no relenting, and I have done with her. Nothing shall change the resolution I have taken, and I should hate myself for ever loving her again. Here she comes. My anger increases at her approach. I shall taunt her with her black guilt, completely put her to the blush, and, after that, bring you a heart wholly freed from her deceitful attractions.

SCENE III.

CÉLIMÈNE, ALCESTE.

ALCESTE. [*Aside*] Grant, Heaven, that I may control my temper.
CÉLIMÈNE. [*Aside*] Ah! [*To* ALCESTE] What is all this trouble that I see you in, and what means those long-drawn sighs, and those black looks which you cast at me?
ALCESTE. That all the wickedness of which a heart is capable is not to be compared to your perfidy; that neither fate, hell, nor Heaven in its wrath, ever produced anything so wicked as you are.
CÉLIMÈNE. These are certainly pretty compliments, which I admire very much.
ALCESTE. Do not jest. This is no time for laughing. Blush rather, you have cause to do so; and I have undeniable proofs of your treachery. This is what the agitations of my mind prognosticated; it was not without cause that my love took alarm; by these frequent suspicions, which were hateful to you, I was trying to discover the misfortune

which my eyes have beheld; and in spite of all your care and your skill in dissembling, my star foretold me what I had to fear. But do not imagine that I will bear unavenged this slight of being insulted. I know that we have no command over our inclinations, that love will everywhere spring up spontaneously, that there is no entering a heart by force, and that every soul is free to name its conqueror: I should thus have no reason to complain if you had spoken to me without dissembling, and rejected my advances from the very beginning; my heart would then have been justified in blaming fortune alone. But to see my love encouraged by a deceitful avowal on your part, is an action so treacherous and perfidious, that it cannot meet with too great a punishment; and I can allow my resentment to do anything. Yes, yes; after such an outrage, fear everything; I am no longer myself, I am mad with rage. My senses, struck by the deadly blow with which you kill me, are no longer governed by reason; I give way to the outbursts of a just wrath, and am no longer responsible for what I may do.

CÉLIMÈNE. Whence comes, I pray, such a passion? Speak! Have you lost your senses?

ALCESTE. Yes, yes, I lost them when, to my misfortune, I beheld you and thus took the poison which kills me, and when I thought to meet with some sincerity in those treacherous charms that bewitched me.

CÉLIMÈNE. Of what treachery have you to complain?

ALCESTE. Ah! how double-faced she is! how well she knows how to dissemble! But I am fully prepared with the means of driving her to extremities. Cast your eyes here and recognize your writing. This picked-up note is sufficient to confound you, and such proof cannot easily be refuted.

CÉLIMÈNE. And this is the cause of your perturbation of spirits?

ALCESTE. You do not blush on beholding this writing!

CÉLIMÈNE. And why should I blush?

ALCESTE. What! You add boldness to craft! Will you disown this note because it bears no name?

CÉLIMÈNE. Why should I disown it, since I wrote it?

ALCESTE. And you can look at it without becoming confused at the crime of which its style accuses you!

CÉLIMÈNE. You are, in truth, a very eccentric man.

ALCESTE. What! You thus out-brave this convincing proof! And the contents so full of tenderness for Oronte, need have nothing in them to outrage me, or to shame you?

CÉLIMÈNE. Oronte! Who told you that this letter is for him?
ALCESTE. The people who put it into my hands this day. But I will even suppose that it is for some one else. Has my heart any less cause to complain of yours? Will you, in fact, be less guilty towards me?
CÉLIMÈNE. But if it is a woman to whom this letter is addressed, how can it hurt you, or what is there culpable in it?
ALCESTE. Hem! The prevarication is ingenious, and the excuse excellent. I must own that I did not expect this turn; and nothing but that was wanting to convince me. Do you dare to have recourse to such palpable tricks? Do you think people entirely destitute of common sense? Come, let us see a little by what subterfuge, with what air, you will support so palpable a falsehood; and how you can apply to a woman every word of this note which evinces so much tenderness! Reconcile, if you can, to hide your deceit, what I am about to read . . .
CÉLIMÈNE. It does not suit me to do so. I think it ridiculous that you should take so much upon yourself, and tell me to my face what you have the daring to say to me!
ALCESTE. No, no, without flying into a rage, take a little trouble to explain these terms.
CÉLIMÈNE. No, I shall do nothing of the kind, and it matters very little to me what you think upon the subject.
ALCESTE. I pray you, show me, and I shall be satisfied, if this letter can be explained as meant for a woman.
CÉLIMÈNE. Not at all. It is for Oronte; and I will have you believe it. I accept all his attentions gladly; I admire what he says, I like him, and I shall agree to whatever you please. Do as you like, and act as you think proper; let nothing hinder you and do not harass me any longer.
ALCESTE. [*Aside*] Heavens! can anything more cruel be conceived, and was ever heart treated like mine? What! I am justly angry with her, I come to complain, and I am quarreled with instead! My grief and my suspicions are excited to the utmost, I am allowed to believe everything, she boasts of everything; and yet, my heart is still sufficiently mean not to be able to break the bonds that hold it fast, and not to arm itself with a generous contempt for the ungrateful object of which it is too much enamored. [*To* CÉLIMÈNE] Perfidious woman, you know well how to take advantage of my great weakness, and to employ for your own purpose that excessive, astonishing, and fatal love which your treacherous looks have inspired! Defend yourself at least from this crime that overwhelms me, and stop pretending to be guilty. Show me,

if you can, that this letter is innocent; my affection will even consent to assist you. At any rate, endeavor to appear faithful, and I shall strive to believe you such.

CÉLIMÈNE. Bah, you are mad with your jealous frenzies, and do not deserve the love which I have for you. I should much like to know what could compel me to stoop for you to the baseness of dissembling; and why, if my heart were disposed towards another, I should not say so candidly. What! does the kind assurance of my sentiments towards you not defend me sufficiently against all your suspicions? Ought they to possess any weight at all with such a guarantee? Is it not insulting me even to listen to them? And since it is with the utmost difficulty that we can resolve to confess our love, since the strict honor of our sex, hostile to our passion, strongly opposes such a confession, ought a lover who sees such an obstacle overcome for his sake, doubt with impunity our avowal? And is he not greatly to blame in not assuring himself of the truth of that which is never said but after a severe struggle with one's self? Begone, such suspicions deserve my anger, and you are not worthy of being cared for. I am silly, and am vexed at my own simplicity in still preserving the least kindness for you. I ought to place my affections elsewhere, and give you a just cause for complaint.

ALCESTE. Ah! you traitress! mine is a strange infatuation for you; those tender expressions are, no doubt, meant only to deceive me. But it matters little, I must submit to my fate; my very soul is wrapt up in you; I will see to the bitter end how your heart will act towards me, and whether it will be black enough to deceive me.

CÉLIMÈNE. No, you do not love me as you ought to love.

ALCESTE. Indeed! Nothing is to be compared to my exceeding love; and, in its eagerness to show itself to the whole world, it goes even so far as to form wishes against you. Yes, I could wish that no one thought you handsome, that you were reduced to a miserable existence; that Heaven, at your birth, had bestowed upon you nothing; that you had no rank, no nobility, no wealth, so that I might openly proffer my heart, and thus make amends to you for the injustice of such a lot; and that, this very day, I might have the joy and the glory of seeing you owe everything to my love.

CÉLIMÈNE. This is wishing me well in a strange way! Heaven grant that you may never have occasion . . . But here comes Monsieur Dubois curiously decked out.

SCENE IV.

CÉLIMÈNE, ALCESTE, DUBOIS.

ALCESTE. What means this strange attire, and that frightened look? What ails you?
DUBOIS. Sir . . .
ALCESTE. Well?
DUBOIS. The most mysterious event.
ALCESTE. What is it?
DUBOIS. Our affairs are turning out badly, sir.
ALCESTE. What?
DUBOIS. Shall I speak out?
ALCESTE. Yes, do, and quickly.
DUBOIS. Is there no one there?
ALCESTE. Curse your trifling! Will you speak?
DUBOIS. Sir, we must beat a retreat.
ALCESTE. What do you mean?
DUBOIS. We must steal away from this quietly.
ALCESTE. And why?
DUBOIS. I tell you that we must leave this place.
ALCESTE. The reason?
DUBOIS. You must go, sir, without staying to take leave.
ALCESTE. But what is the meaning of this strain?
DUBOIS. The meaning is, sir, that you must make yourself scarce.
ALCESTE. I shall knock you on the head to a certainty, booby, if you do not explain yourself more clearly.
DUBOIS. A fellow, sir, with a black dress, and as black a look, got as far as the kitchen to leave a paper with us, scribbled over in such a fashion that Old Nick himself could not have read it. It is about your law-suit, I make no doubt; but the very devil, I believe, could not make head nor tail of it.
ALCESTE. Well! what then? What has the paper to do with the going away of which you speak, you scoundrel?
DUBOIS. I must tell you, sir, that, about an hour afterwards, a gentleman who often calls, came to ask for you quite eagerly, and not finding you at home, quietly told me, knowing how attached I am to you, to let you know . . . Stop a moment, what the deuce is his name?

ALCESTE. Never mind his name, you scoundrel, and tell me what he told you.
DUBOIS. He is one of your friends, in short, that is sufficient. He told me that for your very life you must get away from this, and that you are threatened with arrest.
ALCESTE. But how! has he not specified anything?
DUBOIS. No. He asked me for ink and paper, and has sent you a line from which you can, I think, fathom the mystery!
ALCESTE. Hand it over then.
CÉLIMÈNE. What can all this mean?
ALCESTE. I do not know; but I am anxious to be informed. Have you almost done, devil take you?
DUBOIS. [*After having fumbled for some time for the note*] After all, sir, I have left it on your table.
ALCESTE. I do not know what keeps me from . . .
CÉLIMÈNE. Do not put yourself in a passion, but go and unravel this perplexing business.
ALCESTE. It seems that fate, whatever I may do, has sworn to prevent my having a conversation with you. But, to get the better of her, allow me to see you again, Madam, before the end of the day.

ACT V.
SCENE I.

ALCESTE, PHILINTE.

ALCESTE. I tell you, my mind is made up about it.
PHILINTE. But, whatever this blow may be, does it compel you . . .
ALCESTE. You may talk and argue till doomsday if you like, nothing can avert me from what I have said. The age we live in is too perverse, and I am determined to withdraw altogether from intercourse with the world. What! when honor, probity, decency, and the laws are all against my adversary; when the equity of my claim is everywhere cried up; when my mind is at rest as to the justice of my cause, I meanwhile see myself betrayed by its issue! What! I have got justice on my side, and I lose my case! A wretch, whose scandalous history is well known, comes off triumphant by the blackest falsehood! All good faith yields to his treachery! He finds the means of being in the right, whilst cutting my throat! The weight of his dissimulation, so full of cunning, overthrows the right and turns the scales of justice! He obtains even a decree of court to crown his villainy. And, not content with the wrong he is doing me, there is abroad in society an abominable book, of which the very reading is to be condemned, a book that deserves the utmost severity, and of which the scoundrel has the impudence to proclaim me the author. Upon this, Oronte is observed to mutter, and tries wickedly to support the imposture! He, who holds an honorable position at court, to whom I have done nothing without having been sincere and candid, who came to ask me in spite of myself of my opinion of some of his verses; and because I treat him honestly, and will not betray either him or truth, he assists in overwhelming me with a trumped-up crime. Behold him now my greatest enemy! And I shall never obtain his sincere forgiveness, because I did not think that his

sonnet was good! 'Sdeath! to think that mankind is made thus! The thirst for fame induces them to do such things! This is the good faith, the virtuous zeal, the justice and the honor to be found amongst them! Let us begone; it is too much to endure the vexations they are devising; let us get out of this wood, this cut-throat hole; and since men behave towards each other like real wolves, wretches, you shall never see me again as long as I live.

PHILINTE. I think you are acting somewhat hastily; and the harm done is not so great as you would make it out. Whatever your adversary dares to impute to you has not had the effect of causing you to be arrested. We see his false reports defeating themselves, and this action is likely to hurt him much more than you.

ALCESTE. Him? he does not mind the scandal of such tricks as these. He has a license to be an arrant knave; and this event, far from damaging his position, will obtain him a still better standing tomorrow.

PHILINTE. In short, it is certain that little notice has been taken of the report which his malice spread against you; from that side you have already nothing to fear; and as for your law-suit, of which you certainly have reason to complain, it is easy for you to bring the trial on afresh, and against this decision . . .

ALCESTE. No, I shall leave it as it is. Whatever cruel wrong this verdict may inflict, I shall take particular care not to have it set aside. We see too plainly how right is maltreated in it, and I wish to go down to posterity as a signal proof, as a notorious testimony of the wickedness of the men of our age. It may indeed cost me twenty thousand francs, but at the cost of twenty thousand francs I shall have the right of railing against the iniquity of human nature, and of nourishing an undying hatred of it.

PHILINTE. But after all . . .

ALCESTE. But after all, your pains are thrown away. What can you, sir, say upon this head? Would you have the assurance to wish, to my face, to excuse the villainy of all that is happening?

PHILINTE. No, I agree with you in all that you say. Everything goes by intrigue, and by pure influence. It is only trickery which carries the day in our time, and men ought to act differently. But is their want of equity a reason for wishing to withdraw from their society? All human failings give us, in life, the means of exercising our philosophy. It is the best employment for virtue; and if probity reigned everywhere, if all hearts were candid, just, and tractable, most of our virtues would be useless to us, inasmuch as their functions are to bear, without annoyance, the injustice of others in our good cause; and just in the same way as a heart full of virtue . . .

ALCESTE. I know that you are a most fluent speaker, sir; that you always abound in fine arguments; but you are wasting your time, and all your fine speeches. Reason tells me to retire for my own good. I cannot command my tongue sufficiently; I cannot answer for what I might say, and should very probably get myself into a hundred scrapes. Allow me, without any more words, to wait for Célimène. She must consent to the plan that brings me here. I shall see whether her heart has any love for me; and this very hour will prove it to me.

PHILINTE. Let us go upstairs to Éliante, and wait her coming.

ALCESTE. No, my mind is too harassed. You go and see her, and leave me in this little dark corner with my black care.

PHILINTE. That is strange company to leave you in; I will induce Éliante to come down.

SCENE II.

CÉLIMÈNE, ORONTE, ALCESTE.

ORONTE. Yes, Madam, it remains for you to consider whether, by ties so dear, you will make me wholly yours. I must be absolutely certain of your affection: A lover dislikes to be held in suspense upon such a subject. If the ardor of my affection has been able to move your feelings, you ought not to hesitate to let me see it; and the proof, after all, which I ask of you, is not to allow Alceste to wait upon you any longer; to sacrifice him to my love, and, in short, to banish him from your house this very day.

CÉLIMÈNE. But why are you so incensed against him; you, whom I have so often heard speak of his merits?

ORONTE. There is no need, Madam, of these explanations; the question is, what are your feelings? Please to choose between the one or the other; my resolution depends entirely upon yours.

ALCESTE. [*Coming out of his corner*] Yes, this gentleman is right, Madam, you must make a choice; and his request agrees perfectly with mine. I am equally eager, and the same anxiety brings me here. My love requires a sure proof. Things cannot go on any longer in this way, and the moment has arrived for explaining your feelings.

ORONTE.   I have no wish, sir, in any way to disturb, by an untimely affection, your good fortune.

ALCESTE.   And I have no wish, sir, jealous or not jealous, to share aught in her heart with you.

ORONTE.   If she prefers your affection to mine . . .

ALCESTE.   If she has the slightest inclination towards you . . .

ORONTE.   I swear henceforth not to pretend to it again.

ALCESTE.   I peremptorily swear never to see her again.

ORONTE.   Madam, it remains with you now to speak openly.

ALCESTE.   Madam, you can explain yourself fearlessly.

ORONTE.   You have simply to tell us where your feelings are engaged.

ALCESTE.   You may simply finish the matter, by choosing between us two.

ORONTE.   What! you seem to be at a loss to make such a choice.

ALCESTE.   What! your heart still wavers, and appears uncertain!

CÉLIMÈNE.   Good Heavens, how out of place is this persistence, and how very unreasonable you both show yourselves! It is not that I do not know whom to prefer, nor is it my heart that wavers. It is not at all in doubt between you two; and nothing could be more quickly accomplished than the choice of my affections. But to tell the truth, I feel too confused to pronounce such an avowal before you; I think that disobliging words ought not to be spoken in people's presence; that a heart can give sufficient proof of its attachment without going so far as to break with everyone; and gentler intimations suffice to inform a lover of the ill success of his suit.

ORONTE.   No, no, I do not fear a frank avowal; for my part I consent to it.

ALCESTE.   And I demand it; it is just its very publicity that I claim, and I do not wish you to spare my feelings in the least. Your great study has always been to keep friends with everyone; but no more trifling, no more uncertainty. You must explain yourself clearly, or I shall take your refusal as a verdict; I shall know, for my part, how to interpret your silence, and shall consider it as a confirmation of the worst.

ORONTE.   I owe you many thanks, sir, for this wrath, and I say in every respect as you do.

CÉLIMÈNE.   How you weary me with such a whim! Is there any justice in what you ask? And have I not told you what motive prevents me? I will be judged by Éliante, who is just coming.

SCENE III.

ÉLIANTE, PHILINTE, CÉLIMÈNE, ORONTE, ALCESTE.

CÉLIMÈNE.   Good cousin, I am being persecuted here by people who have concerted to do so. They both demand, with the same warmth, that I should declare whom my heart has chosen, and that, by a decision which I must give before their very faces, I should forbid one of them to tease me any more with his attentions. Say, has ever such a thing been done?
ÉLIANTE.   Pray, do not consult me upon such a matter. You may perhaps address yourself to a wrong person, for I am decidedly for people who speak their mind.
ORONTE.   Madam, it is useless for you to decline.
ALCESTE.   All your evasions here will be badly supported.
ORONTE.   You must speak, you must, and no longer waver.
ALCESTE.   You need do no more than remain silent.
ORONTE.   I desire but one word to end our discussions.
ALCESTE.   To me your silence will convey as much as speech.

SCENE IV.

ARSINOÉ, CÉLIMÈNE, ÉLIANTE, ALCESTE, PHILINTE, ACASTE, CLITANDRE, ORONTE.

ACASTE.   [To CÉLIMÈNE] We have both come, by your leave, Madam, to clear up a certain little matter with you.
CLITANDRE.   [To ORONTE and ALCESTE] Your presence happens fortunately, gentlemen; for this affair concerns you also.
ARSINOÉ.   [To CÉLIMÈNE] No doubt you are surprised at seeing me here, Madam; but these gentlemen are the cause of my intrusion. They both came to see me, and complained of a proceeding which I

could not have credited. I have too high an opinion of your kindness of heart ever to believe you capable of such a crime; my eyes even have refused to give credence to their strongest proofs, and in my friendship, forgetting trivial disagreements, I have been induced to accompany them here, to hear you refute this slander.

ACASTE. Yes, Madam, let us see, with composure, how you will manage to bear this out. This letter has been written by you, to Clitandre.

CLITANDRE. And this tender epistle you have addressed to Acaste.

ACASTE. [*To* ORONTE *and* ALCESTE] This writing is not altogether unknown to you, gentlemen, and I have no doubt that her kindness has before now made you familiar with her hand. But this is well worth the trouble of reading.

> "You are a strange man to condemn my liveliness of spirits, and to reproach me that I am never so merry as when I am not with you. Nothing could be more unjust; and if you do not come very soon to ask my pardon for this offence, I shall never forgive you as long as I live. Our great hulking booby of a Viscount . . ." He ought to have been here. "Our great hulking booby of a Viscount, with whom you begin your complaints, is a man who would not at all suit me; and ever since I watched him for full three-quarters of an hour spitting in a well to make circles in the water, I never could have a good opinion of him. As for the little Marquis . . ." that is myself, ladies and gentlemen, be it said without the slightest vanity, . . . "as for the little Marquis, who held my hand yesterday for a long while, I think that there is nothing so diminutive as his whole person, and his sole merit consists in his cloak and sword. As to the man with the green shoulder knot . . ." [*To* ALCESTE] It is your turn now, sir. "As to the man with the green shoulder knot, he amuses me sometimes with his bluntness and his splenetic behavior; but there are hundreds of times when I think him the greatest bore in the world. Respecting the man with the big waistcoat . . ." [*To* ORONTE] This is your share. "Respecting the man with the big waistcoat, who has thought fit to set up as a wit, and wishes to be an author in spite of everyone, I cannot even take the trouble to listen to what he says; and his prose bores me just as much as his poetry. Take it for granted that I do not always enjoy myself so much as you think; and that I wish for you, more than I care to say, amongst all the entertainments to which I am dragged; and that the presence of those we love is an excellent relish to our pleasures."

CLITANDRE.   Now for myself.

> "Your Clitandre, whom you mention to me, and who has always such a quantity of soft expressions at his command, is the last man for whom I could feel any affection. He must be crazed in persuading himself that I love him; and you are so too in believing that I do not love you. You had better change your fancies for his, and come and see me as often as you can, to help me in bearing the annoyance of being pestered by him."

This shows the model of a lovely character, Madam; and I need not tell you what to call it. It is enough. We shall, both of us, show this admirable sketch of your heart everywhere and to everybody.

ACASTE.   I might also say something, and the subject is tempting; but I deem you beneath my anger; and I will show you that little marquises can find worthier hearts than yours to console themselves.

SCENE V.

CÉLIMÈNE, ÉLIANTE, ARSINOÉ, ALCESTE, ORONTE, PHILINTE.

ORONTE.   What! Am I to be pulled to pieces in this fashion, after all that you have written to me? And does your heart, with all its semblance of love, plight its faith to all mankind by turns! Bah, I have been too great a dupe, but I shall be so no longer. You have done me a service, in showing yourself in your true colors to me. I am the richer by a heart which you thus restore to me, and find my revenge in your loss. [*To* ALCESTE] Sir, I shall no longer be an obstacle to your flame, and you may settle matters with this lady as soon as you please.

SCENE VI.

CÉLIMÈNE, ÉLIANTE, ARSINOÉ, ALCESTE, PHILINTE.

ARSINOÉ.   [*To* CÉLIMÈNE] This is certainly one of the basest actions which I have ever seen; I can no longer be silent, and feel quite upset.

Has any one ever seen the like of it? I do not concern myself much in the affairs of other people, but this gentleman [*pointing to* ALCESTE], who has staked the whole of his happiness on you, an honorable and deserving man like this, and who worshipped you to madness, ought he to have been . . .

ALCESTE. Leave me, I pray you, Madam, to manage my own affairs; and do not trouble yourself unnecessarily. In vain do I see you espouse my quarrel. I am unable to repay you for this great zeal; and if ever I intended to avenge myself by choosing some one else, it would not be you whom I would select.

ARSINOÉ. And do you imagine, sir, that I ever harbored such a thought, and that I am so very anxious to secure you? You must be very vain, indeed, to flatter yourself with such an idea. Célimène's leavings are a commodity, of which no one needs be so very much enamored. Pray, undeceive yourself, and do not carry matters with so high a hand. People like me are not for such as you. You will do much better to remain dangling after her skirts, and I long to see so beautiful a match.

SCENE VII.

CÉLIMÈNE, ÉLIANTE, ALCESTE, PHILINTE.

ALCESTE. [*To* CÉLIMÈNE] Well! I have held my tongue, notwithstanding all I have seen, and I have let everyone have his say before me. Have I controlled myself long enough? and will you now allow me . . .

CÉLIMÈNE. Yes, you may say what you like; you are justified when you complain, and you may reproach me with anything you please. I confess that I am in the wrong; and overwhelmed by confusion I do not seek by any idle excuse to palliate my fault. The anger of the others I have despised; but I admit my guilt towards you. No doubt, your resentment is just; I know how culpable I must appear to you, that everything speaks of my treachery to you and that, in short, you have cause to hate me. Do so, I consent to it.

ALCESTE. But can I do so, you traitress? Can I thus get the better of all my tenderness for you? And although I wish to hate you with all my soul, shall I find a heart quite ready to obey me? [*To* ÉLIANTE *and* PHILINTE] You see what an unworthy passion can do, and I call you both as witnesses of my infatuation. Nor, truth to say, is this all, and you will see me carry it out to the bitter end, to show you that it is wrong to call us wise, and that in all hearts there remains still something of the man. [*To* CÉLIMÈNE] Yes, perfidious creature, I am willing to forget your crimes. I can find, in my own heart, an excuse for all your doings, and hide them under the name of a weakness into which the vices of the age betrayed your youth, provided your heart will second the design which I have formed of avoiding all human creatures, and that you are determined to follow me without delay into the solitude in which I have made a vow to pass my days. It is by that only, that, in everyone's opinion, you can repair the harm done by your letters, and that, after the scandal which every noble heart must abhor, it may still be possible for me to love you.

CÉLIMÈNE. What! I renounce the world before I grow old, and bury myself in your wilderness!

ALCESTE. If your affection responds to mine what need the rest of the world signify to you? Am I not sufficient for you?

CÉLIMÈNE. Solitude is frightful to a widow of twenty. I do not feel my mind sufficiently grand and strong to resolve to adopt such a plan. If the gift of my hand can satisfy your wishes, I might be induced to tie such bonds; and marriage . . .

ALCESTE. No. My heart loathes you now, and this refusal alone effects more than all the rest. As you are not disposed, in those sweet ties, to find all in all in me, as I would find all in all in you, begone, I refuse your offer, and this much-felt outrage frees me for ever from your unworthy toils.

SCENE VIII.

ÉLIANTE, ALCESTE, PHILINTE.

ALCESTE. [*To* ÉLIANTE] Madam, your beauty is adorned by a hundred virtues; and I never saw anything in you but what was sincere. For a long while I thought very highly of you; but allow me to esteem you thus for ever, and suffer my heart in its various troubles not to offer itself for the honor of your acceptance. I feel too unworthy, and begin to perceive that Heaven did not intend me for the marriage bond; that the homage of only the remainder of a heart unworthy of you would be below your merit, and that in short . . .

ÉLIANTE. You may pursue this thought. I am not at all embarrassed with my hand; and here is your friend, who, without giving me much trouble, might possibly accept it if I asked him.

PHILINTE. Ah! Madam, I ask for nothing better than that honor, and I could sacrifice my life and soul for it.

ALCESTE. May you, to taste true contentment, preserve for ever these feelings towards each other! Deceived on all sides, overwhelmed with injustice, I will fly from an abyss where vice is triumphant, and seek out some small secluded nook on earth, where one may enjoy the freedom of being an honest man.

PHILINTE. Come, Madam, let us leave nothing untried to deter him from the design on which his heart is set.

DOVER·THRIFT·EDITIONS

The Importance of Being Earnest

OSCAR WILDE

DOVER PUBLICATIONS, INC.
New York

DOVER THRIFT EDITIONS
Editor: Stanley Appelbaum

Published in Canada by General Publishing Company, Ltd.,
30 Lesmill Road, Don Mills, Toronto, Ontario.
Published in the United Kingdom by Constable and Company, Ltd.

This Dover edition, first published in 1990, contains the
unabridged and unaltered text of *The Importance of Being Earnest*
(first publication: Leonard Smithers & Co., London, 1899).

Manufactured in the United States of America
Dover Publications, Inc.
31 East 2nd Street
Mineola, N.Y. 11501

Library of Congress Cataloging-in-Publication Data

Wilde, Oscar, 1854–1900.
The importance of being earnest / Oscar Wilde.
    p.   cm. — (Dover thrift editions)
ISBN 0-486-26478-5
I. Title. II. Series.
PR5818.I4   1990b
822'.8—dc20   90-36100
                              CIP

Note

OSCAR WILDE (born in Dublin, 1854; died in Paris, 1900) was a writer, editor, lecturer and wit with many strings to his bow. His oeuvre includes charming fairy tales, erotically bizarre fin-de-siècle productions (the novel *The Picture of Dorian Gray,* the play *Salomé*), personal poems of deep sincerity ("The Ballad of Reading Gaol") and society comedies sparkling with paradoxical epigrams that are among the most quotable in the English language.

Of the comedies, the last one to be written is universally considered to be Wilde's most perfect work. This is *The Importance of Being Earnest,* first performed in London in February of 1895, just three months before Wilde was convicted at his notorious third trial. Bankruptcy and a two-year prison term brought his brilliant social career to an end, but his literary achievement was never tarnished. *Earnest,* above all, has given joy to thousands who savor its brilliant lines like familiar music.

The Importance of Being Earnest

London: St. James' Theatre: Lessee and Manager, Mr. George Alexander, February 14, 1895.

Characters

JOHN WORTHING, J.P. [JACK]	Mr. George Alexander
ALGERNON MONCRIEFF	Mr. Allen Aynesworth
REV. CANON CHASUBLE, D.D.	Mr. H. H. Vincent
MERRIMAN (Butler)	Mr. Frank Dyall
LANE (Manservant)	Mr. F. Kinsey Peile
LADY BRACKNELL	Miss Rose Leclercq
HON. GWENDOLEN FAIRFAX	Miss Irene Vanbrugh
CECILY CARDEW	Miss Evelyn Millard
MISS PRISM (Governess)	Mrs. George Canninge

The Scenes of the Play

Act I   Algernon Moncrieff's Flat in Half Moon Street, W.

Act II   The Garden at the Manor House, Woolton.

Act III   Drawing-room of the Manor House, Woolton.

Time—The Present
Place—London

Contents

Act I   1

Act II   21

Act III   43

The Importance of Being Earnest
Act I

SCENE—*Morning-room in* ALGERNON'S *flat in Half Moon Street. The room is luxuriously and artistically furnished. The sound of a piano is heard in the adjoining room.*

[LANE *is arranging afternoon tea on the table, and after the music has ceased,* ALGERNON *enters.*]

ALGERNON. Did you hear what I was playing, Lane?

LANE. I didn't think it polite to listen, sir.

ALGERNON. I'm sorry for that, for your sake. I don't play accurately—anyone can play accurately—but I play with wonderful expression. As far as the piano is concerned, sentiment is my forte. I keep science for Life.

LANE. Yes, sir.

ALGERNON. And, speaking of the science of Life, have you got the cucumber sandwiches cut for Lady Bracknell?

LANE. Yes, sir. [*Hands them on a salver.*]

ALGERNON [*Inspects them, takes two, and sits down on the sofa*]. Oh! . . . by the way, Lane, I see from your book that on Thursday night, when Lord Shoreman and Mr. Worthing were dining with me, eight bottles of champagne are entered as having been consumed.

LANE. Yes, sir; eight bottles and a pint.

ALGERNON. Why is it that at a bachelor's establishment the servants invariably drink the champagne? I ask merely for information.

LANE. I attribute it to the superior quality of the wine, sir. I have often observed that in married households the champagne is rarely of a first-rate brand.

ALGERNON. Good heavens! Is marriage so demoralising as that?

LANE. I believe it *is* a very pleasant state, sir. I have had very little experience of it myself up to the present. I have only been married once. That was in consequence of a misunderstanding between myself and a young person.

ALGERNON [*Languidly*]. I don't know that I am much interested in your family life, Lane.

LANE. No, sir; it is not a very interesting subject. I never think of it myself.

ALGERNON. Very natural, I am sure. That will do, Lane, thank you.

LANE. Thank you, sir. [LANE *goes out.*]

ALGERNON. Lane's views on marriage seem somewhat lax. Really, if the lower orders don't set us a good example, what on earth is the use of them? They seem, as a class, to have absolutely no sense of moral responsibility.

[*Enter* LANE.]

LANE. Mr. Ernest Worthing.

[*Enter* JACK.] [LANE *goes out.*]

ALGERNON. How are you, my dear Ernest? What brings you up to town?

JACK. Oh, pleasure, pleasure! What else should bring one anywhere? Eating as usual, I see, Algy!

ALGERNON [*Stiffly*]. I believe it is customary in good society to take some slight refreshment at five o'clock. Where have you been since last Thursday?

JACK [*Sitting down on the sofa*]. In the country.

ALGERNON. What on earth do you do there?

JACK [*Pulling off his gloves*]. When one is in town one amuses oneself. When one is in the country one amuses other people. It is excessively boring.

ALGERNON. And who are the people you amuse?

JACK [*Airily*]. Oh, neighbours, neighbours.

ALGERNON. Got nice neighbours in your part of Shropshire?

JACK. Perfectly horrid! Never speak to one of them.

ALGERNON. How immensely you must amuse them! [*Goes over and takes sandwich.*] By the way, Shropshire is your county, is it not?

JACK. Eh? Shropshire? Yes, of course. Hallo! Why all these cups? Why cucumber sandwiches? Why such reckless extravagance in one so young? Who is coming to tea?

ALGERNON. Oh! merely Aunt Augusta and Gwendolen.

JACK. How perfectly delightful!

ALGERNON. Yes, that is all very well; but I am afraid Aunt Augusta won't quite approve of your being here.

JACK. May I ask why?

ALGERNON. My dear fellow, the way you flirt with Gwendolen is perfectly disgraceful. It is almost as bad as the way Gwendolen flirts with you.

JACK. I am in love with Gwendolen. I have come up to town expressly to propose to her.
ALGERNON. I thought you had come up for pleasure? . . . I call that business.
JACK. How utterly unromantic you are!
ALGERNON. I really don't see anything romantic in proposing. It is very romantic to be in love. But there is nothing romantic about a definite proposal. Why, one may be accepted. One usually is, I believe. Then the excitement is all over. The very essence of romance is uncertainty. If ever I get married, I'll certainly try to forget the fact.
JACK. I have no doubt about that, dear Algy. The Divorce Court was specially invented for people whose memories are so curiously constituted.
ALGERNON. Oh! there is no use speculating on that subject. Divorces are made in Heaven—[JACK *puts out his hand to take a sandwich.* ALGERNON *at once interferes.*] Please don't touch the cucumber sandwiches. They are ordered specially for Aunt Augusta. [*Takes one and eats it.*]
JACK. Well, you have been eating them all the time.
ALGERNON. That is quite a different matter. She is my aunt. [*Takes plate from below.*] Have some bread and butter. The bread and butter is for Gwendolen. Gwendolen is devoted to bread and butter.
JACK [*Advancing to table and helping himself*]. And very good bread and butter it is too.
ALGERNON. Well, my dear fellow, you need not eat as if you were going to eat it all. You behave as if you were married to her already. You are not married to her already, and I don't think you ever will be.
JACK. Why on earth do you say that?
ALGERNON. Well, in the first place girls never marry the men they flirt with. Girls don't think it right.
JACK. Oh, that is nonsense!
ALGERNON. It isn't. It is a great truth. It accounts for the extraordinary number of bachelors that one sees all over the place. In the second place, I don't give my consent.
JACK. Your consent!
ALGERNON. My dear fellow, Gwendolen is my first cousin. And before I allow you to marry her, you will have to clear up the whole question of Cecily. [*Rings bell.*]
JACK. Cecily! What on earth do you mean? What do you mean, Algy, by Cecily? I don't know anyone of the name of Cecily.
[*Enter* LANE.]

ALGERNON. Bring me that cigarette case Mr. Worthing left in the smoking-room the last time he dined here.

LANE. Yes, sir. [LANE *goes out.*]

JACK. Do you mean to say you have had my cigarette case all this time? I wish to goodness you had let me know. I have been writing frantic letters to Scotland Yard about it. I was very nearly offering a large reward.

ALGERNON. Well, I wish you would offer one. I happen to be more than usually hard up.

JACK. There is no good offering a large reward now that the thing is found.

[*Enter* LANE *with the cigarette case on a salver.* ALGERNON *takes it at once.* LANE *goes out.*]

ALGERNON. I think that is rather mean of you, Ernest, I must say. [*Opens case and examines it.*] However, it makes no matter, for, now that I look at the inscription inside, I find that the thing isn't yours after all.

JACK. Of course it's mine. [*Moving to him.*] You have seen me with it a hundred times, and you have no right whatsoever to read what is written inside. It is a very ungentlemanly thing to read a private cigarette case.

ALGERNON. Oh! it is absurd to have a hard-and-fast rule about what one should read and what one shouldn't. More than half of modern culture depends on what one shouldn't read.

JACK. I am quite aware of the fact, and I don't propose to discuss modern culture. It isn't the sort of thing one should talk of in private. I simply want my cigarette case back.

ALGERNON. Yes; but this isn't your cigarette case. This cigarette case is a present from someone of the name of Cecily, and you said you didn't know anyone of that name.

JACK. Well, if you want to know, Cecily happens to be my aunt.

ALGERNON. Your aunt!

JACK. Yes. Charming old lady she is, too. Lives at Tunbridge Wells. Just give it back to me, Algy.

ALGERNON [*Retreating to back of sofa*]. But why does she call herself little Cecily if she is your aunt and lives at Tunbridge Wells? [*Reading.*] 'From little Cecily with her fondest love.'

JACK [*Moving to sofa and kneeling upon it*]. My dear fellow, what on earth is there in that? Some aunts are tall, some aunts are not tall. That is a matter that surely an aunt may be allowed to decide for herself. You seem to think that every aunt should be exactly like your aunt! That is absurd! For Heaven's sake give me back my cigarette case. [*Follows* ALGERNON *round the room.*]

ALGERNON.   Yes. But why does your aunt call you her uncle? 'From little Cecily, with her fondest love to her dear Uncle Jack.' There is no objection, I admit, to an aunt being a small aunt, but why an aunt, no matter what her size may be, should call her own nephew her uncle, I can't quite make out. Besides, your name isn't Jack at all; it is Ernest.

JACK.   It isn't Ernest; it's Jack.

ALGERNON.   You have always told me it was Ernest. I have introduced you to everyone as Ernest. You answer to the name of Ernest. You look as if your name was Ernest. You are the most earnest looking person I ever saw in my life. It is perfectly absurd your saying that your name isn't Ernest. It's on your cards. Here is one of them. [*Taking it from case.*] 'Mr. Ernest Worthing, B 4, The Albany.' I'll keep this as a proof your name is Ernest if ever you attempt to deny it to me, or to Gwendolen, or to anyone else. [*Puts the card in his pocket.*]

JACK.   Well, my name is Ernest in town and Jack in the country, and the cigarette case was given to me in the country.

ALGERNON.   Yes, but that does not account for the fact that your small Aunt Cecily, who lives at Tunbridge Wells, calls you her dear uncle. Come, old boy, you had much better have the thing out at once.

JACK.   My dear Algy, you talk exactly as if you were a dentist. It is very vulgar to talk like a dentist when one isn't a dentist. It produces a false impression.

ALGERNON.   Well, that is exactly what dentists always do. Now, go on! Tell me the whole thing. I may mention that I have always suspected you of being a confirmed and secret Bunburyist; and I am quite sure of it now.

JACK.   Bunburyist? What on earth do you mean by a Bunburyist?

ALGERNON.   I'll reveal to you the meaning of that incomparable expression as soon as you are kind enough to inform me why you are Ernest in town and Jack in the country.

JACK.   Well, produce my cigarette case first.

ALGERNON.   Here it is. [*Hands cigarette case.*] Now produce your explanation, and pray make it improbable. [*Sits on sofa.*]

JACK.   My dear fellow, there is nothing improbable about my explanation at all. In fact it's perfectly ordinary. Old Mr. Thomas Cardew, who adopted me when I was a little boy, made me in his will guardian to his grand-daughter, Miss Cecily Cardew. Cecily, who addresses me as her uncle from motives of respect that you could not possibly appreciate, lives at my place in the country under the charge of her admirable governess, Miss Prism.

ALGERNON.   Where is that place in the country, by the way?

JACK.   That is nothing to you, dear boy. You are not going to be invited. . . . I may tell you candidly that the place is not in Shropshire.

ALGERNON.   I suspected that, my dear fellow! I have Bunburyed all over Shropshire on two separate occasions. Now, go on. Why are you Ernest in town and Jack in the country?

JACK.   My dear Algy, I don't know whether you will be able to understand my real motives. You are hardly serious enough. When one is placed in the position of guardian, one has to adopt a very high moral tone on all subjects. It's one's duty to do so. And as a high moral tone can hardly be said to conduce very much to either one's health or one's happiness, in order to get up to town I have always pretended to have a younger brother of the name of Ernest, who lives in the Albany, and gets into the most dreadful scrapes. That, my dear Algy, is the whole truth pure and simple.

ALGERNON.   The truth is rarely pure and never simple. Modern life would be very tedious if it were either, and modern literature a complete impossibility!

JACK.   That wouldn't be at all a bad thing.

ALGERNON.   Literary criticism is not your forte, my dear fellow. Don't try it. You should leave that to people who haven't been at a University. They do it so well in the daily papers. What you really are is a Bunburyist. I was quite right in saying you were a Bunburyist. You are one of the most advanced Bunburyists I know.

JACK.   What on earth do you mean?

ALGERNON.   You have invented a very useful younger brother called Ernest, in order that you may be able to come up to town as often as you like. I have invented an invaluable permanent invalid called Bunbury, in order that I may be able to go down into the country whenever I choose. Bunbury is perfectly invaluable. If it wasn't for Bunbury's extraordinary bad health, for instance, I wouldn't be able to dine with you at Willis's to-night, for I have been really engaged to Aunt Augusta for more than a week.

JACK.   I haven't asked you to dine with me anywhere to-night.

ALGERNON.   I know. You are absurdly careless about sending out invitations. It is very foolish of you. Nothing annoys people so much as not receiving invitations.

JACK.   You had much better dine with your Aunt Augusta.

ALGERNON.   I haven't the smallest intention of doing anything of the kind. To begin with, I dined there on Monday, and once a week is quite enough to dine with one's own relations. In the second place, whenever I do dine there I am always treated as a member of the family, and sent down with either no woman at all, or two. In the third place, I know perfectly well whom she will place me next to, to-night. She will place me next Mary Farquhar, who always flirts with her own husband across the dinner-table. That is not very pleasant. Indeed, it is not even decent . . . and that sort of thing is enormously on the increase. The amount of women in London who flirt with their own husbands is perfectly scandalous. It looks so bad. It is simply washing one's clean linen in public. Besides, now that I know you to be a confirmed Bunburyist I naturally want to talk to you about Bunburying. I want to tell you the rules.

JACK. I'm not a Bunburyist at all. If Gwendolen accepts me, I am going to kill my brother, indeed I think I'll kill him in any case. Cecily is a little too much interested in him. It is rather a bore. So I am going to get rid of Ernest. And I strongly advise you to do the same with Mr. . . . with your invalid friend who has the absurd name.

ALGERNON. Nothing will induce me to part with Bunbury, and if you ever get married, which seems to me extremely problematic, you will be very glad to know Bunbury. A man who marries without knowing Bunbury has a very tedious time of it.

JACK. That is nonsense. If I marry a charming girl like Gwendolen, and she is the only girl I ever saw in my life that I would marry, I certainly won't want to know Bunbury.

ALGERNON. Then your wife will. You don't seem to realise, that in married life three is company and two is none.

JACK [*Sententiously*]. That, my dear young friend, is the theory that the corrupt French drama has been propounding for the last fifty years.

ALGERNON. Yes; and that the happy English home has proved in half the time.

JACK. For Heaven's sake, don't try to be cynical. It's perfectly easy to be cynical.

ALGERNON. My dear fellow, it isn't easy to be anything now-a-days. There's such a lot of beastly competition about. [*The sound of an electric bell is heard.*] Ah! that must be Aunt Augusta. Only relatives, or creditors, ever ring in that Wagnerian manner. Now, if I get her out of the way for ten minutes, so that you can have an opportunity for proposing to Gwendolen, may I dine with you to-night at Willis's?

JACK. I suppose so, if you want to.

ALGERNON. Yes, but you must be serious about it. I hate people who are not serious about meals. It is so shallow of them.

[*Enter* LANE.]

LANE. Lady Bracknell and Miss Fairfax.

[ALGERNON *goes forward to meet them. Enter* LADY BRACKNELL *and* GWENDOLEN.]

LADY BRACKNELL. Good afternoon, dear Algernon, I hope you are behaving very well.

ALGERNON. I'm feeling very well, Aunt Augusta.

LADY BRACKNELL. That's not quite the same thing. In fact the two things rarely go together. [*Sees* JACK *and bows to him with icy coldness.*]

ALGERNON [*To* GWENDOLEN]. Dear me, you are smart!

GWENDOLEN. I am always smart! Aren't I, Mr. Worthing?

JACK. You're quite perfect, Miss Fairfax.

GWENDOLEN. Oh! I hope I am not that. It would leave no room for developments, and I intend to develop in many directions. [GWENDOLEN *and* JACK *sit down together in the corner.*]

LADY BRACKNELL. I'm sorry if we are a little late, Algernon, but I was obliged to call on dear Lady Harbury. I hadn't been there since her poor husband's death. I never saw a woman so altered; she looks quite twenty years younger. And now I'll have a cup of tea, and one of those nice cucumber sandwiches you promised me.

ALGERNON. Certainly, Aunt Augusta. [*Goes over to tea-table.*]

LADY BRACKNELL. Won't you come and sit here, Gwendolen?

GWENDOLEN. Thanks, mamma, I'm quite comfortable where I am.

ALGERNON [*Picking up empty plate in horror*]. Good Heavens! Lane! Why are there no cucumber sandwiches? I ordered them specially.

LANE [*Gravely*]. There were no cucumbers in the market this morning, sir. I went down twice.

ALGERNON. No cucumbers!

LANE. No, sir. Not even for ready money.

ALGERNON. That will do, Lane, thank you.

LANE. Thank you, sir. [*Goes out.*]

ALGERNON. I am greatly distressed, Aunt Augusta, about there being no cucumbers, not even for ready money.

LADY BRACKNELL. It really makes no matter, Algernon. I had some crumpets with Lady Harbury, who seems to me to be living entirely for pleasure now.

ALGERNON. I hear her hair has turned quite gold from grief.

LADY BRACKNELL. It certainly has changed its colour. From what cause I, of course, cannot say. [ALGERNON *crosses and hands tea.*]

Thank you. I've quite a treat for you to-night, Algernon. I am going to send you down with Mary Farquhar. She is such a nice woman, and so attentive to her husband. It's delightful to watch them.

ALGERNON.   I am afraid, Aunt Augusta, I shall have to give up the pleasure of dining with you to-night after all.

LADY BRACKNELL [*Frowning*].   I hope not, Algernon. It would put my table completely out. Your uncle would have to dine upstairs. Fortunately he is accustomed to that.

ALGERNON.   It is a great bore, and, I need hardly say, a terrible disappointment to me, but the fact is I have just had a telegram to say that my poor friend Bunbury is very ill again. [*Exchanges glances with* JACK.] They seem to think I should be with him.

LADY BRACKNELL.   It is very strange. This Mr. Bunbury seems to suffer from curiously bad health.

ALGERNON.   Yes; poor Bunbury is a dreadful invalid.

LADY BRACKNELL.   Well, I must say, Algernon, that I think it is high time that Mr. Bunbury made up his mind whether he was going to live or to die. This shilly-shallying with the question is absurd. Nor do I in any way approve of the modern sympathy with invalids. I consider it morbid. Illness of any kind is hardly a thing to be encouraged in others. Health is the primary duty of life. I am always telling that to your poor uncle, but he never seems to take much notice . . . as far as any improvement in his ailments goes. I should be much obliged if you would ask Mr. Bunbury, from me, to be kind enough not to have a relapse on Saturday, for I rely on you to arrange my music for me. It is my last reception and one wants something that will encourage conversation, particularly at the end of the season when everyone has practically said whatever they had to say, which, in most cases, was probably not much.

ALGERNON.   I'll speak to Bunbury, Aunt Augusta, if he is still conscious, and I think I can promise you he'll be all right by Saturday. Of course the music is a great difficulty. You see, if one plays good music, people don't listen, and if one plays bad music people don't talk. But I'll run over the programme I've drawn out, if you will kindly come into the next room for a moment.

LADY BRACKNELL.   Thank you, Algernon. It is very thoughtful of you. [*Rising, and following* ALGERNON.] I'm sure the programme will be delightful, after a few expurgations. French songs I cannot possibly allow. People always seem to think that they are improper, and either look shocked, which is vulgar, or laugh, which is worse. But German sounds a thoroughly respectable language, and indeed, I believe is so. Gwendolen, you will accompany me.

GWENDOLEN. Certainly, mamma.
[LADY BRACKNELL *and* ALGERNON *go into the music-room,* GWENDOLEN *remains behind.*]
JACK. Charming day it has been, Miss Fairfax.
GWENDOLEN. Pray don't talk to me about the weather, Mr. Worthing. Whenever people talk to me about the weather, I always feel quite certain that they mean something else. And that makes me so nervous.
JACK. I do mean something else.
GWENDOLEN. I thought so. In fact, I am never wrong.
JACK. And I would like to be allowed to take advantage of Lady Bracknell's temporary absence . . .
GWENDOLEN. I would certainly advise you to do so. Mamma has a way of coming back suddenly into a room that I have often had to speak to her about.
JACK [*Nervously*]. Miss Fairfax, ever since I met you I have admired you more than any girl . . . I have ever met since . . . I met you.
GWENDOLEN. Yes, I am quite aware of the fact. And I often wish that in public, at any rate, you had been more demonstrative. For me you have always had an irresistible fascination. Even before I met you I was far from indifferent to you. [JACK *looks at her in amazement.*] We live, as I hope you know, Mr. Worthing, in an age of ideals. The fact is constantly mentioned in the more expensive monthly magazines, and has reached the provincial pulpits, I am told: and my ideal has always been to love some one of the name of Ernest. There is something in that name that inspires absolute confidence. The moment Algernon first mentioned to me that he had a friend called Ernest, I knew I was destined to love you.
JACK. You really love me, Gwendolen?
GWENDOLEN. Passionately!
JACK. Darling! You don't know how happy you've made me.
GWENDOLEN. My own Ernest!
JACK. But you don't really mean to say that you couldn't love me if my name wasn't Ernest?
GWENDOLEN. But your name is Ernest.
JACK. Yes, I know it is. But supposing it was something else? Do you mean to say you couldn't love me then?
GWENDOLEN [*Glibly*]. Ah! that is clearly a metaphysical speculation, and like most metaphysical speculations has very little reference at all to the actual facts of real life, as we know them.
JACK. Personally, darling, to speak quite candidly, I don't much care about the name of Ernest . . . I don't think the name suits me at all.

GWENDOLEN. It suits you perfectly. It is a divine name. It has a music of its own. It produces vibrations.
JACK. Well, really, Gwendolen, I must say that I think there are lots of other much nicer names. I think Jack, for instance, a charming name.
GWENDOLEN. Jack? . . . No, there is very little music in the name Jack, if any at all, indeed. It does not thrill. It produces absolutely no vibrations. . . . I have known several Jacks, and they all, without exception, were more than usually plain. Besides, Jack is a notorious domesticity for John! And I pity any woman who is married to a man called John. She would probably never be allowed to know the entrancing pleasure of a single moment's solitude. The only really safe name is Ernest.
JACK. Gwendolen, I must get christened at once—I mean we must get married at once. There is no time to be lost.
GWENDOLEN. Married, Mr. Worthing?
JACK [*Astounded*]. Well . . . surely. You know that I love you, and you led me to believe, Miss Fairfax, that you were not absolutely indifferent to me.
GWENDOLEN. I adore you. But you haven't proposed to me yet. Nothing has been said at all about marriage. The subject has not even been touched on.
JACK. Well . . . may I propose to you now?
GWENDOLEN. I think it would be an admirable opportunity. And to spare you any possible disappointment, Mr. Worthing, I think it only fair to tell you quite frankly beforehand that I am fully determined to accept you.
JACK. Gwendolen!
GWENDOLEN. Yes, Mr. Worthing, what have you got to say to me?
JACK. You know what I have got to say to you.
GWENDOLEN. Yes, but you don't say it.
JACK. Gwendolen, will you marry me? [*Goes on his knees.*]
GWENDOLEN. Of course I will, darling. How long you have been about it! I am afraid you have had very little experience in how to propose.
JACK. My own one, I have never loved anyone in the world but you.
GWENDOLEN. Yes, but men often propose for practice. I know my brother Gerald does. All my girl friends tell me so. What wonderfully blue eyes you have, Ernest! They are quite, quite blue. I hope you will always look at me just like that, especially when there are other people present.
[*Enter* LADY BRACKNELL.]

LADY BRACKNELL. Mr. Worthing! Rise, sir, from this semi-recumbent posture. It is most indecorous.
GWENDOLEN. Mamma! [*He tries to rise; she restrains him.*] I must beg you to retire. This is no place for you. Besides, Mr. Worthing has not quite finished yet.
LADY BRACKNELL. Finished what, may I ask?
GWENDOLEN. I am engaged to Mr. Worthing, mamma. [*They rise together.*]
LADY BRACKNELL. Pardon me, you are not engaged to any one. When you do become engaged to some one, I, or your father, should his health permit him, will inform you of the fact. An engagement should come on a young girl as a surprise, pleasant or unpleasant, as the case may be. It is hardly a matter that she could be allowed to arrange for herself. . . . And now I have a few questions to put to you, Mr. Worthing. While I am making these inquiries, you, Gwendolen, will wait for me below in the carriage.
GWENDOLEN [*Reproachfully*]. Mamma!
LADY BRACKNELL. In the carriage, Gwendolen! [GWENDOLEN *goes to the door. She and* JACK *blow kisses to each other behind* LADY BRACKNELL'S *back.* LADY BRACKNELL *looks vaguely about as if she could not understand what the noise was. Finally turns round.*] Gwendolen, the carriage!
GWENDOLEN. Yes, mamma. [*Goes out, looking back at* JACK.]
LADY BRACKNELL [*Sitting down*]. You can take a seat, Mr. Worthing. [*Looks in her pocket for note-book and pencil.*]
JACK. Thank you, Lady Bracknell, I prefer standing.
LADY BRACKNELL [*Pencil and note-book in hand*]. I feel bound to tell you that you are not down on my list of eligible young men, although I have the same list as the dear Duchess of Bolton has. We work together, in fact. However, I am quite ready to enter your name, should your answers be what a really affectionate mother requires. Do you smoke?
JACK. Well, yes, I must admit I smoke.
LADY BRACKNELL. I am glad to hear it. A man should always have an occupation of some kind. There are far too many idle men in London as it is. How old are you?
JACK. Twenty-nine.
LADY BRACKNELL. A very good age to be married at. I have always been of opinion that a man who desires to get married should know either everything or nothing. Which do you know?
JACK [*After some hesitation*]. I know nothing, Lady Bracknell.
LADY BRACKNELL. I am pleased to hear it. I do not approve of anything

that tampers with natural ignorance. Ignorance is like a delicate exotic fruit; touch it and the bloom is gone. The whole theory of modern education is radically unsound. Fortunately in England, at any rate, education produces no effect whatsoever. If it did, it would prove a serious danger to the upper classes, and probably lead to acts of violence in Grosvenor Square. What is your income?

JACK.   Between seven and eight thousand a year.

LADY BRACKNELL [*Makes a note in her book*].   In land, or in investments?

JACK.   In investments, chiefly.

LADY BRACKNELL.   That is satisfactory. What between the duties expected of one during one's lifetime, and the duties exacted from one after one's death, land has ceased to be either a profit or a pleasure. It gives one position, and prevents one from keeping it up. That's all that can be said about land.

JACK.   I have a country house with some land, of course, attached to it, about fifteen hundred acres, I believe; but I don't depend on that for my real income. In fact, as far as I can make out, the poachers are the only people who make anything out of it.

LADY BRACKNELL.   A country house! How many bedrooms? Well, that point can be cleared up afterwards. You have a town house, I hope? A girl with a simple, unspoiled nature, like Gwendolen, could hardly be expected to reside in the country.

JACK.   Well, I own a house in Belgrave Square, but it is let by the year to Lady Bloxham. Of course, I can get it back whenever I like, at six months' notice.

LADY BRACKNELL.   Lady Bloxham? I don't know her.

JACK.   Oh, she goes about very little. She is a lady considerably advanced in years.

LADY BRACKNELL.   Ah, now-a-days that is no guarantee of respectability of character. What number in Belgrave Square?

JACK.   149.

LADY BRACKNELL [*Shaking her head*].   The unfashionable side. I thought there was something. However, that could easily be altered.

JACK.   Do you mean the fashion, or the side?

LADY BRACKNELL [*Sternly*].   Both, if necessary, I presume. What are your politics?

JACK.   Well, I am afraid I really have none. I am a Liberal Unionist.

LADY BRACKNELL.   Oh, they count as Tories. They dine with us. Or come in the evening, at any rate. Now to minor matters. Are your parents living?

JACK.   I have lost both my parents.

LADY BRACKNELL. To lose one parent, Mr. Worthing, may be regarded as a misfortune; to lose both looks like carelessness. Who was your father? He was evidently a man of some wealth. Was he born in what the Radical papers call the purple of commerce, or did he rise from the ranks of the aristocracy?

JACK. I am afraid I really don't know. The fact is, Lady Bracknell, I said I had lost my parents. It would be nearer the truth to say that my parents seem to have lost me . . . I don't actually know who I am by birth. I was . . . well, I was found.

LADY BRACKNELL. Found!

JACK. The late Mr. Thomas Cardew, an old gentleman of a very charitable and kindly disposition, found me, and gave me the name of Worthing, because he happened to have a first-class ticket for Worthing in his pocket at the time. Worthing is a place in Sussex. It is a seaside resort.

LADY BRACKNELL. Where did the charitable gentleman who had a first-class ticket for this seaside resort find you?

JACK [*Gravely*]. In a hand-bag.

LADY BRACKNELL. A hand-bag?

JACK [*Very seriously*]. Yes, Lady Bracknell. I was in a hand-bag—a somewhat large, black leather hand-bag, with handles to it—an ordinary hand-bag in fact.

LADY BRACKNELL. In what locality did this Mr. James, or Thomas, Cardew come across this ordinary hand-bag?

JACK. In the cloak-room at Victoria Station. It was given to him in mistake for his own.

LADY BRACKNELL. The cloak-room at Victoria Station?

JACK. Yes. The Brighton line.

LADY BRACKNELL. The line is immaterial. Mr. Worthing, I confess I feel somewhat bewildered by what you have just told me. To be born, or at any rate bred, in a hand-bag, whether it had handles or not, seems to me to display a contempt for the ordinary decencies of family life that reminds one of the worst excesses of the French Revolution. And I presume you know what that unfortunate movement led to? As for the particular locality in which the hand-bag was found, a cloak-room at a railway station might serve to conceal a social indiscretion—has probably, indeed, been used for that purpose before now—but it could hardly be regarded as an assured basis for a recognised position in good society.

JACK. May I ask you then what you would advise me to do? I need hardly say I would do anything in the world to ensure Gwendolen's happiness.

LADY BRACKNELL. I would strongly advise you, Mr. Worthing, to try and acquire some relations as soon as possible, and to make a definite effort to produce at any rate one parent, of either sex, before the season is quite over.
JACK. Well, I don't see how I could possibly manage to do that. I can produce the hand-bag at any moment. It is in my dressing-room at home. I really think that should satisfy you, Lady Bracknell.
LADY BRACKNELL. Me, sir! What has it to do with me? You can hardly imagine that I and Lord Bracknell would dream of allowing our only daughter—a girl brought up with the utmost care—to marry into a cloak-room, and form an alliance with a parcel? Good morning, Mr. Worthing!
[LADY BRACKNELL *sweeps out in majestic indignation.*]
JACK. Good morning! [ALGERNON *from the other room, strikes up the Wedding March.* JACK *looks perfectly furious, and goes to the door.*] For goodness' sake don't play that ghastly tune, Algy! How idiotic you are!
[*The music stops and* ALGERNON *enters cheerily.*]
ALGERNON. Didn't it go off all right, old boy? You don't mean to say Gwendolen refused you? I know it is a way she has. She is always refusing people. I think it is most ill-natured of her.
JACK. Oh, Gwendolen is as right as a trivet. As far as she is concerned, we are engaged. Her mother is perfectly unbearable. Never met such a Gorgon . . . I don't really know what a Gorgon is like, but I am quite sure that Lady Bracknell is one. In any case, she is a monster, without being a myth, which is rather unfair. . . . I beg your pardon, Algy, I suppose I shouldn't talk about your own aunt in that way before you.
ALGERNON. My dear boy, I love hearing my relations abused. It is the only thing that makes me put up with them at all. Relations are simply a tedious pack of people, who haven't got the remotest knowledge of how to live, nor the smallest instinct about when to die.
JACK. Oh, that is nonsense!
ALGERNON. It isn't!
JACK. Well, I won't argue about the matter. You always want to argue about things.
ALGERNON. That is exactly what things were originally made for.
JACK. Upon my word, if I thought that, I'd shoot myself . . . [*A pause.*] You don't think there is any chance of Gwendolen becoming like her mother in about a hundred and fifty years, do you Algy?
ALGERNON. All women become like their mothers. That is their tragedy. No man does. That's his.

JACK. Is that clever?
ALGERNON. It is perfectly phrased! and quite as true as any observation in civilised life should be.
JACK. I am sick to death of cleverness. Everybody is clever now-a-days. You can't go anywhere without meeting clever people. The thing has become an absolute public nuisance. I wish to goodness we had a few fools left.
ALGERNON. We have.
JACK. I should extremely like to meet them. What do they talk about?
ALGERNON. The fools? Oh! about the clever people, of course.
JACK. What fools!
ALGERNON. By the way, did you tell Gwendolen the truth about your being Ernest in town, and Jack in the country?
JACK [*In a very patronising manner*]. My dear fellow, the truth isn't quite the sort of thing one tells to a nice, sweet, refined girl. What extraordinary ideas you have about the way to behave to a woman!
ALGERNON. The only way to behave to a woman is to make love to her, if she is pretty, and to some one else if she is plain.
JACK. Oh, that is nonsense.
ALGERNON. What about your brother? What about the profligate Ernest?
JACK. Oh, before the end of the week I shall have got rid of him. I'll say he died in Paris of apoplexy. Lots of people die of apoplexy, quite suddenly, don't they?
ALGERNON. Yes, but it's hereditary, my dear fellow. It's a sort of thing that runs in families. You had much better say a severe chill.
JACK. You are sure a severe chill isn't hereditary, or anything of that kind?
ALGERNON. Of course it isn't!
JACK. Very well, then. My poor brother Ernest is carried off suddenly in Paris, by a severe chill. That gets rid of him.
ALGERNON. But I thought you said that . . . Miss Cardew was a little too much interested in your poor brother Ernest? Won't she feel his loss a good deal?
JACK. Oh, that is all right. Cecily is not a silly, romantic girl, I am glad to say. She has got a capital appetite, goes long walks, and pays no attention at all to her lessons.
ALGERNON. I would rather like to see Cecily.
JACK. I will take very good care you never do. She is excessively pretty, and she is only just eighteen.
ALGERNON. Have you told Gwendolen yet that you have an excessively pretty ward who is only just eighteen?

JACK. Oh! one doesn't blurt these things out to people. Cecily and Gwendolen are perfectly certain to be extremely great friends. I'll bet you anything you like that half an hour after they have met, they will be calling each other sister.

ALGERNON. Women only do that when they have called each other a lot of other things first. Now, my dear boy, if we want to get a good table at Willis's, we really must go and dress. Do you know it is nearly seven?

JACK [*Irritably*]. Oh! it always is nearly seven.

ALGERNON. Well, I'm hungry.

JACK. I never knew you when you weren't. . . .

ALGERNON. What shall we do after dinner? Go to a theatre?

JACK. Oh, no! I loathe listening.

ALGERNON. Well, let us go to the Club?

JACK. Oh, no! I hate talking.

ALGERNON. Well, we might trot round to the Empire at ten?

JACK. Oh, no! I can't bear looking at things. It is so silly.

ALGERNON. Well, what shall we do?

JACK. Nothing!

ALGERNON. It is awfully hard work doing nothing. However, I don't mind hard work where there is no definite object of any kind.

[*Enter* LANE.]

LANE. Miss Fairfax.

[*Enter* GWENDOLEN. LANE *goes out.*]

ALGERNON. Gwendolen, upon my word!

GWENDOLEN. Algy, kindly turn your back. I have something very particular to say to Mr. Worthing.

ALGERNON. Really, Gwendolen, I don't think I can allow this at all.

GWENDOLEN. Algy, you always adopt a strictly immoral attitude towards life. You are not quite old enough to do that. [ALGERNON *retires to the fireplace.*]

JACK. My own darling!

GWENDOLEN. Ernest, we may never be married. From the expression on mamma's face I fear we never shall. Few parents now-a-days pay any regard to what their children say to them. The old-fashioned respect for the young is fast dying out. Whatever influence I ever had over mamma, I lost at the age of three. But although she may prevent us from becoming man and wife, and I may marry someone else, and marry often, nothing that she can possibly do can alter my eternal devotion to you.

JACK. Dear Gwendolen!

GWENDOLEN. The story of your romantic origin, as related to me by mamma, with unpleasing comments, has naturally stirred the deeper fibres of my nature. Your Christian name has an irresistible fascination. The simplicity of your character makes you exquisitely incomprehensible to me. Your town address at the Albany, I have. What is your address in the country?

JACK. The Manor House, Woolton, Hertfordshire.

[ALGERNON, *who has been carefully listening, smiles to himself, and writes the address on his shirt-cuff. Then picks up the Railway Guide.*]

GWENDOLEN. There is a good postal service, I suppose? It may be necessary to do something desperate. That, of course, will require serious consideration. I will communicate with you daily.

JACK. My own one!

GWENDOLEN. How long do you remain in town?

JACK. Till Monday.

GWENDOLEN. Good! Algy, you may turn round now.

ALGERNON. Thanks, I've turned round already.

GWENDOLEN. You may also ring the bell.

JACK. You will let me see you to your carriage, my own darling?

GWENDOLEN. Certainly.

JACK [*To* LANE, *who now enters*]. I will see Miss Fairfax out.

LANE. Yes, sir. [JACK *and* GWENDOLEN *go off.*]

[LANE *presents several letters on a salver to* ALGERNON. *It is to be surmised that they are bills, as* ALGERNON, *after looking at the envelopes, tears them up.*]

ALGERNON. A glass of sherry, Lane.

LANE. Yes, sir.

ALGERNON. To-morrow, Lane, I'm going Bunburying.

LANE. Yes, sir.

ALGERNON. I shall probably not be back till Monday. You can put up my dress clothes, my smoking jacket, and all the Bunbury suits . . .

LANE. Yes, sir. [*Handing sherry.*]

ALGERNON. I hope to-morrow will be a fine day, Lane.

LANE. It never is, sir.

ALGERNON. Lane, you're a perfect pessimist.

LANE. I do my best to give satisfaction, sir.

[*Enter* JACK. LANE *goes off.*]

JACK. There's a sensible, intellectual girl! the only girl I ever cared for in my life. [ALGERNON *is laughing immoderately.*] What on earth are you so amused at?

ALGERNON. Oh, I'm a little anxious about poor Bunbury, that is all.

JACK. If you don't take care, your friend Bunbury will get you into a serious scrape some day.

ALGERNON.   I love scrapes. They are the only things that are never serious.
JACK.   Oh, that's nonsense, Algy. You never talk anything but nonsense.
ALGERNON.   Nobody ever does.
[JACK *looks indignantly at him, and leaves the room,* ALGERNON *lights a cigarette, reads his shirt-cuff and smiles.*]

ACT-DROP

Act II

SCENE—*Garden at the Manor House. A flight of gray stone steps leads up to the house. The garden, an old-fashioned one, full of roses. Time of year, July. Basket chairs, and a table covered with books, are set under a large yew tree.*
[MISS PRISM *discovered seated at the table.* CECILY *is at the back watering flowers.*]

MISS PRISM [*Calling*]. Cecily, Cecily! Surely such a utilitarian occupation as the watering of flowers is rather Moulton's duty than yours? Especially at a moment when intellectual pleasures await you. Your German grammar is on the table. Pray open it at page fifteen. We will repeat yesterday's lesson.

CECILY [*Coming over very slowly*]. But I don't like German. It isn't at all a becoming language. I know perfectly well that I look quite plain after my German lesson.

MISS PRISM. Child, you know how anxious your guardian is that you should improve yourself in every way. He laid particular stress on your German, as he was leaving for town yesterday. Indeed, he always lays stress on your German when he is leaving for town.

CECILY. Dear Uncle Jack is so very serious! Sometimes he is so serious that I think he cannot be quite well.

MISS PRISM [*Drawing herself up*]. Your guardian enjoys the best of health, and his gravity of demeanour is especially to be commended in one so comparatively young as he is. I know no one who has a higher sense of duty and responsibility.

CECILY. I suppose that is why he often looks a little bored when we three are together.

MISS PRISM. Cecily! I am surprised at you. Mr. Worthing has many troubles in his life. Idle merriment and triviality would be out of place in his conversation. You must remember his constant anxiety about that unfortunate young man, his brother.

CECILY. I wish Uncle Jack would allow that unfortunate young man, his brother, to come down here sometimes. We might have a good influence over him, Miss Prism. I am sure you certainly would. You know German, and geology, and things of that kind influence a man very much. [CECILY *begins to write in her diary*.]

MISS PRISM [*Shaking her head*]. I do not think that even I could produce any effect on a character that according to his own brother's admission is irretrievably weak and vacillating. Indeed I am not sure that I would desire to reclaim him. I am not in favour of this modern mania for turning bad people into good people at a moment's notice. As a man sows so let him reap. You must put away your diary, Cecily. I really don't see why you should keep a diary at all.

CECILY. I keep a diary in order to enter the wonderful secrets of my life. If I didn't write them down I should probably forget all about them.

MISS PRISM. Memory, my dear Cecily, is the diary that we all carry about with us.

CECILY. Yes, but it usually chronicles the things that have never happened, and couldn't possibly have happened. I believe that Memory is responsible for nearly all the three-volume novels that Mudie sends us.

MISS PRISM. Do not speak slightingly of the three-volume novel, Cecily. I wrote one myself in earlier days.

CECILY. Did you really, Miss Prism? How wonderfully clever you are! I hope it did not end happily? I don't like novels that end happily. They depress me so much.

MISS PRISM. The good ended happily, and the bad unhappily. That is what Fiction means.

CECILY. I suppose so. But it seems very unfair. And was your novel ever published?

MISS PRISM. Alas! no. The manuscript unfortunately was abandoned. I use the word in the sense of lost or mislaid. To your work, child, these speculations are profitless.

CECILY [*Smiling*]. But I see dear Dr. Chasuble coming up through the garden.

MISS PRISM [*Rising and advancing*]. Dr. Chasuble! This is indeed a pleasure.

[*Enter* CANON CHASUBLE.]

CHASUBLE. And how are we this morning? Miss Prism, you are, I trust, well?

CECILY. Miss Prism has just been complaining of a slight headache. I

think it would do her so much good to have a short stroll with you in the Park, Dr. Chasuble.
MISS PRISM. Cecily, I have not mentioned anything about a headache.
CECILY. No, dear Miss Prism, I know that, but I felt instinctively that you had a headache. Indeed I was thinking about that, and not about my German lesson, when the Rector came in.
CHASUBLE. I hope, Cecily, you are not inattentive.
CECILY. Oh, I am afraid I am.
CHASUBLE. That is strange. Were I fortunate enough to be Miss Prism's pupil, I would hang upon her lips. [MISS PRISM *glares*.] I spoke metaphorically.—My metaphor was drawn from bees. Ahem! Mr. Worthing, I suppose, has not returned from town yet?
MISS PRISM. We do not expect him till Monday afternoon.
CHASUBLE. Ah yes, he usually likes to spend his Sunday in London. He is not one of those whose sole aim is enjoyment, as, by all accounts, that unfortunate young man, his brother, seems to be. But I must not disturb Egeria and her pupil any longer.
MISS PRISM. Egeria? My name is Lætitia, Doctor.
CHASUBLE [*Bowing*]. A classical allusion merely, drawn from the Pagan authors. I shall see you both no doubt at Evensong?
MISS PRISM. I think, dear Doctor, I will have a stroll with you. I find I have a headache after all, and a walk might do it good.
CHASUBLE. With pleasure, Miss Prism, with pleasure. We might go as far as the schools and back.
MISS PRISM. That would be delightful. Cecily, you will read your Political Economy in my absence. The chapter on the Fall of the Rupee you may omit. It is somewhat too sensational. Even these metallic problems have their melodramatic side. [*Goes down the garden with* DR. CHASUBLE.]
CECILY [*Picks up books and throws them back on table*]. Horrid Political Economy! Horrid Geography! Horrid, horrid German!
[*Enter* MERRIMAN *with a card on a salver*.]
MERRIMAN. Mr. Ernest Worthing has just driven over from the station. He has brought his luggage with him.
CECILY [*Takes the card and reads it*]. 'Mr. Ernest Worthing, B 4, The Albany, W.' Uncle Jack's brother! Did you tell him Mr. Worthing was in town?
MERRIMAN. Yes, Miss. He seemed very much disappointed. I mentioned that you and Miss Prism were in the garden. He said he was anxious to speak to you privately for a moment.
CECILY. Ask Mr. Ernest Worthing to come here. I suppose you

had better talk to the housekeeper about a room for him.

MERRIMAN. Yes, Miss. [MERRIMAN *goes off*.]

CECILY. I have never met any really wicked person before. I feel rather frightened. I am so afraid he will look just like everyone else.

[*Enter* ALGERNON, *very gay and débonnaire.*]

He does!

ALGERNON [*Raising his hat*]. You are my little cousin Cecily, I'm sure.

CECILY. You are under some strange mistake. I am not little. In fact, I believe I am more than usually tall for my age. [ALGERNON *is rather taken aback.*] But I am your cousin, Cecily. You, I see from your card, are Uncle Jack's brother, my cousin Ernest, my wicked cousin Ernest.

ALGERNON. Oh! I am not really wicked at all, cousin Cecily. You mustn't think that I am wicked.

CECILY. If you are not, then you have certainly been deceiving us all in a very inexcusable manner. I hope you have not been leading a double life, pretending to be wicked and being really good all the time. That would be hypocrisy.

ALGERNON [*Looks at her in amazement*]. Oh! of course I have been rather reckless.

CECILY. I am glad to hear it.

ALGERNON. In fact, now you mention the subject, I have been very bad in my own small way.

CECILY. I don't think you should be so proud of that, though I am sure it must have been very pleasant.

ALGERNON. It is much pleasanter being here with you.

CECILY. I can't understand how you are here at all. Uncle Jack won't be back till Monday afternoon.

ALGERNON. That is a great disappointment. I am obliged to go up by the first train on Monday morning. I have a business appointment that I am anxious . . . to miss.

CECILY. Couldn't you miss it anywhere but in London?

ALGERNON. No: the appointment is in London.

CECILY. Well, I know, of course, how important it is not to keep a business engagement, if one wants to retain any sense of the beauty of life, but still I think you had better wait till Uncle Jack arrives. I know he wants to speak to you about your emigrating.

ALGERNON. About my what?

CECILY. Your emigrating. He has gone up to buy your outfit.

ALGERNON. I certainly wouldn't let Jack buy my outfit. He has no taste in neckties at all.

CECILY. I don't think you will require neckties. Uncle Jack is sending you to Australia.

ALGERNON. Australia! I'd sooner die.

CECILY. Well, he said at dinner on Wednesday night, that you would have to choose between this world, the next world, and Australia.

ALGERNON. Oh, well! The accounts I have received of Australia and the next world are not particularly encouraging. This world is good enough for me, cousin Cecily.

CECILY. Yes, but are you good enough for it?

ALGERNON. I'm afraid I'm not that. That is why I want you to reform me. You might make that your mission, if you don't mind, cousin Cecily.

CECILY. I'm afraid I've no time, this afternoon.

ALGERNON. Well, would you mind my reforming myself this afternoon?

CECILY. It is rather Quixotic of you. But I think you should try.

ALGERNON. I will. I feel better already.

CECILY. You are looking a little worse.

ALGERNON. That is because I am hungry.

CECILY. How thoughtless of me. I should have remembered that when one is going to lead an entirely new life, one requires regular and wholesome meals. Won't you come in?

ALGERNON. Thank you. Might I have a button-hole first? I never have any appetite unless I have a button-hole first.

CECILY. A Maréchal Niel? [*Picks up scissors.*]

ALGERNON. No, I'd sooner have a pink rose.

CECILY. Why? [*Cuts a flower.*]

ALGERNON. Because you are like a pink rose, cousin Cecily.

CECILY. I don't think it can be right for you to talk to me like that. Miss Prism never says such things to me.

ALGERNON. Then Miss Prism is a short-sighted old lady. [CECILY *puts the rose in his button-hole.*] You are the prettiest girl I ever saw.

CECILY. Miss Prism says that all good looks are a snare.

ALGERNON. They are a snare that every sensible man would like to be caught in.

CECILY. Oh! I don't think I would care to catch a sensible man. I shouldn't know what to talk to him about.

[*They pass into the house.* MISS PRISM *and* DR. CHASUBLE *return.*]

MISS PRISM. You are too much alone, dear Dr. Chasuble. You should get married. A misanthrope I can understand—a womanthrope, never!

CHASUBLE [*With a scholar's shudder*]. Believe me, I do not deserve so neologistic a phrase. The precept as well as the practice of the Primitive Church was distinctly against matrimony.

MISS PRISM [*Sententiously*]. That is obviously the reason why the Primitive Church has not lasted up to the present day. And you do not seem to realise, dear Doctor, that by persistently remaining single, a man converts himself into a permanent public temptation. Men should be more careful; this very celibacy leads weaker vessels astray.

CHASUBLE. But is a man not equally attractive when married?

MISS PRISM. No married man is ever attractive except to his wife.

CHASUBLE. And often, I've been told, not even to her.

MISS PRISM. That depends on the intellectual sympathies of the woman. Maturity can always be depended on. Ripeness can be trusted. Young women are green. [DR. CHASUBLE *starts*.] I spoke horticulturally. My metaphor was drawn from fruits. But where is Cecily?

CHASUBLE. Perhaps she followed us to the schools.

[*Enter* JACK *slowly from the back of the garden. He is dressed in the deepest mourning, with crepe hat-band and black gloves.*]

MISS PRISM. Mr. Worthing!

CHASUBLE. Mr. Worthing?

MISS PRISM. This is indeed a surprise. We did not look for you till Monday afternoon.

JACK [*Shakes* MISS PRISM'S *hand in a tragic manner*]. I have returned sooner than I expected. Dr. Chasuble, I hope you are well?

CHASUBLE. Dear Mr. Worthing, I trust this garb of woe does not betoken some terrible calamity?

JACK. My brother.

MISS PRISM. More shameful debts and extravagance?

CHASUBLE. Still leading his life of pleasure?

JACK [*Shaking his head*]. Dead!

CHASUBLE. Your brother Ernest dead?

JACK. Quite dead.

MISS PRISM. What a lesson for him! I trust he will profit by it.

CHASUBLE. Mr. Worthing, I offer you my sincere condolence. You have at least the consolation of knowing that you were always the most generous and forgiving of brothers.

JACK. Poor Ernest! He had many faults, but it is a sad, sad blow.

CHASUBLE. Very sad, indeed. Were you with him at the end?

JACK. No. He died abroad; in Paris, in fact. I had a telegram last night from the manager of the Grand Hotel.

CHASUBLE. Was the cause of death mentioned?

JACK.   A severe chill, it seems.
MISS PRISM.   As a man sows, so shall he reap.
CHASUBLE [*Raising his hand*].   Charity, dear Miss Prism, charity! None of us are perfect. I myself am peculiarly susceptible to draughts. Will the interment take place here?
JACK.   No. He seemed to have expressed a desire to be buried in Paris.
CHASUBLE.   In Paris! [*Shakes his head.*] I fear that hardly points to any very serious state of mind at the last. You would no doubt wish me to make some slight allusion to this tragic domestic affliction next Sunday. [JACK *presses his hand convulsively.*] My sermon on the meaning of the manna in the wilderness can be adapted to almost any occasion, joyful, or, as in the present case, distressing. [*All sigh.*] I have preached it at harvest celebrations, christenings, confirmations, on days of humiliation and festal days. The last time I delivered it was in the Cathedral, as a charity sermon on behalf of the Society for the Prevention of Discontent among the Upper Orders. The Bishop, who was present, was much struck by some of the analogies I drew.
JACK.   Ah! that reminds me, you mentioned christenings I think, Dr. Chasuble? I suppose you know how to christen all right? [DR. CHASUBLE *looks astounded.*] I mean, of course, you are continually christening, aren't you?
MISS PRISM.   It is, I regret to say, one of the Rector's most constant duties in this parish. I have often spoken to the poorer classes on the subject. But they don't seem to know what thrift is.
CHASUBLE.   But is there any particular infant in whom you are interested, Mr. Worthing? Your brother was, I believe, unmarried, was he not?
JACK.   Oh, yes.
MISS PRISM [*Bitterly*].   People who live entirely for pleasure usually are.
JACK.   But it is not for any child, dear Doctor. I am very fond of children. No! the fact is, I would like to be christened myself, this afternoon, if you have nothing better to do.
CHASUBLE.   But surely, Mr. Worthing, you have been christened already?
JACK.   I don't remember anything about it.
CHASUBLE.   But have you any grave doubts on the subject?
JACK.   I certainly intend to have. Of course, I don't know if the thing would bother you in any way, or if you think I am a little too old now.
CHASUBLE.   Not at all. The sprinkling, and, indeed, the immersion of adults is a perfectly canonical practice.

JACK. Immersion!
CHASUBLE. You need have no apprehensions. Sprinkling is all that is necessary, or indeed I think advisable. Our weather is so changeable. At what hour would you wish the ceremony performed?
JACK. Oh, I might trot round about five if that would suit you?
CHASUBLE. Perfectly, perfectly! In fact I have two similar ceremonies to perform at that time. A case of twins that occurred recently in one of the outlying cottages on your own estate. Poor Jenkins the carter, a most hard-working man.
JACK. Oh! I don't see much fun in being christened along with other babies. It would be childish. Would half-past five do?
CHASUBLE. Admirably! Admirably! [*Takes out watch.*] And now, dear Mr. Worthing, I will not intrude any longer into a house of sorrow. I would merely beg you not to be too much bowed down by grief. What seem to us bitter trials are often blessings in disguise.
MISS PRISM. This seems to me a blessing of an extremely obvious kind.
[*Enter* CECILY *from the house.*]
CECILY. Uncle Jack! Oh, I am pleased to see you back. But what horrid clothes you have got on! Do go and change them.
MISS PRISM. Cecily!
CHASUBLE. My child! my child! [CECILY *goes toward* JACK; *he kisses her brow in a melancholy manner.*]
CECILY. What is the matter, Uncle Jack? Do look happy! You look as if you had toothache, and I have got such a surprise for you. Who do you think is in the dining-room? Your brother!
JACK. Who?
CECILY. Your brother Ernest. He arrived about half an hour ago.
JACK. What nonsense! I haven't got a brother.
CECILY. Oh, don't say that. However badly he may have behaved to you in the past he is still your brother. You couldn't be so heartless as to disown him. I'll tell him to come out. And you will shake hands with him, won't you, Uncle Jack? [*Runs back into the house.*]
CHASUBLE. These are very joyful tidings.
MISS PRISM. After we had all been resigned to his loss, his sudden return seems to me peculiarly distressing.
JACK. My brother is in the dining-room? I don't know what it all means. I think it is perfectly absurd.
[*Enter* ALGERNON *and* CECILY *hand in hand. They come slowly up to* JACK.]
JACK. Good heavens! [*Motions* ALGERNON *away.*]
ALGERNON. Brother John, I have come down from town to tell you that I am very sorry for all the trouble I have given you, and that I

intend to lead a better life in the future. [JACK *glares at him and does not take his hand.*]

CECILY.   Uncle Jack, you are not going to refuse your own brother's hand?

JACK.   Nothing will induce me to take his hand. I think his coming down here disgraceful. He knows perfectly well why.

CECILY.   Uncle Jack, do be nice. There is some good in everyone. Ernest has just been telling me about his poor invalid friend Mr. Bunbury, whom he goes to visit so often. And surely there must be much good in one who is kind to an invalid, and leaves the pleasures of London to sit by a bed of pain.

JACK.   Oh! he has been talking about Bunbury, has he?

CECILY.   Yes, he has told me all about poor Mr. Bunbury, and his terrible state of health.

JACK.   Bunbury! Well, I won't have him talk to you about Bunbury or about anything else. It is enough to drive one perfectly frantic.

ALGERNON.   Of course I admit that the faults were all on my side. But I must say that I think that brother John's coldness to me is peculiarly painful. I expected a more enthusiastic welcome, especially considering it is the first time I have come here.

CECILY.   Uncle Jack, if you don't shake hands with Ernest I will never forgive you.

JACK.   Never forgive me?

CECILY.   Never, never, never!

JACK.   Well, this is the last time I shall ever do it. [*Shakes hands with* ALGERNON *and glares.*]

CHASUBLE.   It's pleasant, is it not, to see so perfect a reconciliation? I think we might leave the two brothers together.

MISS PRISM.   Cecily, you will come with us.

CECILY.   Certainly, Miss Prism. My little task of reconciliation is over.

CHASUBLE.   You have done a beautiful action to-day, dear child.

MISS PRISM.   We must not be premature in our judgments.

CECILY.   I feel very happy. [*They all go off.*]

JACK.   You young scoundrel, Algy, you must get out of this place as soon as possible. I don't allow any Bunburying here.

[*Enter* MERRIMAN.]

MERRIMAN.   I have put Mr. Ernest's things in the room next to yours, sir. I suppose that is all right?

JACK.   What?

MERRIMAN.   Mr. Ernest's luggage, sir. I have unpacked it and put it in the room next to your own.

JACK.   His luggage?

MERRIMAN. Yes, sir. Three portmanteaus, a dressing-case, two hat-boxes, and a large luncheon-basket.

ALGERNON. I am afraid I can't stay more than a week this time.

JACK. Merriman, order the dog-cart at once. Mr. Ernest has been suddenly called back to town.

MERRIMAN. Yes, sir. [*Goes back into the house.*]

ALGERNON. What a fearful liar you are, Jack. I have not been called back to town at all.

JACK. Yes, you have.

ALGERNON. I haven't heard anyone call me.

JACK. Your duty as a gentleman calls you back.

ALGERNON. My duty as a gentleman has never interfered with my pleasures in the smallest degree.

JACK. I can quite understand that.

ALGERNON. Well, Cecily is a darling.

JACK. You are not to talk of Miss Cardew like that. I don't like it.

ALGERNON. Well, I don't like your clothes. You look perfectly ridiculous in them. Why on earth don't you go up and change? It is perfectly childish to be in deep mourning for a man who is actually staying for a whole week with you in your house as a guest. I call it grotesque.

JACK. You are certainly not staying with me for a whole week as a guest or anything else. You have got to leave . . . by the four-five train.

ALGERNON. I certainly won't leave you so long as you are in mourning. It would be most unfriendly. If I were in mourning you would stay with me, I suppose. I should think it very unkind if you didn't.

JACK. Well, will you go if I change my clothes?

ALGERNON. Yes, if you are not too long. I never saw anybody take so long to dress, and with such little result.

JACK. Well, at any rate, that is better than being always over-dressed as you are.

ALGERNON. If I am occasionally a little over-dressed, I make up for it by being always immensely over-educated.

JACK. Your vanity is ridiculous, your conduct an outrage, and your presence in my garden utterly absurd. However, you have got to catch the four-five, and I hope you will have a pleasant journey back to town. This Bunburying, as you call it, has not been a great success for you. [*Goes into the house.*]

ALGERNON. I think it has been a great success. I'm in love with Cecily, and that is everything.

[*Enter* CECILY *at the back of the garden. She picks up the can and begins to water the flowers.*]
    But I must see her before I go, and make arrangements for another Bunbury. Ah, there she is.
CECILY.   Oh, I merely came back to water the roses. I thought you were with Uncle Jack.
ALGERNON.   He's gone to order the dog-cart for me.
CECILY.   Oh, is he going to take you for a nice drive?
ALGERNON.   He's going to send me away.
CECILY.   Then have we got to part?
ALGERNON.   I am afraid so. It's a very painful parting.
CECILY.   It is always painful to part from people whom one has known for a very brief space of time. The absence of old friends one can endure with equanimity. But even a momentary separation from anyone to whom one has just been introduced is almost unbearable.
ALGERNON.   Thank you.
[*Enter* MERRIMAN.]
MERRIMAN.   The dog-cart is at the door, sir. [ALGERNON *looks appealingly at* CECILY.]
CECILY.   It can wait, Merriman . . . for . . . five minutes.
MERRIMAN.   Yes, Miss.   [*Exit* MERRIMAN.]
ALGERNON.   I hope, Cecily, I shall not offend you if I state quite frankly and openly that you seem to me to be in every way the visible personification of absolute perfection.
CECILY.   I think your frankness does you great credit, Ernest. If you will allow me I will copy your remarks into my diary. [*Goes over to table and begins writing in diary.*]
ALGERNON.   Do you really keep a diary? I'd give anything to look at it. May I?
CECILY.   Oh, no. [*Puts her hand over it.*] You see, it is simply a very young girl's record of her own thoughts and impressions, and consequently meant for publication. When it appears in volume form I hope you will order a copy. But pray, Ernest, don't stop. I delight in taking down from dictation. I have reached 'absolute perfection.' You can go on. I am quite ready for more.
ALGERNON [*Somewhat taken aback*].   Ahem! Ahem!
CECILY.   Oh, don't cough, Ernest. When one is dictating one should speak fluently and not cough. Besides, I don't know how to spell a cough. [*Writes as* ALGERNON *speaks.*]
ALGERNON [*Speaking very rapidly*]. Cecily, ever since I first looked upon your wonderful and incomparable beauty, I have dared to love you wildly, passionately, devotedly, hopelessly.

CECILY. I don't think that you should tell me that you love me wildly, passionately, devotedly, hopelessly. Hopelessly doesn't seem to make much sense, does it?
ALGERNON. Cecily!
[*Enter* MERRIMAN.]
MERRIMAN. The dog-cart is waiting, sir.
ALGERNON. Tell it to come round next week, at the same hour.
MERRIMAN [*Looks at* CECILY, *who makes no sign*]. Yes, sir. [MERRIMAN *retires*.]
CECILY. Uncle Jack would be very much annoyed if he knew you were staying on till next week, at the same hour.
ALGERNON. Oh, I don't care about Jack. I don't care for anybody in the whole world but you. I love you, Cecily. You will marry me, won't you?
CECILY. You silly boy! Of course. Why, we have been engaged for the last three months.
ALGERNON. For the last three months?
CECILY. Yes, it will be exactly three months on Thursday.
ALGERNON. But how did we become engaged?
CECILY. Well, ever since dear Uncle Jack first confessed to us that he had a younger brother who was very wicked and bad, you of course have formed the chief topic of conversation between myself and Miss Prism. And of course a man who is much talked about is always very attractive. One feels there must be something in him after all. I daresay it was foolish of me, but I fell in love with you, Ernest.
ALGERNON. Darling! And when was the engagement actually settled?
CECILY. On the 14th of February last. Worn out by your entire ignorance of my existence, I determined to end the matter one way or the other, and after a long struggle with myself I accepted you under this dear old tree here. The next day I bought this little ring in your name, and this is the little bangle with the true lover's knot I promised you always to wear.
ALGERNON. Did I give you this? It's very pretty, isn't it?
CECILY. Yes, you've wonderfully good taste, Ernest. It's the excuse I've always given for your leading such a bad life. And this is the box in which I keep all your dear letters. [*Kneels at table, opens box, and produces letters tied up with blue ribbon.*]
ALGERNON. My letters! But my own sweet Cecily, I have never written you any letters.
CECILY. You need hardly remind me of that, Ernest. I remember only too well that I was forced to write your letters for you. I wrote always three times a week, and sometimes oftener.

ALGERNON. Oh, do let me read them, Cecily?

CECILY. Oh, I couldn't possibly. They would make you far too conceited. [*Replaces box.*] The three you wrote me after I had broken off the engagement are so beautiful, and so badly spelled, that even now I can hardly read them without crying a little.

ALGERNON. But was our engagement ever broken off?

CECILY. Of course it was. On the 22nd of last March. You can see the entry if you like. [*Shows diary.*] 'To-day I broke off my engagement with Ernest. I feel it is better to do so. The weather still continues charming.'

ALGERNON. But why on earth did you break it off? What had I done? I had done nothing at all. Cecily, I am very much hurt indeed to hear you broke it off. Particularly when the weather was so charming.

CECILY. It would hardly have been a really serious engagement if it hadn't been broken off at least once. But I forgave you before the week was out.

ALGERNON [*Crossing to her, and kneeling*]. What a perfect angel you are, Cecily.

CECILY. You dear romantic boy. [*He kisses her, she puts her fingers through his hair.*] I hope your hair curls naturally, does it?

ALGERNON. Yes, darling, with a little help from others.

CECILY. I am so glad.

ALGERNON. You'll never break off our engagement again, Cecily?

CECILY. I don't think I could break it off now that I have actually met you. Besides, of course, there is the question of your name.

ALGERNON. Yes, of course. [*Nervously.*]

CECILY. You must not laugh at me, darling, but it had always been a girlish dream of mine to love some one whose name was Ernest. [ALGERNON *rises*, CECILY *also.*] There is something in that name that seems to inspire absolute confidence. I pity any poor married woman whose husband is not called Ernest.

ALGERNON. But, my dear child, do you mean to say you could not love me if I had some other name?

CECILY. But what name?

ALGERNON. Oh, any name you like—Algernon—for instance . . .

CECILY. But I don't like the name of Algernon.

ALGERNON. Well, my own dear, sweet, loving little darling, I really can't see why you should object to the name of Algernon. It is not at all a bad name. In fact, it is rather an aristocratic name. Half of the chaps who get into the Bankruptcy Court are called Algernon. But seriously, Cecily . . . [*Moving to her.*] . . . if my name was Algy, couldn't you love me?

CECILY [*Rising*]. I might respect you, Ernest, I might admire your character, but I fear that I should not be able to give you my undivided attention.
ALGERNON. Ahem! Cecily! [*Picking up hat.*] Your Rector here is, I suppose, thoroughly experienced in the practice of all the rites and ceremonials of the Church?
CECILY. Oh, yes. Dr. Chasuble is a most learned man. He has never written a single book, so you can imagine how much he knows.
ALGERNON. I must see him at once on a most important christening— I mean on most important business.
CECILY. Oh!
ALGERNON. I shan't be away more than half an hour.
CECILY. Considering that we have been engaged since February the 14th, and that I only met you to-day for the first time, I think it is rather hard that you should leave me for so long a period as half an hour. Couldn't you make it twenty minutes?
ALGERNON. I'll be back in no time. [*Kisses her and rushes down the garden.*]
CECILY. What an impetuous boy he is! I like his hair so much. I must enter his proposal in my diary.
[*Enter* MERRIMAN.]
MERRIMAN. A Miss Fairfax has just called to see Mr. Worthing. On very important business Miss Fairfax states.
CECILY. Isn't Mr. Worthing in his library?
MERRIMAN. Mr. Worthing went over in the direction of the Rectory some time ago.
CECILY. Pray ask the lady to come out here; Mr. Worthing is sure to be back soon. And you can bring tea.
MERRIMAN. Yes, Miss. [*Goes out.*]
CECILY. Miss Fairfax! I suppose one of the many good elderly women who are associated with Uncle Jack in some of his philanthropic work in London. I don't quite like women who are interested in philanthropic work. I think it is so forward of them.
[*Enter* MERRIMAN.]
MERRIMAN. Miss Fairfax.
[*Enter* GWENDOLEN.] [*Exit* MERRIMAN.]
CECILY [*Advancing to meet her*]. Pray let me introduce myself to you. My name is Cecily Cardew.
GWENDOLEN. Cecily Cardew? [*Moving to her and shaking hands.*] What a very sweet name! Something tells me that we are going to be great friends. I like you already more than I can say. My first impressions of people are never wrong.
CECILY. How nice of you to like me so much after we have known

each other such a comparatively short time. Pray sit down.
GWENDOLEN [*Still standing up*]. I may call you Cecily, may I not?
CECILY. With pleasure!
GWENDOLEN. And you will always call me Gwendolen, won't you?
CECILY. If you wish.
GWENDOLEN. Then that is all quite settled, is it not?
CECILY. I hope so. [*A pause. They both sit down together.*]
GWENDOLEN. Perhaps this might be a favourable opportunity for my mentioning who I am. My father is Lord Bracknell. You have never heard of papa, I suppose?
CECILY. I don't think so.
GWENDOLEN. Outside the family circle, papa, I am glad to say, is entirely unknown. I think that is quite as it should be. The home seems to me to be the proper sphere for the man. And certainly once a man begins to neglect his domestic duties he becomes painfully effeminate, does he not? And I don't like that. It makes men so very attractive. Cecily, mamma, whose views on education are remarkably strict, has brought me up to be extremely short-sighted; it is part of her system; so do you mind my looking at you through my glasses?
CECILY. Oh! not at all, Gwendolen. I am very fond of being looked at.
GWENDOLEN [*After examining* CECILY *carefully through a lorgnette*]. You are here on a short visit, I suppose.
CECILY. Oh no! I live here.
GWENDOLEN [*Severely*]. Really? Your mother, no doubt, or some female relative of advanced years, resides here also?
CECILY. Oh no! I have no mother, nor, in fact, any relations.
GWENDOLEN. Indeed!
CECILY. My dear guardian, with the assistance of Miss Prism, has the arduous task of looking after me.
GWENDOLEN. Your guardian?
CECILY. Yes, I am Mr. Worthing's ward.
GWENDOLEN. Oh! It is strange he never mentioned to me that he had a ward. How secretive of him! He grows more interesting hourly. I am not sure, however, that the news inspires me with feelings of unmixed delight. [*Rising and going to her.*] I am very fond of you, Cecily; I have liked you ever since I met you! But I am bound to state that now that I know that you are Mr. Worthing's ward, I cannot help expressing a wish you were—well just a little older than you seem to be—and not quite so very alluring in appearance. In fact, if I may speak candidly——
CECILY. Pray do! I think that whenever one has anything unpleasant to say, one should always be quite candid.

GWENDOLEN. Well, to speak with perfect candour, Cecily, I wish that you were fully forty-two, and more than usually plain for your age. Ernest has a strong upright nature. He is the very soul of truth and honour. Disloyalty would be as impossible to him as deception. But even men of the noblest possible moral character are extremely susceptible to the influence of the physical charms of others. Modern, no less than Ancient History, supplies us with many most painful examples of what I refer to. If it were not so, indeed, History would be quite unreadable.
CECILY. I beg your pardon, Gwendolen, did you say Ernest?
GWENDOLEN. Yes.
CECILY. Oh, but it is not Mr. Ernest Worthing who is my guardian. It is his brother—his elder brother.
GWENDOLEN [*Sitting down again*]. Ernest never mentioned to me that he had a brother.
CECILY. I am sorry to say they have not been on good terms for a long time.
GWENDOLEN. Ah! that accounts for it. And now that I think of it I have never heard any man mention his brother. The subject seems distasteful to most men. Cecily, you have lifted a load from my mind. I was growing almost anxious. It would have been terrible if any cloud had come across a friendship like ours, would it not? Of course you are quite, quite sure that it is not Mr. Ernest Worthing who is your guardian?
CECILY. Quite sure. [*A pause.*] In fact, I am going to be his.
GWENDOLEN [*Enquiringly*]. I beg your pardon?
CECILY [*Rather shy and confidingly*]. Dearest Gwendolen, there is no reason why I should make a secret of it to you. Our little county newspaper is sure to chronicle the fact next week. Mr. Ernest Worthing and I are engaged to be married.
GWENDOLEN [*Quite politely, rising*]. My darling Cecily, I think there must be some slight error. Mr. Ernest Worthing is engaged to me. The announcement will appear in the 'Morning Post' on Saturday at the latest.
CECILY [*Very politely, rising*]. I am afraid you must be under some misconception. Ernest proposed to me exactly ten minutes ago. [*Shows diary.*]
GWENDOLEN [*Examines diary through her lorgnette carefully*]. It is certainly very curious, for he asked me to be his wife yesterday afternoon at 5.30. If you would care to verify the incident, pray do so. [*Produces diary of her own.*] I never travel without my diary. One should always have something sensational to read in the train. I am

so sorry, dear Cecily, if it is any disappointment to you, but I am afraid *I* have the prior claim.

CECILY. It would distress me more than I can tell you, dear Gwendolen, if it caused you any mental or physical anguish, but I feel bound to point out that since Ernest proposed to you he clearly has changed his mind.

GWENDOLEN [*Meditatively*]. If the poor fellow has been entrapped into any foolish promise I shall consider it my duty to rescue him at once, and with a firm hand.

CECILY [*Thoughtfully and sadly*]. Whatever unfortunate entanglement my dear boy may have got into, I will never reproach him with it after we are married.

GWENDOLEN. Do you allude to me, Miss Cardew, as an entanglement? You are presumptuous. On an occasion of this kind it becomes more than a moral duty to speak one's mind. It becomes a pleasure.

CECILY. Do you suggest, Miss Fairfax, that I entrapped Ernest into an engagement? How dare you? This is no time for wearing the shallow mask of manners. When I see a spade I call it a spade.

GWENDOLEN [*Satirically*]. I am glad to say that I have never seen a spade. It is obvious that our social spheres have been widely different.

[*Enter* MERRIMAN, *followed by the footman. He carries a salver, table cloth, and plate stand.* CECILY *is about to retort. The presence of the servants exercises a restraining influence, under which both girls chafe.*]

MERRIMAN. Shall I lay tea here as usual, Miss?

CECILY [*Sternly, in a calm voice*]. Yes, as usual. [MERRIMAN *begins to clear and lay cloth. A long pause.* CECILY *and* GWENDOLEN *glare at each other.*]

GWENDOLEN. Are there many interesting walks in the vicinity, Miss Cardew?

CECILY. Oh! yes! a great many. From the top of one of the hills quite close one can see five counties.

GWENDOLEN. Five counties! I don't think I should like that. I hate crowds.

CECILY [*Sweetly*]. I suppose that is why you live in town? [GWENDOLEN *bites her lip, and beats her foot nervously with her parasol.*]

GWENDOLEN [*Looking around*]. Quite a well-kept garden this is, Miss Cardew.

CECILY. So glad you like it, Miss Fairfax.

GWENDOLEN. I had no idea there were any flowers in the country.

CECILY. Oh, flowers are as common here, Miss Fairfax, as people are in London.

GWENDOLEN. Personally I cannot understand how anybody manages to exist in the country, if anybody who is anybody does. The country always bores me to death.

CECILY. Ah! This is what the newspapers call agricultural depression, is it not? I believe the aristocracy are suffering very much from it just at present. It is almost an epidemic amongst them, I have been told. May I offer you some tea, Miss Fairfax?

GWENDOLEN [*With elaborate politeness*]. Thank you. [*Aside.*] Detestable girl! But I require tea!

CECILY [*Sweetly*]. Sugar?

GWENDOLEN [*Superciliously*]. No, thank you. Sugar is not fashionable any more. [CECILY *looks angrily at her, takes up the tongs and puts four lumps of sugar into the cup.*]

CECILY [*Severely*]. Cake or bread and butter?

GWENDOLEN [*In a bored manner*]. Bread and butter, please. Cake is rarely seen at the best houses now-a-days.

CECILY [*Cuts a very large slice of cake, and puts it on the tray*]. Hand that to Miss Fairfax.

[MERRIMAN *does so, and goes out with footman.* GWENDOLEN *drinks the tea and makes a grimace. Puts down cup at once, reaches out her hand to the bread and butter, looks at it, and finds it is cake. Rises in indignation.*]

GWENDOLEN. You have filled my tea with lumps of sugar, and though I asked most distinctly for bread and butter, you have given me cake. I am known for the gentleness of my disposition, and the extraordinary sweetness of my nature, but I warn you, Miss Cardew, you may go too far.

CECILY [*Rising*]. To save my poor, innocent, trusting boy from the machinations of any other girl there are no lengths to which I would not go.

GWENDOLEN. From the moment I saw you I distrusted you. I felt that you were false and deceitful. I am never deceived in such matters. My first impressions of people are invariably right.

CECILY. It seems to me, Miss Fairfax, that I am trespassing on your valuable time. No doubt you have many other calls of a similar character to make in the neighbourhood.

[*Enter* JACK.]

GWENDOLEN [*Catching sight of him*]. Ernest! My own Ernest!

JACK. Gwendolen! Darling! [*Offers to kiss her.*]

GWENDOLEN [*Drawing back*]. A moment! May I ask if you are engaged to be married to this young lady? [*Points to* CECILY.]

JACK [*Laughing*]. To dear little Cecily! Of course not! What could have put such an idea into your pretty little head?

GWENDOLEN. Thank you. You may. [*Offers her cheek.*]
CECILY [*Very sweetly*].   I knew there must be some misunderstanding, Miss Fairfax. The gentleman whose arm is at present around your waist is my dear guardian, Mr. John Worthing.
GWENDOLEN.   I beg your pardon?
CECILY.   This is Uncle Jack.
GWENDOLEN [*Receding*].   Jack! Oh!
[*Enter* ALGERNON.]
CECILY.   Here is Ernest.
ALGERNON [*Goes straight over to* CECILY *without noticing anyone else*].   My own love! [*Offers to kiss her.*]
CECILY [*Drawing back*].   A moment, Ernest! May I ask you—are you engaged to be married to this young lady?
ALGERNON [*Looking around*].   To what young lady? Good heavens! Gwendolen!
CECILY.   Yes! to good heavens, Gwendolen, I mean to Gwendolen.
ALGERNON [*Laughing*].   Of course not! What could have put such an idea into your pretty little head?
CECILY.   Thank you. [*Presenting her cheek to be kissed.*] You may. [ALGERNON *kisses her.*]
GWENDOLEN.   I felt there was some slight error, Miss Cardew. The gentleman who is now embracing you is my cousin, Mr. Algernon Moncrieff.
CECILY [*Breaking away from* ALGERNON].   Algernon Moncrieff! Oh! [*The two girls move towards each other and put their arms round each other's waist as if for protection.*]
CECILY.   Are you called Algernon?
ALGERNON.   I cannot deny it.
CECILY.   Oh!
GWENDOLEN.   Is your name really John?
JACK [*Standing rather proudly*].   I could deny it if I liked. I could deny anything if I liked. But my name certainly is John. It has been John for years.
CECILY [*To* GWENDOLEN].   A gross deception has been practised on both of us.
GWENDOLEN.   My poor wounded Cecily!
CECILY.   My sweet wronged Gwendolen!
GWENDOLEN [*Slowly and seriously*].   You will call me sister, will you not? [*They embrace.* JACK *and* ALGERNON *groan and walk up and down.*]
CECILY [*Rather brightly*].   There is just one question I would like to be allowed to ask my guardian.

GWENDOLEN.   An admirable idea! Mr. Worthing, there is just one question I would like to be permitted to put to you. Where is your brother Ernest? We are both engaged to be married to your brother Ernest, so it is a matter of some importance to us to know where your brother Ernest is at present.
JACK [*Slowly and hesitatingly*].   Gwendolen—Cecily—it is very painful for me to be forced to speak the truth. It is the first time in my life that I have ever been reduced to such a painful position, and I am really quite inexperienced in doing anything of the kind. However, I will tell you quite frankly that I have no brother Ernest. I have no brother at all. I never had a brother in my life, and I certainly have not the smallest intention of ever having one in the future.
CECILY [*Surprised*].   No brother at all?
JACK [*Cheerily*].   None!
GWENDOLEN [*Severely*].   Had you never a brother of any kind?
JACK [*Pleasantly*].   Never. Not even of any kind.
GWENDOLEN.   I am afraid it is quite clear, Cecily, that neither of us is engaged to be married to anyone.
CECILY.   It is not a very pleasant position for a young girl suddenly to find herself in. Is it?
GWENDOLEN.   Let us go into the house. They will hardly venture to come after us there.
CECILY.   No, men are so cowardly, aren't they?

[*They retire into the house with scornful looks.*]

JACK.   This ghastly state of things is what you call Bunburying, I suppose?
ALGERNON.   Yes, and a perfectly wonderful Bunbury it is. The most wonderful Bunbury I have ever had in my life.
JACK.   Well, you've no right whatsoever to Bunbury here.
ALGERNON.   That is absurd. One has a right to Bunbury anywhere one chooses. Every serious Bunburyist knows that.
JACK.   Serious Bunburyist! Good heavens!
ALGERNON.   Well, one must be serious about something, if one wants to have any amusement in life. I happen to be serious about Bunburying. What on earth you are serious about I haven't got the remotest idea. About everything, I should fancy. You have such an absolutely trivial nature.
JACK.   Well, the only small satisfaction I have in the whole of this wretched business is that your friend Bunbury is quite exploded. You won't be able to run down to the country quite so often as you used to do, dear Algy. And a very good thing too.
ALGERNON.   Your brother is a little off colour, isn't he, dear Jack? You

won't be able to disappear to London quite so frequently as your wicked custom was. And not a bad thing either.

JACK. As for your conduct towards Miss Cardew, I must say that your taking in a sweet, simple, innocent girl like that is quite inexcusable. To say nothing of the fact that she is my ward.

ALGERNON. I can see no possible defence at all for your deceiving a brilliant, clever, thoroughly experienced young lady like Miss Fairfax. To say nothing of the fact that she is my cousin.

JACK. I wanted to be engaged to Gwendolen, that is all. I love her.

ALGERNON. Well, I simply wanted to be engaged to Cecily. I adore her.

JACK. There is certainly no chance of your marrying Miss Cardew.

ALGERNON. I don't think there is much likelihood, Jack, of you and Miss Fairfax being united.

JACK. Well, that is no business of yours.

ALGERNON. If it was my business, I wouldn't talk about it. [*Begins to eat muffins.*] It is very vulgar to talk about one's business. Only people like stock-brokers do that, and then merely at dinner parties.

JACK. How you can sit there, calmly eating muffins when we are in this horrible trouble, I can't make out. You seem to me to be perfectly heartless.

ALGERNON. Well, I can't eat muffins in an agitated manner. The butter would probably get on my cuffs. One should always eat muffins quite calmly. It is the only way to eat them.

JACK. I say it's perfectly heartless your eating muffins at all, under the circumstances.

ALGERNON. When I am in trouble, eating is the only thing that consoles me. Indeed, when I am in really great trouble, as anyone who knows me intimately will tell you, I refuse everything except food and drink. At the present moment I am eating muffins because I am unhappy. Besides, I am particularly fond of muffins. [*Rising.*]

JACK [*Rising*]. Well, that is no reason why you should eat them all in that greedy way. [*Takes muffins from* ALGERNON.]

ALGERNON [*Offering tea-cake*]. I wish you would have tea-cake instead. I don't like tea-cake.

JACK. Good heavens! I suppose a man may eat his own muffins in his own garden.

ALGERNON. But you have just said it was perfectly heartless to eat muffins.

JACK. I said it was perfectly heartless of you, under the circumstances. That is a very different thing.

ALGERNON. That may be. But the muffins are the same. [*He seizes the muffin-dish from* JACK.]

JACK. Algy, I wish to goodness you would go.

ALGERNON. You can't possibly ask me to go without having some dinner. It's absurd. I never go without my dinner. No one ever does, except vegetarians and people like that. Besides I have just made arrangements with Dr. Chasuble to be christened at a quarter to six under the name of Ernest.

JACK. My dear fellow, the sooner you give up that nonsense the better. I made arrangements this morning with Dr. Chasuble to be christened myself at 5.30, and I naturally will take the name of Ernest. Gwendolen would wish it. We can't both be christened Ernest. It's absurd. Besides, I have a perfect right to be christened if I like. There is no evidence at all that I ever have been christened by anybody. I should think it extremely probable I never was, and so does Dr. Chasuble. It is entirely different in your case. You have been christened already.

ALGERNON. Yes, but I have not been christened for years.

JACK. Yes, but you have been christened. That is the important thing.

ALGERNON. Quite so. So I know my constitution can stand it. If you are not quite sure about your ever having been christened, I must say I think it rather dangerous your venturing on it now. It might make you very unwell. You can hardly have forgotten that someone very closely connected with you was very nearly carried off this week in Paris by a severe chill.

JACK. Yes, but you said yourself that a severe chill was not hereditary.

ALGERNON. It usen't to be, I know—but I daresay it is now. Science is always making wonderful improvements in things.

JACK [*Picking up the muffin-dish*]. Oh, that is nonsense; you are always talking nonsense.

ALGERNON. Jack, you are at the muffins again! I wish you wouldn't. There are only two left. [*Takes them.*] I told you I was particularly fond of muffins.

JACK. But I hate tea-cake.

ALGERNON. Why on earth then do you allow tea-cake to be served up for your guests? What ideas you have of hospitality!

JACK. Algernon! I have already told you to go. I don't want you here. Why don't you go?

ALGERNON. I haven't quite finished my tea yet! and there is still one muffin left. [JACK *groans and sinks into a chair.* ALGERNON *still continues eating.*]

ACT-DROP

Act III

SCENE—*Morning-room at the Manor House.*
[GWENDOLEN *and* CECILY *are at the window, looking out into the garden.*]
GWENDOLEN.   The fact that they did not follow us at once into the house, as anyone else would have done, seems to me to show that they have some sense of shame left.
CECILY.   They have been eating muffins. That looks like repentance.
GWENDOLEN [*After a pause*].   They don't seem to notice us at all. Couldn't you cough?
CECILY.   But I haven't a cough.
GWENDOLEN.   They're looking at us. What effrontery!
CECILY.   They're approaching. That's very forward of them.
GWENDOLEN.   Let us preserve a dignified silence.
CECILY.   Certainly. It's the only thing to do now.
[*Enter* JACK *followed by* ALGERNON. *They whistle some dreadful popular air from a British opera.*]
GWENDOLEN.   This dignified silence seems to produce an unpleasant effect.
CECILY.   A most distasteful one.
GWENDOLEN.   But we will not be the first to speak.
CECILY.   Certainly not.
GWENDOLEN.   Mr. Worthing, I have something very particular to ask you. Much depends on your reply.
CECILY.   Gwendolen, your common sense is invaluable. Mr. Moncrieff, kindly answer me the following question: Why did you pretend to be my guardian's brother?
ALGERNON.   In order that I might have an opportunity of meeting you.
CECILY [*To* GWENDOLEN].   That certainly seems a satisfactory explanation, does it not?
GWENDOLEN.   Yes, dear, if you can believe him.

CECILY. I don't. But that does not affect the wonderful beauty of his answer.
GWENDOLEN. True. In matters of grave importance, style, not sincerity is the vital thing. Mr. Worthing, what explanation can you offer to me for pretending to have a brother? Was it in order that you might have an opportunity of coming up to town to see me as often as possible?
JACK. Can you doubt it, Miss Fairfax?
GWENDOLEN. I have the gravest doubts upon the subject. But I intend to crush them. This is not the moment for German scepticism. [*Moving to* CECILY.] Their explanations appear to be quite satisfactory, especially Mr. Worthing's. That seems to me to have the stamp of truth upon it.
CECILY. I am more than content with what Mr. Moncrieff said. His voice alone inspires one with absolute credulity.
GWENDOLEN. Then you think we should forgive them?
CECILY. Yes. I mean no.
GWENDOLEN. True! I had forgotten. There are principles at stake that one cannot surrender. Which of us should tell them? The task is not a pleasant one.
CECILY. Could we not both speak at the same time?
GWENDOLEN. An excellent idea! I nearly always speak at the same time as other people. Will you take the time from me?
CECILY. Certainly. [GWENDOLEN *beats time with uplifted finger.*]
GWENDOLEN and CECILY [*Speaking together*]. Your Christian names are still an insuperable barrier! That is all!
JACK and ALGERNON [*Speaking together*]. Our Christian names! Is that all? But we are going to be christened this afternoon.
GWENDOLEN [*To* JACK]. For my sake you are prepared to do this terrible thing?
JACK. I am.
CECILY [*To* ALGERNON]. To please me you are ready to face this fearful ordeal?
ALGERNON. I am!
GWENDOLEN. How absurd to talk of the equality of the sexes! Where questions of self-sacrifice are concerned, men are infinitely beyond us.
JACK. We are. [*Clasps hands with* ALGERNON.]
CECILY. They have moments of physical courage of which we women know absolutely nothing.
GWENDOLEN [*To* JACK]. Darling!
ALGERNON [*To* CECILY]. Darling! [*They fall into each other's arms.*]

[*Enter* MERRIMAN. *When he enters he coughs loudly, seeing the situation.*]
MERRIMAN.   Ahem! Ahem! Lady Bracknell!
JACK.   Good heavens!
[*Enter* LADY BRACKNELL. *The couples separate in alarm. Exit* MERRIMAN.]
LADY BRACKNELL.   Gwendolen! What does this mean?
GWENDOLEN.   Merely that I am engaged to be married to Mr. Worthing, mamma.
LADY BRACKNELL.   Come here. Sit down. Sit down immediately. Hesitation of any kind is a sign of mental decay in the young, of physical weakness in the old. [*Turns to* JACK.] Apprised, sir, of my daughter's sudden flight by her trusty maid, whose confidence I purchased by means of a small coin, I followed her at once by a luggage train. Her unhappy father is, I am glad to say, under the impression that she is attending a more than usually lengthy lecture by the University Extension Scheme on the Influence of a Permanent Income on Thought. I do not propose to undeceive him. Indeed I have never undeceived him on any question. I would consider it wrong. But of course, you will clearly understand that all communication between yourself and my daughter must cease immediately from this moment. On this point, as indeed on all points, I am firm.
JACK.   I am engaged to be married to Gwendolen, Lady Bracknell!
LADY BRACKNELL.   You are nothing of the kind, sir. And now, as regards Algernon! . . . Algernon!
ALGERNON.   Yes, Aunt Augusta.
LADY BRACKNELL.   May I ask if it is in this house that your invalid friend Mr. Bunbury resides?
ALGERNON [*Stammering*].   Oh! No! Bunbury doesn't live here. Bunbury is somewhere else at present. In fact, Bunbury is dead.
LADY BRACKNELL.   Dead! When did Mr. Bunbury die? His death must have been extremely sudden.
ALGERNON [*Airily*].   Oh! I killed Bunbury this afternoon. I mean poor Bunbury died this afternoon.
LADY BRACKNELL.   What did he die of?
ALGERNON.   Bunbury? Oh, he was quite exploded.
LADY BRACKNELL.   Exploded! Was he the victim of a revolutionary outrage? I was not aware that Mr. Bunbury was interested in social legislation. If so, he is well punished for his morbidity.
ALGERNON.   My dear Aunt Augusta, I mean he was found out! The doctors found out that Bunbury could not live, that is what I mean—so Bunbury died.
LADY BRACKNELL.   He seems to have had great confidence in the opinion of his physicians. I am glad, however, that he made up his

mind at the last to some definite course of action, and acted under proper medical advice. And now that we have finally got rid of this Mr. Bunbury, may I ask, Mr. Worthing, who is that young person whose hand my nephew Algernon is now holding in what seems to me a peculiarly unnecessary manner?

JACK. That lady is Miss Cecily Cardew, my ward. [LADY BRACKNELL *bows coldly to* CECILY.]

ALGERNON. I am engaged to be married to Cecily, Aunt Augusta.

LADY BRACKNELL. I beg your pardon?

CECILY. Mr. Moncrieff and I are engaged to be married, Lady Bracknell.

LADY BRACKNELL [*With a shiver, crossing to the sofa and sitting down*]. I do not know whether there is anything peculiarly exciting in the air of this particular part of Hertfordshire, but the number of engagements that go on seems to me considerably above the proper average that statistics have laid down for our guidance. I think some preliminary enquiry on my part would not be out of place. Mr. Worthing, is Miss Cardew at all connected with any of the larger railway stations in London? I merely desire information. Until yesterday I had no idea that there were any families or persons whose origin was a Terminus. [JACK *looks perfectly furious, but restrains himself.*]

JACK [*In a clear, cold voice*]. Miss Cardew is the granddaughter of the late Mr. Thomas Cardew of 149, Belgrave Square, S.W.; Gervase Park, Dorking, Surrey; and the Sporran, Fifeshire, N.B.

LADY BRACKNELL. That sounds not unsatisfactory. Three addresses always inspire confidence, even in tradesmen. But what proof have I of their authenticity?

JACK. I have carefully preserved the Court Guides of the period. They are open to your inspection, Lady Bracknell.

LADY BRACKNELL [*Grimly*]. I have known strange errors in that publication.

JACK. Miss Cardew's family solicitors are Messrs. Markby, Markby, and Markby.

LADY BRACKNELL. Markby, Markby, and Markby? A firm of the very highest position in their profession. Indeed I am told that one of the Mr. Markbys is occasionally to be seen at dinner parties. So far I am satisfied.

JACK [*Very irritably*]. How extremely kind of you, Lady Bracknell! I have also in my possession, you will be pleased to hear, certificates of Miss Cardew's birth, baptism, whooping cough, registration, vaccination, confirmation, and the measles; both the German and the English variety.

LADY BRACKNELL. Ah! A life crowded with incident, I see; though perhaps somewhat too exciting for a young girl. I am not myself in favour of premature experiences. [*Rises, looks at her watch.*] Gwendolen! the time approaches for our departure. We have not a moment to lose. As a matter of form, Mr. Worthing, I had better ask you if Miss Cardew has any little fortune?

JACK. Oh! about a hundred and thirty thousand pounds in the Funds. That is all. Good-bye, Lady Bracknell. So pleased to have seen you.

LADY BRACKNELL [*Sitting down again*]. A moment, Mr. Worthing. A hundred and thirty thousand pounds! And in the Funds! Miss Cardew seems to me a most attractive young lady, now that I look at her. Few girls of the present day have any really solid qualities, any of the qualities that last, and improve with time. We live, I regret to say, in an age of surfaces. [*To* CECILY.] Come over here, dear. [CECILY *goes across.*] Pretty child! your dress is sadly simple, and your hair seems almost as Nature might have left it. But we can soon alter all that. A thoroughly experienced French maid produces a really marvellous result in a very brief space of time. I remember recommending one to young Lady Lancing, and after three months her own husband did not know her.

JACK. And after six months nobody knew her.

LADY BRACKNELL [*Glares at* JACK *for a few moments. Then bends, with a practised smile, to* CECILY.] Kindly turn round, sweet child. [CECILY *turns completely round.*] No, the side view is what I want. [CECILY *presents her profile.*] Yes, quite as I expected. There are distinct social possibilities in your profile. The two weak points in our age are its want of principle and its want of profile. The chin a little higher, dear. Style largely depends on the way the chin is worn. They are worn very high, just at present. Algernon!

ALGERNON. Yes, Aunt Augusta!

LADY BRACKNELL. There are distinct social possibilities in Miss Cardew's profile.

ALGERNON. Cecily is the sweetest, dearest, prettiest girl in the whole world. And I don't care twopence about social possibilities.

LADY BRACKNELL. Never speak disrespectfully of Society, Algernon. Only people who can't get into it do that. [*To* CECILY.] Dear child, of course you know that Algernon has nothing but his debts to depend upon. But I do not approve of mercenary marriages. When I married Lord Bracknell I had no fortune of any kind. But I never dreamed for a moment of allowing that to stand in my way. Well, I suppose I must give my consent.

ALGERNON. Thank you, Aunt Augusta.

LADY BRACKNELL.   Cecily, you may kiss me!
CECILY [*Kisses her*].   Thank you, Lady Bracknell.
LADY BRACKNELL.   You may also address me as Aunt Augusta for the future.
CECILY.   Thank you, Aunt Augusta.
LADY BRACKNELL.   The marriage, I think, had better take place quite soon.
ALGERNON.   Thank you, Aunt Augusta.
CECILY.   Thank you, Aunt Augusta.
LADY BRACKNELL.   To speak frankly, I am not in favour of long engagements. They give people the opportunity of finding out each other's character before marriage, which I think is never advisable.
JACK.   I beg your pardon for interrupting you, Lady Bracknell, but this engagement is quite out of the question. I am Miss Cardew's guardian, and she cannot marry without my consent until she comes of age. That consent I absolutely decline to give.
LADY BRACKNELL.   Upon what grounds, may I ask? Algernon is an extremely, I may almost say an ostentatiously, eligible young man. He has nothing, but he looks everything. What more can one desire?
JACK.   It pains me very much to have to speak frankly to you, Lady Bracknell, about your nephew, but the fact is that I do not approve at all of his moral character. I suspect him of being untruthful. [ALGERNON *and* CECILY *look at him in indignant amazement.*]
LADY BRACKNELL.   Untruthful! My nephew Algernon? Impossible! He is an Oxonian.
JACK.   I fear there can be no possible doubt about the matter. This afternoon, during my temporary absence in London on an important question of romance, he obtained admission to my house by means of the false pretence of being my brother. Under an assumed name he drank, I've just been informed by my butler, an entire pint bottle of my Perrier-Jouet, Brut, '89; a wine I was specially reserving for myself. Continuing his disgraceful deception, he succeeded in the course of the afternoon in alienating the affections of my only ward. He subsequently stayed to tea, and devoured every single muffin. And what makes his conduct all the more heartless is, that he was perfectly well aware from the first that I have no brother, that I never had a brother, and that I don't intend to have a brother, not even of any kind. I distinctly told him so myself yesterday afternoon.
LADY BRACKNELL.   Ahem! Mr. Worthing, after careful consideration I have decided entirely to overlook my nephew's conduct to you.
JACK.   That is very generous of you, Lady Bracknell. My own decision, however, is unalterable. I decline to give my consent.

LADY BRACKNELL [*To* CECILY]. Come here, sweet child. [CECILY *goes over*.] How old are you, dear?
CECILY. Well, I am really only eighteen, but I always admit to twenty when I go to evening parties.
LADY BRACKNELL. You are perfectly right in making some slight alteration. Indeed, no woman should ever be quite accurate about her age. It looks so calculating. . . . [*In a meditative manner*.] Eighteen, but admitting to twenty at evening parties. Well, it will not be very long before you are of age and free from the restraints of tutelage. So I don't think your guardian's consent is, after all, a matter of any importance.
JACK. Pray excuse me, Lady Bracknell, for interrupting you again, but it is only fair to tell you that according to the terms of her grandfather's will Miss Cardew does not come legally of age till she is thirty-five.
LADY BRACKNELL. That does not seem to me to be a grave objection. Thirty-five is a very attractive age. London society is full of women of the very highest birth who have, of their own free choice, remained thirty-five for years. Lady Dumbleton is an instance in point. To my own knowledge she has been thirty-five ever since she arrived at the age of forty, which was many years ago now. I see no reason why our dear Cecily should not be even still more attractive at the age you mention than she is at present. There will be a large accumulation of property.
CECILY. Algy, could you wait for me till I was thirty-five?
ALGERNON. Of course I could, Cecily. You know I could.
CECILY. Yes, I felt it instinctively, but I couldn't wait all that time. I hate waiting even five minutes for anybody. It always makes me rather cross. I am not punctual myself, I know, but I do like punctuality in others, and waiting, even to be married, is quite out of the question.
ALGERNON. Then what is to be done, Cecily?
CECILY. I don't know, Mr. Moncrieff.
LADY BRACKNELL. My dear Mr. Worthing, as Miss Cardew states positively that she cannot wait till she is thirty-five—a remark which I am bound to say seems to me to show a somewhat impatient nature—I would beg of you to reconsider your decision.
JACK. But my dear Lady Bracknell, the matter is entirely in your own hands. The moment you consent to my marriage with Gwendolen, I will most gladly allow your nephew to form an alliance with my ward.
LADY BRACKNELL [*Rising and drawing herself up*]. You must be quite aware that what you propose is out of the question.

JACK. Then a passionate celibacy is all that any of us can look forward to.

LADY BRACKNELL. That is not the destiny I propose for Gwendolen. Algernon, of course, can choose for himself. [*Pulls out her watch.*] Come dear; [GWENDOLEN *rises*] we have already missed five, if not six, trains. To miss any more might expose us to comment on the platform.

[*Enter* DR. CHASUBLE.]

CHASUBLE. Everything is quite ready for the christenings.

LADY BRACKNELL. The christenings, sir! Is not that somewhat premature?

CHASUBLE [*Looking rather puzzled, and pointing to* JACK *and* ALGERNON]. Both these gentlemen have expressed a desire for immediate baptism.

LADY BRACKNELL. At their age? The idea is grotesque and irreligious! Algernon, I forbid you to be baptised. I will not hear of such excesses. Lord Bracknell would be highly displeased if he learned that that was the way in which you wasted your time and money.

CHASUBLE. Am I to understand then that there are to be no christenings at all this afternoon?

JACK. I don't think that, as things are now, it would be of much practical value to either of us, Dr. Chasuble.

CHASUBLE. I am grieved to hear such sentiments from you, Mr. Worthing. They savour of the heretical views of the Anabaptists, views that I have completely refuted in four of my unpublished sermons. However, as your present mood seems to be one peculiarly secular, I will return to the church at once. Indeed, I have just been informed by the pew-opener that for the last hour and a half Miss Prism has been waiting for me in the vestry.

LADY BRACKNELL [*Starting*]. Miss Prism! Did I hear you mention a Miss Prism?

CHASUBLE. Yes, Lady Bracknell. I am on my way to join her.

LADY BRACKNELL. Pray allow me to detain you for a moment. This matter may prove to be one of vital importance to Lord Bracknell and myself. Is this Miss Prism a female of repellent aspect, remotely connected with education?

CHASUBLE [*Somewhat indignantly*]. She is the most cultivated of ladies, and the very picture of respectability.

LADY BRACKNELL. It is obviously the same person. May I ask what position she holds in your household?

CHASUBLE [*Severely*]. I am a celibate, madam.

JACK [*Interposing*]. Miss Prism, Lady Bracknell, has been for the last three years Miss Cardew's esteemed governess and valued companion.

LADY BRACKNELL.   In spite of what I hear of her, I must see her at once. Let her be sent for.
CHASUBLE [*Looking off*].   She approaches; she is nigh.
[*Enter* MISS PRISM *hurriedly*.]
MISS PRISM.   I was told you expected me in the vestry, dear Canon. I have been waiting for you there for an hour and three-quarters. [*Catches sight of* LADY BRACKNELL, *who has fixed her with a stony glare.* MISS PRISM *grows pale and quails. She looks anxiously round as if desirous to escape.*]
LADY BRACKNELL [*In a severe, judicial voice*].   Prism! [MISS PRISM *bows her head in shame.*] Come here, Prism! [MISS PRISM *approaches in a humble manner.*] Prism! Where is that baby? [*General consternation. The Canon starts back in horror.* ALGERNON *and* JACK *pretend to be anxious to shield* CECILY *and* GWENDOLEN *from hearing the details of a terrible public scandal.*] Twenty-eight years ago, Prism, you left Lord Bracknell's house, Number 104, Upper Grosvenor Street, in charge of a perambulator that contained a baby, of the male sex. You never returned. A few weeks later, through the elaborate investigations of the Metropolitan police, the perambulator was discovered at midnight, standing by itself in a remote corner of Bayswater. It contained the manuscript of a three-volume novel of more than usually revolting sentimentality. [MISS PRISM *starts in involuntary indignation.*] But the baby was not there! [*Everyone looks at* MISS PRISM.] Prism; Where is that baby? [*A pause.*]
MISS PRISM.   Lady Bracknell, I admit with shame that I do not know. I only wish I did. The plain facts of the case are these. On the morning of the day you mention, a day that is for ever branded on my memory, I prepared as usual to take the baby out in its perambulator. I had also with me a somewhat old, but capacious hand-bag in which I had intended to place the manuscript of a work of fiction that I had written during my few unoccupied hours. In a moment of mental abstraction, for which I never can forgive myself, I deposited the manuscript in the bassinette, and placed the baby in the hand-bag.
JACK [*Who has been listening attentively*].   But where did you deposit the hand-bag?
MISS PRISM.   Do not ask me, Mr. Worthing.
JACK.   Miss Prism, this is a matter of no small importance to me. I insist on knowing where you deposited the hand-bag that contained that infant.
MISS PRISM.   I left it in the cloak-room of one of the larger railway stations in London.
JACK.   What railway station?

MISS PRISM [*Quite crushed*].   Victoria. The Brighton line. [*Sinks into a chair.*]
JACK.   I must retire to my room for a moment. Gwendolen, wait here for me.
GWENDOLEN.   If you are not too long, I will wait here for you all my life.
[*Exit* JACK *in great excitement.*]
CHASUBLE.   What do you think this means, Lady Bracknell?
LADY BRACKNELL.   I dare not even suspect, Dr. Chasuble. I need hardly tell you that in families of high position strange coincidences are not supposed to occur. They are hardly considered the thing.
[*Noises heard overhead as if someone was throwing trunks about. Everyone looks up.*]
CECILY.   Uncle Jack seems strangely agitated.
CHASUBLE.   Your guardian has a very emotional nature.
LADY BRACKNELL.   This noise is extremely unpleasant. It sounds as if he was having an argument. I dislike arguments of any kind. They are always vulgar, and often convincing.
CHASUBLE [*Looking up*].   It has stopped now. [*The noise is redoubled.*]
LADY BRACKNELL.   I wish he would arrive at some conclusion.
GWENDOLEN.   This suspense is terrible. I hope it will last.
[*Enter* JACK *with a hand-bag of black leather in his hand.*]
JACK [*Rushing over to* MISS PRISM].   Is this the hand-bag, Miss Prism? Examine it carefully before you speak. The happiness of more than one life depends on your answer.
MISS PRISM [*Calmly*].   It seems to be mine. Yes, here is the injury it received through the upsetting of a Gower Street omnibus in younger and happier days. Here is the stain on the lining caused by the explosion of a temperance beverage, an incident that occurred at Leamington. And here, on the lock, are my initials. I had forgotten that in an extravagant mood I had had them placed there. The bag is undoubtedly mine. I am delighted to have it so unexpectedly restored to me. It has been a great inconvenience being without it all these years.
JACK [*In a pathetic voice*].   Miss Prism, more is restored to you than this hand-bag. I was the baby you placed in it.
MISS PRISM [*Amazed*].   You?
JACK [*Embracing her*].   Yes . . . mother!
MISS PRISM [*Recoiling in indignant astonishment*].   Mr. Worthing! I am unmarried!
JACK.   Unmarried! I do not deny that is a serious blow. But after all, who has the right to cast a stone against one who has suffered?

Cannot repentance wipe out an act of folly? Why should there be one law for men, and another for women? Mother, I forgive you. [*Tries to embrace her again.*]

MISS PRISM [*Still more indignant*]. Mr. Worthing, there is some error. [*Pointing to* LADY BRACKNELL.] There is the lady who can tell you who you really are.

JACK [*After a pause*]. Lady Bracknell, I hate to seem inquisitive, but would you kindly inform me who I am?

LADY BRACKNELL. I am afraid that the news I have to give you will not altogether please you. You are the son of my poor sister, Mrs. Moncrieff, and consequently Algernon's elder brother.

JACK. Algy's elder brother! Then I have a brother after all. I knew I had a brother! I always said I had a brother! Cecily,—how could you have ever doubted that I had a brother. [*Seizes hold of* ALGERNON.] Dr. Chasuble, my unfortunate brother. Miss Prism, my unfortunate brother. Gwendolen, my unfortunate brother. Algy, you young scoundrel, you will have to treat me with more respect in the future. You have never behaved to me like a brother in all your life.

ALGERNON. Well, not till to-day, old boy, I admit. I did my best, however, though I was out of practice. [*Shakes hands.*]

GWENDOLEN [To JACK]. My own! But what own are you? What is your Christian name, now that you have become someone else?

JACK. Good heavens! . . . I had quite forgotten that point. Your decision on the subject of my name is irrevocable, I suppose?

GWENDOLEN. I never change, except in my affections.

CECILY. What a noble nature you have, Gwendolen!

JACK. Then the question had better be cleared up at once. Aunt Augusta, a moment. At the time when Miss Prism left me in the hand-bag, had I been christened already?

LADY BRACKNELL. Every luxury that money could buy, including christening, had been lavished on you by your fond and doting parents.

JACK. Then I was christened! That is settled. Now, what name was I given? Let me know the worst.

LADY BRACKNELL. Being the eldest son you were naturally christened after your father.

JACK [*Irritably*]. Yes, but what was my father's Christian name?

LADY BRACKNELL [*Meditatively*]. I cannot at the present moment recall what the General's Christian name was. But I have no doubt he had one. He was eccentric, I admit. But only in later years. And that was the result of the Indian climate, and marriage, and indigestion, and other things of that kind.

JACK. Algy! Can't you recollect what our father's Christian name was?
ALGERNON. My dear boy, we were never even on speaking terms. He died before I was a year old.
JACK. His name would appear in the Army Lists of the period, I suppose, Aunt Augusta?
LADY BRACKNELL. The General was essentially a man of peace, except in his domestic life. But I have no doubt his name would appear in any military directory.
JACK. The Army Lists of the last forty years are here. These delightful records should have been my constant study. [*Rushes to bookcase and tears the books out.*] M. Generals . . . . Mallam, Maxbohm, Magley, what ghastly names they have—Markby, Migsby, Mobbs, Moncrieff! Lieutenant 1840, Captain, Lieutenant-Colonel, Colonel, General 1869, Christian names, Ernest John. [*Puts book very quietly down and speaks quite calmly.*] I always told you, Gwendolen, my name was Ernest, didn't I? Well, it is Ernest after all. I mean it naturally is Ernest.
LADY BRACKNELL. Yes, I remember that the General was called Ernest. I knew I had some particular reason for disliking the name.
GWENDOLEN. Ernest! My own Ernest! I felt from the first that you could have no other name!
JACK. Gwendolen, it is a terrible thing for a man to find out suddenly that all his life he has been speaking nothing but the truth. Can you forgive me?
GWENDOLEN. I can. For I feel that you are sure to change.
JACK. My own one!
CHASUBLE [*To* MISS PRISM]. Lætitia! [*Embraces her.*]
MISS PRISM [*Enthusiastically*]. Frederick! At last!
ALGERNON. Cecily! [*Embraces her.*] At last!
JACK. Gwendolen! [*Embraces her.*] At last!
LADY BRACKNELL. My nephew, you seem to be displaying signs of triviality.
JACK. On the contrary, Aunt Augusta, I've now realised for the first time in my life the vital Importance of Being Earnest.

TABLEAU

CURTAIN

Lost at hot cockles round a Christmas fire!
The transient hour of fashion too soon spent,
Farewell the tranquil mind, farewell content!
Farewell the plumed head, the cushion'd tête,
That takes the cushion from its proper seat!
The spirit-stirring drum! card drums I mean,
Spadille—odd trick—pam—basto—king and queen!
And you, ye knockers, that, with brazen throat,
The welcome visitors' approach denote;
Farewell all quality of high renown,
Pride, pomp, and circumstance of glorious town!
Farewell! your revels I partake no more,
And Lady Teazle's occupation's o'er!
All this I told our bard; he smiled, and said 'twas clear,
I ought to play deep tragedy next year.
Meanwhile he drew wise morals from his play,
And in these solemn periods stalk'd away:
Blest were the fair like you; her faults who stopt,
And closed her follies when the curtain dropt!
No more in vice or error to engage,
Or play the fool at large on life's great stage.

EPILOGUE

BY MR. COLMAN

SPOKEN BY LADY TEAZLE

I, who was late so volatile and gay,
Like a trade wind must now blow all one way,
Bend all my cares, my studies, and my vows,
To one dull rusty weathercock—my spouse!
So wills our virtuous bard—the motley Bayes
Of crying epilogues and laughing plays!
Old bachelors, who marry smart young wives,
Learn from our play to regulate your lives:
Each bring his dear to town, all faults upon her—
London will prove the very source of honour.
Plunged fairly in, like a cold bath it serves,
When principles relax, to brace the nerves:
Such is my case; and yet I must deplore
That the gay dream of dissipation's o'er.
And say, ye fair, was ever lively wife,
Born with a genius for the highest life,
Like me untimely blasted in her bloom,
Like me condemn'd to such a dismal doom?
Save money—when I just knew how to waste it!
Leave London—just as I began to taste it!
   Must I then watch the early crowing cock,
The melancholy ticking of a clock;
In a lone rustic hall for ever pounded,
With dogs, cats, rats, and squalling brats surrounded?
With humble curate can I now retire,
(While good Sir Peter boozes with the squire),
And at backgammon mortify my soul,
That pants for loo, or flutters at a vole?
Seven's the main! Dear sound that must expire,

SIR PETER. Hey!—What the plague!—Are you ashamed of having done a right thing once in your life?
SNAKE. Ah, sir! consider,—I live by the badness of my character; I have nothing but my infamy to depend on! and if it were once known that I had been betrayed into an honest action, I should lose every friend I have in the world.
SIR OLIVER. Well, well,—we'll not traduce you by saying anything in your praise, never fear.

Exit SNAKE.

SIR PETER. There's a precious rogue!
LADY TEAZLE. See, Sir Oliver, there needs no persuasion now to reconcile your nephew and Maria.
SIR OLIVER. Ay, ay, that's as it should be, and egad we'll have the wedding to-morrow morning.
CHARLES. Thank you, dear uncle!
SIR PETER. What, you rogue! don't you ask the girl's consent first?
CHARLES. Oh, I have done that a long time—a minute ago—and she has looked yes.
MARIA. For shame, Charles!—I protest, Sir Peter, there has not been a word.
SIR OLIVER. Well, then, the fewer the better;—may your love for each other never know abatement!
SIR PETER. And may you live as happily together as Lady Teazle and I intend to do!
CHARLES. Rowley, my old friend, I am sure you congratulate me; and I suspect that I owe you much.
SIR OLIVER. You do indeed, Charles.
ROWLEY. If my efforts to serve you had not succeeded, you would have been in my debt for the attempt; but deserve to be happy, and you overpay me.
SIR PETER. Ay, honest Rowley always said you would reform.
CHARLES. Why, as to reforming, Sir Peter, I'll make no promises, and that I take to be a proof that I intend to set about it; but here shall be my monitor—my gentle guide—ah! can I leave the virtuous path those eyes illumine?

> Though thou, dear maid, shouldst wave thy beauty's sway,
> Thou still must rule, because I will obey:
> An humble fugitive from Folly view,
> No sanctuary near but Love and you;
> [*To the audience.*
> You can, indeed, each anxious fear remove,
> For even Scandal dies if you approve.

Enter SNAKE.

I thought his testimony might be wanted: however, it happens unluckily, that he comes to confront Lady Sneerwell, not to support her.

LADY SNEERWELL. A villain! Treacherous to me at last!—Speak, fellow; have you too conspired against me?

SNAKE. I beg your ladyship ten thousand pardons: you paid me extremely liberally for the lie in question; but I unfortunately have been offered double to speak the truth.

SIR PETER. Plot and counter-plot, egad!

LADY SNEERWELL. The torments of shame and disappointment on you all.—

LADY TEAZLE. Hold, Lady Sneerwell,—before you go, let me thank you for the trouble you and that gentleman have taken, in writing letters from me to Charles, and answering them yourself; and let me also request you to make my respects to the scandalous college, of which you are president, and inform them, that Lady Teazle, licentiate, begs leave to return the diploma they gave her, as she leaves off practice, and kills characters no longer.

LADY SNEERWELL. You too, madam—provoking—insolent—May your husband live these fifty years!

Exit.

SIR PETER. Oons! what a fury!

LADY TEAZLE. A malicious creature, indeed!

SIR PETER. Hey! Not for her last wish?

LADY TEAZLE. Oh no!

SIR OLIVER. Well, sir, and what have you to say now?

JOSEPH. Sir, I am so confounded, to find that Lady Sneerwell could be guilty of suborning Mr. Snake in this manner, to impose on us all, that I know not what to say: however, lest her revengeful spirit should prompt her to injure my brother, I had certainly better follow her directly.

Exit.

SIR PETER. Moral to the last drop!

SIR OLIVER. Ay, and marry her, Joseph, if you can.—Oil and Vinegar, egad! you'll do very well together.

ROWLEY. I believe we have no more occasion for Mr. Snake at present?

SNAKE. Before I go, I beg pardon once for all, for whatever uneasiness I have been the humble instrument of causing to the parties present.

SIR PETER. Well, well, you have made atonement by a good deed at last.

SNAKE. But I must request of the company, that it shall never be known.

sold me judges and generals by the foot, and maiden aunts as cheap as broken china.

CHARLES. To be sure, Sir Oliver, I did make a little free with the family canvas, that's the truth on't. My ancestors may rise in judgment against me, there's no denying it; but believe me sincere when I tell you—and upon my soul I would not say so if I was not—that if I do not appear mortified at the exposure of my follies, it is because I feel at this moment the warmest satisfaction in seeing you, my liberal benefactor.

SIR OLIVER. Charles, I believe you; give me your hand again: the ill-looking little fellow over the settee has made your peace.

CHARLES. Then, sir, my gratitude to the original is still increased.

LADY TEAZLE. Yet, I believe, Sir Oliver, here is one whom Charles is still more anxious to be reconciled to.

SIR OLIVER. Oh, I have heard of his attachment there; and, with the young lady's pardon, if I construe right—that blush——

SIR PETER. Well, child, speak your sentiments!

MARIA. Sir, I have little to say, but that I shall rejoice to hear that he is happy; for me—whatever claim I had to his affection, I willingly resign to one who has a better title.

CHARLES. How, Maria!

SIR PETER. Hey day! what's the mystery now?—While he appeared an incorrigible rake, you would give your hand to no one else; and now that he is likely to reform, I'll warrant you won't have him.

MARIA. His own heart and Lady Sneerwell know the cause.

CHARLES. Lady Sneerwell!

JOSEPH. Brother, it is with great concern I am obliged to speak on this point, but my regard to justice compels me, and Lady Sneerwell's injuries can no longer be concealed. [*Opens the door.*

Enter LADY SNEERWELL.

SIR PETER. So! another French milliner! Egad, he has one in every room in the house, I suppose.

LADY SNEERWELL. Ungrateful Charles! Well may you be surprised, and feel for the indelicate situation your perfidy has forced me into.

CHARLES. Pray, uncle, is this another plot of yours? For, as I have life, I don't understand it.

JOSEPH. I believe, sir, there is but the evidence of one person more necessary to make it extremely clear.

SIR PETER. And that person, I imagine, is Mr. Snake.—Rowley, you were perfectly right to bring him with us, and pray let him appear.

ROWLEY. Walk in, Mr. Snake.

extort a shilling from that benevolent gentleman; and now, egad, I stood a chance of faring worse than my ancestors, and being knocked down without being bid for.

JOSEPH. Charles!

CHARLES. Joseph!

JOSEPH. 'Tis now complete!

CHARLES. Very!

SIR OLIVER. Sir Peter, my friend, and Rowley too—look on that elder nephew of mine. You know what he has already received from my bounty; and you also know how gladly I would have regarded half my fortune as held in trust for him: judge then my disappointment in discovering him to be destitute of faith, charity, and gratitude.

SIR PETER. Sir Oliver, I should be more surprised at this declaration, if I had not myself found him to be mean, treacherous, and hypocritical.

LADY TEAZLE. And if the gentleman pleads not guilty to these, pray let him call *me* to his character.

SIR PETER. Then, I believe, we need add no more: if he knows himself, he will consider it as the most perfect punishment, that he is known to the world.

CHARLES. If they talk this way to honesty, what will they say to me, by and by? [*Aside.*

SIR OLIVER. As for that prodigal, his brother, there——

CHARLES. Ay, now comes my turn: the damned family pictures will ruin me. [*Aside.*

JOSEPH. Sir Oliver—uncle, will you honour me with a hearing?

CHARLES. Now if Joseph would make one of his long speeches, I might recollect myself a little. [*Aside.*

SIR PETER. I suppose you would undertake to justify yourself entirely? [*To* JOSEPH.

JOSEPH. I trust I could.

SIR OLIVER. Well, sir!—and you could justify yourself too, I suppose? [*To* CHARLES.

CHARLES. Not that I know of, Sir Oliver.

SIR OLIVER. What!—Little Premium has been let too much into the secret, I suppose?

CHARLES. True, sir; but they were *family* secrets, and should not be mentioned again, you know.

ROWLEY. Come, Sir Oliver, I know you cannot speak of Charles's follies with anger.

SIR OLIVER. Odds heart, no more I can; nor with gravity either.——Sir Peter, do you know, the rogue bargained with me for all his ancestors;

you compel me, sir, not one moment—this is such insolence! [*Going to push him out.*

Enter CHARLES SURFACE.

CHARLES. Hey day! what's the matter now? What the devil, have you got hold of my little broker here? Zounds, brother! don't hurt little Premium. What's the matter, my little fellow?
JOSEPH. So! he has been with you too, has he?
CHARLES. To be sure he has. Why he's as honest a little—— But sure, Joseph, you have not been borrowing money too, have you?
JOSEPH. Borrowing! no! But, brother, you know we expect Sir Oliver here every——
CHARLES. O Gad, that's true! Noll mustn't find the little broker here, to be sure.
JOSEPH. Yet Mr. Stanley insists——
CHARLES. Stanley! why his name's Premium.
JOSEPH. No, sir, Stanley.
CHARLES. No, no, Premium.
JOSEPH. Well, no matter which—but——
CHARLES. Ay, ay, Stanley or Premium, 'tis the same thing, as you say; for I suppose he goes by half a hundred names, besides A. B. at the coffee-house.

Knocking.

JOSEPH. 'Sdeath! here's Sir Oliver at the door. Now I beg, Mr. Stanley——
CHARLES. Ay, ay, and I beg, Mr. Premium——
SIR OLIVER. Gentlemen——
JOSEPH. Sir, by heaven you shall go!
CHARLES. Ay, out with him, certainly!
SIR OLIVER. This violence——
JOSEPH. Sir, 'tis your own fault.
CHARLES. Out with him, to be sure.

Both forcing SIR OLIVER *out.*

Enter SIR PETER *and* LADY TEAZLE, MARIA, *and* ROWLEY.

SIR PETER. My old friend, Sir Oliver—hey! What in the name of wonder—here are dutiful nephews—assault their uncle at a first visit!
LADY TEAZLE. Indeed, Sir Oliver, 'twas well we came in to rescue you.
ROWLEY. Truly, it was; for I perceive, Sir Oliver, the character of old Stanley was no protection to you.
SIR OLIVER. Nor of Premium either: the necessities of the former could not

field for your roguery in imposing upon Sir Peter, and supplanting your brother, but you must endeavour to seduce his wife? I hate such an avarice of crimes; 'tis an unfair monopoly, and never prospers.

JOSEPH. Well, I admit I have been to blame. I confess I deviated from the direct road of wrong, but I don't think we're so totally defeated neither.

LADY SNEERWELL. No!

JOSEPH. You tell me you have made a trial of Snake since we met, and that you still believe him faithful to us.

LADY SNEERWELL. I do believe so.

JOSEPH. And that he has undertaken, should it be necessary, to swear and prove, that Charles is at this time contracted by vows and honour to your ladyship, which some of his former letters to you will serve to support.

LADY SNEERWELL. This, indeed, might have assisted.

JOSEPH. Come, come; it is not too late yet. [*Knocking at the door.*] But hark! this is probably my uncle, Sir Oliver: retire to that room; we'll consult further when he is gone.

LADY SNEERWELL. Well, but if *he* should find you out too?

JOSEPH. Oh, I have no fear of that. Sir Peter will hold his tongue for his own credit's sake—and you may depend on it I shall soon discover Sir Oliver's weak side!

LADY SNEERWELL. I have no diffidence of your abilities! only be constant to one roguery at a time.

Exit LADY SNEERWELL.

JOSEPH. I will, I will. So! 'tis confounded hard, after such bad fortune, to be baited by one's confederate in evil. Well, at all events my character is so much better than Charles's, that I certainly——hey!—what!—this is not Sir Oliver, but old Stanley again. Plague on't that he should return to tease me just now—I shall have Sir Oliver come and find him here—and——

Enter SIR OLIVER SURFACE.

Gad's life, Mr. Stanley, why have you come back to plague me at this time? You must not stay now, upon my word.

SIR OLIVER. Sir, I hear your Uncle Oliver is expected here, and though he has been so penurious to you, I'll try what he'll do for me.

JOSEPH. Sir, 'tis impossible for you to stay now, so I must beg—— Come any other time, and I promise you, you shall be assisted.

SIR OLIVER. No: Sir Oliver and I must be acquainted.

JOSEPH. Zounds, sir! then I insist on your quitting the room directly.

SIR OLIVER. Nay, sir——

JOSEPH. Sir, I insist on't: here, William! show this gentleman out. Since

SIR PETER. Well, I know not what to think. You remember the letter I found of hers evidently intended for Charles?

ROWLEY. A mere forgery, Sir Peter, laid in your way on purpose. This is one of the points which I intend Snake shall give you conviction of.

SIR PETER. I wish I were once satisfied of that. She looks this way. What a remarkably elegant turn of the head she has! Rowley, I'll go to her.

ROWLEY. Certainly.

SIR PETER. Though when it is known that we are reconciled, people will laugh at me ten times more.

ROWLEY. Let them laugh, and retort their malice only by showing them you are happy in spite of it.

SIR PETER. I'faith, so I will! and, if I'm not mistaken, we may yet be the happiest couple in the country.

ROWLEY. Nay, Sir Peter, he who once lays aside suspicion——

SIR PETER. Hold, Master Rowley! if you have any regard for me, never let me hear you utter anything like a sentiment: I have had enough of them to serve me the rest of my life.

Exeunt.

Scene III.—*The Library*

Enter JOSEPH SURFACE *and* LADY SNEERWELL.

LADY SNEERWELL. Impossible! Will not Sir Peter immediately be reconciled to Charles, and of course no longer oppose his union with Maria? The thought is distraction to me.

JOSEPH. Can passion furnish a remedy?

LADY SNEERWELL. No, nor cunning neither. Oh! I was a fool, an idiot, to league with such a blunderer!

JOSEPH. Sure, Lady Sneerwell, I am the greatest sufferer; yet you see I bear the accident with calmness.

LADY SNEERWELL. Because the disappointment doesn't reach your heart; your interest only attached you to Maria. Had you felt for her what I have for that ungrateful libertine, neither your temper nor hypocrisy could prevent your showing the sharpness of your vexation.

JOSEPH. But why should your reproaches fall on me for this disappointment?

LADY SNEERWELL. Are you not the cause of it? Had you not a sufficient

SIR PETER. And does Sir Oliver know all this?
SIR OLIVER. Every circumstance.
SIR PETER. What, of the closet and the screen, hey?
SIR OLIVER. Yes, yes, and the little French milliner. Oh, I have been vastly diverted with the story! Ha! ha! ha!
SIR PETER. 'Twas very pleasant.
SIR OLIVER. I never laughed more in my life, I assure you: ha! ha! ha!
SIR PETER. Oh, vastly diverting! Ha! ha! ha!
ROWLEY. To be sure, Joseph with his sentiments: ha! ha! ha!
SIR PETER. Yes, yes, his sentiments! Ha! ha! ha! Hypocritical villain!
SIR OLIVER. Ay, and that rogue Charles to pull Sir Peter out of the closet: ha! ha! ha!
SIR PETER. Ha! ha! 'twas devilish entertaining, to be sure!
SIR OLIVER. Ha! ha! ha! Egad, Sir Peter, I should like to have seen your face when the screen was thrown down: ha! ha!
SIR PETER. Yes, yes, my face when the screen was thrown down: ha! ha! ha! Oh, I must never show my head again!
SIR OLIVER. But come, come, it isn't fair to laugh at you neither, my old friend; though, upon my soul, I can't help it.
SIR PETER. Oh, pray don't restrain your mirth on my account: it does not hurt me at all! I laugh at the whole affair myself. Yes, yes, I think being a standing jest for all one's acquaintance a very happy situation. Oh, yes, and then of a morning to read the paragraphs about Mr. S———, Lady T———, and Sir P———, will be so entertaining!
ROWLEY. Without affectation, Sir Peter, you may despise the ridicule of fools: but I see Lady Teazle going towards the next room; I am sure you must desire a reconciliation as earnestly as she does.
SIR OLIVER. Perhaps my being here prevents her coming to you. Well, I'll leave honest Rowley to mediate between you; but he must bring you all presently to Mr. Surface's, where I am now returning, if not to reclaim a libertine, at least to expose hypocrisy.
SIR PETER. Ah, I'll be present at your discovering yourself there with all my heart; though 'tis a vile unlucky place for discoveries.
ROWLEY. We'll follow.

Exit SIR OLIVER.

SIR PETER. She is not coming here, you see, Rowley.
ROWLEY. No, but she has left the door of that room open, you perceive. See, she is in tears.
SIR PETER. Certainly a little mortification appears very becoming in a wife. Don't you think it will do her good to let her pine a little?
ROWLEY. Oh, this is ungenerous in you!

Mrs. Candour. Well, well, we are going, and depend on't we'll make the best report of it we can.

Exit.

Sir Peter. Leave my house!
Crabtree. And tell how hardly you've been treated.

Exit.

Sir Peter. Leave my house!
Sir Benjamin. And how patiently you bear it.

Exit.

Sir Peter. Fiends! vipers! furies! Oh! that their own venom would choke them!
Sir Oliver. They are very provoking, indeed, Sir Peter.

Enter Rowley.

Rowley. I heard high words: what has ruffled you, sir?
Sir Peter. Pshaw! what signifies asking? Do I ever pass a day without my vexations?
Rowley. Well, I'm not inquisitive.
Sir Oliver. Well, Sir Peter, I have seen both my nephews in the manner we proposed.
Sir Peter. A precious couple they are!
Rowley. Yes, and Sir Oliver is convinced that your judgment was right, Sir Peter.
Sir Oliver. Yes, I find Joseph is indeed the man, after all.
Rowley. Ay, as Sir Peter says, he is a man of sentiment.
Sir Oliver. And acts up to the sentiments he professes.
Rowley. It certainly is edification to hear him talk.
Sir Oliver. Oh, he's a model for the young men of the age!——But how's this, Sir Peter? you don't join us in your friend Joseph's praise, as I expected.
Sir Peter. Sir Oliver, we live in a damned wicked world, and the fewer we praise the better.
Rowley. What! do you say so, Sir Peter, who were never mistaken in your life?
Sir Peter. Pshaw! Plague on you both! I see by your sneering you have heard the whole affair. I shall go mad among you!
Rowley. Then, to fret you no longer, Sir Peter, we are indeed acquainted with it all. I met Lady Teazle coming from Mr. Surface's, so humbled, that she deigned to request me to be her advocate with you.

SIR OLIVER. Not a word!
CRABTREE. Not of his being dangerously wounded?
SIR OLIVER. The devil he is!
SIR BENJAMIN. Run through the body——
CRABTREE. Shot in the breast——
SIR BENJAMIN. By one Mr. Surface——
CRABTREE. Ay, the younger.
SIR OLIVER. Hey! what the plague! you seem to differ strangely in your accounts: however, you agree that Sir Peter is dangerously wounded.
SIR BENJAMIN. Oh, yes, we agree there.
CRABTREE. Yes, yes, I believe there can be no doubt of that.
SIR OLIVER. Then, upon my word, for a person in that situation, he is the most imprudent man alive; for here he comes, walking as if nothing at all was the matter.

Enter SIR PETER TEAZLE.

Odds heart, Sir Peter, you are come in good time, I promise you; for we had just given you over.
SIR BENJAMIN. Egad, uncle, this is the most sudden recovery!
SIR OLIVER. Why, man, what do you out of bed with a small sword through your body, and a bullet lodged in your thorax?
SIR PETER. A small sword, and a bullet!
SIR OLIVER. Ay, these gentlemen would have killed you without law, or physic, and wanted to dub me a doctor, to make me an accomplice.
SIR PETER. Why, what is all this?
SIR BENJAMIN. We rejoice, Sir Peter, that the story of the duel is not true, and are sincerely sorry for your other misfortune.
SIR PETER. So, so; all over the town already. [*Aside.*
CRABTREE. Though, Sir Peter, you were certainly vastly to blame to marry at your years.
SIR PETER. Sir, what business is that of yours?
MRS. CANDOUR. Though, indeed, as Sir Peter made so good a husband, he's very much to be pitied.
SIR PETER. Plague on your pity, ma'am! I desire none of it.
SIR BENJAMIN. However, Sir Peter, you must not mind the laughing and jests you will meet with on the occasion.
SIR PETER. Sir, sir, I desire to be master in my own house.
CRABTREE. 'Tis no uncommon case, that's one comfort.
SIR PETER. I insist on being left to myself: without ceremony—I insist on your leaving my house directly.

CRABTREE. Odds life, nephew, allow others to know something too. A pair of pistols lay on the bureau (for Mr. Surface, it seems, had come home the night before late from Salthill, where he had been to see the Montem with a friend, who has a son at Eton), so, unluckily, the pistols were left charged.

SIR BENJAMIN. I heard nothing of this.

CRABTREE. Sir Peter forced Charles to take one, and they fired, it seems, pretty nearly together. Charles's shot took effect, as I tell you, and Sir Peter's missed; but what is very extraordinary, the ball struck against a little bronze Shakspeare that stood over the fireplace, grazed out of the window at a right angle, and wounded the postman, who was just coming to the door with a double letter from Northamptonshire.

SIR BENJAMIN. My uncle's account is more circumstantial, I confess; but I believe mine is the true one, for all that.

LADY SNEERWELL. I am more interested in this affair than they imagine, and must have better information. [*Aside.*

Exit LADY SNEERWELL.

SIR BENJAMIN. Ah! Lady Sneerwell's alarm is very easily accounted for.

CRABTREE. Yes, yes, they certainly do say—but that's neither here nor there.

MRS. CANDOUR. But, pray, where is Sir Peter at present?

CRABTREE. Oh! they brought him home, and he is now in the house, though the servants are ordered to deny him.

MRS. CANDOUR. I believe so, and Lady Teazle, I suppose, attending him.

CRABTREE. Yes, yes; and I saw one of the faculty enter just before me.

SIR BENJAMIN. Hey! who comes here?

CRABTREE. Oh, this is he: the physician, depend on't.

MRS. CANDOUR. Oh, certainly: it must be the physician; and now we shall know.

Enter SIR OLIVER SURFACE.

CRABTREE. Well, doctor, what hopes?

MRS. CANDOUR. Ay, doctor, how's your patient?

SIR BENJAMIN. Now, doctor, isn't it a wound with a small sword?

CRABTREE. A bullet lodged in the thorax, for a hundred.

SIR OLIVER. Doctor! a wound with a small sword! and a bullet in the thorax! Oons! are you mad, good people?

SIR BENJAMIN. Perhaps, sir, you are not a doctor?

SIR OLIVER. Truly, I am to thank you for my degree if I am.

CRABTREE. Only a friend of Sir Peter's, then, I presume. But, sir, you must have heard of his accident?

MRS. CANDOUR. Yes, yes, he was the lover. Mr. Surface, to do him justice, was only the informer.

SIR BENJAMIN. Well, I'll not dispute with you, Mrs. Candour; but, be it which it may, I hope that Sir Peter's wound will not——

MRS. CANDOUR. Sir Peter's wound! Oh, mercy! I didn't hear a word of their fighting.

LADY SNEERWELL. Nor I, a syllable.

SIR BENJAMIN. No! what, no mention of the duel?

MRS. CANDOUR. Not a word.

SIR BENJAMIN. Oh, yes: they fought before they left the room.

LADY SNEERWELL. Pray, let us hear.

MRS. CANDOUR. Ay, do oblige us with the duel.

SIR BENJAMIN. "Sir," says Sir Peter, immediately after the discovery, "you are a most ungrateful fellow."

MRS. CANDOUR. Ay, to Charles——

SIR BENJAMIN. No, no—to Mr. Surface—"a most ungrateful fellow; and old as I am, sir," says he, "I insist on immediate satisfaction."

MRS. CANDOUR. Ay, that must have been to Charles; for 'tis very unlikely Mr. Surface should fight in his own house.

SIR BENJAMIN. Gad's life, ma'am, not at all—"Giving me immediate satisfaction." On this, ma'am, Lady Teazle, seeing Sir Peter in such danger, ran out of the room in strong hysterics, and Charles after her, calling out for hartshorn and water; then, madam, they began to fight with swords——

Enter CRABTREE.

CRABTREE. With pistols, nephew—pistols: I have it from undoubted authority.

MRS. CANDOUR. O, Mr. Crabtree, then it is all true!

CRABTREE. Too true, indeed, madam, and Sir Peter is dangerously wounded—

SIR BENJAMIN. By a thrust in second quite through his left side—

CRABTREE. By a bullet lodged in the thorax.

MRS. CANDOUR. Mercy on me! Poor Sir Peter!

CRABTREE. Yes, madam; though Charles would have avoided the matter, if he could.

MRS. CANDOUR. I knew Charles was the person.

SIR BENJAMIN. My uncle, I see, knows nothing of the matter.

CRABTREE. But Sir Peter taxed him with the basest ingratitude.

SIR BENJAMIN. That I told you, you know—

CRABTREE. Do, nephew, let me speak! and insisted on immediate—

SIR BENJAMIN. Just as I said—

MRS. CANDOUR. Do go again,—I shall be glad to see her, if it be only for a moment, for I am sure she must be in great distress.

Exit MAID.

Dear heart, how provoking! I'm not mistress of half the circumstances! We shall have the whole affair in the newspapers, with the names of the parties at length, before I have dropped the story at a dozen houses.

Enter SIR BENJAMIN BACKBITE.

Oh, Sir Benjamin! you have heard, I suppose——
SIR BENJAMIN. Of Lady Teazle and Mr. Surface——
MRS. CANDOUR. And Sir Peter's discovery——
SIR BENJAMIN. Oh! the strangest piece of business, to be sure!
MRS. CANDOUR. Well, I never was so surprised in my life. I am so sorry for all parties, indeed.
SIR BENJAMIN. Now, I don't pity Sir Peter at all: he was so extravagantly partial to Mr. Surface.
MRS. CANDOUR. Mr. Surface! Why, 'twas with Charles Lady Teazle was detected.
SIR BENJAMIN. No, no, I tell you—Mr. Surface is the gallant.
MRS. CANDOUR. No such thing! Charles is the man. 'Twas Mr. Surface brought Sir Peter on purpose to discover them.
SIR BENJAMIN. I tell you I had it from one——
MRS. CANDOUR. And I have it from one——
SIR BENJAMIN. Who had it from one, who had it——
MRS. CANDOUR. From one immediately——but here comes Lady Sneerwell; perhaps she knows the whole affair.

Enter LADY SNEERWELL.

LADY SNEERWELL. So, my dear Mrs. Candour, here's a sad affair of our friend Lady Teazle.
MRS. CANDOUR. Ay, my dear friend, who would have thought——
LADY SNEERWELL. Well, there is no trusting appearances; though, indeed, she was always too lively for me.
MRS. CANDOUR. To be sure, her manners were a little too free: but then she was so young!
LADY SNEERWELL. And had, indeed, some good qualities.
MRS. CANDOUR. So she had, indeed. But have you heard the particulars?
LADY SNEERWELL. No; but everybody says that Mr. Surface——
SIR BENJAMIN. Ay, there; I told you Mr. Surface was the man.
MRS. CANDOUR. No, no: indeed the assignation was with Charles.
LADY SNEERWELL. With Charles! You alarm me, Mrs. Candour!

ore of pure charity is an expensive article in the catalogue of a man's good qualities; whereas the sentimental French plate I use instead of it makes just as good a show, and pays no tax.

Enter ROWLEY.

ROWLEY. Mr. Surface, your servant: I was apprehensive of interrupting you, though my business demands immediate attention, as this note will inform you.

JOSEPH. Always happy to see Mr. Rowley. [*Reads the letter.*]—Sir Oliver Surface!—My uncle arrived!

ROWLEY. He is, indeed: we have just parted—quite well, after a speedy voyage, and impatient to embrace his worthy nephew.

JOSEPH. I am astonished!—William! stop Mr. Stanley, if he's not gone.

ROWLEY. Oh! he's out of reach, I believe.

JOSEPH. Why did you not let me know this when you came in together?

ROWLEY. I thought you had particular business;—but I must be gone to inform your brother, and appoint him here to meet your uncle. He will be with you in a quarter of an hour.

JOSEPH. So he says. Well, I am strangely overjoyed at his coming.—— Never, to be sure, was anything so damned unlucky. [*Aside.*]

ROWLEY. You will be delighted to see how well he looks.

JOSEPH. Ah! I'm rejoiced to hear it——Just at this time! [*Aside.*

ROWLEY. I'll tell him how impatiently you expect him.

JOSEPH. Do, do; pray give my best duty and affection. Indeed, I cannot express the sensations I feel at the thought of seeing him.—

Exit ROWLEY.

—Certainly his coming just at this time is the cruellest piece of ill-fortune!

Exit.

Scene II.—SIR PETER TEAZLE's

Enter MRS. CANDOUR *and* MAID.

MAID. Indeed, ma'am, my lady will see nobody at present.
MRS. CANDOUR. Did you tell her it was her friend Mrs. Candour?
MAID. Yes, ma'am; but she begs you will excuse her.

age. I will tell you, my good sir, in confidence, what he has done for me has been a mere nothing; though people, I know, have thought otherwise, and, for my part, I never chose to contradict the report.

SIR OLIVER. What! has he never transmitted you bullion—rupees—pagodas?

JOSEPH. Oh, dear sir, nothing of the kind:—No, no—a few presents now and then—china, shawls, congou tea, avadavats, and Indian crackers—little more, believe me.

SIR OLIVER. Here's gratitude for twelve thousand pounds!—Avadavats and Indian crackers! [*Aside.*]

JOSEPH. Then, my dear sir, you have heard, I doubt not, of the extravagance of my brother: there are very few would credit what I have done for that unfortunate young man.

SIR OLIVER. Not I, for one! [*Aside.*]

JOSEPH. The sums I have lent him!—Indeed I have been exceedingly to blame; it was an amiable weakness: however, I don't pretend to defend it,—and now I feel it doubly culpable, since it has deprived me of the pleasure of serving you, Mr. Stanley, as my heart dictates.

SIR OLIVER. Dissembler! [*Aside.*]—Then, sir, you can't assist me?

JOSEPH. At present, it grieves me to say, I cannot; but, whenever I have the ability, you may depend upon hearing from me.

SIR OLIVER. I am extremely sorry——

JOSEPH. Not more than I, believe me;—to pity without the power to relieve, is still more painful than to ask and be denied.

SIR OLIVER. Kind sir, your most obedient humble servant.

JOSEPH. You leave me deeply affected, Mr. Stanley. William, be ready to open the door.

SIR OLIVER. Oh, dear sir, no ceremony.

JOSEPH. Your very obedient.

SIR OLIVER. Sir, your most obsequious.

JOSEPH. You may depend upon hearing from me, whenever I can be of service.

SIR OLIVER. Sweet sir, you are too good!

JOSEPH. In the meantime I wish you health and spirits.

SIR OLIVER. Your ever grateful and perpetual humble servant.

JOSEPH. Sir, yours as sincerely.

SIR OLIVER. Charles, you are my heir! [*Aside.*]

Exit.

JOSEPH. This is one bad effect of a good character; it invites application from the unfortunate, and there needs no small degree of address to gain the reputation of benevolence without incurring the expense. The silver

ROWLEY. As to his way of thinking, I cannot pretend to decide; for, to do him justice, he appears to have as much speculative benevolence as any private gentleman in the kingdom, though he is seldom so sensual as to indulge himself in the exercise of it.

SIR OLIVER. Yet has a string of charitable sentiments at his fingers' ends.

ROWLEY. Or rather, at his tongue's end, Sir Oliver; for I believe there is no sentiment he has such faith in as that "Charity begins at home."

SIR OLIVER. And his, I presume, is of that domestic sort which never stirs abroad at all.

ROWLEY. I doubt you'll find it so;—but he's coming. I mustn't seem to interrupt you; and you know immediately as you leave him, I come in to announce your arrival in your real character.

SIR OLIVER. True; and afterwards you'll meet me at Sir Peter's.

ROWLEY. Without losing a moment.

Exit.

SIR OLIVER. I don't like the complaisance of his features.

Enter JOSEPH SURFACE.

JOSEPH. Sir, I beg you ten thousand pardons for keeping you a moment waiting——Mr. Stanley, I presume.—

SIR OLIVER. At your service.

JOSEPH. Sir, I beg you will do me the honour to sit down—I entreat you, sir!—

SIR OLIVER. Dear sir—there's no occasion——too civil by half! [*Aside.*

JOSEPH. I have not the pleasure of knowing you, Mr. Stanley; but I am extremely happy to see you look so well. You were nearly related to my mother, I think, Mr. Stanley?

SIR OLIVER. I was, sir;—so nearly that my present poverty, I fear, may do discredit to her wealthy children, else I should not have presumed to trouble you.

JOSEPH. Dear sir, there needs no apology:—he that is in distress, though a stranger, has a right to claim kindred with the wealthy. I am sure I wish I was of that class, and had it in my power to offer you even a small relief.

SIR OLIVER. If your uncle, Sir Oliver, were here, I should have a friend.

JOSEPH. I wish he was, sir, with all my heart: you should not want an advocate with him, believe me, sir.

SIR OLIVER. I should not need one—my distresses would recommend me. But I imagined his bounty would enable you to become the agent of his charity.

JOSEPH. My dear sir, you were strangely misinformed. Sir Oliver is a worthy man, a very worthy man; but avarice, Mr. Stanley, is the vice of

ACT V

Scene I.—*The Library*

Enter JOSEPH SURFACE *and* SERVANT.

JOSEPH. Mr. Stanley!—and why should you think I would see him? you must know he comes to ask something.

SERVANT. Sir, I should not have let him in, but that Mr. Rowley came to the door with him.

JOSEPH. Pshaw! blockhead! to suppose that I should now be in a temper to receive visits from poor relations!——Well, why don't you show the fellow up?

SERVANT. I will, sir.——Why, sir, it was not my fault that Sir Peter discovered my lady——

JOSEPH. Go, fool!

Exit SERVANT.

——Sure Fortune never played a man of my policy such a trick before. My character with Sir Peter, my hopes with Maria, destroyed in a moment! I'm in a rare humour to listen to other people's distresses! I shan't be able to bestow even a benevolent sentiment on Stanley.—So! here he comes, and Rowley with him. I must try to recover myself, and put a little charity into my face, however.

Exit.

Enter SIR OLIVER SURFACE *and* ROWLEY.

SIR OLIVER. What! does he avoid us?—That was he, was it not?

ROWLEY. It was, sir. But I doubt you are come a little too abruptly. His nerves are so weak, that the sight of a poor relation may be too much for him. I should have gone first to break it to him.

SIR OLIVER. Oh, plague of his nerves! Yet this is he whom Sir Peter extols as a man of the most benevolent way of thinking!

59

credulous friend, while he affected honourable addresses to his ward—I behold him now in a light so truly despicable, that I shall never again respect myself for having listened to him.

Exit LADY TEAZLE.

JOSEPH. Notwithstanding all this, Sir Peter, Heaven knows——
SIR PETER. That you are a villain! and so I leave you to your conscience.
JOSEPH. You are too rash, Sir Peter; you shall hear me.—The man who shuts out conviction by refusing to——

[*Exeunt* SIR PETER *and* JOSEPH SURFACE *talking.*

Brother, I'm sorry to find you have given that worthy man cause for so much uneasiness.—Sir Peter! there's nothing in the world so noble as a man of sentiment!

Exit CHARLES.

They stand for some time looking at each other.

JOSEPH. Sir Peter—notwithstanding—I confess—that appearances are against me—if you will afford me your patience—I make no doubt—but I shall explain everything to your satisfaction.

SIR PETER. If you please, sir.

JOSEPH. The fact is, sir, that Lady Teazle, knowing my pretensions to your ward Maria—I say, sir,—Lady Teazle, being apprehensive of the jealousy of your temper—and knowing my friendship to the family—she, sir, I say—called here—in order that—I might explain these pretensions—but on your coming—being apprehensive—as I said—of your jealousy—she withdrew—and this, you may depend on it, is the whole truth of the matter.

SIR PETER. A very clear account, upon my word; and I dare swear the lady will vouch for every article of it.

LADY TEAZLE. For not one word of it, Sir Peter!

SIR PETER. How! don't you think it worth while to agree in the lie?

LADY TEAZLE. There is not one syllable of truth in what that gentleman has told you.

SIR PETER. I believe you, upon my soul, ma'am!

JOSEPH.—'Sdeath, madam, will you betray me? [*Aside.*

LADY TEAZLE. Good Mr. Hypocrite, by your leave, I'll speak for myself.

SIR PETER. Ay, let her alone, sir; you'll find she'll make out a better story than you, without prompting.

LADY TEAZLE. Hear me, Sir Peter!—I came hither on no matter relating to your ward, and even ignorant of this gentleman's pretensions to her. But I came seduced by his insidious arguments, at least to listen to his pretended passion, if not to sacrifice your honour to his baseness.

SIR PETER. Now, I believe, the truth is coming indeed!

JOSEPH. The woman's mad!

LADY TEAZLE. No, sir,—she has recovered her senses, and your own arts have furnished her with the means.—Sir Peter, I do not expect you to credit me—but the tenderness you expressed for me, when I am sure you could not think I was a witness to it, has penetrated so to my heart, that had I left the place without the shame of this discovery, my future life should have spoken the sincerity of my gratitude. As for that smooth-tongued hypocrite, who would have seduced the wife of his too

Sir Peter. I! not for the world! [*Apart to* Joseph.]—Ah! Charles, if you associated more with your brother, one might indeed hope for your reformation. He is a man of sentiment.—Well, there is nothing in the world so noble as a man of sentiment!

Charles. Pshaw! he is too moral by half—and so apprehensive of his good name, as he calls it, that I suppose he would as soon let a priest into his house as a girl.

Sir Peter. No, no,—come, come,—you wrong him.—No, no! Joseph is no rake, but he is no such saint either in that respect.——I have a great mind to tell him—we should have a laugh at Joseph. [*Aside.*]

Charles. Oh, hang him! He's a very anchorite, a young hermit.

Sir Peter. Hark'ee—you must not abuse him: he may chance to hear of it again, I promise you.

Charles. Why, you won't tell him?

Sir Peter. No—but—this way. Egad, I'll tell him. [*Aside.*]—Hark'ee—have you a mind to have a good laugh at Joseph?

Charles. I should like it of all things.

Sir Peter. Then, i'faith, we will—I'll be quit with him for discovering me.—He had a girl with him when I called.

Charles. What! Joseph? you jest.

Sir Peter. Hush!—a little French milliner—and the best of the jest is—she's in the room now.

Charles. The devil she is!

Sir Peter. Hush! I tell you! [*Points.*]

Charles. Behind the screen! 'Slife, let's unveil her!

Sir Peter. No, no—he's coming—you shan't, indeed!

Charles. Oh, egad, we'll have a peep at the little milliner!

Sir Peter. Not for the world—Joseph will never forgive me.

Charles. I'll stand by you——

Sir Peter. Odds, here he is!

Joseph Surface *enters just as* Charles Surface *throws down the screen.*

Charles. Lady Teazle, by all that's wonderful!

Sir Peter. Lady Teazle, by all that's damnable!

Charles. Sir Peter, this is one of the smartest French milliners I ever saw. Egad, you seem all to have been diverting yourselves here at hide and seek, and I don't see who is out of the secret.—Shall I beg your ladyship to inform me? Not a word!—Brother, will you be pleased to explain this matter? What! is Morality dumb too?—Sir Peter, though I found you in the dark, perhaps you are not so now! All mute!—Well—though I can make nothing of the affair, I suppose you perfectly understand one another—so I'll leave you to yourselves—[*Going.*]

JOSEPH. Nay, nay, sir, this is no jest.
CHARLES. Egad, I'm serious.—Don't you remember one day when I called here——
JOSEPH. Nay, prithee, Charles——
CHARLES. And found you together——
JOSEPH. Zounds, sir! I insist——
CHARLES. And another time when your servant——
JOSEPH. Brother, brother, a word with you!—Gad, I must stop him. [*Aside.*
CHARLES. Informed, I say, that——
JOSEPH. Hush! I beg your pardon, but Sir Peter has overheard all we have been saying. I knew you would clear yourself, or I should not have consented.
CHARLES. How, Sir Peter! Where is he?
JOSEPH. Softly; there! [*Points to the closet.*
CHARLES. Oh, 'fore Heaven, I'll have him out. Sir Peter, come forth!
JOSEPH. No, no——
CHARLES. I say, Sir Peter, come into court.—[*Pulls in* SIR PETER.]—What! my old guardian!—What! turn inquisitor, and take evidence incog.?
SIR PETER. Give me your hand, Charles—I believe I have suspected you wrongfully; but you mustn't be angry with Joseph—'twas my plan!
CHARLES. Indeed!
SIR PETER. But I acquit you. I promise you I don't think near so ill of you as I did: what I have heard has given me great satisfaction.
CHARLES. Egad, then, 'twas lucky you didn't hear any more—wasn't it, Joseph? [*Apart to* JOSEPH.
SIR PETER. Ah! you would have retorted on him.
CHARLES. Ay, ay, that was a joke.
SIR PETER. Yes, yes, I know his honour too well.
CHARLES. But you might as well have suspected *him* as *me* in this matter, for all that—mightn't he, Joseph? [*Apart to* JOSEPH.
SIR PETER. Well, well, I believe you.
JOSEPH. Would they were both well out of the room! [*Aside.*

Enter SERVANT, *and whispers* JOSEPH SURFACE.

SIR PETER. And in future perhaps we may not be such strangers.
JOSEPH. Gentlemen, I beg pardon—I must wait on you downstairs: here is a person come on particular business.
CHARLES. Well, you can see him in another room. Sir Peter and I have not met a long time, and I have something to say to him.
JOSEPH. They must not be left together. [*Aside.*]—I'll send this man away, and return directly.——Sir Peter, not a word of the French milliner. [*Apart to* SIR PETER, *and goes out.*

JOSEPH. In, in, my good Sir Peter.—'Fore gad, I wish I had a key to the door.

Enter CHARLES SURFACE.

CHARLES. Holla! brother, what has been the matter? Your fellow would not let me up at first. What! have you had a Jew or a wench with you?

JOSEPH. Neither, brother, I assure you.

CHARLES. But what has made Sir Peter steal off? I thought he had been with you.

JOSEPH. He *was*, brother; but hearing you were coming, he did not choose to stay.

CHARLES. What! was the old gentleman afraid I wanted to borrow money of him?

JOSEPH. No, sir: but I am sorry to find, Charles, you have lately given that worthy man grounds for great uneasiness.

CHARLES. Yes, they tell me I do that to a great many worthy men.—But how so, pray?

JOSEPH. To be plain with you, brother—he thinks you are endeavouring to gain Lady Teazle's affections from him.

CHARLES. Who, I? O Lud! not I, upon my word.—Ha! ha! ha! ha! so the old fellow has found out that he has got a young wife, has he?—or, what is worse, Lady Teazle has found out she has an old husband?

JOSEPH. This is no subject to jest on, brother. He who can laugh——

CHARLES. True, true, as you were going to say—then, seriously, I never had the least idea of what you charge me with, upon my honour.

JOSEPH. Well, it will give Sir Peter great satisfaction to hear this. [*Aloud.*

CHARLES. To be sure, I once thought the lady seemed to have taken a fancy to me; but, upon my soul, I never gave her the least encouragement:—besides, you know my attachment to Maria.

JOSEPH. But sure, brother, even if Lady Teazle had betrayed the fondest partiality for you——

CHARLES. Why, look'ee, Joseph, I hope I shall never deliberately do a dishonourable action; but if a pretty woman was purposely to throw herself in my way—and that pretty woman married to a man old enough to be her father——

JOSEPH. Well!

CHARLES. Why, I believe I should be obliged to borrow a little of your morality, that's all.—But, brother, do you know now that you surprise me exceedingly, by naming *me* with Lady Teazle; for, 'faith, I always understood you were her favourite.

JOSEPH. Oh, for shame, Charles! This retort is foolish.

CHARLES. Nay, I swear I have seen you exchange such significant glances——

SERVANT. Your brother, sir, is speaking to a gentleman in the street, and says he knows you are within.

JOSEPH. 'Sdeath, blockhead, I'm not within—I'm out for the day.

SIR PETER. Stay—hold—a thought has struck me:—you shall be at home.

JOSEPH. Well, well, let him up.

[*Exit* SERVANT.]

He'll interrupt Sir Peter, however. [*Aside*.

SIR PETER. Now, my good friend, oblige me, I entreat you.—Before Charles comes, let me conceal myself somewhere—then do you tax him on the point we have been talking, and his answer may satisfy me at once.

JOSEPH. Oh, fie, Sir Peter! would you have me join in so mean a trick?—to trepan my brother too?

SIR PETER. Nay, you tell me you are sure he is innocent; if so, you do him the greatest service by giving him an opportunity to clear himself, and you will set my heart at rest. Come, you shall not refuse me: here, behind this screen will be—Hey! what the devil! there seems to be one listener there already—I'll swear I saw a petticoat!

JOSEPH. Ha! ha! ha! Well, this is ridiculous enough. I'll tell you, Sir Peter, though I hold a man of intrigue to be a most despicable character, yet, you know, it does not follow that one is to be an absolute Joseph either! Hark'ee, 'tis a little French milliner—a silly rogue that plagues me,—and having some character to lose, on your coming, sir, she ran behind the screen.

SIR PETER. Ah! you rogue! But, egad, she has overheard all I have been saying of my wife.

JOSEPH. Oh, 'twill never go any farther, you may depend upon it.

SIR PETER. No! then, faith, let her hear it out.—Here's a closet will do as well.

JOSEPH. Well, go in there.

SIR PETER. Sly rogue! sly rogue! [*Going into the closet*.

JOSEPH. A narrow escape, indeed! and a curious situation I'm in, to part man and wife in this manner.

LADY TEAZLE. [*Peeping*.]—Couldn't I steal off?

JOSEPH. Keep close, my angel!

SIR PETER. [*Peeping*.]—Joseph, tax him home.

JOSEPH. Back, my dear friend!

LADY TEAZLE. Couldn't you lock Sir Peter in?

JOSEPH. Be still, my life!

SIR PETER. [*Peeping*.]—You're sure the little milliner won't blab?

JOSEPH. Oh, 'tis not to be credited. There may be a man capable of such baseness, to be sure; but, for my part, till you can give me positive proofs, I cannot but doubt it. However, if it should be proved on him, he is no longer a brother of mine—I disclaim kindred with him: for the man who can break the laws of hospitality, and tempt the wife of his friend, deserves to be branded as the pest of society.

SIR PETER. What a difference there is between you! What noble sentiments!

JOSEPH. Yet, I cannot suspect Lady Teazle's honour.

SIR PETER. I am sure I wish to think well of her, and to remove all ground of quarrel between us. She has lately reproached me more than once with having made no settlement on her; and, in our last quarrel, she almost hinted that she should not break her heart if I was dead. Now, as we seem to differ in our ideas of expense, I have resolved she shall have her own way, and be her own mistress in that respect for the future; and if I were to die, she will find I have not been inattentive to her interest while living. Here, my friend, are the drafts of two deeds, which I wish to have your opinion on.—By one, she will enjoy eight hundred a year independent while I live; and, by the other, the bulk of my fortune at my death.

JOSEPH. This conduct, Sir Peter, is indeed truly generous.——I wish it may not corrupt my pupil. [*Aside.*]

SIR PETER. Yes, I am determined she shall have no cause to complain, though I would not have her acquainted with the latter instance of my affection yet awhile.

JOSEPH. Nor I, if I could help it. [*Aside.*]

SIR PETER. And now, my dear friend, if you please, we will talk over the situation of your affairs with Maria.

JOSEPH. [*Softly.*]—Oh, no, Sir Peter; another time, if you please.

SIR PETER. I am sensibly chagrined at the little progress you seem to make in her affections.

JOSEPH. I beg you will not mention it. What are my disappointments when your happiness is in debate! [*Softly.*]—'Sdeath, I shall be ruined every way. [*Aside.*]

SIR PETER. And though you are so averse to my acquainting Lady Teazle with your passion for Maria, I'm sure she's not your enemy in the affair.

JOSEPH. Pray, Sir Peter, now, oblige me. I am really too much affected by the subject we have been speaking of, to bestow a thought on my own concerns. The man who is entrusted with his friend's distresses can never——

Enter SERVANT.

Well, sir?

JOSEPH. Indeed! I am very sorry to hear it.

SIR PETER. Ay, 'tis too plain she has not the least regard for me; but, what's worse, I have pretty good authority to suppose she has formed an attachment to another.

JOSEPH. Indeed! you astonish me!

SIR PETER. Yes; and, between ourselves, I think I've discovered the person.

JOSEPH. How! you alarm me exceedingly.

SIR PETER. Ay, my dear friend, I knew you would sympathise with me!

JOSEPH. Yes—believe me, Sir Peter, such a discovery would hurt me just as much as it would you.

SIR PETER. I am convinced of it.—Ah! it is a happiness to have a friend whom we can trust even with one's family secrets. But have you no guess who I mean?

JOSEPH. I haven't the most distant idea. It can't be Sir Benjamin Backbite!

SIR PETER. Oh no! What say you to Charles?

JOSEPH. My brother! impossible!

SIR PETER. Oh! my dear friend, the goodness of your own heart misleads you. You judge of others by yourself.

JOSEPH. Certainly, Sir Peter, the heart that is conscious of its own integrity is ever slow to credit another's treachery.

SIR PETER. True—but your brother has no sentiment—you never hear him talk so.

JOSEPH. Yet, I can't but think Lady Teazle herself has too much principle.

SIR PETER. Ay,—but what is principle against the flattery of a handsome, lively young fellow?

JOSEPH. That's very true.

SIR PETER. And there's, you know, the difference of our ages makes it very improbable that she should have any very great affection for me; and if she were to be frail, and I were to make it public, why the town would only laugh at me, the foolish old bachelor, who had married a girl.

JOSEPH. That's true, to be sure—they would laugh.

SIR PETER. Laugh—ay, and make ballads, and paragraphs, and the devil knows what of me.

JOSEPH. No—you must never make it public.

SIR PETER. But then again—that the nephew of my old friend, Sir Oliver, should be the person to attempt such a wrong, hurts me more nearly.

JOSEPH. Ay, there's the point.—When ingratitude barbs the dart of injury, the wound has double danger in it.

SIR PETER. Ay—I, that was, in a manner, left his guardian; in whose house he had been so often entertained; who never in my life denied him—my advice.

LADY TEAZLE. I doubt they do indeed; and I will fairly own to you, that if I could be persuaded to do wrong, it would be by Sir Peter's ill-usage sooner than your *honourable logic*, after all.

JOSEPH. Then, by this hand, which he is unworthy of—— [*Taking her hand.*

Enter SERVANT.

'Sdeath, you blockhead—what do you want?

SERVANT. I beg your pardon, sir, but I thought you would not choose Sir Peter to come up without announcing him.

JOSEPH. Sir Peter!—Oons—the devil!

LADY TEAZLE. Sir Peter! O Lud—I'm ruined—I'm ruined!

SERVANT. Sir, 'twasn't I let him in.

LADY TEAZLE. Oh! I'm quite undone! What will become of me? Now, Mr. Logic—Oh! he's on the stairs—I'll get behind here—and if ever I'm so imprudent again—— [*Goes behind the screen.*

JOSEPH. Give me that book. [*Sits down.* SERVANT *pretends to adjust his hair.*

Enter SIR PETER.

SIR PETER. Ay, ever improving himself—Mr. Surface, Mr. Surface——

JOSEPH. Oh! my dear Sir Peter, I beg your pardon—[*Gaping—throws away the book.*]—I have been dozing over a stupid book.—Well, I am much obliged to you for this call. You haven't been here, I believe, since I fitted up this room.—Books, you know, are the only things in which I am a coxcomb.

SIR PETER. 'Tis very neat indeed.—Well, well, that's proper; and you can make even your screen a source of knowledge—hung, I perceive, with maps?

JOSEPH. Oh, yes, I find great use in that screen.

SIR PETER. I daresay you must, certainly, when you want to find anything in a hurry.

JOSEPH. Ay, or to hide anything in a hurry either. [*Aside.*

SIR PETER. Well, I have a little private business——

JOSEPH. You need not stay [*to the* SERVANT].

SERVANT. No, sir.

Exit.

JOSEPH. Here's a chair, Sir Peter—I beg——

SIR PETER. Well, now we are alone, there is a subject, my dear friend, on which I wish to unburthen my mind to you—a point of the greatest moment to my peace; in short, my dear friend, Lady Teazle's conduct of late has made me extremely unhappy.

a husband entertains a groundless suspicion of his wife, and withdraws his confidence from her, the original compact is broken, and she owes it to the honour of her sex to outwit him.

LADY TEAZLE. Indeed!—so that if he suspects me without cause, it follows, that the best way of curing his jealousy is to give him reason for't.

JOSEPH. Undoubtedly—for your husband should never be deceived in you,—and in that case it becomes you to be frail in compliment to his discernment.

LADY TEAZLE. To be sure, what you say is very reasonable, and when the consciousness of my innocence——

JOSEPH. Ah! my dear madam, there is the great mistake: 'tis this very conscious innocence that is of the greatest prejudice to you. What is it makes you negligent of forms, and careless of the world's opinion?—why, the consciousness of your own innocence. What makes you thoughtless in your conduct, and apt to run into a thousand little imprudences?—why, the consciousness of your own innocence. What makes you impatient of Sir Peter's temper, and outrageous at his suspicions?—why, the consciousness of your innocence.

LADY TEAZLE. 'Tis very true!

JOSEPH. Now, my dear Lady Teazle, if you would but once make a trifling *faux pas*, you can't conceive how cautious you would grow, and how ready to humour and agree with your husband.

LADY TEAZLE. Do you think so?

JOSEPH. Oh! I am sure on't; and then you would find all scandal would cease at once, for, in short, your character at present is like a person in a plethora, absolutely dying from too much health.

LADY TEAZLE. So, so; then I perceive your prescription is, that I must sin in my own defence, and part with my virtue to secure my reputation?

JOSEPH. Exactly so, upon my credit, ma'am.

LADY TEAZLE. Well, certainly this is the oddest doctrine, and the newest receipt for avoiding calumny!

JOSEPH. An infallible one, believe me. Prudence, like experience, must be paid for.

LADY TEAZLE. Why, if my understanding were once convinced——

JOSEPH. Oh, certainly, madam, your understanding should be convinced.—Yes, yes—Heaven forbid I should persuade you to do anything you thought wrong. No, no, I have too much honour to desire it.

LADY TEAZLE. Don't you think we may as well leave *honour* out of the question?

JOSEPH. Ah! the ill effects of your country education, I see, still remain with you.

JOSEPH. Hold!—See whether it is or not before you go to the door: I have a particular message for you, if it should be my brother.
SERVANT. 'Tis her ladyship, sir; she always leaves her chair at the milliner's in the next street.
JOSEPH. Stay, stay; draw that screen before the window—that will do;—my opposite neighbour is a maiden lady of so anxious a temper.—

SERVANT *draws the screen, and exit.*

I have a difficult hand to play in this affair. Lady Teazle has lately suspected my views on Maria; but she must by no means be let into that secret,—at least, till I have her more in my power.

Enter LADY TEAZLE.

LADY TEAZLE. What, sentiment in soliloquy now? Have you been very impatient?—O Lud! don't pretend to look grave.—I vow I couldn't come before.
JOSEPH. Oh, madam, punctuality is a species of constancy, a very unfashionable quality in a lady.
LADY TEAZLE. Upon my word, you ought to pity me. Do you know Sir Peter is grown so ill-natured to me of late, and so jealous of Charles too—that's the best of the story, isn't it?
JOSEPH. I am glad my scandalous friends keep that up. [*Aside.*
LADY TEAZLE. I am sure I wish he would let Maria marry him, and then perhaps he would be convinced; don't you, Mr. Surface?
JOSEPH. Indeed I do not. [*Aside.*]—Oh, certainly I do! for then my dear Lady Teazle would also be convinced, how wrong her suspicions were of my having any design on the silly girl.
LADY TEAZLE. Well, well, I'm inclined to believe you. But isn't it provoking, to have the most ill-natured things said of one?—And there's my friend Lady Sneerwell has circulated I don't know how many scandalous tales of me, and all without any foundation too—that's what vexes me.
JOSEPH. Ay, madam, to be sure, that is the provoking circumstance—without foundation; yes, yes, there's the mortification, indeed; for when a scandalous story is believed against one, there certainly is no comfort like the consciousness of having deserved it.
LADY TEAZLE. No, to be sure, then I'd forgive their malice; but to attack me, who am really so innocent, and who never say an ill-natured thing of anybody—that is, of any friend; and then Sir Peter too, to have him so peevish, and so suspicious, when I know the integrity of my own heart—indeed 'tis monstrous!
JOSEPH. But, my dear Lady Teazle, 'tis your own fault if you suffer it. When

ROWLEY. And I left a hosier and two tailors in the hall, who, I'm sure, won't be paid, and this hundred would satisfy them.

SIR OLIVER. Well, well, I'll pay his debts, and his benevolence too.—But now I am no more a broker, and you shall introduce me to the elder brother as old Stanley.

ROWLEY. Not yet a while; Sir Peter, I know, means to call there about this time.

Enter TRIP.

TRIP. Oh, gentlemen, I beg pardon for not showing you out; this way——Moses, a word.

Exeunt TRIP *and* MOSES.

SIR OLIVER. There's a fellow for you—would you believe it, that puppy intercepted the Jew on our coming, and wanted to raise money before he got to his master.

ROWLEY. Indeed!

SIR OLIVER. Yes, they are now planning an annuity business.—Ah! Master Rowley, in my days servants were content with the follies of their masters, when they were worn a little threadbare; but now, they have their vices, like their birthday clothes, with the gloss on.

Exeunt.

Scene III.—A Library

JOSEPH SURFACE *and a* SERVANT.

JOSEPH. No letter from Lady Teazle?

SERVANT. No, sir.

JOSEPH. I am surprised she has not sent, if she is prevented from coming. Sir Peter certainly does not suspect me. Yet, I wish I may not lose the heiress, through the scrape I have drawn myself into with the wife; however, Charles's imprudence and bad character are great points in my favour.

Knocking heard without.

SERVANT. Sir, I believe that must be Lady Teazle.

ROWLEY. There's no making you serious a moment.
CHARLES. Yes, faith, I am so now. Here, my honest Rowley, here, get me this changed directly, and take a hundred pounds of it immediately to old Stanley.
ROWLEY. A hundred pounds! Consider only——
CHARLES. Gad's life, don't talk about it: poor Stanley's wants are pressing, and if you don't make haste, we shall have some one call that has a better right to the money.
ROWLEY. Ah! there's the point! I never will cease dunning you with the old proverb——
CHARLES. "Be just before you're generous."—Why, so I would if I could; but Justice is an old lame hobbling beldame, and I can't get her to keep pace with Generosity for the soul of me.
ROWLEY. Yet, Charles, believe me, one hour's reflection——
CHARLES. Ay, ay, it's all very true; but, hark'ee, Rowley, while I have, by Heaven I'll give; so damn your economy, and now for hazard.

Exeunt.

Scene II.—*The Parlour*

Enter SIR OLIVER SURFACE *and* MOSES.

MOSES. Well, sir, I think, as Sir Peter said, you have seen Mr. Charles in high glory; 'tis great pity he's so extravagant.
SIR OLIVER. True, but he would not sell my picture.
MOSES. And loves wine and women so much.
SIR OLIVER. But he would not sell my picture.
MOSES. And games so deep.
SIR OLIVER. But he would not sell my picture.——Oh, here's Rowley.

Enter ROWLEY.

ROWLEY. So, Sir Oliver, I find you have made a purchase——
SIR OLIVER. Yes, yes, our young rake has parted with his ancestors like old tapestry.
ROWLEY. And here has he commissioned me to re-deliver you part of the purchase-money—I mean, though, in your necessitous character of old Stanley.
MOSES. Ah! there is the pity of all; he is so damned charitable.

CHARLES. Zounds! no!—I tell you once more.
SIR OLIVER. Then never mind the difference, we'll balance that another time—but give me your hand on the bargain; you are an honest fellow, Charles—I beg pardon, sir, for being so free.—Come, Moses.
CHARLES. Egad, this is a whimsical old fellow! But hark'ee, Premium, you'll prepare lodgings for these gentlemen.
SIR OLIVER. Yes, yes, I'll send for them in a day or two.
CHARLES. But, hold; do now send a genteel conveyance for them, for, I assure you, they were most of them used to ride in their own carriages.
SIR OLIVER. I will, I will—for all but Oliver.
CHARLES. Ay, all but the little nabob.
SIR OLIVER. You're fixed on that?
CHARLES. Peremptorily.
SIR OLIVER. A dear extravagant rogue! [*Aside.*]—Good-day!—Come, Moses.——Let me hear now who calls him profligate!

Exeunt SIR OLIVER SURFACE *and* MOSES.

CARELESS. Why, this is the oddest genius of the sort I ever saw!
CHARLES. Egad, he's the prince of brokers, I think. I wonder how Moses got acquainted with so honest a fellow.—Hah! here's Rowley; do, Careless, say I'll join the company in a few moments.
CARELESS. I will—but don't let that old blockhead persuade you to squander any of that money on old musty debts, or any such nonsense; for tradesmen, Charles, are the most exorbitant fellows.
CHARLES. Very true, and paying them is only encouraging them.
CARELESS. Nothing else.
CHARLES. Ay, ay, never fear. [*Exit* CARELESS.]—Soh! this was an odd old fellow, indeed.——Let me see—two-thirds of this is mine by right, five hundred and thirty odd pounds. 'Fore Heaven! I find one's ancestors are more valuable relations than I took them for!—Ladies and gentlemen, your most obedient and very grateful servant.——

Enter ROWLEY.

Hah! old Rowley! egad, you are just come in time to take leave of your old acquaintance.
ROWLEY. Yes, I heard they were a-going. But I wonder you can have such spirits under so many distresses.
CHARLES. Why, there's the point! my distresses are so many, that I can't afford to part with my spirits; but I shall be rich and splenetic, all in good time. However, I suppose you are surprised that I am not more sorrowful at parting with so many near relations; to be sure 'tis very affecting: but you see they never move a muscle, so why should I?

CHARLES. Here's a jolly fellow—I don't know what relation, but he was mayor of Manchester: take him at eight pounds.

SIR OLIVER. No, no; six will do for the mayor.

CHARLES. Come, make it guineas, and I'll throw you the two aldermen there into the bargain.

SIR OLIVER. They're mine.

CHARLES. Careless, knock down the mayor and aldermen.——But plague on't, we shall be all day retailing in this manner; do let us deal wholesale: what say you, little Premium? Give us three hundred pounds for the rest of the family in the lump.

CARELESS. Ay, ay, that will be the best way.

SIR OLIVER. Well, well, anything to accommodate you;—they are mine. But there is one portrait which you have always passed over.

CARELESS. What, that ill-looking little fellow over the settee?

SIR OLIVER. Yes, sir, I mean that, though I don't think him so ill-looking a little fellow, by any means.

CHARLES. What, that?—Oh! that's my Uncle Oliver; 'twas done before he went to India.

CARELESS. Your Uncle Oliver!—Gad, then you'll never be friends, Charles. That, now, to me, is as stern a looking rogue as ever I saw; an unforgiving eye, and a damned disinheriting countenance! an inveterate knave, depend on't. Don't you think so, little Premium?

SIR OLIVER. Upon my soul, sir, I do not; I think it is as honest a looking face as any in the room, dead or alive;—but I suppose Uncle Oliver goes with the rest of the lumber?

CHARLES. No, hang it; I'll not part with poor Noll. The old fellow has been very good to me, and, egad, I'll keep his picture while I've a room to put it in.

SIR OLIVER. The rogue's my nephew after all! [*Aside*.]—But, sir, I have somehow taken a fancy to that picture.

CHARLES. I'm sorry for't, for you certainly will not have it.—Oons, haven't you got enough of them?

SIR OLIVER. I forgive him everything! [*Aside*.]—But, sir, when I take a whim in my head I don't value money. I'll give you as much for that as for all the rest.

CHARLES. Don't tease me, master broker; I tell you I'll not part with it, and there's an end of it.

SIR OLIVER. How like his father the dog is! [*Aside*.]—Well, well, I have done.——I did not perceive it before, but I think I never saw such a striking resemblance—[*Aside*.]——Here is a draft for your sum.

CHARLES. Why, 'tis for eight hundred pounds.

SIR OLIVER. You will not let Sir Oliver go?

Raveline, a marvellous good general in his day, I assure you. He served in all the Duke of Marlborough's wars, and got that cut over his eye at the battle of Malplaquet.—What say you, Mr. Premium?—look at him—there's a hero, not cut out of his feathers, as your modern clipt captains are, but enveloped in wig and regimentals, as a general should be.—What do you bid?

MOSES. Mr. Premium would have *you* speak.

CHARLES. Why, then, he shall have him for ten pounds, and I'm sure that's not dear for a staff-officer.

SIR OLIVER. Heaven deliver me! his famous Uncle Richard for ten pounds! [*Aside.*]—Well, sir, I take him at that.

CHARLES. Careless, knock down my Uncle Richard.—Here, now, is a maiden sister of his, my great-aunt Deborah, done by Kneller, thought to be in his best manner, and a very formidable likeness.—There she is, you see, a shepherdess feeding her flock.—You shall have her for five pounds ten—the sheep are worth the money.

SIR OLIVER. Ah! poor Deborah! a woman who set such a value on herself! [*Aside.*]—Five pounds ten—she's mine.

CHARLES. Knock down my Aunt Deborah!—Here, now, are two that were a sort of cousins of theirs. You see, Moses, these pictures were done some time ago, when beaux wore wigs, and the ladies their own hair.

SIR OLIVER. Yes, truly, head-dresses appear to have been a little lower in those days.

CHARLES. Well, take that couple for the same.

MOSES. 'Tis good bargain.

CHARLES. Careless!—This, now, is a grandfather of my mother's, a learned judge, well known on the western circuit.—What do you rate him at, Moses?

MOSES. Four guineas.

CHARLES. Four guineas!—Gad's life, you don't bid me the price of his wig.—Mr. Premium, you have more respect for the woolsack; do let us knock his lordship down at fifteen.

SIR OLIVER. By all means.

CARELESS. Gone!

CHARLES. And there are two brothers of his, William and Walter Blunt, Esquires, both members of parliament, and noted speakers, and what's very extraordinary, I believe, this is the first time they were ever bought or sold.

SIR OLIVER. That is very extraordinary, indeed! I'll take them at your own price, for the honour of parliament.

CARELESS. Well said, little Premium!—I'll knock them down at forty.

ACT IV

Scene I.—*Picture Room at* CHARLES'S

Enter CHARLES SURFACE, SIR OLIVER SURFACE, MOSES, *and* CARELESS.

CHARLES. Walk in, gentlemen, pray walk in;—here they are, the family of the Surfaces, up to the Conquest.

SIR OLIVER. And, in my opinion, a goodly collection.

CHARLES. Ay, ay, these are done in the true spirit of portrait painting;—no *volontier grace* and expression. Not like the works of your modern Raphaels, who give you the strongest resemblance, yet contrive to make your portrait independent of you; so that you may sink the original and not hurt the picture.—No, no; the merit of these is the inveterate likeness—all stiff and awkward as the originals, and like nothing in human nature besides.

SIR OLIVER. Ah! we shall never see such figures of men again.

CHARLES. I hope not.——Well, you see, Master Premium, what a domestic character I am; here I sit of an evening surrounded by my family.——But, come, get to your pulpit, Mr. Auctioneer; here's an old gouty chair of my father's will answer the purpose.

CARELESS. Ay, ay, this will do.——But, Charles, I haven't a hammer; and what's an auctioneer without his hammer?

CHARLES. Egad, that's true;—what parchment have we here?—Oh, our genealogy in full. Here, Careless,—you shall have no common bit of mahogany, here's the family tree for you, you rogue,—this shall be your hammer, and now you may knock down my ancestors with their own pedigree.

SIR OLIVER. What an unnatural rogue!—an *ex post facto* parricide! [*Aside.*

CARELESS. Yes, yes, here's a bit of your generation indeed;—faith, Charles, this is the most convenient thing you could have found for the business, for 'twill serve not only as a hammer, but a catalogue into the bargain.——Come, begin——A-going, a-going, a-going!

CHARLES. Bravo, Careless!—Well, here's my great-uncle, Sir Richard

CHARLES. Not much, indeed; unless you have a mind to the family pictures. I have got a room full of ancestors above, and if you have a taste for paintings, egad, you shall have 'em a bargain.
SIR OLIVER. Hey! what the devil! sure, you wouldn't sell your forefathers, would you?
CHARLES. Every man of them to the best bidder.
SIR OLIVER. What! your great-uncles and aunts?
CHARLES. Ay, and my great-grandfathers and grandmothers too.
SIR OLIVER. Now I give him up. [*Aside.*] What the plague, have you no bowels for your own kindred? Odd's life, do you take me for Shylock in the play, that you would raise money of me on your own flesh and blood?
CHARLES. Nay, my little broker, don't be angry: what need you care if you have your money's worth?
SIR OLIVER. Well, I'll be the purchaser: I think I can dispose of the family canvas. Oh, I'll never forgive him this! never! [*Aside.*

Enter CARELESS.

CARELESS. Come, Charles, what keeps you?
CHARLES. I can't come yet: i'faith we are going to have a sale above stairs; here's little Premium will buy all my ancestors.
CARELESS. Oh, burn your ancestors!
CHARLES. No, he may do that afterwards, if he pleases. Stay, Careless, we want you: egad, you shall be auctioneer; so come along with us.
CARELESS. Oh, have with you, if that's the case. Handle a hammer as well as a dice-box!
SIR OLIVER. Oh, the profligates! [*Aside.*]
CHARLES. Come, Moses, you shall be appraiser, if we want one. Gad's life, little Premium, you don't seem to like the business?
SIR OLIVER. Oh yes, I do, vastly. Ha! ha! ha! yes, yes, I think it a rare joke to sell one's family by auction—ha! ha!—Oh, the prodigal! [*Aside.*
CHARLES. To be sure! when a man wants money, where the plague should he get assistance if he can't make free with his own relations?

Exeunt.

SIR OLIVER. Then I believe I should be the most unwelcome dun you ever had in your life.

CHARLES. What! I suppose you're afraid that Sir Oliver is too good a life?

SIR OLIVER. No, indeed, I am not; though I have heard he is as hale and healthy as any man of his years in Christendom.

CHARLES. There again now you are misinformed. No, no, the climate has hurt him considerably, poor Uncle Oliver! Yes, yes, he breaks apace, I'm told—and is so much altered lately, that his nearest relations don't know him.

SIR OLIVER. No! ha! ha! ha! so much altered lately, that his nearest relations don't know him! ha! ha! ha! egad—ha! ha! ha!

CHARLES. Ha! ha!—you're glad to hear that, little Premium?

SIR OLIVER. No, no, I'm not.

CHARLES. Yes, yes, you are—ha! ha! ha!—You know that mends your chance.

SIR OLIVER. But I'm told Sir Oliver is coming over?—nay, some say he is actually arrived?

CHARLES. Pshaw! sure I must know better than you whether he's come or not. No, no, rely on't he's at this moment at Calcutta—isn't he, Moses?

MOSES. Oh yes, certainly.

SIR OLIVER. Very true, as you say, you must know better than I, though I have it from pretty good authority—haven't I, Moses?

MOSES. Yes, most undoubted!

SIR OLIVER. But, sir, as I understand you want a few hundreds immediately—is there nothing you could dispose of?

CHARLES. How do you mean?

SIR OLIVER. For instance, now, I have heard that your father left behind him a great quantity of massy old plate?

CHARLES. O Lud!—that's gone long ago.—Moses can tell you how better than I can.

SIR OLIVER. Good lack! all the family race cups and corporation bowls! [*Aside.*]—Then it was also supposed that his library was one of the most valuable and complete——

CHARLES. Yes, yes, so it was—vastly too much so for a private gentleman. For my part, I was always of a communicative disposition, so I thought it a shame to keep so much knowledge to myself.

SIR OLIVER. Mercy upon me! Learning that had run in the family like an heirloom! [*Aside.*] Pray, what are become of the books?

CHARLES. You must inquire of the auctioneer, Master Premium, for I don't believe even Moses can direct you.

MOSES. I know nothing of books.

SIR OLIVER. So, so, nothing of the family property left, I suppose?

SIR OLIVER. Exceeding frank, upon my word.—I see, sir, you are not a man of many compliments.
CHARLES. Oh no, sir! plain dealing in business I always think best.
SIR OLIVER. Sir, I like you the better for it—however, you are mistaken in one thing; I have no money to lend, but I believe I could procure some of a friend; but then he's an unconscionable dog, isn't he, Moses?
MOSES. But you can't help that.
SIR OLIVER. And must sell stock to accommodate you—mustn't he, Moses?
MOSES. Yes, indeed! You know I always speak the truth, and scorn to tell a lie!
CHARLES. Right. People that speak truth generally do: but these are trifles, Mr. Premium. What! I know money isn't to be bought without paying for't!
SIR OLIVER. Well—but what security could you give? You have no land, I suppose?
CHARLES. Not a mole-hill, nor a twig, but what's in the bough-pots out of the window!
SIR OLIVER. Nor any stock, I presume?
CHARLES. Nothing but live stock—and that's only a few pointers and ponies. But pray, Mr. Premium, are you acquainted at all with any of my connections?
SIR OLIVER. Why, to say truth, I am.
CHARLES. Then you must know that I have a dev'lish rich uncle in the East Indies, Sir Oliver Surface, from whom I have the greatest expectations?
SIR OLIVER. That you have a wealthy uncle I have heard; but how your expectations will turn out is more, I believe, than you can tell.
CHARLES. Oh no!—there can be no doubt. They tell me I'm a prodigious favourite, and that he talks of leaving me everything.
SIR OLIVER. Indeed! this is the first I've heard of it.
CHARLES. Yes, yes, 'tis just so—Moses knows 'tis true, don't you, Moses?
MOSES. Oh yes! I'll swear to't.
SIR OLIVER. Egad, they'll persuade me presently I'm at Bengal. [*Aside*.
CHARLES. Now I propose, Mr. Premium, if it's agreeable to you, a post-obit on Sir Oliver's life; though at the same time the old fellow has been so liberal to me, that I give you my word, I should be very sorry to hear that anything had happened to him.
SIR OLIVER. Not more than I should, I assure you. But the bond you mention happens to be just the worst security you could offer me—for I might live to a hundred, and never see the principal.
CHARLES. Oh yes, you would—the moment Sir Oliver dies, you know, you would come on me for the money.

MOSES. *Success to usury!*
CARELESS. Right, Moses—usury is prudence and industry, and deserves to succeed.
SIR OLIVER. Then—*here's all the success it deserves!*
CARELESS. No, no, that won't do! Mr. Premium, you have demurred at the toast, and must drink it in a pint bumper.
1ST GENTLEMAN. A pint bumper, at least.
MOSES. Oh, pray, sir, consider—Mr. Premium's a gentleman.
CARELESS. And therefore loves good wine.
2ND GENTLEMAN. Give Moses a quart glass—this is mutiny, and a high contempt for the chair.
CARELESS. Here, now for't! I'll see justice done, to the last drop of my bottle.
SIR OLIVER. Nay, pray, gentlemen—I did not expect this usage.
CHARLES. No, hang it, you shan't! Mr. Premium's a stranger.
SIR OLIVER. Odd! I wish I was well out of their company. [*Aside.*

CARELESS. Plague on 'em then!—if they don't drink, we'll not sit down with them. Come, Harry, the dice are in the next room—Charles, you'll join us when you have finished your business with the gentlemen?
CHARLES. I will! I will!

Exeunt.

Careless!

CARELESS. [*Returning.*] Well!
CHARLES. Perhaps I may want you.
CARELESS. Oh, you know I am always ready: word, note, or bond, 'tis all the same to me.

Exit.

MOSES. Sir, this is Mr. Premium, a gentleman of the strictest honour and secrecy; and always performs what he undertakes. Mr. Premium, this is——
CHARLES. Pshaw! have done.—Sir, my friend Moses is a very honest fellow, but a little slow at expression: he'll be an hour giving us our titles. Mr. Premium, the plain state of the matter is this: I am an extravagant young fellow who wants to borrow money—you I take to be a prudent old fellow, who have got money to lend.—I am blockhead enough to give 50 per cent sooner than not have it; and you, I presume, are rogue enough to take a hundred if you can get it. Now, sir, you see we are acquainted at once, and may proceed to business without further ceremony.

Chorus.   Let the toast pass, etc.

        Here's to the maid with a bosom of snow;
           Now to her that's as brown as a berry:
        Here's to the wife with a face full of woe,
           And now to the girl that is merry.

Chorus.   Let the toast pass, etc.

        For let 'em be clumsy, or let 'em be slim,
           Young or ancient, I care not a feather;
        So fill a pint bumper quite up to the brim,
           And let us e'en toast them together.

Chorus.   Let the toast pass, etc.

ALL. Bravo! bravo!

Enter TRIP, *and whispers* CHARLES SURFACE.

CHARLES. Gentlemen, you must excuse me a little. Careless, take the chair, will you?

CARELESS. Nay, prithee, Charles, what now? This is one of your peerless beauties, I suppose, has dropt in by chance?

CHARLES. No, faith! To tell you the truth, 'tis a Jew and a broker, who are come by appointment.

CARELESS. Oh, damn it! let's have the Jew in.

1ST GENTLEMAN. Ay, and the broker too, by all means.

2ND GENTLEMAN. Yes, yes, the Jew and the broker.

CHARLES. Egad, with all my heart! Trip, bid the gentlemen walk in—though there's one of them a stranger, I can tell you.

Exit TRIP.

CARELESS. Charles, let us give them some generous Burgundy, and perhaps they'll grow conscientious.

CHARLES. Oh, hang 'em, no! wine does but draw forth a man's natural qualities; and to make them drink would only be to whet their knavery.

Enter TRIP, SIR OLIVER SURFACE, *and* MOSES.

CHARLES. So, honest Moses, walk in: walk in, pray, Mr. Premium—that's the gentleman's name, isn't it, Moses?

MOSES. Yes, sir.

CHARLES. Set chairs, Trip—sit down, Mr. Premium—glasses, Trip—sit down, Moses. Come, Mr. Premium, I'll give you a sentiment; here's *Success to usury!*—Moses, fill the gentleman a bumper.

for the course by keeping him from corn? For my part, egad, I am never so successful as when I am a little merry: let me throw on a bottle of Champagne, and I never lose—at least, I never feel my losses, which is exactly the same thing.
2ND GENTLEMAN. Ay, that I believe.
CHARLES. And then, what man can pretend to be a believer in love, who is an abjurer of wine? 'Tis the test by which the lover knows his own heart. Fill a dozen bumpers to a dozen beauties, and she that floats atop is the maid that has bewitched you.
CARELESS. Now then, Charles, be honest, and give us your real favourite.
CHARLES. Why, I have withheld her only in compassion to you. If I toast her, you must give a round of her peers, which is impossible—on earth.
CARELESS. Oh! then we'll find some canonised vestals or heathen goddesses that will do, I warrant!
CHARLES. Here then, bumpers, you rogues! bumpers! Maria! Maria!—
SIR HARRY. Maria who?
CHARLES. Oh, damn the surname—'tis too formal to be registered in Love's calendar; but now, Sir Harry, beware, we must have beauty superlative.
CARELESS. Nay, never study, Sir Harry: we'll stand to the toast, though your mistress should want an eye, and you know you have a song will excuse you.
SIR HARRY. Egad, so I have! and I'll give him the song instead of the lady.

SONG

Here's to the maiden of bashful fifteen;
   Here's to the widow of fifty;
Here's to the flaunting extravagant quean,
   And here's to the housewife that's thrifty.

Chorus.　　　　　Let the toast pass,—
        Drink to the lass,
I'll warrant she'll prove an excuse for the glass.

Here's to the charmer whose dimples we prize;
   Now to the maid who has none, sir:
Here's to the girl with a pair of blue eyes,
   And here's to the nymph with but *one*, sir.

TRIP. Oh, with all my heart! I'll insure my place, and my life too, if you please.
SIR OLIVER. It's more than I would your neck. [*Aside.*
MOSES. But is there nothing you could deposit?
TRIP. Why, nothing capital of my master's wardrobe has dropped lately; but I could give you a mortgage on some of his winter clothes, with equity of redemption before November—or you shall have the reversion of the French velvet, or a post-obit on the blue and silver:—these, I should think, Moses, with a few pair of point ruffles, as a collateral security—hey, my little fellow?
MOSES. Well, well.

Bell rings.

TRIP. Egad, I heard the bell! I believe, gentlemen, I can now introduce you. Don't forget the annuity, little Moses! This way, gentlemen. I'll insure my place, you know.
SIR OLIVER. If the man be a shadow of the master, this is the temple of dissipation indeed!

Exeunt.

Scene III.—CHARLES SURFACE, CARELESS, *etc. etc., at a table with wine, etc.*

CHARLES. 'Fore heaven, 'tis true!—there's the great degeneracy of the age. Many of our acquaintance have taste, spirit, and politeness; but, plague on't, they won't drink.
CARELESS. It is so indeed, Charles! they give into all the substantial luxuries of the table, and abstain from nothing but wine and wit. Oh, certainly society suffers by it intolerably; for now, instead of the social spirit of raillery that used to mantle over a glass of bright Burgundy, their conversation is become just like the Spa water they drink, which has all the pertness and flatulence of Champagne, without the spirit or flavour.
1ST GENTLEMAN. But what are they to do who love play better than wine?
CARELESS. True: there's Sir Harry diets himself for gaming, and is now under a hazard regimen.
CHARLES. Then he'll have the worst of it. What! you wouldn't train a horse

MOSES. Mr. Premium.
TRIP. Premium—very well.

Exit TRIP, *taking snuff.*

SIR OLIVER. To judge by the servants, one wouldn't believe the master was ruined. But what!—sure, this was my brother's house?
MOSES. Yes, sir; Mr. Charles bought it of Mr. Joseph, with the furniture, pictures, etc., just as the old gentleman left it. Sir Peter thought it a piece of extravagance in him.
SIR OLIVER. In my mind, the other's economy in selling it to him was more reprehensible by half.

Enter TRIP.

TRIP. My master says you must wait, gentlemen: he has company, and can't speak with you yet.
SIR OLIVER. If he knew who it was wanted to see him, perhaps he would not send such a message?
TRIP. Yes, yes, sir; he knows you are here—I did not forget little Premium: no, no, no.
SIR OLIVER. Very well; and I pray, sir, what may be your name?
TRIP. Trip, sir; my name is Trip, at your service.
SIR OLIVER. Well then, Mr. Trip, you have a pleasant sort of place here, I guess?
TRIP. Why, yes—here are three or four of us pass our time agreeably enough; but then our wages are sometimes a little in arrear—and not very great either—but fifty pounds a year, and find our own bags and bouquets.
SIR OLIVER. Bags and bouquets! halters and bastinadoes! [*Aside.*
TRIP. And, *à-propos*, Moses—have you been able to get me that little bill discounted?
SIR OLIVER. Wants to raise money too!—mercy on me! Has his distresses too, I warrant, like a lord, and affects creditors and duns. [*Aside.*
MOSES. 'Twas not to be done, indeed, Mr. Trip.
TRIP. Good lack, you surprise me! My friend Brush has indorsed it, and I thought when he put his name at the back of a bill 'twas the same as cash.
MOSES. No! 'twouldn't do.
TRIP. A small sum—but twenty pounds. Hark'ee, Moses, do you think you couldn't get it me by way of annuity?
SIR OLIVER. An annuity! ha! ha! a footman raise money by way of annuity! Well done, luxury, egad! [*Aside.*
MOSES. Well, but you must insure your place.

SIR PETER. No, no, madam: 'tis evident you never cared a pin for me, and I was a madman to marry you—a pert, rural coquette, that had refused half the honest 'squires in the neighbourhood.

LADY TEAZLE. And I am sure I was a fool to marry you—an old dangling bachelor, who was single at fifty, only because he never could meet with any one who would have him.

SIR PETER. Ay, ay, madam; but you were pleased enough to listen to me: you never had such an offer before.

LADY TEAZLE. No! didn't I refuse Sir Tivy Terrier, who everybody said would have been a better match? for his estate is just as good as yours, and he has broke his neck since we have been married.

SIR PETER. I have done with you, madam! You are an unfeeling, ungrateful—but there's an end of everything. I believe you capable of everything that is bad.—Yes, madam, I now believe the reports relative to you and Charles, madam.—Yes, madam, *you* and Charles are—not without grounds——

LADY TEAZLE. Take care, Sir Peter! you had better not insinuate any such thing! I'll not be suspected without cause, I promise you.

SIR PETER. Very well, madam! very well! A separate maintenance as soon as you please. Yes, madam, or a divorce!—I'll make an example of myself for the benefit of all old bachelors.—Let us separate, madam.

LADY TEAZLE. Agreed! agreed!—And now, my dear Sir Peter, we are of a mind once more, we may be the happiest couple—and never differ again, you know—ha! ha! ha! Well, you are going to be in a passion, I see, and I shall only interrupt you—so, bye—bye.

Exit.

SIR PETER. Plagues and tortures! Can't I make her angry either! Oh, I am the most miserable fellow! but I'll not bear her presuming to keep her temper: no! she may break my heart, but she shan't keep her temper.

Exit.

Scene II.—CHARLES SURFACE'S *House*

Enter TRIP, MOSES, *and* SIR OLIVER SURFACE.

TRIP. Here, Master Moses! if you'll stay a moment, I'll try whether—what's the gentleman's name?

SIR OLIVER. Mr. Moses, what is my name?

LADY TEAZLE. I assure you, Sir Peter, good-nature becomes you—you look now as you did before we were married, when you used to walk with me under the elms, and tell me stories of what a gallant you were in your youth, and chuck me under the chin, you would; and ask me if I thought I could love an old fellow, who would deny me nothing—didn't you?

SIR PETER. Yes, yes, and you were as kind and attentive——

LADY TEAZLE. Ay—so I was, and would always take your part, when my acquaintance used to abuse you, and turn you into ridicule.

SIR PETER. Indeed!

LADY TEAZLE. Ay, and when my cousin Sophy has called you a stiff, peevish old bachelor, and laughed at me for thinking of marrying one who might be my father, I have always defended you, and said, I didn't think you so ugly by any means, and I dared say you'd make a very good sort of a husband.

SIR PETER. And you prophesied right; and we shall now be the happiest couple——

LADY TEAZLE. And never differ again?

SIR PETER. No, never!—though at the same time, indeed, my dear Lady Teazle, you must watch your temper very seriously; for in all our little quarrels, my dear, if you recollect, my love, you always began first.

LADY TEAZLE. I beg your pardon, my dear Sir Peter: indeed, you always gave the provocation.

SIR PETER. Now see, my angel! take care—contradicting isn't the way to keep friends.

LADY TEAZLE. Then don't you begin it, my love!

SIR PETER. There, now! you—you are going on. You don't perceive, my life, that you are just doing the very thing which you know always makes me angry.

LADY TEAZLE. Nay, you know if you will be angry without any reason, my dear——

SIR PETER. There! now you want to quarrel again.

LADY TEAZLE. No, I am sure I don't:—but if you will be so peevish——

SIR PETER. There now! who begins first?

LADY TEAZLE. Why you, to be sure. I said nothing—but there's no bearing your temper.

SIR PETER. No, no, madam: the fault's in your own temper.

LADY TEAZLE. Ay, you are just what my cousin Sophy said you would be.

SIR PETER. Your cousin Sophy is a forward, impertinent gipsy.

LADY TEAZLE. You are a great bear, I'm sure, to abuse my relations.

SIR PETER. Now may all the plagues of marriage be doubled on me, if ever I try to be friends with you any more!

LADY TEAZLE. So much the better.

understanding severely condemns his vices, my heart suggests some pity for his distresses.

Sir Peter. Well, well, pity him as much as you please; but give your heart and hand to a worthier object.

Maria. Never to his brother!

Sir Peter. Go—perverse and obstinate! but take care, madam; you have never yet known what the authority of a guardian is: don't compel me to inform you of it.

Maria. I can only say, you shall not have just reason. 'Tis true, by my father's will, I am for a short period bound to regard you as his substitute; but must cease to think you so, when you would compel me to be miserable.

Exit Maria.

Sir Peter. Was ever man so crossed as I am? everything conspiring to fret me! I had not been involved in matrimony a fortnight, before her father, a hale and hearty man, died, on purpose, I believe, for the pleasure of plaguing me with the care of his daughter. But here comes my helpmate! She appears in great good humour. How happy I should be if I could tease her into loving me, though but a little!

Enter Lady Teazle.

Lady Teazle. Lud! Sir Peter, I hope you haven't been quarrelling with Maria? It is not using me well to be ill-humoured when I am not by.

Sir Peter. Ah! Lady Teazle, you might have the power to make me good-humoured at all times.

Lady Teazle. I am sure I wish I had; for I want you to be in a charming sweet temper at this moment. Do be good-humoured now, and let me have two hundred pounds, will you?

Sir Peter. Two hundred pounds! what, ain't I to be in a good humour without paying for it? But speak to me thus, and i'faith there's nothing I could refuse you. You shall have it; but seal me a bond for the repayment.

Lady Teazle. Oh no—there—my note of hand will do as well. [*Offering her hand.*

Sir Peter. And you shall no longer reproach me with not giving you an independent settlement. I mean shortly to surprise you:—but shall we always live thus, hey?

Lady Teazle. If you please. I'm sure I don't care how soon we leave off quarrelling, provided you'll own you were tired first.

Sir Peter. Well—then let our future contest be, who shall be most obliging.

MOSES. Very much.

ROWLEY. And lament that a young man now must be at years of discretion before he is suffered to ruin himself?

MOSES. Ay, great pity!

SIR PETER. And abuse the public for allowing merit to an act, whose only object is to snatch misfortune and imprudence from the rapacious gripe of usury, and give the minor a chance of inheriting his estate without being undone by coming into possession.

SIR OLIVER. So—so—Moses shall give me further instructions as we go together.

SIR PETER. You will not have much time, for your nephew lives hard by.

SIR OLIVER. Oh! never fear: my tutor appears so able, that though Charles lived in the next street, it must be my own fault if I am not a complete rogue before I turn the corner.

Exeunt SIR OLIVER SURFACE *and* MOSES.

SIR PETER. So, now, I think Sir Oliver will be convinced: you are partial, Rowley, and would have prepared Charles for the other plot.

ROWLEY. No, upon my word, Sir Peter.

SIR PETER. Well, go bring me this Snake, and I'll hear what he has to say presently.—I see Maria, and want to speak with her. [*Exit* ROWLEY.] I should be glad to be convinced my suspicions of Lady Teazle and Charles were unjust. I have never yet opened my mind on this subject to my friend Joseph—I am determined I will do it—he will give me his opinion sincerely.

Enter MARIA.

So, child, has Mr. Surface returned with you?

MARIA. No, sir; he was engaged.

SIR PETER. Well, Maria, do you not reflect, the more you converse with that amiable young man, what return his partiality for you deserves?

MARIA. Indeed, Sir Peter, your frequent importunity on this subject distresses me extremely—you compel me to declare, that I know no man who has ever paid me a particular attention, whom I would not prefer to Mr. Surface.

SIR PETER. So—here's perverseness!—No, no, Maria, 'tis Charles only whom you would prefer. 'Tis evident his vices and follies have won your heart.

MARIA. This is unkind, sir. You know I have obeyed you in neither seeing nor corresponding with him: I have heard enough to convince me that he is unworthy my regard. Yet I cannot think it culpable, if, while my

ROWLEY. Well, this is taking Charles rather at a disadvantage, to be sure;—however, Moses, you understand Sir Peter, and will be faithful?

MOSES. You may depend upon me;—this is near the time I was to have gone.

SIR OLIVER. I'll accompany you as soon as you please, Moses—— But hold! I have forgot one thing—how the plague shall I be able to pass for a Jew?

MOSES. There's no need—the principal is Christian.

SIR OLIVER. Is he? I'm very sorry to hear it. But then again, ain't I rather too smartly dressed to look like a money-lender?

SIR PETER. Not at all; 'twould not be out of character, if you went in your own carriage—would it, Moses?

MOSES. Not in the least.

SIR OLIVER. Well—but how must I talk?—there's certainly some cant of usury and mode of treating that I ought to know.

SIR PETER. Oh! there's not much to learn. The great point, as I take it, is to be exorbitant enough in your demands—hey, Moses?

MOSES. Yes, that's a very great point.

SIR OLIVER. I'll answer for't I'll not be wanting in that. I'll ask him 8 or 10 per cent on the loan, at least.

MOSES. If you ask him no more than that, you'll be discovered immediately.

SIR OLIVER. Hey!—what the plague!—how much then?

MOSES. That depends upon the circumstances. If he appears not very anxious for the supply, you should require only 40 or 50 per cent; but if you find him in great distress, and want the moneys very bad, you may ask double.

SIR PETER. A good honest trade you're learning, Sir Oliver!

SIR OLIVER. Truly, I think so—and not unprofitable.

MOSES. Then, you know, you haven't the moneys yourself, but are forced to borrow them for him of an old friend.

SIR OLIVER. Oh! I borrow it of a friend, do I?

MOSES. And your friend is an unconscionable dog: but you can't help that.

SIR OLIVER. My friend an unconscionable dog?

MOSES. Yes, and he himself has not the moneys by him, but is forced to sell stock at a great loss.

SIR OLIVER. He is forced to sell stock at a great loss, is he? Well, that's very kind of him.

SIR PETER. I'faith, Sir Oliver—Mr. Premium, I mean, you'll soon be master of the trade. But, Moses! would not you have him run out a little against the Annuity Bill? That would be in character, I should think.

has done everything in his power to bring your nephew to a proper sense of his extravagance.

SIR PETER. Pray let us have him in.

ROWLEY. Desire Mr. Moses to walk upstairs. [*Apart to* SERVANT.

SIR PETER. But, pray, why should you suppose he will speak the truth?

ROWLEY. Oh! I have convinced him that he has no chance of recovering certain sums advanced to Charles, but through the bounty of Sir Oliver, who he knows is arrived; so that you may depend on his fidelity to his own interests: I have also another evidence in my power, one Snake, whom I have detected in a matter little short of forgery, and shall speedily produce him to remove some of your prejudices.

SIR PETER. I have heard too much on that subject.

ROWLEY. Here comes the honest Israelite.—

Enter MOSES.

—This is Sir Oliver.

SIR OLIVER. Sir, I understand you have lately had great dealings with my nephew, Charles.

MOSES. Yes, Sir Oliver, I have done all I could for him; but he was ruined before he came to me for assistance.

SIR OLIVER. That was unlucky, truly; for you have had no opportunity of showing your talents.

MOSES. None at all; I hadn't the pleasure of knowing his distresses till he was some thousands worse than nothing.

SIR OLIVER. Unfortunate, indeed!—But I suppose you have done all in your power for him, honest Moses?

MOSES. Yes, he knows that;—this very evening I was to have brought him a gentleman from the city, who does not know him, and will, I believe, advance him some money.

SIR PETER. What,—one Charles has never had money from before?

MOSES. Yes,—Mr. Premium, of Crutched Friars, formerly a broker.

SIR PETER. Egad, Sir Oliver, a thought strikes me!——Charles, you say, does not know Mr. Premium?

MOSES. Not at all.

SIR PETER. Now then, Sir Oliver, you may have a better opportunity of satisfying yourself than by an old romancing tale of a poor relation: go with my friend Moses, and represent Premium, and then, I'll answer for it, you'll see your nephew in all his glory.

SIR OLIVER. Egad, I like this idea better than the other, and I may visit Joseph afterwards as old Stanley.

SIR PETER. True—so you may.

ACT III

Scene I.—SIR PETER TEAZLE's

Enter SIR PETER TEAZLE, SIR OLIVER SURFACE, *and* ROWLEY.

SIR PETER. Well, then, we will see this fellow first, and have our wine afterwards:—but how is this, Master Rowley? I don't see the jet of your scheme.

ROWLEY. Why, sir, this Mr. Stanley, whom I was speaking of, is nearly related to them by their mother. He was a merchant in Dublin, but has been ruined by a series of undeserved misfortunes. He has applied, by letter, to Mr. Surface and Charles: from the former he has received nothing but evasive promises of future service, while Charles has done all that his extravagance has left him power to do; and he is, at this time, endeavouring to raise a sum of money, part of which, in the midst of his own distresses, I know he intends for the service of poor Stanley.

SIR OLIVER. Ah!—he is my brother's son.

SIR PETER. Well, but how is Sir Oliver personally to——

ROWLEY. Why, sir, I will inform Charles and his brother, that Stanley has obtained permission to apply personally to his friends, and as they have neither of them ever seen him, let Sir Oliver assume his character, and he will have a fair opportunity of judging, at least, of the benevolence of their dispositions; and believe me, sir, you will find in the youngest brother, one, who, in the midst of folly and dissipation, has still, as our immortal bard expresses it,—"a heart to pity, and a hand, open as day, for melting charity."

SIR PETER. Pshaw! What signifies his having an open hand or purse either, when he has nothing left to give? Well, well—make the trial, if you please. But where is the fellow whom you brought for Sir Oliver to examine, relative to Charles's affairs?

ROWLEY. Below, waiting his commands, and no one can give him better intelligence. This, Sir Oliver, is a friendly Jew, who, to do him justice, mistake me, Sir Peter; I don't mean to defend Charles's errors: but before I form my judgment of either of them, I intend to make a trial of their hearts; and my friend Rowley and I have planned something for the purpose.

ROWLEY. And Sir Peter shall own for once he has been mistaken.

SIR PETER. Oh! my life on Joseph's honour.

SIR OLIVER. Well—come, give us a bottle of good wine, and we'll drink the lads' health, and tell you our scheme.

SIR PETER. *Allons* then!

SIR OLIVER. And don't, Sir Peter, be so severe against your old friend's son. Odds my life! I am not sorry that he has run out of the course a little: for my part, I hate to see prudence clinging to the green suckers of youth; 'tis like ivy round a sapling, and spoils the growth of the tree.

Exeunt.

ROWLEY. Then, my life on't, you will reclaim him.——Ah, sir! it gives me new life to find that *your* heart is not turned against him; and that the son of my good old master has one friend, however, left.

SIR OLIVER. What, shall I forget, Master Rowley, when I was at his years myself?—Egad, my brother and I were neither of us very prudent youths; and yet, I believe, you have not seen many better men than your old master was.

ROWLEY. Sir, 'tis this reflection gives me assurance that Charles may yet be a credit to his family.—But here comes Sir Peter.

SIR OLIVER. Egad, so he does.—Mercy on me!—he's greatly altered—and seems to have a settled married look! One may read *husband* in his face at this distance!

Enter SIR PETER TEAZLE.

SIR PETER. Hah! Sir Oliver—my old friend! Welcome to England a thousand times!

SIR OLIVER. Thank you—thank you, Sir Peter! and i'faith I am glad to find you well, believe me.

SIR PETER. Oh! 'tis a long time since we met—fifteen years, I doubt, Sir Oliver, and many a cross accident in the time.

SIR OLIVER. Ay, I have had my share.—But, what! I find you are married, hey?—Well, well—it can't be helped—and so—I wish you joy with all my heart.

SIR PETER. Thank you, thank you, Sir Oliver.—Yes, I have entered into—the happy state;—but we'll not talk of that now.

SIR OLIVER. True, true, Sir Peter: old friends should not begin on grievances at first meeting—no, no, no.—

ROWLEY. Take care, pray, sir.—

SIR OLIVER. Well—so one of my nephews is a wild fellow, hey?

SIR PETER. Wild!—Ah! my old friend, I grieve for your disappointment there; he's a lost young man, indeed. However, his brother will make you amends; Joseph is, indeed, what a youth should be. Everybody in the world speaks well of him.

SIR OLIVER. I am sorry to hear it; he has too good a character to be an honest fellow. Everybody speaks well of him!—Pshaw! then he has bowed as low to knaves and fools as to the honest dignity of genius and virtue.

SIR PETER. What, Sir Oliver! do you blame him for not making enemies?

SIR OLIVER. Yes, if he has merit enough to deserve them.

SIR PETER. Well, well—you'll be convinced when you know him. 'Tis edification to hear him converse; he professes the noblest sentiments.

SIR OLIVER. Oh! plague of his sentiments! If he salutes me with a scrap of morality in his mouth, I shall be sick directly.—But, however, don't

JOSEPH. But we had best not return together.

LADY TEAZLE. Well—don't stay; for Maria shan't come to hear any more of your reasoning, I promise you.

Exit LADY TEAZLE.

JOSEPH. A curious dilemma my politics have run me into! I wanted, at first, only to ingratiate myself with Lady Teazle, that she might not be my enemy with Maria; and I have, I don't know how, become her serious lover. Sincerely I begin to wish I had never made such a point of gaining so very good a character, for it has led me into so many cursed rogueries that I doubt I shall be exposed at last.

Exit.

Scene III.—SIR PETER TEAZLE'S

Enter ROWLEY *and* SIR OLIVER SURFACE.

SIR OLIVER. Ha! ha! ha! So my old friend is married, hey?—a young wife out of the country.—Ha! ha! ha! that he should have stood bluff to old bachelor so long, and sink into a husband at last.

ROWLEY. But you must not rally him on the subject, Sir Oliver: 'tis a tender point, I assure you, though he has been married only seven months.

SIR OLIVER. Then he has been just half a year on the stool of repentance!—Poor Peter!——But you say he has entirely given up Charles,—never sees him, hey?

ROWLEY. His prejudice against him is astonishing, and I am sure, greatly increased by a jealousy of him with Lady Teazle, which he has industriously been led into by a scandalous society in the neighbourhood, who have contributed not a little to Charles's ill name. Whereas, the truth is, I believe, if the lady is partial to either of them, his brother is the favourite.

SIR OLIVER. Ay, I know there are a set of malicious, prating, prudent gossips, both male and female, who murder characters to kill time; and will rob a young fellow of his good name, before he has years to know the value of it.—But I am not to be prejudiced against my nephew by such, I promise you.—No, no,—if Charles has done nothing false or mean, I shall compound for his extravagance.

nothing could excuse the intemperance of their tongues, but a natural and uncontrollable bitterness of mind.

JOSEPH. Undoubtedly, madam; and it has always been a sentiment of mine, that to propagate a malicious truth wantonly is more despicable than to falsify from revenge. But can you, Maria, feel thus for others, and be unkind to me alone?—Is hope to be denied the tenderest passion?

MARIA. Why will you distress me by renewing the subject?

JOSEPH. Ah, Maria! you would not treat me thus, and oppose your guardian Sir Peter's will, but that I see that profligate Charles is still a favoured rival.

MARIA. Ungenerously urged!—But whatever my sentiments are for that unfortunate young man, be assured I shall not feel more bound to give him up because his distresses have lost him the regard even of a brother.

JOSEPH. Nay, but, Maria, do not leave me with a frown: by all that's honest, I swear———Gad's life, here's Lady Teazle!—[*Aside.*]———You must not—no, you shall not—for, though I have the greatest regard for Lady Teazle———

MARIA. Lady Teazle!

JOSEPH. Yet were Sir Peter to suspect———

Enter LADY TEAZLE, *and comes forward.*

LADY TEAZLE. What is this, pray? Do you take her for me?—Child, you are wanted in the next room.—[*Exit* MARIA.]—What is all this, pray?

JOSEPH. Oh, the most unlucky circumstance in nature! Maria has somehow suspected the tender concern I have for your happiness, and threatened to acquaint Sir Peter with her suspicions, and I was just endeavouring to reason with her when you came in.

LADY TEAZLE. Indeed! but you seemed to adopt a very tender mode of reasoning—do you usually argue on your knees?

JOSEPH. Oh, she's a child, and I thought a little bombast——— But, Lady Teazle, when are you to give me your judgment on my library, as you promised?

LADY TEAZLE. No, no; I begin to think it would be imprudent, and you know I admit you as a lover no farther than fashion sanctions.

JOSEPH. True—a mere platonic cicisbeo—what every wife is entitled to.

LADY TEAZLE. Certainly, one must not be out of the fashion.—However, I have so much of my country prejudices left, that, though Sir Peter's ill-humour may vex me ever so, it never shall provoke me to———

JOSEPH. The only revenge in your power.—Well—I applaud your moderation.

LADY TEAZLE. Go—you are an insinuating wretch.———But we shall be missed—let us join the company.

reputation of as much importance as poaching on manors, and pass an act for the preservation of fame, I believe there are many would thank them for the bill.

LADY SNEERWELL. O Lud! Sir Peter; would you deprive us of our privileges?

SIR PETER. Ay, madam; and then no person should be permitted to kill characters and run down reputations, but qualified old maids and disappointed widows.

LADY SNEERWELL. Go, you monster!

MRS. CANDOUR. But, surely, you would not be quite so severe on those who only report what they hear?

SIR PETER. Yes, madam, I would have law merchant for them too; and in all cases of slander currency, whenever the drawer of the lie was not to be found, the injured parties should have a right to come on any of the indorsers.

CRABTREE. Well, for my part, I believe there never was a scandalous tale without some foundation.

SIR PETER. Oh, nine out of ten of the malicious inventions are founded on some ridiculous misrepresentation!

LADY SNEERWELL. Come, ladies, shall we sit down to cards in the next room?

Enter a SERVANT, *who whispers* SIR PETER.

SIR PETER. I'll be with them directly.—I'll get away unperceived. [*Apart.*

LADY SNEERWELL. Sir Peter, you are not going to leave us?

SIR PETER. Your ladyship must excuse me; I'm called away by particular business. But I leave my character behind me.

Exit SIR PETER.

SIR BENJAMIN. Well—certainly, Lady Teazle, that lord of yours is a strange being: I could tell you some stories of him would make you laugh heartily if he were not your husband.

LADY TEAZLE. Oh, pray don't mind that;—come, do let's hear them. [*Joins the rest of the company going into the next room.*

JOSEPH. Maria, I see you have no satisfaction in this society.

MARIA. How is it possible I should?—If to raise malicious smiles at the infirmities or misfortunes of those who have never injured us be the province of wit or humour, Heaven grant me a double portion of dulness!

JOSEPH. Yet they appear more ill-natured than they are,—they have no malice at heart.

MARIA. Then is their conduct still more contemptible; for, in my opinion,

LADY TEAZLE. Nay, I vow Lady Stucco is very well with the dessert after dinner; for she's just like the French fruit one cracks for mottoes—made up of paint and proverb.
MRS. CANDOUR. Well, I never will join in ridiculing a friend; and so I constantly tell my cousin Ogle, and you all know what pretensions she has to be critical on beauty.
CRABTREE. Oh, to be sure! she has herself the oddest countenance that ever was seen; 'tis a collection of features from all the different countries of the globe.
SIR BENJAMIN. So she has, indeed—an Irish front—
CRABTREE. Caledonian locks—
SIR BENJAMIN. Dutch nose—
CRABTREE. Austrian lips—
SIR BENJAMIN. Complexion of a Spaniard—
CRABTREE. And teeth *à la Chinois*—
SIR BENJAMIN. In short, her face resembles a *table d'hôte* at Spa—where no two guests are of a nation—
CRABTREE. Or a congress at the close of a general war—wherein all the members, even to her eyes, appear to have a different interest, and her nose and chin are the only parties likely to join issue.
MRS. CANDOUR. Ha! ha! ha!
SIR PETER. Mercy on my life!—a person they dine with twice a week. [*Aside*.
LADY SNEERWELL. Go, go; you are a couple of provoking toads.
MRS. CANDOUR. Nay, but I vow you shall not carry the laugh off so—for give me leave to say, that Mrs. Ogle——
SIR PETER. Madam, madam, I beg your pardon—there's no stopping these good gentlemen's tongues.—But when I tell you, Mrs. Candour, that the lady they are abusing is a particular friend of mine, I hope you'll not take her part.
LADY SNEERWELL. Ha! ha! ha! Well said, Sir Peter! but you are a cruel creature,—too phlegmatic yourself for a jest, and too peevish to allow wit in others.
SIR PETER. Ah! madam, true wit is more nearly allied to good-nature than your ladyship is aware of.
LADY TEAZLE. True, Sir Peter: I believe they are so near akin that they can never be united.
SIR BENJAMIN. Or rather, madam, suppose them to be man and wife, because one seldom sees them together.
LADY TEAZLE. But Sir Peter is such an enemy to scandal, I believe he would have it put down by parliament.
SIR PETER. 'Fore heaven, madam, if they were to consider the sporting with

Enter SIR PETER TEAZLE.

SIR PETER. Ladies, your most obedient.—Mercy on me! here is the whole set! a character dead at every word, I suppose. [*Aside.*
MRS. CANDOUR. I am rejoiced you are come, Sir Peter. They have been so censorious—and Lady Teazle as bad as any one.
SIR PETER. It must be very distressing to *you*, Mrs. Candour, I dare swear.
MRS. CANDOUR. Oh, they will allow good qualities to nobody; not even good-nature to our friend Mrs. Pursy.
LADY TEAZLE. What, the fat dowager who was at Mrs. Quadrille's last night?
MRS. CANDOUR. Nay, her bulk is her misfortune; and when she takes such pains to get rid of it, you ought not to reflect on her.
LADY SNEERWELL. That's very true, indeed.
LADY TEAZLE. Yes, I know she almost lives on acids and small whey; laces herself by pulleys; and often in the hottest noon in summer, you may see her on a little squat pony, with her hair plaited up behind like a drummer's, and puffing round the Ring on a full trot.
MRS. CANDOUR. I thank you, Lady Teazle, for defending her.
SIR PETER. Yes, a good defence, truly!
MRS. CANDOUR. Truly, Lady Teazle is as censorious as Miss Sallow.
CRABTREE. Yes, and she is a curious being to pretend to be censorious—an awkward gawky, without any one good point under heaven.
MRS. CANDOUR. Positively you shall not be so very severe. Miss Sallow is a near relation of mine by marriage, and as for her person, great allowance is to be made; for, let me tell you, a woman labours under many disadvantages who tries to pass for a girl at six and thirty.
LADY SNEERWELL. Though, surely, she is handsome still—and for the weakness in her eyes, considering how much she reads by candlelight, it is not to be wondered at.
MRS. CANDOUR. True, and then as to her manner; upon my word I think it is particularly graceful, considering she never had the least education: for you know her mother was a Welsh milliner, and her father a sugar-baker at Bristol.
SIR BENJAMIN. Ah! you are both of you too good-natured!
SIR PETER. Yes, damned good-natured! This their own relation! mercy on me! [*Aside.*
MRS. CANDOUR. For my part, I own I cannot bear to hear a friend ill-spoken of.
SIR PETER. No, to be sure!
SIR BENJAMIN. Oh! you are of a moral turn. Mrs. Candour and I can sit for an hour and hear Lady Stucco talk sentiment.

CRABTREE. I am very glad you think so, ma'am.
MRS. CANDOUR. She has a charming fresh colour.
LADY TEAZLE. Yes, when it is fresh put on.
MRS. CANDOUR. O fie! I'll swear her colour is natural: I have seen it come and go.
LADY TEAZLE. I dare swear you have, ma'am: it goes off at night, and comes again in the morning.
SIR BENJAMIN. True, ma'am, it not only comes and goes, but, what's more—egad, her maid can fetch and carry it!
MRS. CANDOUR. Ha! ha! ha! how I hate to hear you talk so! But surely now, her sister *is*, or *was*, very handsome.
CRABTREE. Who? Mrs. Evergreen? O Lord! she's six and fifty if she's an hour!
MRS. CANDOUR. Now positively you wrong her; fifty-two or fifty-three is the utmost—and I don't think she looks more.
SIR BENJAMIN. Ah! there's no judging by her looks, unless one could see her face.
LADY SNEERWELL. Well, well, if Mrs. Evergreen *does* take some pains to repair the ravages of time, you must allow she effects it with great ingenuity; and surely that's better than the careless manner in which the widow Ochre chalks her wrinkles.
SIR BENJAMIN. Nay now, Lady Sneerwell, you are severe upon the widow. Come, come, 'tis not that she paints so ill—but when she has finished her face, she joins it so badly to her neck, that she looks like a mended statue, in which the connoisseur sees at once that the head's modern, though the trunk's antique.
CRABTREE. Ha! ha! ha! well said, nephew!
MRS. CANDOUR. Ha! ha! ha! well, you make me laugh; but I vow I hate you for it.—What do you think of Miss Simper?
SIR BENJAMIN. Why, she has very pretty teeth.
LADY TEAZLE. Yes, and on that account, when she is neither speaking nor laughing (which very seldom happens), she never absolutely shuts her mouth, but leaves it always on a jar, as it were,—thus. [*Shows her teeth.*
MRS. CANDOUR. How can you be so ill-natured?
LADY TEAZLE. Nay, I allow even that's better than the pains Mrs. Prim takes to conceal her losses in front. She draws her mouth till it positively resembles the aperture of a poor's box, and all her words appear to slide out edgewise as it were,—thus—*How do you do, madam? Yes, madam.*
LADY SNEERWELL. Very well, Lady Teazle; I see you can be a little severe.
LADY TEAZLE. In defence of a friend it is but justice.—But here comes Sir Peter to spoil our pleasantry.

Scene II.—At LADY SNEERWELL'S

Enter LADY SNEERWELL, MRS. CANDOUR, CRABTREE, SIR BENJAMIN BACKBITE, *and* JOSEPH SURFACE.

LADY SNEERWELL. Nay, positively, we will hear it.
JOSEPH. Yes, yes, the epigram, by all means.
SIR BENJAMIN. O plague on't, uncle! 'tis mere nonsense.
CRABTREE. No, no; 'fore Gad, very clever for an extempore!
SIR BENJAMIN. But, ladies, you should be acquainted with the circumstance. You must know, that one day last week, as Lady Betty Curricle was taking the dust in Hyde Park, in a sort of duodecimo phaeton, she desired me to write some verses on her ponies; upon which I took out my pocket-book, and in one moment produced the following:

> Sure never were seen two such beautiful ponies;
> Other horses are clowns, but these macaronies:
> To give them this title I'm sure can't be wrong,
> Their legs are so slim, and their tails are so long.

CRABTREE. There, ladies, done in the smack of a whip, and on horseback too.
JOSEPH. A very Phoebus, mounted—indeed, Sir Benjamin.
SIR BENJAMIN. O dear, sir! trifles—trifles.

Enter LADY TEAZLE *and* MARIA.

MRS. CANDOUR. I must have a copy.
LADY SNEERWELL. Lady Teazle, I hope we shall see Sir Peter?
LADY TEAZLE. I believe he'll wait on your ladyship presently.
LADY SNEERWELL. Maria, my love, you look grave. Come, you shall sit down to piquet with Mr. Surface.
MARIA. I take very little pleasure in cards—however, I'll do as you please.
LADY TEAZLE. I am surprised Mr. Surface should sit down with her; I thought he would have embraced this opportunity of speaking to me, before Sir Peter came. [*Aside.*
MRS. CANDOUR. Now, I'll die, but you are so scandalous, I'll forswear your society.
LADY TEAZLE. What's the matter, Mrs. Candour?
MRS. CANDOUR. They'll not allow our friend Miss Vermillion to be handsome.
LADY SNEERWELL. O surely she is a pretty woman.

LADY TEAZLE. For my part, I should think you would like to have your wife thought a woman of taste.

SIR PETER. Ay—there again—taste—Zounds! madam, you had no taste when you married me!

LADY TEAZLE. That's very true indeed, Sir Peter; and after having married you, I should never pretend to taste again, I allow. But now, Sir Peter, if we have finished our daily jangle, I presume I may go to my engagement at Lady Sneerwell's.

SIR PETER. Ay, there's another precious circumstance—a charming set of acquaintance you have made there.

LADY TEAZLE. Nay, Sir Peter, they are all people of rank and fortune, and remarkably tenacious of reputation.

SIR PETER. Yes, egad, they are tenacious of reputation with a vengeance; for they don't choose anybody should have a character but themselves!—Such a crew! Ah! many a wretch has rid on a hurdle who has done less mischief than these utterers of forged tales, coiners of scandal, and clippers of reputation.

LADY TEAZLE. What! would you restrain the freedom of speech?

SIR PETER. Ah! they have made you just as bad as any one of the society.

LADY TEAZLE. Why, I believe I do bear a part with a tolerable grace. But I vow I bear no malice against the people I abuse.—When I say an ill-natured thing, 'tis out of pure good humour; and I take it for granted, they deal exactly in the same manner with me. But, Sir Peter, you know you promised to come to Lady Sneerwell's too.

SIR PETER. Well, well, I'll call in just to look after my own character.

LADY TEAZLE. Then indeed you must make haste after me, or you'll be too late. So, good-bye to ye.

Exit LADY TEAZLE.

SIR PETER. So—I have gained much by my intended expostulation: yet, with what a charming air she contradicts everything I say, and how pleasingly she shows her contempt for my authority! Well, though I can't make her love me, there is great satisfaction in quarrelling with her; and I think she never appears to such advantage as when she is doing everything in her power to plague me.

Exit.

Lady Teazle. No, no, I don't; 'twas a very disagreeable one, or I should never have married you.

Sir Peter. Yes, yes, madam, you were then in somewhat a humbler style:—the daughter of a plain country squire. Recollect, Lady Teazle, when I saw you first sitting at your tambour, in a pretty figured linen gown, with a bunch of keys at your side; your hair combed smooth over a roll, and your apartment hung round with fruits in worsted, of your own working.

Lady Teazle. O, yes! I remember it very well, and a curious life I led.—My daily occupation to inspect the dairy, superintend the poultry, make extracts from the family receipt-book,—and comb my aunt Deborah's lapdog.

Sir Peter. Yes, yes, ma'am, 'twas so indeed.

Lady Teazle. And then, you know, my evening amusements! To draw patterns for ruffles, which I had not materials to make up; to play Pope Joan with the curate; to read a sermon to my aunt; or to be stuck down to an old spinet to strum my father to sleep after a fox-chase.

Sir Peter. I am glad you have so good a memory. Yes, madam, these were the recreations I took you from; but now you must have your coach—vis-à-vis—and three powdered footmen before your chair; and, in the summer, a pair of white cats to draw you to Kensington Gardens. No recollection, I suppose, when you were content to ride double, behind the butler, on a dock'd coach-horse.

Lady Teazle. No—I swear I never did that: I deny the butler and the coach-horse.

Sir Peter. This, madam, was your situation; and what have I done for you? I have made you a woman of fashion, of fortune, of rank; in short, I have made you my wife.

Lady Teazle. Well, then,—and there is but one thing more you can make me to add to the obligation, and that is——

Sir Peter. My widow, I suppose?

Lady Teazle. Hem! hem!

Sir Peter. I thank you, madam—but don't flatter yourself; for though your ill conduct may disturb my peace, it shall never break my heart, I promise you: however, I am equally obliged to you for the hint.

Lady Teazle. Then why will you endeavour to make yourself so disagreeable to me, and thwart me in every little elegant expense?

Sir Peter. 'Slife, madam, I say, had you any of these little elegant expenses when you married me?

Lady Teazle. Lud, Sir Peter! would you have me be out of the fashion?

Sir Peter. The fashion, indeed! what had you to do with the fashion before you married me?

ACT II

Scene I—SIR PETER TEAZLE's

Enter SIR PETER *and* LADY TEAZLE.

SIR PETER. Lady Teazle, Lady Teazle, I'll not bear it!
LADY TEAZLE. Sir Peter, Sir Peter, you may bear it or not, as you please; but I ought to have my own way in everything, and what's more, I will, too. What! though I was educated in the country, I know very well that women of fashion in London are accountable to nobody after they are married.
SIR PETER. Very well, ma'am, very well;—so a husband is to have no influence, no authority?
LADY TEAZLE. Authority! No, to be sure:—if you wanted authority over me, you should have adopted me, and not married me: I am sure you were old enough.
SIR PETER. Old enough!—ay—there it is. Well, well, Lady Teazle, though my life may be made unhappy by your temper, I'll not be ruined by your extravagance.
LADY TEAZLE. My extravagance! I'm sure I'm not more extravagant than a woman of fashion ought to be.
SIR PETER. No, no, madam, you shall throw away no more sums on such unmeaning luxury. 'Slife! to spend as much to furnish your dressing-room with flowers in winter as would suffice to turn the Pantheon into a greenhouse, and give a fête champêtre at Christmas.
LADY TEAZLE. And am I to blame, Sir Peter, because flowers are dear in cold weather? You should find fault with the climate, and not with me. For my part, I'm sure, I wish it was spring all the year round, and that roses grew under our feet!
SIR PETER. Oons! madam—if you had been born to this, I shouldn't wonder at your talking thus; but you forget what your situation was when I married you.

ROWLEY. I am sorry to find you so violent against the young man, because this may be the most critical period of his fortune. I came hither with news that will surprise you.

SIR PETER. What! let me hear.

ROWLEY. Sir Oliver *is* arrived, and at this moment in town.

SIR PETER. How! you astonish me! I thought you did not expect him this month.

ROWLEY. I did not; but his passage has been remarkably quick.

SIR PETER. Egad, I shall rejoice to see my old friend. 'Tis fifteen years since we met.—We have had many a day together:—but does he still enjoin us not to inform his nephews of his arrival?

ROWLEY. Most strictly. He means, before it is known, to make some trial of their dispositions.

SIR PETER. Ah! there needs no art to discover their merits—he shall have his way: but, pray, does he know I am married?

ROWLEY. Yes, and will soon wish you joy.

SIR PETER. What, as we drink health to a friend in a consumption. Ah! Oliver will laugh at me. We used to rail at matrimony together, and he has been steady to his text.—Well, he must be soon at my house, though!—I'll instantly give orders for his reception.—But, Master Rowley, don't drop a word that Lady Teazle and I ever disagree.

ROWLEY. By no means.

SIR PETER. For I should never be able to stand Noll's jokes; so I'd have him think, Lord forgive me! that we are a very happy couple.

ROWLEY. I understand you:—but then you must be very careful not to differ while he is in the house with you.

SIR PETER. Egad, and so we must—and that's impossible. Ah! Master Rowley, when an old bachelor marries a young wife, he deserves—no—the crime carries its punishment along with it.

Exeunt.

the worst of it is, I doubt I love her, or I should never bear all this. However, I'll never be weak enough to own it.

Enter ROWLEY.

ROWLEY. Oh! Sir Peter, your servant: how is it with you, sir?
SIR PETER. Very bad, Master Rowley, very bad. I meet with nothing but crosses and vexations.
ROWLEY. What can have happened to trouble you since yesterday?
SIR PETER. A good question to a married man!
ROWLEY. Nay, I'm sure your lady, Sir Peter, can't be the cause of your uneasiness.
SIR PETER. Why, has anybody told you she was dead?
ROWLEY. Come, come, Sir Peter, you love her, notwithstanding your tempers don't exactly agree.
SIR PETER. But the fault is entirely hers, Master Rowley. I am, myself, the sweetest-tempered man alive, and hate a teasing temper; and so I tell her a hundred times a day.
ROWLEY. Indeed!
SIR PETER. Ay; and what is very extraordinary, in all our disputes she is always in the wrong! But Lady Sneerwell, and the set she meets at her house, encourage the perverseness of her disposition.—Then, to complete my vexation, Maria, my ward, whom I ought to have the power over, is determined to turn rebel too, and absolutely refuses the man whom I have long resolved on for her husband; meaning, I suppose, to bestow herself on his profligate brother.
ROWLEY. You know, Sir Peter, I have always taken the liberty to differ with you on the subject of these two young gentlemen. I only wish you may not be deceived in your opinion of the elder. For Charles, my life on't! he will retrieve his errors yet. Their worthy father, once my honoured master, was, at his years, nearly as wild a spark; yet, when he died, he did not leave a more benevolent heart to lament his loss.
SIR PETER. You are wrong, Master Rowley. On their father's death, you know, I acted as a kind of guardian to them both, till their uncle Sir Oliver's liberality gave them an early independence: of course, no person could have more opportunities of judging of their hearts, and I was never mistaken in my life. Joseph is indeed a model for the young men of the age. He is a man of sentiment, and acts up to the *sentiments* he professes; but for the other, take my word for't, if he had any grain of virtue by descent, he has dissipated it with the rest of his inheritance. Ah! my old friend, Sir Oliver, will be deeply mortified when he finds how part of his bounty has been misapplied.

some empty bottles that were overlooked, and the family pictures, which I believe are framed in the wainscots——

SIR BENJAMIN. And I'm very sorry, also, to hear some bad stories against him. [*Going.*]

CRABTREE. Oh! he has done many mean things, that's certain.

SIR BENJAMIN. But, however, as he's your brother—— [*Going.*]

CRABTREE. We'll tell you all another opportunity.

Exeunt CRABTREE *and* SIR BENJAMIN.

LADY SNEERWELL. Ha! ha! 'tis very hard for them to leave a subject they have not quite run down.

JOSEPH. And I believe the abuse was no more acceptable to your ladyship than Maria.

LADY SNEERWELL. I doubt her affections are further engaged than we imagine. But the family are to be here this evening, so you may as well dine where you are, and we shall have an opportunity of observing further; in the meantime, I'll go and plot mischief, and you shall study sentiment.

Exeunt.

Scene II.—SIR PETER'S *House*

Enter SIR PETER.

SIR PETER. When an old bachelor marries a young wife, what is he to expect? 'Tis now six months since Lady Teazle made me the happiest of men—and I have been the most miserable dog ever since! We tifted a little going to church, and fairly quarrelled before the bells had done ringing. I was more than once nearly choked with gall during the honeymoon, and had lost all comfort in life before my friends had done wishing me joy. Yet I chose with caution—a girl bred wholly in the country, who never knew luxury beyond one silk gown, nor dissipation above the annual gala of a race ball. Yet now she plays her part in all the extravagant fopperies of the fashion and the town, with as ready a grace as if she had never seen a bush or a grass-plot out of Grosvenor Square! I am sneered at by all my acquaintance, and paragraphed in the newspapers. She dissipates my fortune, and contradicts all my humours; yet,

JOSEPH. Not that I know of, indeed, sir.
CRABTREE. He has been in the East Indies a long time. You can scarcely remember him, I believe?—Sad comfort whenever he returns, to hear how your brother has gone on!
JOSEPH. Charles has been imprudent, sir, to be sure; but I hope no busy people have already prejudiced Sir Oliver against him. He may reform.
SIR BENJAMIN. To be sure he may: for my part, I never believed him to be so utterly void of principle as people say; and though he has lost all his friends, I am told nobody is better spoken of by the Jews.
CRABTREE. That's true, egad, nephew. If the Old Jewry was a ward, I believe Charles would be an alderman:—no man more popular there, 'fore Gad! I hear he pays as many annuities as the Irish tontine; and that whenever he is sick, they have prayers for the recovery of his health in all the synagogues.
SIR BENJAMIN. Yet no man lives in greater splendour. They tell me, when he entertains his friends he will sit down to dinner with a dozen of his own securities; have a score of tradesmen waiting in the antechamber, and an officer behind every guest's chair.
JOSEPH. This may be entertainment to you, gentlemen, but you pay very little regard to the feelings of a brother.
MARIA. Their malice is intolerable.—Lady Sneerwell, I must wish you a good morning: I'm not very well.

Exit MARIA.

MRS. CANDOUR. O dear! she changes colour very much.
LADY SNEERWELL. Do, Mrs. Candour, follow her: she may want assistance.
MRS. CANDOUR. That I will, with all my soul, ma'am.—Poor dear girl, who knows what her situation may be!

Exit MRS. CANDOUR.

LADY SNEERWELL. 'Twas nothing but that she could not bear to hear Charles reflected on, notwithstanding their difference.
SIR BENJAMIN. The young lady's *penchant* is obvious.
CRABTREE. But, Benjamin, you must not give up the pursuit for that:—follow her, and put her into good humour. Repeat her some of your own verses. Come, I'll assist you.
SIR BENJAMIN. Mr. Surface, I did not mean to hurt you; but depend on't your brother is utterly undone.
CRABTREE. O Lud, ay! undone as ever man was.—Can't raise a guinea!—
SIR BENJAMIN. And everything sold, I'm told, that was movable.—
CRABTREE. I have seen one that was at his house.—Not a thing left but

MRS. CANDOUR. Impossible!

CRABTREE. Ask Sir Benjamin.

SIR BENJAMIN. 'Tis very true, ma'am; everything is fixed, and the wedding liveries bespoke.

CRABTREE. Yes—and they do say there were pressing reasons for it.

LADY SNEERWELL. Why, I have heard something of this before.

MRS. CANDOUR. It can't be—and I wonder any one should believe such a story, of so prudent a lady as Miss Nicely.

SIR BENJAMIN. O Lud! ma'am, that's the very reason 'twas believed at once. She has always been so cautious and so reserved, that everybody was sure there was some reason for it at bottom.

MRS. CANDOUR. Why, to be sure, a tale of scandal is as fatal to the credit of a prudent lady of her stamp, as a fever is generally to those of the strongest constitutions. But there is a sort of puny sickly reputation, that is always ailing, yet will outlive the robuster characters of a hundred prudes.

SIR BENJAMIN. True, madam,—there are valetudinarians in reputation as well as constitution; who, being conscious of their weak part, avoid the least breath of air, and supply their want of stamina by care and circumspection.

MRS. CANDOUR. Well, but this may be all a mistake. You know, Sir Benjamin, very trifling circumstances often give rise to the most injurious tales.

CRABTREE. That they do, I'll be sworn, ma'am.—Did you ever hear how Miss Piper came to lose her love and her character last summer at Tunbridge?—Sir Benjamin, you remember it?

SIR BENJAMIN. Oh, to be sure!—the most whimsical circumstance.

LADY SNEERWELL. How was it, pray?

CRABTREE. Why, one evening, at Mrs. Ponto's assembly, the conversation happened to turn on the breeding Nova Scotia sheep in this country. Says a young lady in company, "I have known instances of it—for Miss Letitia Piper, a first cousin of mine, had a Nova Scotia sheep that produced her twins."—"What!" cries the Lady Dowager Dundizzy (who you know is as deaf as a post), "has Miss Piper had twins?"—This mistake, as you may imagine, threw the whole company into a fit of laughter. However, 'twas the next morning everywhere reported, and in a few days believed by the whole town, that Miss Letitia Piper had actually been brought to bed of a fine boy and a girl; and in less than a week there were some people who could name the father, and the farmhouse where the babies were put to nurse.

LADY SNEERWELL. Strange, indeed!

CRABTREE. Matter of fact, I assure you.—O Lud! Mr. Surface, pray is it true that your uncle, Sir Oliver, is coming home?

JOSEPH. Doubtless, ma'am—a very great one.

Enter SERVANT.

SERVANT. Mr. Crabtree and Sir Benjamin Backbite.

Exit SERVANT.

LADY SNEERWELL. So, Maria, you see your lover pursues you; positively you shan't escape.

Enter CRABTREE *and* SIR BENJAMIN BACKBITE.

CRABTREE. Lady Sneerwell, I kiss your hand—Mrs. Candour, I don't believe you are acquainted with my nephew, Sir Benjamin Backbite? Egad! ma'am, he has a pretty wit, and is a pretty poet too; isn't he, Lady Sneerwell?

SIR BENJAMIN. O fie, uncle!

CRABTREE. Nay, egad it's true; I back him at a rebus or a charade against the best rhymer in the kingdom.—Has your ladyship heard the epigram he wrote last week on Lady Frizzle's feather catching fire?—Do, Benjamin, repeat it, or the charade you made last night extempore at Mrs. Drowzie's conversazione. Come now;—your first is the name of a fish, your second a great naval commander, and——

SIR BENJAMIN. Uncle, now—pr'ythee—

CRABTREE. I'faith, ma'am, 'twould surprise you to hear how ready he is at all these fine sort of things.

LADY SNEERWELL. I wonder, Sir Benjamin, you never publish anything.

SIR BENJAMIN. To say truth, ma'am, 'tis very vulgar to print; and as my little productions are mostly satires and lampoons on particular people, I find they circulate more by giving copies in confidence to the friends of the parties.—However, I have some love elegies, which, when favoured with this lady's smiles, I mean to give the public.

CRABTREE. 'Fore heaven, ma'am, they'll immortalise you!—you will be handed down to posterity, like Petrarch's Laura, or Waller's Sacharissa.

SIR BENJAMIN. Yes, madam, I think you will like them, when you shall see them on a beautiful quarto page, where a neat rivulet of text shall meander through a meadow of margin.—'Fore Gad they will be the most elegant things of their kind!

CRABTREE. But, ladies, that's true—have you heard the news?

MRS. CANDOUR. What, sir, do you mean the report of——

CRABTREE. No, ma'am, that's not it—Miss Nicely is going to be married to her own footman.

Miss Gadabout had eloped with Sir Filigree Flirt. But, Lord! there's no minding what one hears; though, to be sure, I had this from very good authority.

MARIA. Such reports are highly scandalous.

MRS. CANDOUR. So they are, child—shameful, shameful! But the world is so censorious, no character escapes.——Lord, now who would have suspected your friend, Miss Prim, of an indiscretion? Yet such is the ill-nature of people, that they say her uncle stopt her last week, just as she was stepping into the York diligence with her dancing-master.

MARIA. I'll answer for't there are no grounds for that report.

MRS. CANDOUR. Ah, no foundation in the world, I dare swear; no more, probably, than for the story circulated last month, of Mrs. Festino's affair with Colonel Cassino;—though, to be sure, that matter was never rightly cleared up.

JOSEPH. The licence of invention some people take is monstrous indeed.

MARIA. 'Tis so,—but, in my opinion, those who report such things are equally culpable.

MRS. CANDOUR. To be sure they are; tale-bearers are as bad as the tale-makers—'tis an old observation, and a very true one: but what's to be done, as I said before? how will you prevent people from talking? To-day, Mrs. Clackitt assured me, Mr. and Mrs. Honeymoon were at last become mere man and wife, like the rest of their acquaintance. She likewise hinted that a certain widow, in the next street, had got rid of her dropsy and recovered her shape in a most surprising manner. And at the same time, Miss Tattle, who was by, affirmed, that Lord Buffalo had discovered his lady at a house of no extraordinary fame; and that Sir H. Boquet and Tom Saunter were to measure swords on a similar provocation.——But, Lord, do you think I would report these things?—No, no! tale-bearers, as I said before, are just as bad as the tale-makers.

JOSEPH. Ah! Mrs. Candour, if everybody had your forbearance and good-nature!

MRS. CANDOUR. I confess, Mr. Surface, I cannot bear to hear people attacked behind their backs; and when ugly circumstances come out against our acquaintance, I own I always love to think the best.——By the by, I hope 'tis not true that your brother is absolutely ruined?

JOSEPH. I am afraid his circumstances are very bad indeed, ma'am.

MRS. CANDOUR. Ah! I heard so—but you must tell him to keep up his spirits; everybody almost is in the same way—Lord Spindle, Sir Thomas Splint, Captain Quinze, and Mr. Nickit—all up, I hear, within this week; so if Charles is undone, he'll find half his acquaintance ruined too, and that, you know, is a consolation.

LADY SNEERWELL. Pshaw!—there's no possibility of being witty without a little ill-nature: the malice of a good thing is the barb that makes it stick.—What's your opinion, Mr. Surface?

JOSEPH. To be sure, madam; that conversation, where the spirit of raillery is suppressed, will ever appear tedious and insipid.

MARIA. Well, I'll not debate how far scandal may be allowable; but in a man, I am sure, it is always contemptible. We have pride, envy, rivalship, and a thousand motives to depreciate each other; but the male slanderer must have the cowardice of a woman before he can traduce one.

Enter SERVANT.

SERVANT. Madam, Mrs. Candour is below, and if your ladyship's at leisure, will leave her carriage.

LADY SNEERWELL. Beg her to walk in.—[*Exit* SERVANT.]—Now, Maria, here is a character to your taste; for though Mrs. Candour is a little talkative, everybody allows her to be the best-natured and best sort of woman.

MARIA. Yes,—with a very gross affectation of good nature and benevolence, she does more mischief than the direct malice of old Crabtree.

JOSEPH. I'faith that's true, Lady Sneerwell: whenever I hear the current running against the characters of my friends, I never think them in such danger as when Candour undertakes their defence.

LADY SNEERWELL. Hush!—here she is!—

Enter MRS. CANDOUR.

MRS. CANDOUR. My dear Lady Sneerwell, how have you been this century?——Mr. Surface, what news do you hear?—though indeed it is no matter, for I think one hears nothing else but scandal.

JOSEPH. Just so, indeed, ma'am.

MRS. CANDOUR. Oh, Maria! child,—what, is the whole affair off between you and Charles?——His extravagance, I presume—the town talks of nothing else.

MARIA. I am very sorry, ma'am, the town has so little to do.

MRS. CANDOUR. True, true, child: but there's no stopping people's tongues. I own I was hurt to hear it, as I indeed was to learn, from the same quarter, that your guardian, Sir Peter, and Lady Teazle have not agreed lately as well as could be wished.

MARIA. 'Tis strangely impertinent for people to busy themselves so.

MRS. CANDOUR. Very true, child:—but what's to be done? People will talk—there's no preventing it. Why, it was but yesterday I was told that

JOSEPH. Egad, that's true!—I'll keep that sentiment till I see Sir Peter;—however, it certainly is a charity to rescue Maria from such a libertine, who, if he is to be reclaimed, can be so only by a person of your ladyship's superior accomplishments and understanding.
SNAKE. I believe, Lady Sneerwell, here's company coming: I'll go and copy the letter I mentioned to you.—Mr. Surface, your most obedient.

Exit SNAKE.

JOSEPH. Sir, your very devoted.—Lady Sneerwell, I am very sorry you have put any further confidence in that fellow.
LADY SNEERWELL. Why so?
JOSEPH. I have lately detected him in frequent conference with old Rowley, who was formerly my father's steward, and has never, you know, been a friend of mine.
LADY SNEERWELL. And do you think he would betray us?
JOSEPH. Nothing more likely:—take my word for't, Lady Sneerwell, that fellow hasn't virtue enough to be faithful even to his own villany.——Ah! Maria!

Enter MARIA.

LADY SNEERWELL. Maria, my dear, how do you do?——What's the matter?
MARIA. Oh! there is that disagreeable lover of mine, Sir Benjamin Backbite, has just called at my guardian's, with his odious uncle, Crabtree; so I slipt out, and ran hither to avoid them.
LADY SNEERWELL. Is that all?
JOSEPH. If my brother Charles had been of the party, madam, perhaps you would not have been so much alarmed.
LADY SNEERWELL. Nay, now you are severe; for I dare swear the truth of the matter is, Maria heard *you* were here.—But, my dear, what has Sir Benjamin done, that you would avoid him so?
MARIA. Oh, he has done nothing—but 'tis for what he has said: his conversation is a perpetual libel on all his acquaintance.
JOSEPH. Ay, and the worst of it is, there is no advantage in not knowing him—for he'll abuse a stranger just as soon as his best friend; and his uncle's as bad.
LADY SNEERWELL. Nay, but we should make allowance,—Sir Benjamin is a wit and a poet.
MARIA. For my part, I confess, madam, wit loses its respect with me, when I see it in company with malice.—What do you think, Mr. Surface?
JOSEPH. Certainly, madam; to smile at the jest which plants a thorn in another's breast is to become a principal in the mischief.

quaintance, he passes for a youthful miracle of prudence, good sense, and benevolence.

SNAKE. Yes; yet Sir Peter vows he has not his equal in England—and above all, he praises him as a man of sentiment.

LADY SNEERWELL. True—and with the assistance of his sentiment and hypocrisy, he has brought Sir Peter entirely into his interest with regard to Maria; while poor Charles has no friend in the house, though, I fear, he has a powerful one in Maria's heart, against whom we must direct our schemes.

Enter SERVANT.

SERVANT. Mr. Surface.
LADY SNEERWELL. Show him up.

Exit SERVANT.

Enter JOSEPH SURFACE.

JOSEPH. My dear Lady Sneerwell, how do you do to-day? Mr. Snake, your most obedient.

LADY SNEERWELL. Snake has just been rallying me on our mutual attachment; but I have informed him of our real views. You know how useful he has been to us, and, believe me, the confidence is not ill placed.

JOSEPH. Madam, it is impossible for me to suspect a man of Mr. Snake's sensibility and discernment.

LADY SNEERWELL. Well, well, no compliments now; but tell me when you saw your mistress, Maria—or, what is more material to me, your brother.

JOSEPH. I have not seen either since I left you; but I can inform you that they never meet. Some of your stories have taken a good effect on Maria.

LADY SNEERWELL. Ah! my dear Snake! the merit of this belongs to you: but do your brother's distresses increase?

JOSEPH. Every hour. I am told he has had another execution in the house yesterday. In short, his dissipation and extravagance exceed anything I have ever heard of.

LADY SNEERWELL. Poor Charles!

JOSEPH. True, madam; notwithstanding his vices, one can't help feeling for him. Poor Charles! I'm sure I wish it were in my power to be of any essential service to him; for the man who does not share in the distresses of a brother, even though merited by his own misconduct, deserves—

LADY SNEERWELL. O Lud! you are going to be moral, and forget that you are among friends.

LADY SNEERWELL. Yes, my dear Snake; and I am no hypocrite to deny the satisfaction I reap from the success of my efforts. Wounded myself in the early part of my life by the envenomed tongue of slander, I confess I have since known no pleasure equal to the reducing others to the level of my own injured reputation.

SNAKE. Nothing can be more natural. But, Lady Sneerwell, there is one affair in which you have lately employed me, wherein, I confess, I am at a loss to guess your motives.

LADY SNEERWELL. I conceive you mean with respect to my neighbour, Sir Peter Teazle, and his family?

SNAKE. I do. Here are two young men, to whom Sir Peter has acted as a kind of guardian since their father's death; the eldest possessing the most amiable character, and universally well spoken of—the youngest, the most dissipated and extravagant young fellow in the kingdom, without friends or character: the former an avowed admirer of your ladyship's, and apparently your favourite: the latter attached to Maria, Sir Peter's ward, and confessedly beloved by her. Now, on the face of these circumstances, it is utterly unaccountable to me, why you, the widow of a city knight, with a good jointure, should not close with the passion of a man of such character and expectations as Mr. Surface; and more so why you should be so uncommonly earnest to destroy the mutual attachment subsisting between his brother Charles and Maria.

LADY SNEERWELL. Then at once to unravel this mystery, I must inform you, that love has no share whatever in the intercourse between Mr. Surface and me.

SNAKE. No!

LADY SNEERWELL. His real attachment is to Maria, or her fortune; but finding in his brother a favoured rival, he has been obliged to mask his pretensions, and profit by my assistance.

SNAKE. Yet still I am more puzzled why you should interest yourself in his success.

LADY SNEERWELL. How dull you are! Cannot you surmise the weakness which I hitherto, through shame, have concealed even from you? Must I confess, that Charles, that libertine, that extravagant, that bankrupt in fortune and reputation, that he it is for whom I'm thus anxious and malicious, and to gain whom I would sacrifice everything?

SNAKE. Now, indeed, your conduct appears consistent: but how came you and Mr. Surface so confidential?

LADY SNEERWELL. For our mutual interest. I have found him out a long time since. I know him to be artful, selfish, and malicious—in short, a sentimental knave; while with Sir Peter, and indeed with all his ac-

ACT I

Scene I.—LADY SNEERWELL's *House*

Discovered LADY SNEERWELL *at the dressing-table;* SNAKE *drinking chocolate.*

LADY SNEERWELL. The paragraphs, you say, Mr. Snake, were all inserted?
SNAKE. They were, madam; and as I copied them myself in a feigned hand, there can be no suspicion whence they came.
LADY SNEERWELL. Did you circulate the report of Lady Brittle's intrigue with Captain Boastall?
SNAKE. That's in as fine a train as your ladyship could wish. In the common course of things, I think it must reach Mrs. Clackitt's ears within four and twenty hours; and then, you know, the business is as good as done.
LADY SNEERWELL. Why, truly, Mrs. Clackitt has a very pretty talent, and a great deal of industry.
SNAKE. True, madam, and has been tolerably successful in her day. To my knowledge she has been the cause of six matches being broken off, and three sons disinherited; of four forced elopements, and as many close confinements; nine separate maintenances, and two divorces. Nay, I have more than once traced her causing a *tête-à-tête* in the *Town and Country Magazine*, when the parties, perhaps, had never seen each other's face before in the course of their lives.
LADY SNEERWELL. She certainly has talents, but her manner is gross.
SNAKE. 'Tis very true. She generally designs well, has a free tongue and a bold invention; but her colouring is too dark, and her outlines often extravagant. She wants that delicacy of tint, and mellowness of sneer, which distinguishes your ladyship's scandal.
LADY SNEERWELL. You are partial, Snake.
SNAKE. Not in the least—everybody allows that Lady Sneerwell can do more with a word or a look than many can with the most laboured detail, even when they happen to have a little truth on their side to support it.

DRAMATIS PERSONÆ

As originally acted at Drury Lane Theatre, May 8, 1777

SIR PETER TEAZLE	*Mr. King.*
SIR OLIVER SURFACE	*Mr. Yates.*
JOSEPH SURFACE	*Mr. Palmer.*
CHARLES	*Mr. Smith.*
CRABTREE	*Mr. Parsons.*
SIR BENJAMIN BACKBITE	*Mr. Dodd.*
ROWLEY	*Mr. Aickin.*
MOSES	*Mr. Baddeley.*
TRIP	*Mr. Lamash.*
SNAKE	*Mr. Packer.*
CARELESS	*Mr. Farren.*
SIR HARRY BUMPER	*Mr. Gawdry.*
LADY TEAZLE	*Mrs. Abington.*
MARIA	*Miss P. Hopkins.*
LADY SNEERWELL	*Miss Sherry.*
MRS. CANDOUR	*Miss Pope.*

Can stop the full springtide of calumny?
Knows he the world so little, and its trade?
Alas! the devil's sooner raised than laid
So strong, so swift, the monster there's no gagging:
Cut Scandal's head off, still the tongue is wagging.
Proud of your smiles once lavishly bestow'd,
Again our young Don Quixote takes the road;
To show his gratitude he draws his pen,
And seeks this hydra, Scandal, in his den.
For your applause all perils he would through—
He'll fight—that's write—a cavalliero true,
Till every drop of blood—that's ink—is spilt for you.

PROLOGUE

Written by Mr. Garrick

A School for Scandal! tell me, I beseech you,
Needs there a school this modish art to teach you?
No need of lessons now, the knowing think;
We might as well be taught to eat and drink.
Caused by a dearth of scandal, should the vapours
Distress our fair ones—let them read the papers;
Their powerful mixtures such disorders hit;
Crave what you will—there's *quantum sufficit.*
"Lord!" cries my Lady *Wormwood* (who loves tattle,
And puts much salt and pepper in her prattle),
Just ris'n at noon, all night at cards when threshing
Strong tea and scandal—"Bless me, how refreshing!
Give me the papers, *Lisp*—how bold and free! (*sips*)
Last night Lord L. (sips) *was caught with Lady D.*
For aching heads what charming *sal volatile!* (*sips*)
If Mrs. B. will still continue flirting,
We hope she'll draw, *or we'll* undraw *the curtain.*
Fine satire, poz—in public all abuse it,
But, by ourselves, (*sips*) our praise we can't refuse it.
Now, *Lisp*, read you—there, at that dash and star":
"Yes, ma'am—*A certain lord had best beware,*
Who lives not twenty miles from Grosvenor Square;
For should he Lady W. find willing,
Wormwood is bitter"—"Oh! that's me, the villain!
Throw it behind the fire, and never more
Let that vile paper come within my door."
Thus at our friends we laugh, who feel the dart;
To reach our feelings, we ourselves must smart.
Is our young bard so young, to think that he

But yield a theme, thy warmest praises wrong;
Just to her merit, though thou canst not raise
Thy feeble verse, behold th' acknowledged praise
Has spread conviction through the envious train,
And cast a fatal gloom o'er Scandal's reign!
And lo! each pallid hag, with blister'd tongue,
Mutters assent to all thy zeal has sung—
Owns all the colours just—the outline true;
Thee my inspirer, and my *model*—CREWE!

They move in meaning, and they pause in thought!
But dost thou farther watch, with charm'd surprise,
The mild irresolution of her eyes,
Curious to mark how frequent they repose,
In brief eclipse and momentary close—
Ah! seest thou not an ambush'd Cupid there,
Too tim'rous of his charge, with jealous care
Veils and unveils those beams of heav'nly light,
Too full, too fatal else, for mortal sight?
Nor yet, such pleasing vengeance fond to meet,
In pard'ning dimples hope a safe retreat.
What though her peaceful breast should ne'er allow
Subduing frowns to arm her alter'd brow,
By Love, I swear, and by his gentle wiles,
More fatal still the mercy of her smiles!
Thus lovely, thus adorn'd, possessing all
Of bright or fair that can to woman fall,
The height of vanity might well be thought
Prerogative in her, and Nature's fault.
Yet gentle *Amoret*, in mind supreme
As well as charms, rejects the vainer theme;
And half mistrustful of her beauty's store,
She barbs with wit those darts too keen before:—
Read in all knowledge that her sex should reach,
Though *Greville*, or the *Muse*, should deign to teach,
Fond to improve, nor tim'rous to discern
How far it is a woman's grace to learn;
In *Millar's* dialect she would not prove
Apollo's priestess, but Apollo's love,
Graced by those signs, which truth delights to own,
The timid blush, and mild submitted tone:
Whate'er she says, though sense appear throughout,
Displays the tender hue of female doubt;
Deck'd with that charm, how lovely wit appears,
How graceful *science*, when that robe she wears!
Such too her talents, and her bent of mind,
As speak a sprightly heart by thought refined,
A taste for mirth, by contemplation school'd,
A turn for ridicule, by candour ruled,
A scorn of folly, which she tries to hide;
An awe of talent, which she owns with pride!
    Peace! idle Muse,—no more thy strain prolong,

The perfect model, which I boast, supply:—
Vain Muse! couldst thou the humblest sketch create
Of her, or slightest charm couldst imitate—
Could thy blest strain in kindred colours trace
The faintest wonder of her form and face—
Poets would study the immortal line,
And *Reynolds* own *his* art subdued by thine;
That art, which well might added lustre give
To Nature's best, and Heaven's superlative:
On *Granby's* cheek might bid new glories rise,
Or point a purer beam from *Devon's* eyes!
Hard is the task to shape that beauty's praise,
Whose judgment scorns the homage flattery pays!
But praising Amoret we cannot err,
No tongue o'ervalues Heaven, or flatters her!
Yet she by Fate's perverseness—she alone
Would doubt our truth, nor deem such praise her own!
Adorning Fashion, unadorn'd by dress,
Simple from taste, and not from carelessness;
Discreet in gesture, in deportment mild,
Not stiff with prudence, nor uncouthly wild:
No state has *Amoret!* no studied mien;
She frowns no *goddess*, and she moves *no queen.*
The softer charm that in her manner lies
Is framed to captivate, yet not surprise;
It justly suits th' expression of her face,—
'Tis less than dignity, and more than grace!
On her pure cheek the native hue is such,
That form'd by heav'n to be admired so much,
The hand divine, with a less partial care,
Might well have fix'd a fainter crimson there,
And bade the gentle inmate of her breast,—
Inshrined Modesty!—supply the rest.
But who the peril of her lips shall paint?
Strip them of smiles—still, still all words are faint!
But moving Love himself appears to teach
Their action, though denied to rule her speech;
And thou who seest her speak and dost not hear,
Mourn not her distant accents 'scape thine ear;
Viewing those lips, thou still may'st make pretence
To judge of what she says, and swear 'tis sense:
Cloth'd with such grace, with such expression fraught,

A PORTRAIT

Addressed to Mrs. Crewe, with the Comedy
of the School for Scandal

BY R. B. SHERIDAN, ESQ.

TELL me, ye prim adepts in Scandal's school,
Who rail by precept, and detract by rule,
Lives there no character, so tried, so known,
So deck'd with grace, and so unlike your own,
That even you assist her fame to raise,
Approve by envy, and by silence praise!—
Attend!—a model shall attract your view—
Daughters of calumny, I summon you!
You shall decide if this a portrait prove,
Or fond creation of the Muse and Love.—
Attend, ye virgin critics, shrewd and sage,
Ye matron censors of this childish age,
Whose peering eye and wrinkled front declare
A fixt antipathy to young and fair;
By cunning, cautious; or by nature, cold,
In maiden madness, virulently bold!—
Attend! ye skilled to coin the precious tale,
Creating proof, where inuendos fail!
Whose practised memories, cruelly exact,
Omit no circumstance, except the fact!—
Attend, all ye who boast,—or old or young,—
The living libel of a slanderous tongue!
So shall my theme as far contrasted be,
As saints by fiends, or hymns by calumny.
Come, gentle Amoret (for 'neath that name,
In worthier verse is sung thy beauty's fame);
Come—for but thee who seeks the Muse? and while
Celestial blushes check thy conscious smile,
With timid grace, and hesitating eye,

Contents

"A Portrait"	ix
Prologue	xiii
Dramatis Personae	xv
ACT I	1
ACT II	13
ACT III	25
ACT IV	41
ACT V	59
Epilogue	77

Note

PARLIAMENTARY ORATOR, adviser to the Prince of Wales (later George IV), manager of Drury Lane Theatre, versifier, wit and bon vivant, Dublin-born Richard Brinsley Sheridan (1751-1816) is best remembered for his comedies, particularly *The Rivals, The Critic* and *The School for Scandal*. The best-known and most frequently revived British play of the eighteenth century, *The School for Scandal* (first performed 1777) has an excellent plot, unforgettable characters, grand theatrical situations (including the auction of ancestors and the famous screen scene) and, above all, a feast of perfectly pointed and phrased humor.

The author of the Prologue, David Garrick (1717-1779), was the premier actor of his day and a former manager of Drury Lane. The writer of the Epilogue, George Colman the elder (1732-1794), was a playwright and manager of the Haymarket Theatre. Frances Anne Crewe (died 1818), to whom *The School for Scandal* is dedicated, was a baroness, a great hostess and friend of statesmen, writers and artists.

DOVER THRIFT EDITIONS
Editor: Stanley Appelbaum

Published in Canada by General Publishing Company, Ltd.,
30 Lesmill Road, Don Mills, Toronto, Ontario.
Published in the United Kingdom by Constable and Company, Ltd.,
3 The Lanchesters, 162–164 Fulham Palace Road, London W6 9ER.

This Dover edition, first published in 1991, is an
unabridged republication of *The School for Scandal* as published in the
volume *The School for Scandal and The Rivals by Richard Brinsley Sheridan*
by Macmillan and Co., Limited, London, in 1926.
A new Note has been prepared specially for the present edition.

Manufactured in the United States of America
Dover Publications, Inc.
31 East 2nd Street
Mineola, N.Y. 11501

Library of Congress Cataloging-in-Publication Data

Sheridan, Richard Brinsley, 1751–1816.
The school for scandal / Richard Brinsley Sheridan.
p.   cm. — (Dover thrift editions)
ISBN 0-486-26687-7 (pbk.)
I. Title. II. Series.
PR3682.S3   1991
822'.6—dc20   90-19747
                                  CIP

DOVER · THRIFT · EDITIONS

The School for Scandal

RICHARD BRINSLEY SHERIDAN

DOVER PUBLICATIONS, INC.
New York

DOVER·THRIFT·EDITIONS

A Doll's House
HENRIK IBSEN

DOVER PUBLICATIONS, INC.
New York

DOVER THRIFT EDITIONS
GENERAL EDITOR: STANLEY APPELBAUM
EDITOR OF THIS VOLUME: PHILIP SMITH

Published in Canada by General Publishing Company, Ltd., 30 Lesmill Road, Don Mills, Toronto, Ontario.

Published in the United Kingdom by Constable and Company, Ltd., 3 The Lanchesters, 162–164 Fulham Palace Road, London W6 9ER.

This Dover edition, first published in 1992, is an unabridged, slightly corrected republication of an anonymous, undated English translation published by Bartholomew House, Inc., New York. The Note has been specially prepared for this edition.

Manufactured in the United States of America
Dover Publications, Inc., 31 East 2nd Street, Mineola, N.Y. 11501

Library of Congress Cataloging-in-Publication Data

Ibsen, Henrik, 1828–1906.
  [Dukkehjem. English]
  A doll's house — Dover thrift ed.
    p. cm.
  "An unabridged, slightly corrected republication of an anonymous, undated English translation published by Bartholomew House, Inc., New York"—T.p. verso.
  ISBN 0-486-27062-9 (pbk.)
PT8861.A31   1992
839.8'226—dc20
                                        91-37873
                                              CIP

Note

ONE OF THE most enduringly popular dramas of the Norwegian poet and playwright Henrik Ibsen (1828–1906), *A Doll's House* (1879) was in its day a startlingly bold exposition of the hypocrisy and concealed struggle within a seemingly happy marriage. Ibsen's characterization of Nora scandalized nineteenth-century audiences, for it suggested that the naivete and childlike impulsiveness of a middle-class housewife— touchstones of the sentimental romanticism of the era—were in fact part of a willful facade erected to achieve a slight autonomy in a society in which women were virtually powerless. This shocking assertion, along with other of the dramatist's innovations, ignited a debate in which "Ibsenism" was alternately touted as the liberation of the theater from the delusions of romantic idealism and denounced as a degenerate attack upon traditional family values.

Although social and artistic developments have lessened the shock value of *A Doll's House*, it still retains power in its depiction of material dependency in affairs of the "heart" and in its forceful demonstration of the ways in which role-playing and expectation in human relationships can stifle an individual's inner reality.

Dramatis Personæ

TORVALD HELMER.
NORA, *his wife*.
DR. RANK.
MRS. LINDE.
NILS KROGSTAD.
HELMER'S *three young children*.
ANNE, *their nurse*.
A HOUSEMAID.
A PORTER.

The action takes place in HELMER'S *house*.

Contents

ACT I	1
ACT II	29
ACT III	51

Act I

SCENE—*A room furnished comfortably and tastefully but not extravagantly. At the back a door to the right leads to the entrance hall; another to the left leads to* HELMER'S *study. Between the doors stands a piano. In the middle of the left-hand wall is a door and beyond a window. Near the window are a round table, armchairs and a small sofa. In the right-hand wall, at the farther end, another door; and on the same side, nearer the footlights, a stove, two easy chairs and a rocking chair; between the stove and the door a small table. Engravings on the walls; a cabinet with china and other small objects; a small bookcase with well-bound books. The floors are carpeted, and a fire burns in the stove. It is winter.*

A bell rings in the hall; shortly afterward the door is heard to open. Enter NORA, *humming a tune and in high spirits. She is in outdoor dress and carries a number of parcels; these she lays on the table to the right. She leaves the outer door open after her, and through it is seen a* PORTER *who is carrying a Christmas tree and a basket, which he gives to the* MAID *who has opened the door.*

NORA. Hide the Christmas tree carefully, Helen. Be sure the children do not see it till this evening, when it is dressed. [*To the* PORTER, *taking out her purse.*] How much?

POR. Sixpence.

NORA. There is a shilling. No, keep the change. [*The* PORTER *thanks her and goes out.* NORA *shuts the door. She is laughing to herself as she takes off her hat and coat. She takes a packet of macaroons from her pocket and eats one or two, then goes cautiously to her husband's door and listens.*] Yes, he is in. [*Still humming, she goes to the table on the right.*]

HEL. [*calls out from his room*]. Is that my little lark twittering out there?

NORA [*busy opening some of the parcels*]. Yes, it is!

HEL. Is it my little squirrel bustling about?
NORA. Yes!
HEL. When did my squirrel come home?
NORA. Just now. [*Puts the bag of macaroons into her pocket and wipes her mouth.*] Come in here, Torvald, and see what I have bought.
HEL. Don't disturb me. [*A little later he opens the door and looks into the room, pen in hand.*] Bought, did you say? All these things? Has my little spendthrift been wasting money again?
NORA. Yes, but, Torvald, this year we really can let ourselves go a little. This is the first Christmas that we have not needed to economize.
HEL. Still, you know, we can't spend money recklessly.
NORA. Yes, Torvald, we may be a wee bit more reckless now, mayn't we? Just a tiny wee bit! You are going to have a big salary and earn lots and lots of money.
HEL. Yes, after the new year; but then it will be a whole quarter before the salary is due.
NORA. Pooh! We can borrow till then.
HEL. Nora! [*Goes up to her and takes her playfully by the ear.*] The same little featherhead! Suppose, now, that I borrowed fifty pounds today and you spent it all in the Christmas week and then on New Year's Eve a slate fell on my head and killed me and——
NORA [*putting her hands over his mouth*]. Oh! don't say such horrid things.
HEL. Still, suppose that happened,—what then?
NORA. If that were to happen, I don't suppose I should care whether I owed money or not.
HEL. Yes, but what about the people who had lent it?
NORA. They? Who would bother about them? I should not know who they were.
HEL. That is like a woman! But seriously, Nora, you know what I think about that. No debt, no borrowing. There can be no freedom or beauty about a home life that depends on borrowing and debt. We two have kept bravely on the straight road so far, and we will go on the same way for the short time longer that there need be any struggle.
NORA [*moving toward the stove*]. As you please, Torvald.
HEL. [*following her*]. Come, come, my little skylark must not droop her

wings. What is this! Is my little squirrel out of temper? [*Taking out his purse.*] Nora, what do you think I have got here?

NORA [*turning round quickly*]. Money!

HEL. There you are. [*Gives her some money.*] Do you think I don't know what a lot is wanted for housekeeping at Christmas time?

NORA [*counting*]. Ten shillings—a pound—two pounds! Thank you, thank you, Torvald; that will keep me going for a long time.

HEL. Indeed it must.

NORA. Yes, yes, it will. But come here and let me show you what I have bought. And all so cheap! Look, here is a new suit for Ivar and a sword, and a horse and a trumpet for Bob, and a doll and dolly's bedstead for Emmy—they are very plain, but anyway she will soon break them in pieces. And here are dress lengths and handkerchiefs for the maids; old Anne ought really to have something better.

HEL. And what is in this parcel?

NORA [*crying out*]. No, no! You mustn't see that till this evening.

HEL. Very well. But now tell me, you extravagant little person, what would you like for yourself?

NORA. For myself? Oh, I am sure I don't want anything.

HEL. Yes, but you must. Tell me something reasonable that you would particularly like to have.

NORA. No, I really can't think of anything—unless, Torvald——

HEL. Well?

NORA [*playing with his coat buttons and without raising her eyes to his*]. If you really want to give me something, you might—you might——

HEL. Well, out with it!

NORA [*speaking quickly*]. You might give me money, Torvald. Only just as much as you can afford; and then one of these days I will buy something with it.

HEL. But, Nora——

NORA. Oh, do! dear Torvald; please, please do! Then I will wrap it up in beautiful gilt paper and hang it on the Christmas tree. Wouldn't that be fun?

HEL. What are little people called that are always wasting money?

NORA. Spendthrifts—I know. Let us do as I suggest, Torvald, and then I shall have time to think what I am most in want of. That is a very sensible plan, isn't it?

HEL. [*smiling*]. Indeed it is—that is to say, if you were really to save out of the money I give you and then really buy something for yourself. But if you spend it all on the housekeeping and any number of unnecessary things, then I merely have to pay up again.

NORA. Oh, but, Torvald——

HEL. You can't deny it, my dear little Nora. [*Puts his arm around her waist.*] It's a sweet little spendthrift, but she uses up a deal of money. One would hardly believe how expensive such little persons are!

NORA. It's a shame to say that. I do really save all I can.

HEL. [*laughing*]. That's very true—all you can. But you can't save anything!

NORA [*smiling quietly and happily*]. You haven't any idea how many expenses we skylarks and squirrels have, Torvald.

HEL. You are an odd little soul. Very like your father. You always find some new way of wheedling money out of me, and as soon as you have got it it seems to melt in your hands. You never know where it has gone. Still, one must take you as you are. It is in the blood; for indeed it is true that you can inherit these things, Nora.

NORA. Ah, I wish I had inherited many of Papa's qualities.

HEL. And I would not wish you to be anything but just what you are, my sweet little skylark. But, do you know, it strikes me that you are looking rather—what shall I say?—rather uneasy today.

NORA. Do I?

HEL. You do, really. Look straight at me.

NORA [*looks at him*]. Well?

HEL. [*wagging his finger at her*]. Hasn't Miss Sweet Tooth been breaking rules in town today?

NORA. No; what makes you think that?

HEL. Hasn't she paid a visit to the confectioner's?

NORA. No, I assure you, Torvald——

HEL. Not been nibbling sweets?

NORA. No, certainly not.

HEL. Not even taken a bite at a macaroon or two?

NORA. No, Torvald, I assure you, really——

HEL. There, there, of course I was only joking.

NORA [*going to the table on the right*]. I should not think of going against your wishes.

HEL. No, I am sure of that; besides, you gave me your word. [*Going up to her.*] Keep your little Christmas secrets to yourself, my darling.

They will all be revealed tonight when the Christmas tree is lit, no doubt.

NORA. Did you remember to invite Doctor Rank?

HEL. No. But there is no need; as a matter of course he will come to dinner with us. However, I will ask him when he comes in this morning. I have ordered some good wine. Nora, you can't think how I am looking forward to this evening.

NORA. So am I! And how the children will enjoy themselves, Torvald!

HEL. It is splendid to feel that one has a perfectly safe appointment and a big enough income. It's delightful to think of, isn't it?

NORA. It's wonderful!

HEL. Do you remember last Christmas? For a full three weeks beforehand you shut yourself up every evening till long after midnight, making ornaments for the Christmas tree and all the other fine things that were to be a surprise to us. It was the dullest three weeks I ever spent!

NORA. I didn't find it dull.

HEL. [*smiling*]. But there was precious little result, Nora.

NORA. Oh, you shouldn't tease me about that again. How could I help the cat's going in and tearing everything to pieces?

HEL. Of course you couldn't, poor little girl. You had the best of intentions to please us all, and that's the main thing. But it is a good thing that our hard times are over.

NORA. Yes, it is really wonderful.

HEL. This time I needn't sit here and be dull all alone and you needn't ruin your dear eyes and your pretty little hands——

NORA [*clapping her hands*]. No, Torvald, I needn't any longer, need I! It's wonderfully lovely to hear you say so! [*Taking his arm.*] Now I will tell you how I have been thinking we ought to arrange things, Torvald. As soon as Christmas is over—— [*A bell rings in the hall.*] There's the bell. [*She tidies the room a little.*] There's someone at the door. What a nuisance!

HEL. If it is a caller, remember I am not at home.

MAID [*in the doorway*]. A lady to see you, ma'am—a stranger.

NORA. Ask her to come in.

MAID [*to* HELMER]. The doctor came at the same time, sir.

HEL. Did he go straight into my room?

MAID. Yes sir.

[HELMER *goes into his room. The* MAID *ushers in* MRS. LINDE, *who is in traveling dress, and shuts the door.*]

MRS. L. [*in a dejected and timid voice*]. How do you do, Nora?
NORA [*doubtfully*]. How do you do——
MRS. L. You don't recognize me, I suppose.
NORA. No, I don't know—yes, to be sure, I seem to—— [*Suddenly.*] Yes! Christine! Is it really you?
MRS. L. Yes, it is I.
NORA. Christine! To think of my not recognizing you! And yet how could I? [*In a gentle voice.*] How you have altered, Christine!
MRS. L. Yes, I have indeed. In nine, ten long years——
NORA. Is it so long since we met? I suppose it is. The last eight years have been a happy time for me, I can tell you. And so now you have come into the town and have taken this long journey in winter—that was plucky of you.
MRS. L. I arrived by steamer this morning.
NORA. To have some fun at Christmas time, of course. How delightful! We will have such fun together! But take off your things. You are not cold, I hope. [*Helps her.*] Now we will sit down by the stove and be cozy. No, take this armchair; I will sit here in the rocking chair. [*Takes her hands.*] Now you look like your old self again; it was only the first moment—— You are a little paler, Christine, and perhaps a little thinner.
MRS. L. And much, much older, Nora.
NORA. Perhaps a little older; very, very little; certainly not much. [*Stops suddenly and speaks seriously.*] What a thoughtless creature I am, chattering away like this. My poor, dear Christine, do forgive me.
MRS. L. What do you mean, Nora?
NORA [*gently*]. Poor Christine, you are a widow.
MRS. L. Yes; it is three years ago now.
NORA. Yes, I knew; I saw it in the papers. I assure you, Christine, I meant ever so often to write to you at the time, but I always put it off and something always prevented me.
MRS. L. I quite understand, dear.
NORA. It was very bad of me, Christine. Poor thing, how you must have suffered. And he left you nothing?
MRS. L. No.
NORA. And no children?

Mrs. L. No.

Nora. Nothing at all, then?

Mrs. L. Not even any sorrow or grief to live upon.

Nora [*looking incredulously at her*]. But, Christine, is that possible?

Mrs. L. [*smiles sadly and strokes her hair*]. It sometimes happens, Nora.

Nora. So you are quite alone. How dreadfully sad that must be. I have three lovely children. You can't see them just now, for they are out with their nurse. But now you must tell me all about it.

Mrs. L. No, no; I want to hear about you.

Nora. No, you must begin. I mustn't be selfish today; today I must only think of your affairs. But there is one thing I must tell you. Do you know we have just had a great piece of good luck?

Mrs. L. No, what is it?

Nora. Just fancy, my husband has been made manager of the bank!

Mrs. L. Your husband? What good luck!

Nora. Yes, tremendous! A barrister's profession is such an uncertain thing, especially if he won't undertake unsavory cases; and naturally Torvald has never been willing to do that, and I quite agree with him. You may imagine how pleased we are! He is to take up his work in the bank at the new year, and then he will have a big salary and lots of commissions. For the future we can live quite differently—we can do just as we like. I feel so relieved and so happy, Christine! It will be splendid to have heaps of money and not need to have any anxiety, won't it?

Mrs. L. Yes, anyhow I think it would be delightful to have what one needs.

Nora. No, not only what one needs but heaps and heaps of money.

Mrs. L. [*smiling*]. Nora, Nora, haven't you learned sense yet? In our schooldays you were a great spendthrift.

Nora [*laughing*]. Yes, that is what Torvald says now. [*Wags her finger at her.*] But "Nora, Nora" is not so silly as you think. We have not been in a position for me to waste money. We have both had to work.

Mrs. L. You too?

Nora. Yes; odds and ends, needlework, crochet work, embroidery and that kind of thing. [*Dropping her voice.*] And other things as well. You know Torvald left his office when we were married? There was no prospect of promotion there, and he had to try and earn more than before. But during the first year he overworked himself dreadfully. You see, he had to make money every way he could; and he worked early and late; but he couldn't stand it and fell dreadfully ill, and the doctors said it was necessary for him to go south.

MRS. L. You spent a whole year in Italy, didn't you?

NORA. Yes. It was no easy matter to get away, I can tell you. It was just after Ivar was born, but naturally we had to go. It was a wonderfully beautiful journey, and it saved Torvald's life. But it cost a tremendous lot of money, Christine.

MRS. L. So I should think.

NORA. It cost about two hundred and fifty pounds. That's a lot, isn't it?

MRS. L. Yes, and in emergencies like that it is lucky to have the money.

NORA. I ought to tell you that we had it from Papa.

MRS. L. Oh, I see. It was just about that time that he died, wasn't it?

NORA. Yes; and, just think of it, I couldn't go and nurse him. I was expecting little Ivar's birth every day and I had my poor sick Torvald to look after. My dear, kind father—I never saw him again, Christine. That was the saddest time I have known since our marriage.

MRS. L. I know how fond you were of him. And then you went off to Italy?

NORA. Yes; you see, we had money then, and the doctors insisted on our going, so we started a month later.

MRS. L. And your husband came back quite well?

NORA. As sound as a bell!

MRS. L. But—the doctor?

NORA. What doctor?

MRS. L. I thought your maid said the gentleman who arrived here just as I did was the doctor.

NORA. Yes, that was Doctor Rank, but he doesn't come here professionally. He is our greatest friend and comes in at least once every day. No, Torvald has not had an hour's illness since then, and our children are strong and healthy and so am I. [*Jumps up and claps her hands.*] Christine! Christine! It's good to be alive and happy! But how horrid of me; I am talking of nothing but my own affairs. [*Sits on a stool near her and rests her arms on her knees.*] You mustn't be angry with me. Tell me, is it really true that you did not love your husband? Why did you marry him?

MRS. L. My mother was alive then and was bedridden and helpless, and I had to provide for my two younger brothers; so I did not think I was justified in refusing his offer.

NORA. No, perhaps you were quite right. He was rich at that time, then?
MRS. L. I believe he was quite well off. But his business was a precarious one, and when he died it all went to pieces and there was nothing left.
NORA. And then?
MRS. L. Well, I had to turn my hand to anything I could find—first a small shop, then a small school and so on. The last three years have seemed like one long working day, with no rest. Now it is at an end, Nora. My poor mother needs me no more, for she is gone; and the boys do not need me either; they have got situations and can shift for themselves.
NORA. What a relief you must feel it.
MRS. L. No indeed; I only feel my life unspeakably empty. No one to live for any more. [*Gets up restlessly.*] That was why I could not stand the life in my little backwater any longer. I hope it may be easier here to find something which will busy me and occupy my thoughts. If only I could have the good luck to get some regular work—office work of some kind——
NORA. But, Christine, that is so frightfully tiring, and you look tired out now. You had far better go away to some watering place.
MRS. L. [*walking to the window*]. I have no father to give me money for a journey, Nora.
NORA [*rising*]. Oh, don't be angry with me.
MRS. L. [*going up to her*]. It is you that must not be angry with me, dear. The worst of a position like mine is that it makes one so bitter. No one to work for and yet obliged to be always on the lookout for chances. One must live, and so one becomes selfish. When you told me of the happy turn your fortunes have taken—you will hardly believe it—I was delighted not so much on your account as on my own.
NORA. How do you mean? Oh, I understand. You mean that perhaps Torvald could get you something to do.
MRS. L. Yes, that was what I was thinking of.
NORA. He must, Christine. Just leave it to me; I will broach the subject very cleverly—I will think of something that will please him very much. It will make me so happy to be of some use to you.
MRS. L. How kind you are, Nora, to be so anxious to help me! It is

doubly kind in you, for you know so little of the burdens and troubles of life.

Nora. I? I know so little of them?

Mrs. L. [*smiling*]. My dear! Small household cares and that sort of thing! You are a child, Nora.

Nora [*tosses her head and crosses the stage*]. You ought not to be so superior.

Mrs. L. No?

Nora. You are just like the others. They all think that I am incapable of anything really serious——

Mrs. L. Come, come.

Nora. —that I have gone through nothing in this world of cares.

Mrs. L. But, my dear Nora, you have just told me all your troubles.

Nora. Pooh!—those were trifles. [*Lowering her voice.*] I have not told you the important thing.

Mrs. L. The important thing? What do you mean?

Nora. You look down upon me altogether, Christine—but you ought not to. You are proud, aren't you, of having worked so hard and so long for your mother?

Mrs. L. Indeed, I don't look down on anyone. But it is true that I am both proud and glad to think that I was privileged to make the end of my mother's life almost free from care.

Nora. And you are proud to think of what you have done for your brothers.

Mrs. L. I think I have the right to be.

Nora. I think so too. But now listen to this; I too have something to be proud and glad of.

Mrs. L. I have no doubt you have. But what do you refer to?

Nora. Speak low. Suppose Torvald were to hear! He mustn't on any account—no one in the world must know, Christine, except you.

Mrs. L. But what is it?

Nora. Come here. [*Pulls her down on the sofa beside her.*] Now I will show you that I too have something to be proud and glad of. It was I who saved Torvald's life.

Mrs. L. "Saved"? How?

Nora. I told you about our trip to Italy. Torvald would never have recovered if he had not gone there.

Mrs. L. Yes, but your father gave you the necessary funds.

NORA [*smiling*]. Yes, that is what Torvald and the others think, but——
MRS. L. But——
NORA. Papa didn't give us a shilling. It was I who procured the money.
MRS. L. You? All that large sum?
NORA. Two hundred and fifty pounds. What do you think of that?
MRS. L. But, Nora, how could you possibly do it? Did you win a prize in the lottery?
NORA [*contemptuously*]. In the lottery? There would have been no credit in that.
MRS. L. But where did you get it from, then?
NORA [*humming and smiling with an air of mystery*]. Hm, hm! Aha!
MRS. L. Because you couldn't have borrowed it.
NORA. Couldn't I? Why not?
MRS. L. No, a wife cannot borrow without her husband's consent.
NORA [*tossing her head*]. Oh, if it is a wife who has any head for business—a wife who has the wit to be a little bit clever——
MRS. L. I don't understand it at all, Nora.
NORA. There is no need you should. I never said I had borrowed the money. I may have got it some other way. [*Lies back on the sofa.*] Perhaps I got it from some other admirers. When anyone is as attractive as I am——
MRS. L. You are a mad creature.
NORA. Now you know you're full of curiosity, Christine.
MRS. L. Listen to me, Nora dear. Haven't you been a little bit imprudent?
NORA [*sits up straight*]. Is it imprudent to save your husband's life?
MRS. L. It seems to me imprudent, without his knowledge, to——
NORA. But it was absolutely necessary that he should not know! My goodness, can't you understand that? It was necessary he should have no idea what a dangerous condition he was in. It was to me that the doctors came and said that his life was in danger and that the only thing to save him was to live in the south. Do you suppose I didn't try, first of all, to get what I wanted as if it were for myself? I told him how much I should love to travel abroad like other young wives; I tried tears and entreaties with him; I told him that he ought to remember the condition I was in and that he ought to be kind and indulgent to me; I even hinted that he might raise a loan. That

nearly made him angry, Christine. He said I was thoughtless and that it was his duty as my husband not to indulge me in my whims and caprices—as I believe he called them. Very well, I thought, you must be saved—and that was how I came to devise a way out of the difficulty.

MRS. L. And did your husband never get to know from your father that the money had not come from him?

NORA. No, never. Papa died just at that time. I had meant to let him into the secret and beg him never to reveal it. But he was so ill then—alas, there never was any need to tell him.

MRS. L. And since then have you never told your secret to your husband?

NORA. Good heavens, no! How could you think so? A man who has such strong opinions about these things! And besides, how painful and humiliating it would be for Torvald, with his manly independence, to know that he owed me anything! It would upset our mutual relations altogether; our beautiful happy home would no longer be what it is now.

MRS. L. Do you mean never to tell him about it?

NORA [*meditatively and with a half-smile*]. Yes—someday, perhaps, after many years, when I am no longer as nice looking as I am now. Don't laugh at me! I mean, of course, when Torvald is no longer as devoted to me as he is now; when my dancing and dressing-up and reciting have palled on him; then it may be a good thing to have something in reserve—— [*Breaking off.*] What nonsense! That time will never come. Now what do you think of my great secret, Christine? Do you still think I am of no use? I can tell you, too, that this affair has caused me a lot of worry. It has been by no means easy for me to meet my engagements punctually. I may tell you that there is something that is called, in business, quarterly interest and another thing called payment in installments, and it is always so dreadfully difficult to manage them. I have had to save a little here and there, where I could, you understand. I have not been able to put aside much from my housekeeping money, for Torvald must have a good table. I couldn't let my children be shabbily dressed; I have felt obliged to use up all he gave me for them, the sweet little darlings!

MRS. L. So it has all had to come out of your own necessaries of life, poor Nora?

NORA. Of course. Besides, I was the one responsible for it. Whenever Torvald has given me money for new dresses and such things I have never spent more than half of it; I have always bought the simplest and cheapest things. Thank heaven any clothes look well on me, and so Torvald has never noticed it. But it was often very hard on me, Christine—because it is delightful to be really well dressed, isn't it?

MRS. L. Quite so.

NORA. Well, then I have found other ways of earning money. Last winter I was lucky enough to get a lot of copying to do, so I locked myself up and sat writing every evening until quite late at night. Many a time I was desperately tired, but all the same it was a tremendous pleasure to sit there working and earning money. It was like being a man.

MRS. L. How much have you been able to pay off in that way?

NORA. I can't tell you exactly. You see, it is very difficult to keep an account of a business matter of that kind. I only know that I have paid every penny that I could scrape together. Many a time I was at my wits' end. [*Smiles.*] Then I used to sit here and imagine that a rich old gentleman had fallen in love with me——

MRS. L. What! Who was it?

NORA. Be quiet!—that he had died and that when his will was opened it contained, written in big letters, the instruction: "The lovely Mrs. Nora Helmer is to have all I possess paid over to her at once in cash."

MRS. L. But, my dear Nora—who could the man be?

NORA. Good gracious, can't you understand? There was no old gentleman at all; it was only something that I used to sit here and imagine, when I couldn't think of any way of procuring money. But it's all the same now; the tiresome old person can stay where he is as far as I am concerned; I don't care about him or his will either, for I am free from care now. [*Jumps up.*] My goodness, it's delightful to think of, Christine! Free from care! To be able to be free from care, quite free from care; to be able to play and romp with the children; to be able to keep the house beautifully and have everything just as Torvald likes it! And, think of it, soon the spring will come and the big blue sky! Perhaps we shall be able to take a little trip—perhaps I shall see the sea again! Oh, it's a wonderful thing to be alive and be happy. [*A bell is heard in the hall.*]

MRS. L. [*rising*]. There is the bell; perhaps I had better go.

NORA. No, don't go; no one will come in here; it is sure to be for Torvald.
SERVANT [*at the hall door*]. Excuse me, ma'am—there is a gentleman to see the master, and as the doctor is with him——
NORA. Who is it?
KROG. [*at the door*]. It is I, Mrs. Helmer. [MRS. LINDE *starts, trembles and turns to the window.*]
NORA [*takes a step toward him and speaks in a strained, low voice*]. You? What is it? What do you want to see my husband about?
KROG. Bank business—in a way. I have a small post in the bank, and I hear your husband is to be our chief now.
NORA. Then it is——
KROG. Nothing but dry business matters, Mrs. Helmer; absolutely nothing else.
NORA. Be so good as to go into the study then. [*She bows indifferently to him and shuts the door into the hall, then comes back and makes up the fire in the stove.*]
MRS. L. Nora—who was that man?
NORA. A lawyer of the name of Krogstad.
MRS. L. Then it really was he.
NORA. Do you know the man?
MRS. L. I used to—many years ago. At one time he was a solicitor's clerk in our town.
NORA. Yes, he was.
MRS. L. He is greatly altered.
NORA. He made a very unhappy marriage.
MRS. L. He is a widower now, isn't he?
NORA. With several children. There now, it is burning up. [*Shuts the door of the stove and moves the rocking chair aside.*]
MRS. L. They say he carries on various kinds of business.
NORA. Really! Perhaps he does; I don't know anything about it. But don't let us think of business; it is so tiresome.
DR. RANK [*comes out of* HELMER'S *study. Before he shuts the door he calls to him*]. No, my dear fellow, I won't disturb you; I would rather go in to your wife for a little while. [*Shuts the door and sees* MRS. LINDE.] I beg your pardon; I am afraid I am disturbing you too.
NORA. No, not at all. [*Introducing him.*] Doctor Rank, Mrs. Linde.
RANK. I have often heard Mrs. Linde's name mentioned here. I think I passed you on the stairs when I arrived, Mrs. Linde?

Mrs. L. Yes, I go up very slowly; I can't manage stairs well.
Rank. Ah! Some slight internal weakness?
Mrs. L. No, the fact is I have been overworking myself.
Rank. Nothing more than that? Then I suppose you have come to town to amuse yourself with our entertainments?
Mrs. L. I have come to look for work.
Rank. Is that a good cure for overwork?
Mrs. L. One must live, Doctor Rank.
Rank. Yes, the general opinion seems to be that it is necessary.
Nora. Look here, Doctor Rank—you know you want to live.
Rank. Certainly. However wretched I may feel, I want to prolong the agony as long as possible. All my patients are like that. And so are those who are morally diseased; one of them, and a bad case too, is at this very moment with Helmer——
Mrs. L. [*sadly*]. Ah!
Nora. Whom do you mean?
Rank. A lawyer of the name of Krogstad, a fellow you don't know at all. He suffers from a diseased moral character, Mrs. Helmer, but even he began talking of its being highly important that he should live.
Nora. Did he? What did he want to speak to Torvald about?
Rank. I have no idea; I only heard that it was something about the bank.
Nora. I didn't know this—what's his name?—Krogstad had anything to do with the bank.
Rank. Yes, he has some sort of appointment there. [*To* Mrs. Linde.] I don't know whether you find also in your part of the world that there are certain people who go zealously snuffing about to smell out moral corruption and, as soon as they have found some, put the person concerned into some lucrative position where they can keep their eye on him. Healthy natures are left out in the cold.
Mrs. L. Still I think the sick are those who most need taking care of.
Rank [*shrugging his shoulders*]. Yes, there you are. That is the sentiment that is turning society into a sick house.

[Nora, *who has been absorbed in her thoughts, breaks out into smothered laughter and claps her hands.*]

Rank. Why do you laugh at that? Have you any notion what society really is?
Nora. What do I care about tiresome society? I am laughing at

something quite different, something extremely amusing. Tell me, Doctor Rank, are all the people who are employed in the bank dependent on Torvald now?

RANK. Is that what you find so extremely amusing?

NORA [*smiling and humming*]. That's my affair! [*Walking about the room.*] It's perfectly glorious to think that we have—that Torvald has so much power over so many people. [*Takes the packet from her pocket.*] Doctor Rank, what do you say to a macaroon?

RANK. What, macaroons? I thought they were forbidden here.

NORA. Yes, but these are some Christine gave me.

MRS. L. What! I?

NORA. Oh well, don't be alarmed! You couldn't know that Torvald had forbidden them. I must tell you that he is afraid they will spoil my teeth. But, bah!—once in a way—— That's so, isn't it, Doctor Rank? By your leave! [*Puts a macaroon into his mouth.*] You must have one too, Christine. And I shall have one, just a little one—or at most two. [*Walking about.*] I am tremendously happy. There is just one thing in the world now that I should dearly love to do.

RANK. Well, what is that?

NORA. It's something I should dearly love to say if Torvald could hear me.

RANK. Well, why can't you say it?

NORA. No, I daren't; it's so shocking.

MRS. L. Shocking?

RANK. Well, I should not advise you to say it. Still, with us you might. What is it you would so much like to say if Torvald could hear you?

NORA. I should just love to say— Well, I'm damned!

RANK. Are you mad?

MRS. L. Nora dear!

RANK. Say it, here he is!

NORA [*hiding the packet*]. Hush! Hush! Hush!

[HELMER *comes out of his room with his coat over his arm and his hat in his hand.*]

NORA. Well, Torvald dear, have you got rid of him?

HEL. Yes, he has just gone.

NORA. Let me introduce you—this is Christine, who has come to town.

Hel. Christine? Excuse me, but I don't know——
Nora. Mrs. Linde, dear; Christine Linde.
Hel. Of course. A school friend of my wife's, I presume?
Mrs. L. Yes, we have known each other since then.
Nora. And just think, she has taken a long journey in order to see you.
Hel. What do you mean?
Mrs. L. No, really, I——
Nora. Christine is tremendously clever at bookkeeping, and she is frightfully anxious to work under some clever man, so as to perfect herself——
Hel. Very sensible, Mrs. Linde.
Nora. And when she heard you had been appointed manager of the bank—the news was telegraphed, you know—she traveled here as quick as she could. Torvald, I am sure you will be able to do something for Christine, for my sake, won't you?
Hel. Well, it is not altogether impossible. I presume you are a widow, Mrs. Linde?
Mrs. L. Yes.
Hel. And have had some experience of bookkeeping?
Mrs. L. Yes, a fair amount.
Hel. Ah well, it's very likely I may be able to find something for you.
Nora [*clapping her hands*]. What did I tell you?
Hel. You have just come at a fortunate moment, Mrs. Linde.
Mrs. L. How am I to thank you?
Hel. There is no need. [*Puts on his coat.*] But today you must excuse me——
Rank. Wait a minute; I will come with you. [*Brings his fur coat from the hall and warms it at the fire.*]
Nora. Don't be long away, Torvald dear.
Hel. About an hour, not more.
Nora. Are you going too, Christine?
Mrs. L. [*putting on her cloak*]. Yes, I must go and look for a room.
Hel. Oh well, then, we can walk down the street together.
Nora [*helping her*]. What a pity it is we are so short of space here; I am afraid it is impossible for us——
Mrs. L. Please don't think of it! Good-by, Nora dear, and many thanks.
Nora. Good-by for the present. Of course you will come back this evening. And you too, Doctor Rank. What do you say? If you are well

enough? Oh, you must be! Wrap yourself up well. [*They go to the door all talking together. Children's voices are heard on the staircase.*]

NORA. There they are. There they are! [*She runs to open the door. The* NURSE *comes in with the children.*] Come in! Come in! [*Stoops and kisses them.*] Oh, you sweet blessings! Look at them, Christine! Aren't they darlings?

RANK. Don't let us stand here in the draught.

HEL. Come along, Mrs. Linde; the place will only be bearable for a mother now!

[RANK, HELMER *and* MRS. LINDE *go downstairs. The* NURSE *comes forward with the children;* NORA *shuts the hall door.*]

NORA. How fresh and well you look! Such red cheeks!—like apples and roses. [*The children all talk at once while she speaks to them.*] Have you had great fun? That's splendid! What, you pulled both Emmy and Bob along on the sledge? Both at once? That *was* good. You are a clever boy, Ivar. Let me take her for a little, Anne. My sweet little baby doll! [*Takes the baby from the* MAID *and dances it up and down.*] Yes, yes, Mother will dance with Bob too. What! Have you been snowballing? I wish I had been there too! No, no, I will take their things off, Anne; please let me do it, it is such fun. Go in now, you look half frozen. There is some hot coffee for you on the stove.

[*The* NURSE *goes into the room on the left.* NORA *takes off the children's things and throws them about while they all talk to her at once.*]

NORA. *Really!* Did a big dog run after you? But it didn't bite you? No, dogs don't bite nice little dolly children. You mustn't look at the parcels, Ivar. What are they? Ah, I daresay you would like to know. No, no—it's something nasty! Come, let us have a game! What shall we play at? Hide and seek? Yes, we'll play hide and seek. Bob shall hide first. Must I hide? Very well, I'll hide first. [*She and the children laugh and shout and romp in and out of the room; at last* NORA *hides under the table; the children rush in and look for her but do not see her; they hear her smothered laughter, run to the table, lift up the cloth and find her. Shouts of laughter. She crawls forward and pretends to frighten them. Fresh laughter. Meanwhile there has been a knock at the hall door but none of them has noticed it. The door is half opened and* KROGSTAD *appears. He waits a little; the game goes on.*]

KROG. Excuse me, Mrs. Helmer.
NORA [*with a stifled cry turns round and gets up onto her knees*]. Ah! What do you want?
KROG. Excuse me, the outer door was ajar; I suppose someone forgot to shut it.
NORA [*rising*]. My husband is out, Mr. Krogstad.
KROG. I know that.
NORA. What do you want here then?
KROG. A word with you.
NORA. With me? [*To the children, gently.*] Go in to Nurse. What? No, the strange man won't do Mother any harm. When he has gone we will have another game. [*She takes the children into the room on the left and shuts the door after them.*] You want to speak to me?
KROG. Yes, I do.
NORA. Today? It is not the first of the month yet.
KROG. No, it is Christmas Eve, and it will depend on yourself what sort of a Christmas you will spend.
NORA. What do you want? Today it is absolutely impossible for me——
KROG. We won't talk about that till later on. This is something different. I presume you can give me a moment?
NORA. Yes—yes, I can—although——
KROG. Good. I was in Olsen's Restaurant and saw your husband going down the street——
NORA. Yes?
KROG. With a lady.
NORA. What then?
KROG. May I make so bold as to ask if it was a Mrs. Linde?
NORA. It was.
KROG. Just arrived in town?
NORA. Yes, today.
KROG. She is a great friend of yours, isn't she?
NORA. She is. But I don't see——
KROG. I knew her too, once upon a time.
NORA. I am aware of that.
KROG. Are you? So you know all about it; I thought as much. Then I can ask you, without beating about the bush—is Mrs. Linde to have an appointment in the bank?
NORA. What right have you to question me, Mr. Krogstad? You, one of

my husband's subordinates! But since you ask, you shall know. Yes, Mrs. Linde *is* to have an appointment. And it was I who pleaded her cause, Mr. Krogstad, let me tell you that.

KROG. I was right in what I thought then.

NORA [*walking up and down the stage*]. Sometimes one has a tiny little bit of influence, I should hope. Because one is a woman it does not necessarily follow that—— When anyone is in a subordinate position, Mr. Krogstad, they should really be careful to avoid offending anyone who—who——

KROG. Who has influence?

NORA. Exactly.

KROG. [*changing his tone*]. Mrs. Helmer, you will be so good as to use your influence on my behalf.

NORA. What? What do you mean?

KROG. You will be so kind as to see that I am allowed to keep my subordinate position in the bank.

NORA. What do you mean by that? Who proposes to take your post away from you?

KROG. Oh, there is no necessity to keep up the pretense of ignorance. I can quite understand that your friend is not very anxious to expose herself to the chance of rubbing shoulders with me, and I quite understand, too, whom I have to thank for being turned off.

NORA. But I assure you——

KROG. Very likely; but, to come to the point, the time has come when I should advise you to use your influence to prevent that.

NORA. But, Mr. Krogstad, I *have* no influence.

KROG. Haven't you? I thought you said yourself just now——

NORA. Naturally I did not mean you to put that construction on it. I! What should make you think I have any influence of that kind with my husband?

KROG. Oh, I have known your husband from our student days. I don't suppose he is any more unassailable than other husbands.

NORA. If you speak slightingly of my husband, I shall turn you out of the house.

KROG. You are bold, Mrs. Helmer.

NORA. I am not afraid of you any longer. As soon as the New Year comes I shall in a very short time be free of the whole thing.

KROG. [*controlling himself*]. Listen to me, Mrs. Helmer. If necessary, I am prepared to fight for my small post in the bank as if I were fighting for my life.

NORA. So it seems.

KROG. It is not only for the sake of the money; indeed, that weighs least with me in the matter. There is another reason—well, I may as well tell you. My position is this. I daresay you know, like everybody else, that once, many years ago, I was guilty of an indiscretion.

NORA. I think I have heard something of the kind.

KROG. The matter never came into court, but every way seemed to be closed to me after that. So I took to the business that you know of. I had to do something; and, honestly, I don't think I've been one of the worst. But now I must cut myself free from all that. My sons are growing up; for their sake I must try and win back as much respect as I can in the town. This post in the bank was like the first step up for me—and now your husband is going to kick me downstairs again into the mud.

NORA. But you must believe me, Mr. Krogstad; it is not in my power to help you at all.

KROG. Then it is because you haven't the will, but I have means to compel you.

NORA. You don't mean that you will tell my husband that I owe you money?

KROG. Hm! Suppose I were to tell him?

NORA. It would be perfectly infamous of you. [*Sobbing.*] To think of his learning my secret, which has been my joy and pride, in such an ugly, clumsy way—that he should learn it from you! And it would put me in a horribly disagreeable position.

KROG. Only disagreeable?

NORA [*impetuously*]. Well, do it then!—and it will be the worse for you. My husband will see for himself what a blackguard you are, and you certainly won't keep your post then.

KROG. I asked you if it was only a disagreeable scene at home that you were afraid of?

NORA. If my husband does get to know of it, of course he will at once pay you what is still owing, and we shall have nothing more to do with you.

KROG. [*coming a step nearer*]. Listen to me, Mrs. Helmer. Either you have a very bad memory or you know very little of business. I shall be obliged to remind you of a few details.

NORA. What do you mean?

KROG. When your husband was ill you came to me to borrow two hundred and fifty pounds.

NORA. I didn't know anyone else to go to.

KROG. I promised to get you that amount——

NORA. Yes, and you did so.

KROG. I promised to get you that amount on certain conditions. Your mind was so taken up with your husband's illness and you were so anxious to get the money for your journey that you seem to have paid no attention to the conditions of our bargain. Therefore it will not be amiss if I remind you of them. Now I promised to get the money on the security of a bond which I drew up.

NORA. Yes, and which I signed.

KROG. Good. But below your signature there were a few lines constituting your father a surety for the money; those lines your father should have signed.

NORA. Should? He did sign them.

KROG. I had left the date blank; that is to say your father should himself have inserted the date on which he signed the paper. Do you remember that?

NORA. Yes, I think I remember.

KROG. Then I gave you the bond to send by post to your father. Is that not so?

NORA. Yes.

KROG. And you naturally did so at once, because five or six days afterward you brought me the bond with your father's signature. And then I gave you the money.

NORA. Well, haven't I been paying it off regularly?

KROG. Fairly so, yes. But—to come back to the matter in hand—that must have been a very trying time for you, Mrs. Helmer?

NORA. It was, indeed.

KROG. Your father was very ill, wasn't he?

NORA. He was very near his end.

KROG. And died soon afterward?

NORA. Yes.

KROG. Tell me, Mrs. Helmer, can you by any chance remember what day your father died?—on what day of the month, I mean.

NORA. Papa died on the twenty-ninth of September.

KROG. That is correct; I have ascertained it for myself. And, as that is so, there is a discrepancy [*taking a paper from his pocket*] which I cannot account for.

NORA. What discrepancy? I don't know——

KROG. The discrepancy consists, Mrs. Helmer, in the fact that your father signed this bond three days after his death.

NORA. What do you mean? I don't understand.

KROG. Your father died on the twenty-ninth of September. But look here; your father has dated his signature the second of October. It is a discrepancy, isn't it? [NORA *is silent.*] Can you explain it to me? [NORA *is still silent.*] It is a remarkable thing, too, that the words "second of October," as well as the year, are not written in your father's handwriting but in one that I think I know. Well, of course it can be explained; your father may have forgotten to date his signature and someone else may have dated it haphazard before they knew of his death. There is no harm in that. It all depends on the signature of the name, and *that* is genuine, I suppose, Mrs. Helmer? It was your father himself who signed his name here?

NORA [*after a short pause, throws her head up and looks defiantly at him*]. No, it was not. It was I that wrote Papa's name.

KROG. Are you aware that is a dangerous confession?

NORA. In what way? You shall have your money soon.

KROG. Let me ask you a question: why did you not send the paper to your father?

NORA. It was impossible; Papa was so ill. If I had asked him for his signature, I should have had to tell him what the money was to be used for; and when he was so ill himself I couldn't tell him that my husband's life was in danger—it was impossible.

KROG. It would have been better for you if you had given up your trip abroad.

NORA. No, that was impossible. That trip was to save my husband's life; I couldn't give that up.

KROG. But did it never occur to you that you were committing a fraud on me?

NORA. I couldn't take that into account; I didn't trouble myself about you at all. I couldn't bear you because you put so many heartless difficulties in my way although you knew what a dangerous condition my husband was in.

KROG. Mrs. Helmer, you evidently do not realize clearly what it is that you have been guilty of. But I can assure you that my one false step, which lost me all my reputation, was nothing more or nothing worse than what you have done.

NORA. You? Do you ask me to believe that you were brave enough to run a risk to save your wife's life?

KROG. The law cares nothing about motives.

NORA. Then it must be a very foolish law.

KROG. Foolish or not, it is the law by which you will be judged if I produce this paper in court.

NORA. I don't believe it. Is a daughter not to be allowed to spare her dying father anxiety and care? Is a wife not to be allowed to save her husband's life? I don't know much about law, but I am certain that there must be laws permitting such things as that. Have you no knowledge of such laws—you who are a lawyer? You must be a very poor lawyer, Mr. Krogstad.

KROG. Maybe. But matters of business—such business as you and I have had together—do you think I don't understand that? Very well. Do as you please. But let me tell you this—if I lose my position a second time, you shall lose yours with me. [*He bows and goes out through the hall.*]

NORA [*appears buried in thought for a short time, then tosses her head*]. Nonsense! Trying to frighten me like that! I am not so silly as he thinks. [*Begins to busy herself putting the children's things in order.*] And yet—— No, it's impossible! I did it for love's sake.

THE CHILDREN [*in the doorway on the left*]. Mother, the stranger man has gone out through the gate.

NORA. Yes, dears, I know. But don't tell anyone about the stranger man. Do you hear? Not even Papa.

CHILDREN. No, Mother; but will you come and play again?

NORA. No, no—not now.

CHILDREN. But, Mother, you promised us.

NORA. Yes, but I can't now. Run away in; I have such a lot to do. Run away in, my sweet little darlings. [*She gets them into the room by degrees and shuts the door on them, then sits down on the sofa, takes up a piece of needlework and sews a few stitches but soon stops.*] No! [*Throws down the work, gets up, goes to the hall door and calls out.*] Helen! bring the tree in. [*Goes to the table on the left, opens a drawer and stops again.*] No, no! It is quite impossible!

MAID [*coming in with the tree*]. Where shall I put it, ma'am?
NORA. Here, in the middle of the floor.
MAID. Shall I get you anything else?
NORA. No, thank you. I have all I want.

[*Exit* MAID.]

NORA [*begins dressing the tree*]. A candle here—and flowers here—— The horrible man! It's all nonsense—there's nothing wrong. The tree shall be splendid! I will do everything I can think of to please you, Torvald! I will sing for you, dance for you—— [HELMER *comes in with some papers under his arm.*] Oh, are you back already?
HEL. Yes. Has anyone been here?
NORA. Here? No.
HEL. That is strange. I saw Krogstad going out of the gate.
NORA. Did you? Oh yes, I forgot, Krogstad was here for a moment.
HEL. Nora, I can see from your manner that he has been here begging you to say a good word for him.
NORA. Yes.
HEL. And you were to appear to do it of your own accord; you were to conceal from me the fact of his having been here; didn't he beg that of you too?
NORA. Yes, Torvald, but——
HEL. Nora, Nora, and you would be a party to that sort of thing? To have any talk with a man like that and give him any sort of promise? And to tell me a lie into the bargain?
NORA. A lie?
HEL. Didn't you tell me no one had been here? [*Shakes his finger at her.*] My little songbird must never do that again. A songbird must have a clean beak to chirp with—no false notes! [*Puts his arm around her waist.*] That is so, isn't it? Yes, I am sure it is. [*Lets her go.*] We will say no more about it. [*Sits down by the stove.*] How warm and snug it is here! [*Turns over his papers.*]
NORA [*after a short pause during which she busies herself with the Christmas tree*]. Torvald!
HEL. Yes.
NORA. I am looking forward tremendously to the fancy-dress ball at the Stenborgs' the day after tomorrow.
HEL. And I am tremendously curious to see what you are going to surprise me with.

NORA. It was very silly of me to want to do that.
HEL. What do you mean?
NORA. I can't hit upon anything that will do; everything I think of seems so silly and insignificant.
HEL. Does my little Nora acknowledge that at last?
NORA [*standing behind his chair with her arms on the back of it*]. Are you very busy, Torvald?
HEL. Well——
NORA. What are all those papers?
HEL. Bank business.
NORA. Already?
HEL. I have got authority from the retiring manager to undertake the necessary changes in the staff and in the rearrangement of the work, and I must make use of the Christmas week for that, so as to have everything in order for the new year.
NORA. Then that was why this poor Krogstad——
HEL. Hm!
NORA [*leans against the back of his chair and strokes his hair*]. If you hadn't been so busy, I should have asked you a tremendously big favor, Torvald.
HEL. What is that? Tell me.
NORA. There is no one has such good taste as you. And I do so want to look nice at the fancy-dress ball. Torvald, couldn't you take me in hand and decide what I shall go as and what sort of a dress I shall wear?
HEL. Aha! So my obstinate little woman is obliged to get someone to come to her rescue?
NORA. Yes, Torvald, I can't get along a bit without your help.
HEL. Very well, I will think it over; we shall manage to hit upon something.
NORA. That is nice of you. [*Goes to the Christmas tree. A short pause.*] How pretty the red flowers look! But tell me, was it really something very bad that this Krogstad was guilty of?
HEL. He forged someone's name. Have you any idea what that means?
NORA. Isn't it possible that he was driven to do it by necessity?
HEL. Yes; or, as in so many cases, by imprudence. I am not so heartless as to condemn a man altogether because of a single false step of that kind.

NORA. No, you wouldn't, would you, Torvald?

HEL. Many a man has been able to retrieve his character if he has openly confessed his fault and taken his punishment.

NORA. Punishment?

HEL. But Krogstad did nothing of that sort; he got himself out of it by a cunning trick, and that is why he has gone under altogether.

NORA. But do you think it would——

HEL. Just think how a guilty man like that has to lie and play the hypocrite with everyone, how he has to wear a mask in the presence of those near and dear to him, even before his own wife and children. And about the children—that is the most terrible part of it all, Nora.

NORA. How?

HEL. Because such an atmosphere of lies infects and poisons the whole life of a home. Each breath the children take in such a house is full of the germs of evil.

NORA [*coming nearer him*]. Are you sure of that?

HEL. My dear, I have often seen it in the course of my life as a lawyer. Almost everyone who has gone to the bad early in life has had a deceitful mother.

NORA. Why do you only say—mother?

HEL. It seems most commonly to be the mother's influence, though naturally a bad father's would have the same result. Every lawyer is familiar with the fact. This Krogstad, now, has been persistently poisoning his own children with lies and dissimulation; that is why I say he has lost all moral character. [*Holds out his hands to her.*] That is why my sweet little Nora must promise me not to plead his cause. Give me your hand on it. Come, come, what is this? Give me your hand. There now, that's settled. I assure you it would be quite impossible for me to work with him; I literally feel physically ill when I am in the company of such people.

NORA [*takes her hand out of his and goes to the opposite side of the Christmas tree*]. How hot it is in here, and I have such a lot to do.

HEL. [*getting up and putting his papers in order*]. Yes, and I must try and read through some of these before dinner, and I must think about your costume too. And it is just possible I may have something ready in gold paper to hang up on the tree. [*Puts his hand on her head.*] My precious little singing bird! [*He goes into his room and shuts the door after him.*]

NORA [*after a pause, whispers*]. No, no—it isn't true. It's impossible; it must be impossible.

[*The* NURSE *opens the door on the left.*]

NURSE. The little ones are begging so hard to be allowed to come in to Mamma.

NORA. No, no, no! Don't let them come in to me! You stay with them, Anne.

NURSE. Very well, ma'am. [*Shuts the door.*]

NORA [*pale with terror*]. Deprave my little children? Poison my home? [*A short pause. Then she tosses her head.*] It's not true. It can't possibly be true.

Act II

THE SAME SCENE—*The Christmas tree is in the corner by the piano, stripped of its ornaments and with burned-down candle ends on its disheveled branches.* NORA'S *cloak and hat are lying on the sofa. She is alone in the room, walking about uneasily. She stops by the sofa and takes up her cloak.*

NORA [*drops the cloak*]. Someone is coming now. [*Goes to the door and listens.*] No—it is no one. Of course no one will come today, Christmas Day—nor tomorrow either. But perhaps—— [*Opens the door and looks out.*] No, nothing in the letter box; it is quite empty. [*Comes forward.*] What rubbish! Of course he can't be in earnest about it. Such a thing couldn't happen; it is impossible—I have three little children.

[*Enter the* NURSE *from the room on the left, carrying a big cardboard box.*]

NURSE. At last I have found the box with the fancy dress.
NORA. Thanks; put it on the table.
NURSE [*in doing so*]. But it is very much in want of mending.
NORA. I should like to tear it into a hundred thousand pieces.
NURSE. What an idea! It can easily be put in order—just a little patience.
NORA. Yes, I will go and get Mrs. Linde to come and help me with it.
NURSE. What, out again? In this horrible weather? You will catch cold, ma'am, and make yourself ill.
NORA. Well, worse than that might happen. How are the children?
NURSE. The poor little souls are playing with their Christmas presents, but——
NORA. Do they ask much for me?
NURSE. You see, they are so accustomed to having their mamma with them.

NORA. Yes—but, Nurse, I shall not be able to be so much with them now as I was before.

NURSE. Oh well, young children easily get accustomed to anything.

NORA. Do you think so? Do you think they would forget their mother if she went away altogether?

NURSE. Good heavens!—went away altogether?

NORA. Nurse, I want you to tell me something I have often wondered about—how could you have the heart to put your own child out among strangers?

NURSE. I was obliged to if I wanted to be little Nora's nurse.

NORA. Yes, but how could you be willing to do it?

NURSE. What, when I was going to get such a good place by it? A poor girl who has got into trouble should be glad to. Besides, that wicked man didn't do a single thing for me.

NORA. But I suppose your daughter has quite forgotten you.

NURSE. No, indeed she hasn't. She wrote to me when she was confirmed and when she was married.

NORA [*putting her arms round her neck*]. Dear old Anne, you were a good mother to me when I was little.

NURSE. Little Nora, poor dear, had no other mother but me.

NORA. And if my little ones had no other mother, I am sure you would—— What nonsense I am talking! [*Opens the box.*] Go in to them. Now I must—— You will see tomorrow how charming I shall look.

NURSE. I am sure there will be no one at the ball so charming as you, ma'am. [*Goes into the room on the left.*]

NORA [*begins to unpack the box but soon pushes it away from her*]. If only I dared go out. If only no one would come. If only I could be sure nothing would happen here in the meantime. Stuff and nonsense! No one will come. Only I mustn't think about it. I will brush my muff. What lovely, lovely gloves! Out of my thoughts, out of my thoughts! One, two, three, four, five, six—— [*Screams.*] Ah! there is someone coming. [*Makes a movement toward the door but stands irresolute.*]

[*Enter* MRS. LINDE *from the hall, where she has taken off her cloak and hat.*]

NORA. Oh, it's you, Christine. There is no one else out there, is there? How good of you to come!

MRS. L. I heard you were up asking for me.

NORA. Yes, I was passing by. As a matter of fact, it is something you could help me with. Let us sit down here on the sofa. Look here. Tomorrow evening there is to be a fancy-dress ball at the Stenborgs', who live above us, and Torvald wants me to go as a Neapolitan fishergirl and dance the tarantella that I learnt at Capri.

MRS. L. I see; you are going to keep up the character.

NORA. Yes, Torvald wants me to. Look, here is the dress; Torvald had it made for me there, but now it is all so torn, and I haven't any idea——

MRS. L. We will easily put that right. It is only some of the trimming come unsewn here and there. Needle and thread? Now then, that's all we want.

NORA. It *is* nice of you.

MRS. L. [*sewing*]. So you are going to be dressed up tomorrow, Nora. I will tell you what—I shall come in for a moment and see you in your fine feathers. But I have completely forgotten to thank you for a delightful evening yesterday.

NORA [*gets up and crosses the stage*]. Well, I don't think yesterday was as pleasant as usual. You ought to have come down to town a little earlier, Christine. Certainly Torvald does understand how to make a house dainty and attractive.

MRS. L. And so do you, it seems to me; you are not your father's daughter for nothing. But tell me, is Doctor Rank always as depressed as he was yesterday?

NORA. No; yesterday it was very noticeable. I must tell you that he suffers from a very dangerous disease. He has consumption of the spine, poor creature. His father was a horrible man who committed all sorts of excesses, and that is why his son was sickly from childhood, do you understand?

MRS. L. [*dropping her sewing*]. But, my dearest Nora, how do you know anything about such things?

NORA [*walking about*]. Pooh! When you have three children you get visits now and then from—from married women who know something of medical matters, and they talk about one thing and another.

MRS. L. [*goes on sewing. A short silence*]. Does Doctor Rank come here every day?

NORA. Every day regularly. He is Torvald's most intimate friend and a friend of mine too. He is just like one of the family.

Mrs. L. But tell me this—is he perfectly sincere? I mean, isn't he the kind of man that is very anxious to make himself agreeable?

Nora. Not in the least. What makes you think that?

Mrs. L. When you introduced him to me yesterday he declared he had often heard my name mentioned in this house, but afterward I noticed that your husband hadn't the slightest idea who I was. So how could Doctor Rank——

Nora. That is quite right, Christine. Torvald is so absurdly fond of me that he wants me absolutely to himself, as he says. At first he used to seem almost jealous if I mentioned any of the dear folks at home, so naturally I gave up doing so. But I often talk about such things with Doctor Rank because he likes hearing about them.

Mrs. L. Listen to me, Nora. You are still very like a child in many things, and I am older than you in many ways and have a little more experience. Let me tell you this—you ought to make an end of it with Doctor Rank.

Nora. What ought I to make an end of?

Mrs. L. Of two things, I think. Yesterday you talked some nonsense about a rich admirer who was to leave you money——

Nora. An admirer who doesn't exist, unfortunately! But what then?

Mrs. L. Is Doctor Rank a man of means?

Nora. Yes, he is.

Mrs. L. And has no one to provide for?

Nora. No, no one; but——

Mrs. L. And comes here every day?

Nora. Yes, I told you so.

Mrs. L. But how can this well-bred man be so tactless?

Nora. I don't understand you at all.

Mrs. L. Don't prevaricate, Nora. Do you suppose I don't guess who lent you the two hundred and fifty pounds?

Nora. Are you out of your senses? How can you think of such a thing! A friend of ours, who comes here every day! Do you realize what a horribly painful position that would be?

Mrs. L. Then it really isn't he?

Nora. No, certainly not. It would never have entered into my head for a moment. Besides, he had no money to lend then; he came into his money afterward.

Mrs. L. Well, I think that was lucky for you, my dear Nora.

NORA. No, it would never have come into my head to ask Doctor Rank. Although I am quite sure that if I had asked him——
MRS. L. But of course you won't.
NORA. Of course not. I have no reason to think it could possibly be necessary. But I am quite sure that if I told Doctor Rank——
MRS. L. Behind your husband's back?
NORA. I must make an end of it with the other one, and that will be behind his back too. I *must* make an end of it with him.
MRS. L. Yes, that is what I told you yesterday, but——
NORA [*walking up and down*]. A man can put a thing like that straight much easier than a woman.
MRS. L. One's husband, yes.
NORA. Nonsense! [*Standing still.*] When you pay off a debt you get your bond back, don't you?
MRS. L. Yes, as a matter of course.
NORA. And can tear it into a hundred thousand pieces and burn it up—the nasty dirty paper!
MRS. L. [*looks hard at her, lays down her sewing and gets up slowly*]. Nora, you are concealing something from me.
NORA. Do I look as if I were?
MRS. L. Something has happened to you since yesterday morning. Nora, what is it?
NORA [*going nearer to her*]. Christine! [*Listens.*] Hush! There's Torvald come home. Do you mind going in to the children for the present? Torvald can't bear to see dressmaking going on. Let Anne help you.
MRS. L. [*gathering some of the things together*]. Certainly—but I am not going away from here till we have had it out with one another. [*She goes into the room on the left as* HELMER *comes in from the hall.*]
NORA [*going up to* HELMER]. I have wanted you so much, Torvald dear.
HEL. Was that the dressmaker?
NORA. No, it was Christine; she is helping me to put my dress in order. You will see I shall look quite smart.
HEL. Wasn't that a happy thought of mine, now?
NORA. Splendid! But don't you think it is nice of me, too, to do as you wish?
HEL. Nice?—because you do as your husband wishes? Well, well, you little rogue, I am sure you did not mean it in that way. But I am not going to disturb you; you will want to be trying on your dress, I expect.

NORA. I suppose you are going to work.
HEL. Yes. [*Shows her a bundle of papers.*] Look at that. I have just been in to the bank. [*Turns to go into his room.*]
NORA. Torvald.
HEL. Yes.
NORA. If your little squirrel were to ask you for something very, very prettily——
HEL. What then?
NORA. Would you do it?
HEL. I should like to hear what it is first.
NORA. Your squirrel would run about and do all her tricks if you would be nice and do what she wants.
HEL. Speak plainly.
NORA. Your skylark would chirp, chirp about in every room, with her song rising and falling——
HEL. Well, my skylark does that anyhow.
NORA. I would play the fairy and dance for you in the moonlight, Torvald.
HEL. Nora—you surely don't mean that request you made of me this morning?
NORA [*going near him*]. Yes, Torvald, I beg you so earnestly——
HEL. Have you really the courage to open up that question again?
NORA. Yes, dear, you *must* do as I ask; you *must* let Krogstad keep his post in the bank.
HEL. My dear Nora, it is his post that I have arranged Mrs. Linde shall have.
NORA. Yes, you have been awfully kind about that, but you could just as well dismiss some other clerk instead of Krogstad.
HEL. This is simply incredible obstinacy! Because you chose to give him a thoughtless promise that you would speak for him I am expected to——
NORA. That isn't the reason, Torvald. It is for your own sake. This fellow writes in the most scurrilous newspapers; you have told me so yourself. He can do you an unspeakable amount of harm. I am frightened to death of him.
HEL. Ah, I understand; it is recollections of the past that scare you.
NORA. What do you mean?
HEL. Naturally you are thinking of your father.

NORA. Yes—yes, of course. Just recall to your mind what these malicious creatures wrote in the papers about Papa and how horribly they slandered him. I believe they would have procured his dismissal if the Department had not sent you over to inquire into it and if you had not been so kindly disposed and helpful to him.

HEL. My little Nora, there is an important difference between your father and me. Your father's reputation as a public official was not above suspicion. Mine is, and I hope it will continue to be so as long as I hold my office.

NORA. You never can tell what mischief these men may contrive. We ought to be so well off, so snug and happy here in our peaceful home, and have no cares—you and I and the children, Torvald! That is why I beg you so earnestly——

HEL. And it is just by interceding for him that you make it impossible for me to keep him. It is already known at the bank that I mean to dismiss Krogstad. Is it to get about now that the new manager has changed his mind at his wife's bidding?

NORA. And what if it did?

HEL. Of course!—if only this obstinate little person can get her way! Do you suppose I am going to make myself ridiculous before my whole staff, to let people think I am a man to be swayed by all sorts of outside influence? I should very soon feel the consequences of it, I can tell you! And besides, there is one thing that makes it quite impossible for me to have Krogstad in the bank as long as I am manager.

NORA. Whatever is that?

HEL. His moral failings I might perhaps have overlooked if necessary——

NORA. Yes, you could—couldn't you?

HEL. And I hear he is a good worker too. But I knew him when we were boys. It was one of those rash friendships that so often prove an incubus in afterlife. I may as well tell you plainly, we were once on very intimate terms with one another. But this tactless fellow lays no restraint on himself when other people are present. On the contrary, he thinks it gives him the right to adopt a familiar tone with me, and every minute it is "I say, Helmer, old fellow!" and that sort of thing. I assure you it is extremely painful for me. He would make my position in the bank intolerable.

NORA. Torvald, I don't believe you mean that.
HEL. Don't you? Why not?
NORA. Because it is such a narrow-minded way of looking at things.
HEL. What are you saying? Narrow-minded? Do you think I am narrow-minded?
NORA. No, just the opposite, dear—and it is exactly for that reason——
HEL. It's the same thing. You say my point of view is narrow-minded, so I must be so too. Narrow-minded! Very well—I must put an end to this. [*Goes to the hall door and calls.*] Helen!
NORA. What are you going to do?
HEL. [*looking among his papers*]. Settle it. [*Enter* MAID.] Look here; take this letter and go downstairs with it at once. Find a messenger and tell him to deliver it and be quick. The address is on it, and here is the money.
MAID. Very well, sir. [*Exit with the letter.*]
HEL. [*putting his papers together*]. Now then, little Miss Obstinate.
NORA [*breathlessly*]. Torvald—what was that letter?
HEL. Krogstad's dismissal.
NORA. Call her back, Torvald! There is still time. Oh, Torvald, call her back! Do it for my sake—for your own sake—for the children's sake! Do you hear me, Torvald? Call her back! You don't know what that letter can bring upon us.
HEL. It's too late.
NORA. Yes, it's too late.
HEL. My dear Nora, I can forgive the anxiety you are in, although really it is an insult to me. It is, indeed. Isn't it an insult to think that I should be afraid of a starving quill driver's vengeance? But I forgive you nevertheless, because it is such eloquent witness to your great love for me. [*Takes her in his arms.*] And that is as it should be, my own darling Nora. Come what will, you may be sure I shall have both courage and strength if they be needed. You will see I am man enough to take everything upon myself.
NORA [*in a horror-stricken voice*]. What do you mean by that?
HEL. Everything, I say.
NORA [*recovering herself*]. You will never have to do that.
HEL. That's right. Well, we will share it, Nora, as man and wife should. That is how it shall be. [*Caressing her.*] Are you content now?

There! there!—not these frightened dove's eyes! The whole thing is only the wildest fancy! Now you must go and play through the tarantella and practice with your tambourine. I shall go into the inner office and shut the door, and I shall hear nothing; you can make as much noise as you please. [*Turns back at the door.*] And when Rank comes tell him where he will find me. [*Nods to her, takes his papers and goes into his room and shuts the door after him.*]

NORA [*bewildered with anxiety, stands as if rooted to the spot and whispers*]. He was capable of doing it. He will do it. He will do it in spite of everything. No, not that! Never, never! Anything rather than that! Oh, for some help, some way out of it! [*The doorbell rings.*] Doctor Rank! Anything rather than that—anything, whatever it is! [*She puts her hands over her face, pulls herself together, goes to the door and opens it.* RANK *is standing without, hanging up his coat. During the following dialogue it begins to grow dark.*]

NORA. Good day, Doctor Rank. I knew your ring. But you mustn't go in to Torvald now; I think he is busy with something.

RANK. And you?

NORA [*brings him in and shuts the door after him*]. Oh, you know very well I always have time for you.

RANK. Thank you. I shall make use of as much of it as I can.

NORA. What do you mean by that? As much of it as you can?

RANK. Well, does that alarm you?

NORA. It was such a strange way of putting it. Is anything likely to happen?

RANK. Nothing but what I have long been prepared for. But I certainly didn't expect it to happen so soon.

NORA [*gripping him by the arm*]. What have you found out? Doctor Rank, you must tell me.

RANK [*sitting down by the stove*]. It is all up with me. And it can't be helped.

NORA [*with a sigh of relief*]. Is it about yourself?

RANK. Who else? It is no use lying to one's self. I am the most wretched of all my patients, Mrs. Helmer. Lately I have been taking stock of my internal economy. Bankrupt! Probably within a month I shall lie rotting in the churchyard.

NORA. What an ugly thing to say!

RANK. The thing itself is cursedly ugly, and the worst of it is that I shall have to face so much more that is ugly before that. I shall only make one more examination of myself; when I have done that I shall know pretty certainly when it will be that the horrors of dissolution will begin. There is something I want to tell you. Helmer's refined nature gives him an unconquerable disgust at everything that is ugly; I won't have him in my sickroom.

NORA. Oh, but, Doctor Rank——

RANK. I won't have him there. Not on any account. I bar my door to him. As soon as I am quite certain that the worst has come I shall send you my card with a black cross on it, and then you will know that the loathsome end has begun.

NORA. You are quite absurd today. And I wanted you so much to be in a really good humor.

RANK. With death stalking beside me? To have to pay this penalty for another man's sin! Is there any justice in that? And in every single family, in one way or another, some such inexorable retribution is being exacted.

NORA [*putting her hands over her ears*]. Rubbish! Do talk of something cheerful.

RANK. Oh, it's a mere laughing matter, the whole thing. My poor innocent spine has to suffer for my father's youthful amusements.

NORA [*sitting at the table on the left*]. I suppose you mean that he was too partial to asparagus and pâté de foie gras, don't you?

RANK. Yes, and to truffles.

NORA. Truffles, yes. And oysters too, I suppose?

RANK. Oysters, of course; that goes without saying.

NORA. And heaps of port and champagne. It is sad that all these nice things should take their revenge on our bones.

RANK. Especially that they should revenge themselves on the unlucky bones of those who have not had the satisfaction of enjoying them.

NORA. Yes, that's the saddest part of it all.

RANK [*with a searching look at her*]. Hm!

NORA [*after a short pause*]. Why did you smile?

RANK. No, it was you that laughed.

NORA. No, it was you that smiled, Doctor Rank!

RANK [*rising*]. You are a greater rascal than I thought.

NORA. I am in a silly mood today.

RANK. So it seems.

NORA [*putting her hands on his shoulders*]. Dear, dear Doctor Rank, death mustn't take you away from Torvald and me.
RANK. It is a loss you would easily recover from. Those who are gone are soon forgotten.
NORA [*looking at him anxiously*]. Do you believe that?
RANK. People form new ties, and then——
NORA. Who will form new ties?
RANK. Both you and Helmer, when I am gone. You yourself are already on the highroad to it, I think. What did that Mrs. Linde want here last night?
NORA. Oho! You don't mean to say that you are jealous of poor Christine?
RANK. Yes, I am. She will be my successor in this house. When I am done for, this woman will——
NORA. Hush! Don't speak so loud. She is in that room.
RANK. Today again. There, you see.
NORA. She has only come to sew my dress for me. Bless my soul, how unreasonable you are! [*Sits down on the sofa.*] Be nice now, Doctor Rank, and tomorrow you will see how beautifully I shall dance, and you can imagine I am doing it all for you—and for Torvald too, of course. [*Takes various things out of the box.*] Doctor Rank, come and sit down here, and I will show you something.
RANK [*sitting down*]. What is it?
NORA. Just look at those!
RANK. Silk stockings.
NORA. Flesh colored. Aren't they lovely? It is so dark here now, but tomorrow—— No, no, no! You must only look at the feet. Oh well, you may have leave to look at the legs too.
RANK. Hm!
NORA. Why are you looking so critical? Don't you think they will fit me?
RANK. I have no means of forming an opinion about that.
NORA [*looks at him for a moment*]. For shame! [*Hits him lightly on the ear with the stockings.*] That's to punish you. [*Folds them up again.*]
RANK. And what other nice things am I to be allowed to see?
NORA. Not a single thing more, for being so naughty. [*She looks among the things, humming to herself.*]
RANK [*after a short silence*]. When I am sitting here talking to you as

intimately as this I cannot imagine for a moment what would have become of me if I had never come into this house.

NORA [*smiling*]. I believe you do feel thoroughly at home with us.

RANK [*in a lower voice, looking straight in front of him*]. And to be obliged to leave it all——

NORA. Nonsense, you are not going to leave it.

RANK [*as before*]. And not be able to leave behind one the slightest token of one's gratitude, scarcely even a fleeting regret—nothing but an empty place which the firstcomer can fill as well as any other.

NORA. And if I asked you now for a—— No!

RANK. For what?

NORA. For a big proof of your friendship——

RANK. Yes, yes!

NORA. I mean a tremendously big favor——

RANK. Would you really make me so happy for once?

NORA. Ah, but you don't know what it is yet.

RANK. No—but tell me.

NORA. I really can't, Doctor Rank. It is something out of all reason; it means advice and help and a favor——

RANK. The bigger a thing it is, the better. I can't conceive what it is you mean. Do tell me. Haven't I your confidence?

NORA. More than anyone else. I know you are my truest and best friend, and so I will tell you what it is. Well, Doctor Rank, it is something you must help me to prevent. You know how devotedly, how inexpressibly deeply Torvald loves me; he would never for a moment hesitate to give his life for me.

RANK [*leaning toward her*]. Nora—do you think he is the only one——

NORA [*with a slight start*]. The only one——?

RANK. The only one who would gladly give his life for your sake.

NORA [*sadly*]. Is that it?

RANK. I was determined you should know it before I went away, and there will never be a better opportunity than this. Now you know it, Nora. And now you know, too, that you can trust me as you would trust no one else.

NORA [*rises deliberately and quietly*]. Let me pass.

RANK [*makes room for her to pass him but sits still*]. Nora!

NORA [*at the hall door*]. Helen, bring in the lamp. [*Goes over to the stove.*] Dear Doctor Rank, that was really horrid of you.

RANK. To have loved you as much as anyone else does? Was that horrid?

NORA. No, but to go and tell me so. There was really no need——

RANK. What do you mean? Did you know? [MAID *enters with lamp, puts it down on the table and goes out.*] Nora—Mrs. Helmer—tell me, had you any idea of this?

NORA. Oh, how do I know whether I had or whether I hadn't? I really can't tell you. To think you could be so clumsy, Doctor Rank! We were getting on so nicely.

RANK. Well, at all events you know that you can command me body and soul. So won't you speak out?

NORA [*looking at him*]. After what happened?

RANK. I beg you to let me know what it is.

NORA. I can't tell you anything now.

RANK. Yes, yes. You mustn't punish me in that way. Let me have permission to do for you whatever a man may do.

NORA. You can do nothing for me now. Besides, I really don't need any help at all. You will find that the whole thing is merely fancy on my part. It really is so—of course it is! [*Sits down in the rocking chair and looks at him with a smile.*] You are a nice sort of man, Doctor Rank! Don't you feel ashamed of yourself now the lamp has come?

RANK. Not a bit. But perhaps I had better go—forever?

NORA. No indeed, you shall not. Of course you must come here just as before. You know very well Torvald can't do without you.

RANK. Yes, but you?

NORA. Oh, I am always tremendously pleased when you come.

RANK. It is just that that put me on the wrong track. You are a riddle to me. I have often thought that you would almost as soon be in my company as in Helmer's.

NORA. Yes—you see, there are some people one loves best and others whom one would almost always rather have as companions.

RANK. Yes, there is something in that.

NORA. When I was at home of course I loved Papa best. But I always thought it tremendous fun if I could steal down into the maids' room, because they never moralized at all and talked to each other about such entertaining things.

RANK. I see—it is *their* place I have taken.

NORA [*jumping up and going to him*]. Oh, dear, nice Doctor Rank, I never meant that at all. But surely you can understand that being with Torvald is a little like being with Papa——

[*Enter* MAID *from the hall.*]

MAID. If you please, ma'am. [*Whispers and hands her a card.*]
NORA [*glancing at the card*]. Oh! [*Puts it in her pocket.*]
RANK. Is there anything wrong?
NORA. No, no, not in the least. It is only something—it is my new dress——
RANK. What? Your dress is lying there.
NORA. Oh yes, that one; but this is another. I ordered it. Torvald mustn't know about it.
RANK. Oho! Then that was the great secret.
NORA. Of course. Just go in to him; he is sitting in the inner room. Keep him as long as——
RANK. Make your mind easy; I won't let him escape. [*Goes into* HELMER'S *room.*]
NORA [*to the* MAID]. And he is standing waiting in the kitchen?
MAID. Yes; he came up the back stairs.
NORA. But didn't you tell him no one was in?
MAID. Yes, but it was no good.
NORA. He won't go away?
MAID. No; he says he won't until he has seen you, ma'am.
NORA. Well, let him come in—but quietly. Helen, you mustn't say anything about it to anyone. It is a surprise for my husband.
MAID. Yes, ma'am, I quite understand. [*Exit.*]
NORA. This dreadful thing is going to happen! It will happen in spite of me! No, no, no, it can't happen—it shan't happen! [*She bolts the door of* HELMER'S *room. The* MAID *opens the hall door for* KROGSTAD *and shuts it after him. He is wearing a fur coat, high boots and a fur cap.*]
NORA [*advancing toward him*]. Speak low—my husband is at home.
KROG. No matter about that.
NORA. What do you want of me?
KROG. An explanation of something.
NORA. Make haste then. What is it?
KROG. You know, I suppose, that I have got my dismissal.
NORA. I couldn't prevent it, Mr. Krogstad. I fought as hard as I could on your side, but it was no good.

KROG. Does your husband love you so little then? He knows what I can expose you to, and yet he ventures——
NORA. How can you suppose that he has any knowledge of the sort?
KROG. I didn't suppose so at all. It would not be the least like our dear Torvald Helmer to show so much courage——
NORA. Mr. Krogstad, a little respect for my husband, please.
KROG. Certainly—all the respect he deserves. But since you have kept the matter so carefully to yourself, I make bold to suppose that you have a little clearer idea than you had yesterday of what it actually is that you have done?
NORA. More than you could ever teach me.
KROG. Yes, such a bad lawyer as I am.
NORA. What is it you want of me?
KROG. Only to see how you were, Mrs. Helmer. I have been thinking about you all day long. A mere cashier, a quill driver, a—well, a man like me—even he has a little of what is called feeling, you know.
NORA. Show it then; think of my little children.
KROG. Have you and your husband thought of mine? But never mind about that. I only wanted to tell you that you need not take this matter too seriously. In the first place there will be no accusation made on my part.
NORA. No, of course not; I was sure of that.
KROG. The whole thing can be arranged amicably; there is no reason why anyone should know anything about it. It will remain a secret between us three.
NORA. My husband must never get to know anything about it.
KROG. How will you be able to prevent it? Am I to understand that you can pay the balance that is owing?
NORA. No, not just at present.
KROG. Or perhaps that you have some expedient for raising the money soon?
NORA. No expedient that I mean to make use of.
KROG. Well, in any case it would have been of no use to you now. If you stood there with ever so much money in your hand, I would never part with your bond.
NORA. Tell me what purpose you mean to put it to.
KROG. I shall only preserve it—keep it in my possession. No one who is

not concerned in the matter shall have the slightest hint of it. So that if the thought of it has driven you to any desperate resolution——
NORA. It has.
KROG. If you had it in your mind to run away from your home——
NORA. I had.
KROG. Or even something worse——
NORA. How could you know that?
KROG. Give up the idea.
NORA. How did you know I had thought of *that*?
KROG. Most of us think of that at first. I did too—but I hadn't the courage.
NORA [*faintly*]. No more than I.
KROG. [*in a tone of relief*]. No, that's it, isn't it—you hadn't the courage either?
NORA. No, I haven't—I haven't.
KROG. Besides, it would have been a great piece of folly. Once the first storm at home is over—— I have a letter for your husband in my pocket.
NORA. Telling him everything?
KROG. In as lenient a manner as I possibly could.
NORA [*quickly*]. He mustn't get the letter. Tear it up. I will find some means of getting money.
KROG. Excuse me, Mrs. Helmer, but I think I told you just now——
NORA. I am not speaking of what I owe you. Tell me what sum you are asking my husband for, and I will get the money.
KROG. I am not asking your husband for a penny.
NORA. What do you want then?
KROG. I will tell you. I want to rehabilitate myself, Mrs. Helmer; I want to get on, and in that your husband must help me. For the last year and a half I have not had a hand in anything dishonorable, and all that time I have been struggling in most restricted circumstances. I was content to work my way up step by step. Now I am turned out, and I am not going to be satisfied with merely being taken into favor again. I want to get on, I tell you. I want to get into the bank again, in a higher position. Your husband must make a place for me——
NORA. That he will never do!
KROG. He will; I know him; he dare not protest. And as soon as I am in there again with him then you will see! Within a year I shall be the

manager's right hand. It will be Nils Krogstad and not Torvald Helmer who manages the bank.
NORA. That's a thing you will never see!
KROG. Do you mean that you will——
NORA. I have courage enough for it now.
KROG. Oh, you can't frighten me. A fine, spoilt lady like you——
NORA. You will see, you will see.
KROG. Under the ice, perhaps? Down into the cold, coal-black water? And then, in the spring, to float up to the surface, all horrible and unrecognizable, with your hair fallen out——
NORA. You can't frighten me.
KROG. Nor you me. People don't do such things, Mrs. Helmer. Besides, what use would it be? I should have him completely in my power all the same.
NORA. Afterward? When I am no longer——
KROG. Have you forgotten that it is I who have the keeping of your reputation? [NORA *stands speechlessly looking at him.*] Well, now, I have warned you. Do not do anything foolish. When Helmer has had my letter I shall expect a message from him. And be sure you remember that it is your husband himself who has forced me into such ways as this again. I will never forgive him for that. Good-by, Mrs. Helmer. [*Exit through the hall.*]
NORA [*goes to the hall door, opens it slightly and listens*]. He is going. He is not putting the letter in the box. Oh no, no! that's impossible! [*Opens the door by degrees.*] What is that? He is standing outside. He is not going downstairs. Is he hesitating? Can he—— [*A letter drops in the box; then* KROGSTAD'S *footsteps are heard, till they die away as he goes downstairs.* NORA *utters a stifled cry and runs across the room to the table by the sofa. A short pause.*]
NORA. In the letter box. [*Steals across to the hall door.*] There it lies—Torvald, Torvald, there is no hope for us now!

[MRS. LINDE *comes in from the room on the left, carrying the dress.*]

MRS. L. There, I can't see anything more to mend now. Would you like to try it on?
NORA [*in a hoarse whisper*]. Christine, come here.
MRS. L. [*throwing the dress down on the sofa*]. What is the matter with you? You look so agitated!

NORA. Come here. Do you see that letter? There, look—you can see it through the glass in the letter box.
MRS. L. Yes, I see it.
NORA. That letter is from Krogstad.
MRS. L. Nora—it was Krogstad who lent you the money!
NORA. Yes, and now Torvald will know all about it.
MRS. L. Believe me, Nora, that's the best thing for both of you.
NORA. You don't know all. I forged a name.
MRS. L. Good heavens!
NORA. I only want to say this to you, Christine—you must be my witness.
MRS. L. Your witness? What do you mean? What am I to——
NORA. If I should go out of my mind—and it might easily happen——
MRS. L. Nora!
NORA. Or if anything else should happen to me—anything, for instance, that might prevent my being here——
MRS. L. Nora! Nora! you are quite out of your mind.
NORA. And if it should happen that there were someone who wanted to take all the responsibility, all the blame, you understand——
MRS. L. Yes, yes—but how can you suppose——
NORA. Then you must be my witness, that it is not true, Christine. I am not out of my mind at all; I am in my right senses now, and I tell you no one else has known anything about it; I, and I alone, did the whole thing. Remember that.
MRS. L. I will, indeed. But I don't understand all this.
NORA. How should you understand it? A wonderful thing is going to happen.
MRS. L. A wonderful thing?
NORA. Yes, a wonderful thing! But it is so terrible. Christine, it *mustn't* happen, not for all the world.
MRS. L. I will go at once and see Krogstad.
NORA. Don't go to him; he will do you some harm.
MRS. L. There was a time when he would gladly do anything for my sake.
NORA. He?
MRS. L. Where does he live?
NORA. How should I know? Yes—[*feeling in her pocket*]—here is his card. But the letter, the letter!

HEL. [*calls from his room, knocking at the door*]. Nora!
NORA [*cries out anxiously*]. Oh, what's that? What do you want?
HEL. Don't be so frightened. We are not coming in; you have locked the door. Are you trying on your dress?
NORA. Yes, that's it. I look so nice, Torvald.
MRS. L. [*who has read the card*]. I see he lives at the corner here.
NORA. Yes, but it's no use. It is hopeless. The letter is lying there in the box.
MRS. L. And your husband keeps the key?
NORA. Yes, always.
MRS. L. Krogstad must ask for his letter back unread, he must find some pretense——
NORA. But it is just at this time that Torvald generally——
MRS. L. You must delay him. Go in to him in the meantime. I will come back as soon as I can. [*She goes out hurriedly through the hall door.*]
NORA [*goes to* HELMER'S *door, opens it and peeps in*]. Torvald!
HEL. [*from the inner room*]. Well? May I venture at last to come into my own room again? Come along, Rank, now you will see—— [*Halting in the doorway.*] But what is this?
NORA. What is what, dear?
HEL. Rank led me to expect a splendid transformation.
RANK [*in the doorway*]. I understood so, but evidently I was mistaken.
NORA. Yes, nobody is to have the chance of admiring me in my dress until tomorrow.
HEL. But, my dear Nora, you look so worn out. Have you been practicing too much?
NORA. No, I have not practiced at all.
HEL. But you will need to——
NORA. Yes, indeed I shall, Torvald. But I can't get on a bit without you to help me; I have absolutely forgotten the whole thing.
HEL. Oh, we will soon work it up again.
NORA. Yes, help me, Torvald. Promise that you will! I am so nervous about it—all the people—— You must give yourself up to me entirely this evening. Not the tiniest bit of business—you mustn't even take a pen in your hand. Will you promise, Torvald dear?
HEL. I promise. This evening I will be wholly and absolutely at your service, you helpless little mortal. Ah, by the way, first of all I will just—— [*Goes toward the hall door.*]

NORA. What are you going to do there?
HEL. Only see if any letters have come.
NORA. No, no! Don't do that, Torvald!
HEL. Why not?
NORA. Torvald, please don't. There is nothing there.
HEL. Well, let me look. [*Turns to go to the letter box.* NORA, *at the piano, plays the first bars of the tarantella.* HELMER *stops in the doorway.*] Aha!
NORA. I can't dance tomorrow if I don't practice with you.
HEL. [*going up to her*]. Are you really so afraid of it, dear?
NORA. Yes, so dreadfully afraid of it. Let me practice at once; there is time now, before we go to dinner. Sit down and play for me, Torvald dear; criticize me and correct me as you play.
HEL. With great pleasure, if you wish me to. [*Sits down at the piano.*]
NORA [*takes out of the box a tambourine and a long variegated shawl. She hastily drapes the shawl round her. Then she springs to the front of the stage and calls out*]. Now play for me! I am going to dance!

[HELMER *plays and* NORA *dances.* RANK *stands by the piano behind* HELMER *and looks on.*]

HEL. [*as he plays*]. Slower, slower!
NORA. I can't do it any other way.
HEL. Not so violently, Nora!
NORA. This is the way.
HEL. [*stops playing*]. No, no—that is not a bit right.
NORA [*laughing and swinging the tambourine*]. Didn't I tell you so?
RANK. Let me play for her.
HEL. [*getting up*]. Yes, do. I can correct her better then.

[RANK *sits down at the piano and plays.* NORA *dances more and more wildly.* HELMER *has taken up a position by the stove and during her dance gives her frequent instructions. She does not seem to hear him; her hair comes down and falls over her shoulders; she pays no attention to it but goes on dancing. Enter* MRS. LINDE.]

MRS. L. [*standing as if spellbound in the doorway*]. Oh!
NORA [*as she dances*]. Such fun, Christine!
HEL. My dear darling Nora, you are dancing as if your life depended on it.
NORA. So it does.

Hel. Stop, Rank; this is sheer madness. Stop, I tell you! [Rank *stops playing, and* Nora *suddenly stands still.* Helmer *goes up to her.*] I could never have believed it. You have forgotten everything I taught you.

Nora [*throwing away the tambourine*]. There, you see.

Hel. You will want a lot of coaching.

Nora. Yes, you see how much I need it. You must coach me up to the last minute. Promise me that, Torvald!

Hel. You can depend on me.

Nora. You must not think of anything but me, either today or tomorrow; you mustn't open a single letter—not even open the letter box——

Hel. Ah, you are still afraid of that fellow——

Nora. Yes, indeed I am.

Hel. Nora, I can tell from your looks that there is a letter from him lying there.

Nora. I don't know; I think there is; but you must not read anything of that kind now. Nothing horrid must come between us till this is all over.

Rank [*whispers to* Helmer]. You mustn't contradict her.

Hel. [*taking her in his arms*]. The child shall have her way. But tomorrow night, after you have danced——

Nora. Then you will be free. [*The* Maid *appears in the doorway to the right.*]

Maid. Dinner is served, ma'am.

Nora. We will have champagne, Helen.

Maid. Very good, ma'am. [*Exit.*]

Hel. Hullo!—are we going to have a banquet?

Nora. Yes, a champagne banquet till the small hours. [*Calls out.*] And a few macaroons, Helen—lots, just for once!

Hel. Come, come, don't be so wild and nervous. Be my own little skylark, as you used.

Nora. Yes, dear, I will. But go in now, and you too, Doctor Rank. Christine, you must help me to do up my hair.

Rank [*whispers to* Helmer *as they go out*]. I suppose there is nothing—she is not expecting anything?

Hel. Far from it, my dear fellow; it is simply nothing more than this childish nervousness I was telling you of. [*They go into the right-hand room.*]

NORA. Well!
MRS. L. Gone out of town.
NORA. I could tell from your face.
MRS. L. He is coming home tomorrow evening. I wrote a note for him.
NORA. You should have let it alone; you must prevent nothing. After all, it is splendid to be waiting for a wonderful thing to happen.
MRS. L. What is it that you are waiting for?
NORA. Oh, you wouldn't understand. Go in to them, I will come in a moment. [MRS. LINDE *goes into the dining room.* NORA *stands still for a little while, as if to compose herself. Then she looks at her watch.*] Five o'clock. Seven hours till midnight; and then four-and-twenty hours till the next midnight. Then the tarantella will be over. Twenty-four and seven? Thirty-one hours to live.
HEL. [*from the doorway on the right*]. Where's my little skylark?
NORA [*going to him with her arms outstretched*]. Here she is!

Act III

THE SAME SCENE—*The table has been placed in the middle of the stage with chairs round it. A lamp is burning on the table. The door into the hall stands open. Dance music is heard in the room above.* MRS. LINDE *is sitting at the table idly turning over the leaves of a book; she tries to read but does not seem able to collect her thoughts. Every now and then she listens intently for a sound at the outer door.*

MRS. L. [*looking at her watch*]. Not yet—and the time is nearly up. If only he does not—— [*Listens again.*] Ah, there he is. [*Goes into the hall and opens the outer door carefully. Light footsteps are heard on the stairs. She whispers.*] Come in. There is no one here.
KROG. [*in the doorway*]. I found a note from you at home. What does this mean?
MRS. L. It is absolutely necessary that I should have a talk with you.
KROG. Really? And it is absolutely necessary that it should be here?
MRS. L. It is impossible where I live; there is no private entrance to my rooms. Come in; we are quite alone. The maid is asleep, and the Helmers are at the dance upstairs.
KROG. [*coming into the room*]. Are the Helmers really at a dance tonight?
MRS. L. Yes, why not?
KROG. Certainly—why not?
MRS. L. Now, Nils, let us have a talk.
KROG. Can we two have anything to talk about?
MRS. L. We have a great deal to talk about.
KROG. I shouldn't have thought so.
MRS. L. No, you have never properly understood me.
KROG. Was there anything else to understand except what was obvious

to all the world—a heartless woman jilts a man when a more lucrative chance turns up?

Mrs. L. Do you believe I am as absolutely heartless as all that? And do you believe it with a light heart?

Krog. Didn't you?

Mrs. L. Nils, did you really think that?

Krog. If it were as you say, why did you write to me as you did at the time?

Mrs. L. I could do nothing else. As I had to break with you, it was my duty also to put an end to all that you felt for me.

Krog. [*wringing his hands*]. So that was it. And all this—only for the sake of money!

Mrs. L. You mustn't forget that I had a helpless mother and two little brothers. We couldn't wait for you, Nils; your prospects seemed hopeless then.

Krog. That may be so, but you had no right to throw me over for anyone else's sake.

Mrs. L. Indeed, I don't know. Many a time did I ask myself if I had the right to do it.

Krog. [*more gently*]. When I lost you it was as if all the solid ground went from under my feet. Look at me now—I am a shipwrecked man clinging to a bit of wreckage.

Mrs. L. But help may be near.

Krog. It *was* near, but then you came and stood in my way.

Mrs. L. Unintentionally, Nils. It was only today that I learned it was your place I was going to take in the bank.

Krog. I believe you, if you say so. But now that you know it, are you not going to give it up to me?

Mrs. L. No, because that would not benefit you in the least.

Krog. Oh, benefit, benefit—I would have done it whether or no.

Mrs. L. I have learned to act prudently. Life and hard, bitter necessity have taught me that.

Krog. And life has taught me not to believe in fine speeches.

Mrs. L. Then life has taught you something very reasonable. But deeds you must believe in.

Krog. What do you mean by that?

Mrs. L. You said you were like a shipwrecked man clinging to some wreckage.

Krog. I had good reason to say so.

Mrs. L. Well, I am like a shipwrecked woman clinging to some wreckage—no one to mourn for, no one to care for.

Krog. It was your own choice.

Mrs. L. There was no other choice—then.

Krog. Well, what now?

Mrs. L. Nils, how would it be if we two shipwrecked people could join forces?

Krog. What are you saying?

Mrs. L. Two on the same piece of wreckage would stand a better chance than each on their own.

Krog. Christine!

Mrs. L. What do you suppose brought me to town?

Krog. Do you mean that you gave me a thought?

Mrs. L. I could not endure life without work. All my life, as long as I can remember, I have worked, and it has been my greatest and only pleasure. But now I am quite alone in the world—my life is so dreadfully empty and I feel so forsaken. There is not the least pleasure in working for one's self. Nils, give me someone and something to work for.

Krog. I don't trust that. It is nothing but a woman's overstrained sense of generosity that prompts you to make such an offer of yourself.

Mrs. L. Have you ever noticed anything of the sort in me?

Krog. Could you really do it? Tell me—do you know all about my past life?

Mrs. L. Yes.

Krog. And do you know what they think of me here?

Mrs. L. You seemed to me to imply that with me you might have been quite another man.

Krog. I am certain of it.

Mrs. L. Is it too late now?

Krog. Christine, are you saying this deliberately? Yes, I am sure you are. I see it in your face. Have you really the courage, then——

Mrs. L. I want to be a mother to someone, and your children need a mother. We two need each other. Nils, I have faith in your real character—I can dare anything with you.

Krog. [*grasps her hands*]. Thanks, thanks, Christine! Now I shall find a way to clear myself in the eyes of the world. Ah, but I forgot——

Mrs. L. [*listening*]. Hush! The tarantella! Go, go!

Krog. Why? What is it?

Mrs. L. Do you hear them up there? When that is over we may expect them back.

Krog. Yes, yes—I will go. But it is all no use. Of course you are not aware what steps I have taken in the matter of the Helmers.

Mrs. L. Yes, I know all about that.

Krog. And in spite of that have you the courage to——

Mrs. L. I understand very well to what lengths a man like you might be driven by despair.

Krog. If I could only undo what I have done!

Mrs. L. You cannot. Your letter is lying in the letter box now.

Krog. Are you sure of that?

Mrs. L. Quite sure, but——

Krog. [*with a searching look at her*]. Is that what it all means?—that you want to save your friend at any cost? Tell me frankly. Is that it?

Mrs. L. Nils, a woman who has once sold herself for another's sake doesn't do it a second time.

Krog. I will ask for my letter back.

Mrs. L. No, no.

Krog. Yes, of course I will. I will wait here till Helmer comes; I will tell him he must give me my letter back—that it only concerns my dismissal—that he is not to read it——

Mrs. L. No, Nils, you must not recall your letter.

Krog. But, tell me, wasn't it for that very purpose that you asked me to meet you here?

Mrs. L. In my first moment of fright it was. But twenty-four hours have elapsed since then, and in that time I have witnessed incredible things in this house. Helmer must know all about it. This unhappy secret must be disclosed; they must have a complete understanding between them, which is impossible with all this concealment and falsehood going on.

Krog. Very well, if you will take the responsibility. But there is one thing I can do in any case, and I shall do it at once

Mrs. L. [*listening*]. You must be quick and go! The dance is over; we are not safe a moment longer.

Krog. I will wait for you below.

Mrs. L. Yes, do. You must see me back to my door.

KROG. I have never had such an amazing piece of good fortune in my life! [*Goes out through the outer door. The door between the room and the hall remains open.*]

MRS. L. [*tidying up the room and laying her hat and cloak ready*]. What a difference! What a difference! Someone to work for and live for—a home to bring comfort into. That I will do, indeed. I wish they would be quick and come. [*Listens.*] Ah, there they are now. I must put on my things. [*Takes up her hat and cloak.* HELMER'S *and* NORA'S *voices are heard outside; a key is turned, and* HELMER *brings* NORA *almost by force into the hall. She is in an Italian costume with a large black shawl round her; he is in evening dress and a black domino which is flying open.*]

NORA [*hanging back in the doorway and struggling with him*]. No, no, no!—don't take me in. I want to go upstairs again; I don't want to leave so early.

HEL. But, my dearest Nora——

NORA. Please, Torvald dear—please, *please*—only an hour more.

HEL. Not a single minute, my sweet Nora. You know that was our agreement. Come along into the room; you are catching cold standing there. [*He brings her gently into the room in spite of her resistance.*]

MRS. L. Good evening.

NORA. Christine!

HEL. You here so late, Mrs. Linde?

MRS. L. Yes, you must excuse me; I was so anxious to see Nora in her dress.

NORA. Have you been sitting here waiting for me?

MRS. L. Yes; unfortunately I came too late—you had already gone upstairs—and I thought I couldn't go away again without having seen you.

HEL. [*taking off* NORA'S *shawl*]. Yes, take a good look at her. I think she is worth looking at. Isn't she charming, Mrs. Linde?

MRS. L. Yes, indeed she is.

HEL. Doesn't she look remarkably pretty? Everyone thought so at the dance. But she is terribly self-willed, this sweet little person. What are we to do with her? You will hardly believe that I had almost to bring her away by force.

NORA. Torvald, you will repent not having let me stay, even if it were only for half an hour.

HEL. Listen to her, Mrs. Linde! She had danced her tarantella, and it had been a tremendous success, as it deserved—although possibly the performance was a trifle too realistic—a little more so, I mean, than was strictly compatible with the limitations of art. But never mind about that! The chief thing is, she had made a success—she had made a tremendous success. Do you think I was going to let her remain there after that and spoil the effect? No indeed! I took my charming little Capri maiden—my capricious little Capri maiden, I should say—on my arm, took one quick turn round the room, a curtsey on either side, and, as they say in novels, the beautiful apparition disappeared. An exit ought always to be effective, Mrs. Linde; but that is what I cannot make Nora understand. Pooh! this room is hot. [*Throws his domino on a chair and opens the door of his room.*] Hullo! it's all dark in here. Oh, of course—excuse me. [*He goes in and lights some candles.*]

NORA [*in a hurried and breathless whisper*]. Well?

MRS. L. [*in a low voice*]. I have had a talk with him.

NORA. Yes, and——

MRS. L. Nora, you must tell your husband all about it.

NORA [*in an expressionless voice*]. I knew it.

MRS. L. You have nothing to be afraid of as far as Krogstad is concerned, but you must tell him.

NORA. I won't tell him.

MRS. L. Then the letter will.

NORA. Thank you, Christine. Now I know what I must do. Hush!

HEL. [*coming in again*]. Well, Mrs. Linde, have you admired her?

MRS. L. Yes, and now I will say good night.

HEL. What, already? Is this yours, this knitting?

MRS. L. [*taking it*]. Yes, thank you. I had very nearly forgotten it.

HEL. So you knit?

MRS. L. Of course.

HEL. Do you know, you ought to embroider.

MRS. L. Really? Why?

HEL. Yes, it's far more becoming. Let me show you. You hold the embroidery thus in your left hand and use the needle with the right—like this—with a long easy sweep. Do you see?

MRS. L. Yes, perhaps——

HEL. Yes, but in the case of knitting—that can never be anything but ungraceful; look here—the arms close together, the knitting needles going up and down—it has a sort of Chinese effect.... That was really excellent champagne they gave us.

Mrs. L. Well—good night, Nora, and don't be self-willed any more.

Hel. That's right, Mrs. Linde.

Mrs. L. Good night, Mr. Helmer.

Hel. [*accompanying her to the door*]. Good night, good night. I hope you will get home all right. I should be very happy to—— But you haven't any great distance to go. Good night, good night. [*She goes out; he shuts the door after her and comes in again.*] Ah!—at last we have got rid of her. She is a frightful bore, that woman.

Nora. Aren't you very tired, Torvald?

Hel. No, not in the least.

Nora. Nor sleepy?

Hel. Not a bit. On the contrary I feel extraordinarily lively. And you?—you really look both tired and sleepy.

Nora. Yes, I am very tired. I want to go to sleep at once.

Hel. There, you see it was quite right of me not to let you stay there any longer.

Nora. Everything you do is quite right, Torvald.

Hel. [*kissing her on the forehead*]. Now my little skylark is speaking reasonably. Did you notice what good spirits Rank was in this evening?

Nora. Really? Was he? I didn't speak to him at all.

Hel. And I very little, but I have not for a long time seen him in such good form. [*Looks for a while at her and then goes nearer to her.*] It is delightful to be at home by ourselves again, to be all alone with you—you fascinating, charming little darling!

Nora. Don't look at me like that, Torvald.

Hel. Why shouldn't I look at my dearest treasure?—at all the beauty that is mine, all my very own?

Nora [*going to the other side of the table*]. You mustn't say things like that to me tonight.

Hel. [*following her*]. You have still got the tarantella in your blood, I see. And it makes you more captivating than ever. Listen—the guests are beginning to go now. [*In a lower voice.*] Nora—soon the whole house will be quiet.

Nora. Yes, I hope so.

Hel. Yes, my own darling Nora. Do you know, when I am out at a party with you like this, why I speak so little to you, keep away from you and only send a stolen glance in your direction now and then?—do you know why I do that? It is because I make believe to myself that we are secretly in love and you are my secretly promised bride and that no one suspects there is anything between us.

NORA. Yes, yes—I know very well your thoughts are with me all the time.

HEL. And when we are leaving and I am putting the shawl over your beautiful young shoulders—on your lovely neck—then I imagine that you are my young bride and that we have just come from our wedding and I am bringing you, for the first time, into our home—to be alone with you for the first time—quite alone with my shy little darling! All this evening I have longed for nothing but you. When I watched the seductive figures of the tarantella my blood was on fire; I could endure it no longer, and that was why I brought you down so early——

NORA. Go away, Torvald! You must let me go. I won't——

HEL. What's that? You're joking, my little Nora! You won't—you won't? Am I not your husband? [*A knock is heard at the outer door.*]

NORA [*starting*]. Did you hear——

HEL. [*going into the hall*]. Who is it?

RANK [*outside*]. It is I. May I come in for a moment?

HEL. [*in a fretful whisper*]. Oh, what does he want now? [*Aloud.*] Wait a minute. [*Unlocks the door.*] Come, that's kind of you not to pass by our door.

RANK. I thought I heard your voice, and I felt as if I should like to look in. [*With a swift glance round.*] Ah yes!—these dear familiar rooms. You are very happy and cosy in here, you two.

HEL. It seems to me that you looked after yourself pretty well upstairs too.

RANK. Excellently. Why shouldn't I? Why shouldn't one enjoy everything in this world?—at any rate as much as one can and as long as one can. The wine was capital——

HEL. Especially the champagne.

RANK. So you noticed that too? It is almost incredible how much I managed to put away!

NORA. Torvald drank a great deal of champagne tonight too.

RANK. Did he?

NORA. Yes, and he is always in such good spirits afterward.
RANK. Well, why should one not enjoy a merry evening after a well-spent day?
HEL. Well-spent? I am afraid I can't take credit for that.
RANK [*clapping him on the back*]. But I can, you know!
HEL. Exactly.
NORA. Doctor Rank, you must have been occupied with some scientific investigation today.
HEL. Just listen!—little Nora talking about scientific investigations!
NORA. And may I congratulate you on the result?
RANK. Indeed you may.
NORA. Was it favorable, then?
RANK. The best possible, for both doctor and patient—certainty.
NORA [*quickly and searchingly*]. Certainty?
RANK. Absolute certainty. So wasn't I entitled to make a merry evening of it after that?
NORA. Yes, you certainly were, Doctor Rank.
HEL. I think so too, so long as you don't have to pay for it in the morning.
RANK. Oh well, one can't have anything in this life without paying for it.
NORA. Doctor Rank—are you fond of fancy-dress balls?
RANK. Yes, if there is a fine lot of pretty costumes.
NORA. Tell me—what shall we two wear at the next?
HEL. Little featherbrain!—are you thinking of the next already?
RANK. We two? Yes, I can tell you. You shall go as a good fairy——
HEL. Yes, but what do you suggest as an appropriate costume for that?
RANK. Let your wife go dressed just as she is in everyday life.
HEL. That was really very prettily turned. But can't you tell us what you will be?
RANK. Yes, my dear friend, I have quite made up my mind about that.
HEL. Well?
RANK. At the next fancy-dress ball I shall be invisible.
HEL. That's a good joke!
RANK. There is a big black hat—have you ever heard of hats that make you invisible? If you put one on, no one can see you.
HEL. [*suppressing a smile*]. Yes, you are quite right.
RANK. But I am clean forgetting what I came for. Helmer, give me a cigar—one of the dark Havanas.

HEL. With the greatest pleasure. [*Offers him his case.*]

RANK [*takes a cigar and cuts off the end*]. Thanks.

NORA [*striking a match*]. Let me give you a light.

RANK. Thank you. [*She holds the match for him to light his cigar.*] And now good-by!

HEL. Good-by, good-by, dear old man!

NORA. Sleep well, Doctor Rank.

RANK. Thank you for that wish.

NORA. Wish me the same.

RANK. You? Well, if you want me to sleep well! And thanks for the light. [*He nods to them both and goes out.*]

HEL. [*in a subdued voice*]. He has drunk more than he ought.

NORA [*absently*]. Maybe. [HELMER *takes a bunch of keys out of his pocket and goes into the hall.*] Torvald! What are you going to do there?

HEL. Empty the letter box; it is quite full; there will be no room to put the newspaper in tomorrow morning.

NORA. Are you going to work tonight?

HEL. You know quite well I'm not. What is this? Someone has been at the lock.

NORA. At the lock?

HEL. Yes, someone has. What can it mean? I should never have thought the maid—— Here is a broken hairpin. Nora, it is one of yours.

NORA [*quickly*]. Then it must have been the children.

HEL. Then you must get them out of those ways. There, at last I have got it open. [*Takes out the contents of the letter box and calls to the kitchen.*] Helen! Helen, put out the light over the front door. [*Goes back into the room and shuts the door into the hall. He holds out his hand full of letters.*] Look at that—look what a heap of them there are. [*Turning them over.*] What on earth is that?

NORA [*at the window*]. The letter—— No! Torvald, no!

HEL. Two cards—of Rank's.

NORA. Of Doctor Rank's?

HEL. [*looking at them*]. Doctor Rank. They were on the top. He must have put them in when he went out.

NORA. Is there anything written on them?

HEL. There is a black cross over the name. Look there—what

an uncomfortable idea! It looks as if he were announcing his own death.

NORA. It is just what he is doing.

HEL. What? Do you know anything about it? Has he said anything to you?

NORA. Yes. He told me that when the cards came it would be his leave-taking from us. He means to shut himself up and die.

HEL. My poor old friend. Certainly I knew we should not have him very long with us. But so soon! And so he hides himself away like a wounded animal.

NORA. If it has to happen, it is best it should be without a word—don't you think so, Torvald?

HEL. [*walking up and down*]. He had so grown into our lives. I can't think of him as having gone out of them. He, with his sufferings and his loneliness, was like a cloudy background to our sunlit happiness. Well, perhaps it is best so. For him, anyway. [*Standing still.*] And perhaps for us too, Nora. We two are thrown quite upon each other now. [*Puts his arms round her.*] My darling wife, I don't feel as if I could hold you tight enough. Do you know, Nora, I have often wished that you might be threatened by some great danger, so that I might risk my life's blood and everything for your sake.

NORA [*disengages herself and says firmly and decidedly*]. Now you must read your letters, Torvald.

HEL. No, no; not tonight. I want to be with you, my darling wife.

NORA. With the thought of your friend's death——

HEL. You are right; it has affected us both. Something ugly has come between us—the thought of the horrors of death. We must try and rid our minds of that. Until then—we will each go to our own room.

NORA [*hanging on his neck*]. Good night, Torvald—good night!

HEL. [*kissing her on the forehead*]. Good night, my little singing bird. Sleep sound, Nora. Now I will read my letters through. [*He takes his letters and goes into his room, shutting the door after him.*]

NORA [*gropes distractedly about, seizes* HELMER'S *domino, throws it about her while she says in quick, hoarse, spasmodic whispers*]. Never to see him again. Never! Never! [*Puts her shawl over her head.*] Never to see my children again either—never again. Never! Never! Ah! the icy black water—the unfathomable depths—if only it were over! He has got it now—now he is reading it. Good-by, Torvald and my children! [*She is about to rush out through the hall when* HELMER *opens his door hurriedly and stands with an open letter in his hand.*]

HEL. Nora!

NORA. Ah!

HEL. What is this? Do you know what is in this letter?

NORA. Yes, I know. Let me go! Let me get out!

HEL. [*holding her back*]. Where are you going?

NORA [*trying to get free*]. You shan't save me, Torvald!

HEL. [*reeling*]. True? Is this true, that I read here? Horrible! No, no—it is impossible that it is true.

NORA. It is true. I have loved you above everything else in the world.

HEL. Oh, don't let us have any silly excuses.

NORA [*taking a step toward him*]. Torvald!

HEL. Miserable creature—what have you done?

NORA. Let me go. You shall not suffer for my sake. You shall not take it upon yourself.

HEL. No tragedy airs, please. [*Locks the hall door.*] Here you shall stay and give me an explanation. Do you understand what you have done? Answer me! Do you understand what you have done?

NORA [*looks steadily at him and says with a growing look of coldness in her face*]. Yes, now I am beginning to understand thoroughly.

HEL. [*walking about the room*]. What a horrible awakening! All these eight years—she who was my joy and pride—a hypocrite, a liar—worse, worse—a criminal! The unutterable ugliness of it all! For shame! For shame! [NORA *is silent and looks steadily at him. He stops in front of her.*] I ought to have suspected that something of the sort would happen. I ought to have foreseen it. All your father's want of principle—be silent!—all your father's want of principle has come out in you. No religion, no morality, no sense of duty—— How I am punished for having winked at what he did! I did it for your sake, and this is how you repay me.

NORA. Yes, that's just it.

HEL. Now you have destroyed all my happiness. You have ruined all my future. It is horrible to think of! I am in the power of an unscrupulous man; he can do what he likes with me, ask anything he likes of me, give me any orders he pleases—I dare not refuse. And I must sink to such miserable depths because of a thoughtless woman!

NORA. When I am out of the way you will be free.
HEL. No fine speeches, please. Your father always had plenty of those ready too. What good would it be to me if you were out of the way, as you say? Not the slightest. He can make the affair known everywhere; and if he does, I may be falsely suspected of having been a party to your criminal action. Very likely people will think I was behind it all—that it was I who prompted you! And I have to thank you for all this—you whom I have cherished during the whole of our married life. Do you understand now what it is you have done for me?
NORA [*coldly and quietly*]. Yes.
HEL. It is so incredible that I can't take it in. But we must come to some understanding. Take off that shawl. Take it off, I tell you. I must try and appease him in some way or another. The matter must be hushed up at any cost. And as for you and me, it must appear as if everything between us were just as before—but naturally only in the eyes of the world. You will still remain in my house, that is a matter of course. But I shall not allow you to bring up the children; I dare not trust them to you. To think that I should be obliged to say so to one whom I have loved so dearly and whom I still—— No, that is all over. From this moment happiness is not the question; all that concerns us is to save the remains, the fragments, the appearance——

[*A ring is heard at the front-door bell.*]

HEL. [*with a start*]. What is that? So late! Can the worst—can he—— Hide yourself, Nora. Say you are ill.

[NORA *stands motionless.* HELMER *goes and unlocks the hall door.*]

MAID [*half dressed, comes to the door*]. A letter for the mistress.
HEL. Give it to me. [*Takes the letter and shuts the door.*] Yes, it is from him. You shall not have it; I will read it myself.
NORA. Yes, read it.
HEL. [*standing by the lamp*]. I scarcely have the courage to do it. It may mean ruin for the both of us. No, I must know. [*Tears open the letter, runs his eye over a few lines, looks at a paper enclosed and gives a shout of joy.*] Nora! [*She looks at him questioningly.*] Nora! No, I must read it once again. Yes, it is true! I am saved! Nora, I am saved!
NORA. And I?

HEL. You too, of course; we are both saved, both you and I. Look, he sends you your bond back. He says he regrets and repents—that a happy change in his life—— Never mind what he says! We are saved, Nora! No one can do anything to you. Oh, Nora, Nora—— No, first I must destroy these hateful things. Let me see. [*Takes a look at the bond.*] No, no, I won't look at it. The whole thing shall be nothing but a bad dream to me. [*Tears up the bond and both letters, throws them all into the stove and watches them burn.*] There—now it doesn't exist any longer. He says that since Christmas Eve you—— These must have been three dreadful days for you, Nora.

NORA. I have fought a hard fight these three days.

HEL. And suffered agonies and seen no way out, but—— No, we won't call any of the horrors to mind. We will only shout with joy and keep saying, "It's all over! It's all over!" Listen to me, Nora. You don't seem to realize that it is all over. What is this?—such a cold, set face! My poor little Nora, I quite understand; you don't feel as if you could believe that I have forgiven you. But it is true, Nora, I swear it; I have forgiven you everything. I know that what you did you did out of love for me.

NORA. That is true.

HEL. You have loved me as a wife ought to love her husband. Only you had not sufficient knowledge to judge of the means you used. But do you suppose you are any the less dear to me because you don't understand how to act on your own responsibility? No, no; only lean on me; I will advise and direct you. I should not be a man if this womanly helplessness did not just give you a double attractiveness in my eyes. You must not think any more about the hard things I said in my first moment of consternation, when I thought everything was going to overwhelm me. I have forgiven you, Nora; I swear to you I have forgiven you.

NORA. Thank you for your forgiveness. [*She goes out through the door to the right.*]

HEL. No, don't go. [*Looks in.*] What are you doing in there?

NORA [*from within*]. Taking off my fancy dress.

HEL. [*standing at the open door*]. Yes, do. Try and calm yourself and make your mind easy again, my frightened little singing bird. Be at rest and feel secure; I have broad wings to shelter you under. [*Walks up and down by the door.*] How warm and cosy our home is, Nora. Here is shelter for you; here I will protect you like a hunted dove that I have saved from a hawk's claws; I will bring peace to your poor beating heart. It will come, little by little, Nora, believe me. Tomorrow morning you will look upon it all quite differently; soon everything will be just as it was before. Very soon you won't need me to assure you that I have forgiven you; you will yourself feel the certainty that I have done so. Can you suppose I should ever think of such a thing as repudiating you or even reproaching you? You have no idea what a true man's heart is like, Nora. There is something so indescribably sweet and satisfying, to a man, in the knowledge that he has forgiven his wife—forgiven her freely and with all his heart. It seems as if that had made her, as it were, doubly his own; he has given her a new life, so to speak, and she has in a way become both wife and child to him. So you shall be for me after this, my little scared, helpless darling. Have no anxiety about anything, Nora; only be frank and open with me, and I will serve as will and conscience both to you—— What is this? Not gone to bed? Have you changed your things?

NORA [*in everyday dress*]. Yes, Torvald, I have changed my things now.

HEL. But what for?—so late as this.

NORA. I shall not sleep tonight.

HEL. But, my dear Nora——

NORA [*looking at her watch*]. It is not so very late. Sit down here, Torvald. You and I have much to say to one another. [*She sits down at one side of the table.*]

HEL. Nora—what is this?—this cold, set face?

NORA. Sit down. It will take some time; I have a lot to talk over with you.

HEL. [*sits down at the opposite side of the table*]. You alarm me, Nora!—and I don't understand you.

NORA. No, that is just it. You don't understand me, and I have never understood you either—before tonight. No, you mustn't interrupt me. You must simply listen to what I say. Torvald, this is a settling of accounts.

HEL. What do you mean by that?

NORA [*after a short silence*]. Isn't there one thing that strikes you as strange in our sitting here like this?

HEL. What is that?

NORA. We have been married now eight years. Does it not occur to you that this is the first time we two, you and I, husband and wife, have had a serious conversation?

HEL. What do you mean, serious?

NORA. In all these eight years—longer than that—from the very beginning of our acquaintance we have never exchanged a word on any serious subject.

HEL. Was it likely that I would be continually and forever telling you about worries that you could not help me to bear?

NORA. I am not speaking about business matters. I say that we have never sat down in earnest together to try and get at the bottom of anything.

HEL. But, dearest Nora, would it have been any good to you?

NORA. That is just it; you have never understood me. I have been greatly wronged, Torvald—first by Papa and then by you.

HEL. What! By us two—by us two who have loved you better than anyone else in the world?

NORA [*shaking her head*]. You have never loved me. You have only thought it pleasant to be in love with me.

HEL. Nora, what do I hear you saying?

NORA. It is perfectly true, Torvald. When I was at home with Papa he told me his opinion about everything, and so I had the same opinions; and if I differed from him I concealed the fact, because he would not have liked it. He called me his doll child, and he played with me just as I used to play with my dolls. And when I came to live with you——

HEL. What sort of an expression is that to use about our marriage?

NORA [*undisturbed*]. I mean that I was simply transferred from Papa's hands to yours. You arranged everything according to your own taste, and so I got the same tastes as you—or else I pretended to. I am really not quite sure which—I think sometimes the one and sometimes the other. When I look back on it it seems to me as if I have been living here like a poor woman—just from hand to mouth. I have existed merely to perform tricks for you, Torvald. But you would have it so. You and Papa have committed a great sin against me. It is your fault that I have made nothing of my life.

HEL. How unreasonable and how ungrateful you are, Nora! Have you not been happy here?

NORA. No, I have never been happy. I thought I was, but it has never really been so.

HEL. Not—not happy!

NORA. No, only merry. And you have always been so kind to me. But our home has been nothing but a playroom. I have been your doll wife, just as at home I was Papa's doll child; and here the children have been my dolls. I thought it great fun when you played with me, just as they thought it great fun when I played with them. That is what our marriage has been, Torvald.

HEL. There is some truth in what you say—exaggerated and strained as your view of it is. But for the future it shall be different. Playtime shall be over and lesson time shall begin.

NORA. Whose lessons? Mine or the children's?

HEL. Both yours and the children's, my darling Nora.

NORA. Alas, Torvald, you are not the man to educate me into being a proper wife for you.

HEL. And you can say that!

NORA. And I—how am I fitted to bring up the children?

HEL. Nora!

NORA. Didn't you say so yourself a little while ago—that you dare not trust me to bring them up?

HEL. In a moment of anger! Why do you pay any heed to that?

NORA. Indeed, you were perfectly right. I am not fit for the task. There is another task I must undertake first. I must try and educate myself—you are not the man to help me in that. I must do that for myself. And that is why I am going to leave you now.

HEL. [*springing up*]. What do you say?

NORA. I must stand quite alone if I am to understand myself and everything about me. It is for that reason that I cannot remain with you any longer.

HEL. Nora, Nora!

NORA. I am going away from here now, at once. I am sure Christine will take me in for the night.

HEL. You are out of your mind! I won't allow it! I forbid you!

NORA. It is no use forbidding me anything any longer. I will take with me what belongs to myself. I will take nothing from you, either now or later.

HEL. What sort of madness is this?

NORA. Tomorrow I shall go home—I mean to my old home. It will be easiest for me to find something to do there.

HEL. You blind, foolish woman!

NORA. I must try and get some sense, Torvald.

HEL. To desert your home, your husband and your children! And you don't consider what people will say!

NORA. I cannot consider that at all. I only know that it is necessary for me.

HEL. It's shocking. This is how you would neglect your most sacred duties.

NORA. What do you consider my most sacred duties?

HEL. Do I need to tell you that? Are they not your duties to your husband and your children?

NORA. I have other duties just as sacred.

HEL. That you have not. What duties could those be?

NORA. Duties to myself.

HEL. Before all else you are a wife and a mother.

NORA. I don't believe that any longer. I believe that before all else I am a reasonable human being just as you are—or, at all events, that I must try and become one. I know quite well, Torvald, that most people would think you right and that views of that kind are to be found in books; but I can no longer content myself with what most people say or with what is found in books. I must think over things for myself and get to understand them.

HEL. Can you understand your place in your own home? Have you not a reliable guide in such matters as that?—have you no religion?

NORA. I am afraid, Torvald, I do not exactly know what religion is.

HEL. What are you saying?

NORA. I know nothing but what the clergyman said when I went to be confirmed. He told us that religion was this and that and the other. When I am away from all this and am alone I will look into that matter too. I will see if what the clergyman said is true, or at all events if it is true for me.

HEL. This is unheard of in a girl of your age! But if religion cannot lead you aright, let me try and awaken your conscience. I suppose you have some moral sense? Or—answer me—am I to think you have none?

NORA. I assure you, Torvald, that is not an easy question to answer. I really don't know. The thing perplexes me altogether. I only know that you and I look at it in quite a different light. I am learning, too, that the law is quite another thing from what I supposed; but I find it impossible to convince myself that the law is right. According to it a woman has no right to spare her old dying father or to save her husband's life. I can't believe that.

HEL. You talk like a child. You don't understand the conditions of the world in which you live.

NORA. No, I don't. But now I am going to try. I am going to see if I can make out who is right, the world or I.

HEL. You are ill, Nora; you are delirious; I almost think you are out of your mind.

NORA. I have never felt my mind so clear and certain as tonight.

HEL. And is it with a clear and certain mind that you forsake your husband and your children?

NORA. Yes, it is.

HEL. Then there is only one possible explanation.

NORA. What is that?

HEL. You do not love me any more.

NORA. No, that is just it.

HEL. Nora!—and you can say that?

NORA. It gives me great pain, Torvald, for you have always been so kind to me, but I cannot help it. I do not love you any more.

HEL. [*regaining his composure*]. Is that a clear and certain conviction too?

NORA. Yes, absolutely clear and certain. That is the reason why I will not stay here any longer.

HEL. And can you tell me what I have done to forfeit your love?

NORA. Yes, indeed I can. It was to-night, when the wonderful thing did not happen; then I saw you were not the man I had thought you.

HEL. Explain yourself better—I don't understand you.

NORA. I have waited so patiently for eight years; for, goodness knows, I knew very well that wonderful things don't happen every day. Then this horrible misfortune came upon me, and then I felt quite certain that the wonderful thing was going to happen at last. When

Krogstad's letter was lying out there never for a moment did I imagine that you would consent to accept this man's conditions. I was so absolutely certain that you would say to him: Publish the thing to the whole world. And when that was done——

HEL. Yes, what then?—when I had exposed my wife to shame and disgrace?

NORA. When that was done I was so absolutely certain you would come forward and take everything upon yourself and say: I am the guilty one.

HEL. Nora!

NORA. You mean that I would never have accepted such a sacrifice on your part? No, of course not. But what would my assurances have been worth against yours? That was the wonderful thing which I hoped for and feared, and it was to prevent that that I wanted to kill myself.

HEL. I would gladly work night and day for you, Nora—bear sorrow and want for your sake. But no man would sacrifice his honor for the one he loves.

NORA. It is a thing hundreds of thousands of women have done.

HEL. Oh, you think and talk like a heedless child.

NORA. Maybe. But you neither think nor talk like the man I could bind myself to. As soon as your fear was over—and it was not fear for what threatened me but for what might happen to you—when the whole thing was past, as far as you were concerned it was exactly as if nothing at all had happened. Exactly as before, I was your little skylark, your doll, which you would in the future treat with doubly gentle care because it was so brittle and fragile. [*Getting up.*] Torvald—it was then it dawned upon me that for eight years I had been living here with a strange man and had borne him three children. Oh, I can't bear to think of it! I could tear myself into little bits!

HEL. [*sadly*]. I see, I see. An abyss has opened between us—there is no denying it. But, Nora, would it not be possible to fill it up?

NORA. As I am now, I am no wife for you.

HEL. I have it in me to become a different man.

NORA. Perhaps—if your doll is taken away from you.

HEL. But to part!—to part from you! No, no, Nora; I can't understand that idea.

NORA [*going out to the right*]. That makes it all the more certain that it must be done. [*She comes back with her cloak and hat and a small bag which she puts on a chair by the table.*]

HEL. Nora. Nora, not now! Wait till tomorrow.

NORA [*putting on her cloak*]. I cannot spend the night in a strange man's room.

HEL. But can't we live here like brother and sister?

NORA [*putting on her hat*]. You know very well that would not last long. [*Puts the shawl round her.*] Good-by, Torvald. I won't see the little ones. I know they are in better hands than mine. As I am now, I can be of no use to them.

HEL. But someday, Nora—someday?

NORA. How can I tell? I have no idea what is going to become of me.

HEL. But you are my wife, whatever becomes of you.

NORA. Listen, Torvald. I have heard that when a wife deserts her husband's house, as I am doing now, he is legally freed from all obligations toward her. In any case I set you free from all your obligations. You are not to feel yourself bound in the slightest way, any more than I shall. There must be perfect freedom on both sides. See, here is your ring back. Give me mine.

HEL. That too?

NORA. That too.

HEL. Here it is.

NORA. That's right. Now it is all over. I have put the keys here. The maids know all about everything in the house—better than I do. Tomorrow, after I have left her, Christine will come here and pack up my own things that I brought with me from home. I will have them sent after me.

HEL. All over! All over! Nora, shall you never think of me again?

NORA. I know I shall often think of you and the children and this house.

HEL. May I write to you, Nora?

NORA. No—never. You must not do that.

HEL. But at least let me send you——

NORA. Nothing—nothing.

HEL. Let me help you if you are in want.

NORA. No. I can receive nothing from a stranger.

Hel. Nora—can I never be anything more than a stranger to you?

Nora [*taking her bag*]. Ah, Torvald, the most wonderful thing of all would have to happen.

Hel. Tell me what that would be!

Nora. Both you and I would have to be so changed that—— Oh, Torvald, I don't believe any longer in wonderful things happening.

Hel. But I will believe in it. Tell me. So changed that——

Nora. That our life together would be a real wedlock. Good-by. [*She goes out through the hall.*]

Hel. [*sinks down on a chair at the door and buries his face in his hands*]. Nora! Nora! [*Looks round and rises.*] Empty! She is gone. [*A hope flashes across his mind.*] The most wonderful thing of all——?

[*The sound of a door shutting is heard from below.*]